The British Campaign for Soviet Jewry 1966-1991: Human Rights and Exit Permits.

By John Cooper

ISBN: 978-1-914933-46-2

Published By: -

i2i

PUBLISHING

i2i Publishing. Manchester.
www.i2ipublishing.co.uk

Contents

4

Acknowledgements

Among those who generously shared their recollections of the Soviet Jewry Campaign and in some cases their correspondence were Andrew Balcombe, Doreen Gainsford, Zelda Harris, Gordon Hausmann, Jerry Lewis, Barbara Oberman, Maurice Samuelson and Enid Wurtman. I would like also to thank Rita Eker for some photographs and for sight of her scrapbooks relating to the 35's campaign for Natan Sharansky.

No book of this nature could have been written without the assistance of the archivists and librarians of the British Library, the London Metropolitan Archives, the National Archives, Special Collections at the University of Southampton, and the Central Archives for the History of the Jewish People, Jerusalem.

I would like to thank Colin Shindler for reading the early chapters of this book; for the advice of an anonymous reviewer; and my brother Rabbi Dr Martin Cooper for his help.

I am very grateful to Roy Clayton for his scrupulous editing of the manuscript and to my publisher Lionel Ross for all his painstaking efforts to enhance it.

If there are any errors of fact or judgement in the book, the faults are mine,

To my wife Judy I owe an enormous debt for sustaining me through the stops and starts of writing this book through the Covid years.

I dedicate this book to our grandchildren, Dov, Kayla, Shira, Ella, Jodie, Avi and Leo.

John Cooper
London January 2023

Timeline

1917
Oct. October Bolshevik Revolution
1918
Nationalisation of the property of the Orthodox Church and houses of worship of other faiths
Pogroms 1918 to 1921 kill over 100,000 Jews
1922
Mar.-Apl. Party Congress and Stalin becomes General Secretary
1924
Jan. Death of Lenin
1936
Aug. First of Stalin's show trials of Zinoviev, Kamenev and others, followed by more victims and trials in 1937 and 1938
1939
Aug. Nazi-Soviet Pact
Sept. Soviets invade Eastern Poland
1941
22 June. German invasion of the Soviet Union
1942
Spring. Establishment of the Jewish Anti-Fascist Committee
1943
Sept. Concordat between Stalin and the Russian Orthodox Church
1948
May. Foundation of the State of Israel
Nov. Dissolution of the Jewish Anti-Fascist Committee
1949
28 Jan. Opening of the Anti-Cosmopolitan Campaign in the *Pravda*
1952
8 May. Opening of the trial of the leaders of the Jewish Anti-Fascist Committee
Nov. Opening of the Slansky Trial in Czechoslovakia, when defendants were charged with cosmopolitanism and Zionism

The Israeli government founds the Lishkato to facilitate emigration from the Soviet Union
1953
Jan. Discovery of the alleged 'Doctors Plot'
Mar. Death of Stalin
Sept. Khrushchev confirmed as First Secretary of the Communist Party
1956
Feb. Khrushchev's secret speech to the Party Congress and the start of the 'Thaw'
1959
1959-1961 Khrushchev's anti-religious campaign
1961
May. Foundation of Amnesty International
1963
Publication of Betty Friedan's *Femine Mystique* sparks the formation of the Feminist movement
1964
27 April. Formation of Student Struggle for Soviet Jewry in the United States
1966
Jan. Establishment of the Universities Committee for Soviet Jewry in London
1967
5 June 1967 start of the Six Day War
1968
May. Insurrection in Paris sparks an international Student revolt
1970 April. Union of Councils for Soviet Jews created
December. After the first Leningrad trial for an alleged hijacking of an aircraft, Edward Kutsnetsov and Mark Dymshits were sentenced to death, intensifying the Soviet Jewry Campaign
1971
May. Formation of the Women's Campaign for Soviet Jewry (35's)
Aug. National Conference on Soviet Jewry started work
1972
September. First preparatory meeting in Helsinki for the Conference on Security and Cooperation in Europe (CSCE)

1973
Oct. Yom Kippur War begins 6 October
1975
Jan. Congress passed the Jackson-Vanik Amendment
August. 1 August the Helsinki Final Act was signed by President Ford and Leonid Brezhnev
December. National Council for Soviet Jewry established
1976
May. Anatoly Shcharansky suggests formation of Human Rights Watch which was established on 12 May 1976
December. On 21 December Professor Bernard Fain and Dr Vladimir Prestin were arrested for organizing a Jewish Cultural Symposium
The International Covenant on Civil and Political Rights and the International Covenant on
Economic and Social Rights came into force but were open for signature ten years earlier
1977
February. On 3 February the human rights activist Alexander Ginzburg was arrested, followed a few days later by Dr Yuri Orlov of the Moscow Human Rights Watch
March
Shcharansky, the human rights and Jewish cultural activist, was arrested on 15 March
June. On 1 June Iosif Begun was arrested for teaching Hebrew and sentenced to two years in internal exile.
August. On 5 August Dr Victor Brailovsky took over the running of the Scientific Seminar from Professor Abzel
1978
June. 21 June Vladimir Slepak sentenced to five years internal exile
On the same day 21 June Ida Nudel was tried and received a sentence of four years in internal exile
July. 14 July Shcharansky sentenced to thirteen years in prison and labour camps

1979
December. Soviet invasion of Afghanistan
1980
November. Opening of the Madrid Follow-Up Conference on 11 November
On 13 November Dr Brailovsky was arrested and later sentenced to five years in internal exile
1981
Dr Alexander Paritsky of Kharkovwas sentenced to three years in a Siberian labour camp for organizing Jewish cultural activities
1983
Nov. Opening in November of the Vienna Follow-Up Conference
1985
March. On 11 March Mikhail Gorbachev became General Secretary of the Communist party
1986
Feb. Shcharansky freed in a spy swap on 11 February
Apl. Nuclear explosion at Chernobyl
1987
Sept.-Oct. Dr Brailovsky, Ida Nudel and Vladimir Slepak were given exit visas
Dec. On 6 December 1987 the biggest rally ever of American Jews was held in Washington
1989
Opening of the Helsinki Follow-Up Conference
1990
The mass emigration of Soviet Jewry gained momentum when 181,802 Jews left the Soviet Union
1991
June. Yeltsin is elected President of Russia
Aug. Most republics in the USSR declare their independence
Dec. Ukrainian independence is confirmed in a referendum.
The USSR is declared disbanded

Introduction

The international campaign to aid the emigration of Soviet
Jewry to Israel or to safe havens in the West was one of the
most iconic episodes in Jewish history since the foundation
of the state in 1948 and was significant in being a
transnational movement which bound the worldwide
Jewish community to Israel from the 1970s until the early
1990s. Modern Jewish history as such did not necessarily
diverge in different directions with the establishment of the
state of Israel in 1948. The British campaign was significant
in that it drew in all sections of the Anglo-Jewish
community into a political movement, including new ones
such as students and women in large numbers; and because
of the wider issues with which it was associated it also
attracted uncommitted Jews and sympathetic gentiles. It
was also a movement with a long time span, stretching
from the late 1960s until 1990. It was a movement very
much bound up with the fate of the new state of Israel, with
whose continued existence the destiny of the Jewish people
seemed so much to be tied. The Jewish state seemed so
isolated and vulnerable in the months before the Six Day
War in 1967 that the euphoria which greeted Israel's
overwhelming victory hardened into a new mood of
resolution and determination in the diaspora to assist the
Jews in the Soviet Union, many of whom displayed their
Jewish identity by openly celebrating Israel's victory.

This feeling of growing concern for their brethren in
the Soviet Union in the West in the 1960s was not entirely
spontaneous but had been stirred by agents of Lishkat
Kesher, a section of the Israeli Foreign Ministry. More
generally it was due to the general revival of ethnic
consciousness in the 1960s; and a new awareness of the
'singled out' condition of the Jews following the Holocaust.
Devotees of peoplehood sought 'to be Jewish through
identification with the Jewish people as a corporate entity,
its history, culture and tradition, but without necessarily
accepting the authoritative character of halakhah [Jewish
law] or the centrality of halakhah in defining their

Jewishness'. At any rate, it was 'common usage' in the Soviet Union to accept anyone as Jewish if they had a Jewish father, even if this was not the case with their mother. Although there was a gradual revival of religion among some Soviet Jews, this civil religion of Jewish peoplehood was an ideal shared ideology and common ground for reaching many of the heavily assimilated Jewish communities in the Soviet Union. As Jonathan Sachs suggested, 'Solidarity between the Jews of the West, Israel, the Soviet Union, and threatened diaspora communities has become more than the object of activism. It has become the carrier of [Jewish] identity'.[1]

For a long time the younger generation in the West was troubled by the belief that their parents' generation had miserably failed to save many of their fellow Jews in Central and Eastern Europe from the onslaught of the Holocaust; and some of the motivation which stirred Jewish students and women in Britain must be ascribed to this source, but this is to fail to set the British movement for Soviet Jewry in the wider context of the 1960s and 1970s. These were decades of sexual revolution, student revolts, women's liberation, and the mushrooming of human rights organizations. The various sections of the Anglo-Jewish Soviet Jewry campaign fitted well into this more general picture. Moreover, the switch from stressing the right to family reunification and the right to emigrate more generally to emphasising the human rights of Soviet Jews by the Anglo-Jewish campaigners in the mid-1970s chimed well with the flourishing of human rights groups set up in the West to aid different groups of dissenters in the Soviet Union and elsewhere; and attracted support for Jewish individuals trapped in the USSR from all strata of British society including journalists, scientists, ballet stars, actors, and religious activists.

---

[1]Jonathan Sacks, One People? Tradition Modernity, and Jewish Unity (London, 2001). Moshe Rosman, How Jewish is Jewish History (Oxford, 2007), p.80.

The most significant events in the Jewish history of the second half of the twentieth century were the three wars Israel fought for its independence in 1948 and for survival in the Six Day War of 1967 and the Yom Kippur War of 1973; the emergence of American Jewry with the financial and political clout to flex its muscles on the political stage; and the international campaign to facilitate the emigration of Soviet Jewry. Israel in its early years was regarded by its enemies as a Crusader kingdom, bereft of manpower, which would capitulate if isolated and subjected to enough pressure. Zionist leaders in Palestine had hoped to draw on the vast Jewish population reserves of Eastern Europe but six million of them perished in the Shoah; and after the foundation of the state, they turned their attention to the surviving remnant in the Soviet Union, who were subjected to the stifling of their religious and cultural rights. If action was not taken, the Jews of the Soviet Union would assimilate and disappear in a generation or two.

Moreover, it is necessary to set the story of the British movement for Soviet Jewry in the context of the changing relationship of Britain and the Soviet Union on security matters and trade. The main players on such issues were the United States and the Soviet Union, so it was necessary for the British groups involved in the struggle to keep in close contact with their counterparts in the National Conference on Soviet Jewry and the Union of Councils for Soviet Jews.

Although there are a number of good accounts of the Soviet Jewry movement in the United States, there is no comparable volume for Anglo-Jewry. One of the few overall accounts by Daphne Gerlis only deals with the history of one group, the Women's Campaign for Soviet Jewry, better known as the 35's, and omits a detailed assessment of other important organizations, such as the National Council for Soviet Jewry and the students from its survey. Packed with nuggets of important information from participants in the Women's Campaign, it does not

always document its sources.[2] A more up-to-date book by
Mark Hurst, which is amply documented, only devotes a
single chapter to the Women's Campaign and then only
covers the early years of the 35's.[3] Then there is a wide-
ranging international survey of the beginning of the
movement, but it only deals with the early years from 1948
until 1967.[4] This volume may be supplemented by an
informative article by Dave Rich on 'The Activist
Challenge: Women, Students and the Board of Deputies'.[5]
There is also an informative and useful general history of
the subsequent decade of the movement by Colin Shindler
entitled *Exit Visa: Detente, Human Rights, and the Jewish
Emigration Movement in the USSR.*[6]

My own account of the British Soviet Jewry campaign
opens with a chapter on Soviet Jewry under Stalin to
delineate his attempt to wipe out religious observance
among Jews and any cultural identity in the guise of
Zionism. During the 1930s, he staged show trials of a
number of Jews among the Old Bolsheviks, who held
important positions in the Soviet state, and there were
countless other Jewish victims of his subsequent liquidation
of the early cadres who joined the Communist party. Once
the Stalin-Hitler pact had been signed in 1939, it was easy

---

[2]Daphne Gerlis, Those Wonderful Women in Black: The Story of the Women's Campaign for Soviet Jewry (London, 1996).

[3]Mark Hurst, British Human Rights Organizations and Soviet Dissent 1965-1985 (London,2016).

[4]Yaacov Ro'i, The Struggle for Soviet Jewish Emigration 1948-1967 (Cambridge,1991).

[5]Dave Rich, 'The Activist Challenge: Women, Students, and the Board of Deputies of British Jews in the British Campaign for Soviet Jewry', vol.29 Jewish History (2015):163-85.

[6]Colin Shindler, Exit Visa: Detente, Human Rights and the Jewish Emigration Movement in the USSR (Gillingham,1978).

for Stalin to ventilate his antisemitism more openly. When in June 1941, the German armies invaded the Soviet Union, Stalin switched his allegiance to an alliance with the Western powers and set up the Jewish Anti-Fascist Committee in 1942 to curry favour with Jewish groups outside his own country and to raise funds. After the defeat of Germany in 1945, Stalin regarded Jews as potential traitors in a war with the United States and ordered a trial of the leading Jewish intellectuals in the anti-Fascist Committee in 1952, but many of them retracted their evidence, so the trial was held in secret and the majority of the defendants were executed. To support this policy Stalin orchestrated an anti-cosmopolitan campaign in the press. These events led to a more vicious attempt to associate a group of mostly Jewish doctors with an imaginary plot to murder some of the country's top politicians which was only thwarted by Stalin's sudden death in 1953. Khrushchev continued with Stalin's anti-religious vendetta, his policy of removing Jews from prestigious positions, and he also staged trials of individuals for economic crimes, featuring a disproportionate number of Jews. Both Soviet leaders inhibited Jewish cultural expression.

In chapter two I discuss how Shaul Avigur was asked by Prime Minister Moshe Sharett in 1952 to set up a secret organization, popularly known as *Lishkat Kesher* (Liaison Bureau), which reported to him. Its tasks were to make contact with Jews in the Soviet Union and later in 1954 to rouse Western Jewish communities from their apathy about this issue and to educate potential campaigners in the realities of Jewish life for Russian Jews. In Britain, Israeli representatives made contact with the poet and novelist Emanuel Litvinoff, who was encouraged to deliver a letter to the Chief Rabbi of Moscow in 1958 asking him to invite Nahum Goldmann as president of the World Jewish Congress on an official visit, an overture which was rebuffed. The Israelis encouraged Litvinoff to write up an account of his trip which caused a stir, subsequently subsidising the publication of a scholarly journal entitled

Jews in Eastern Europe which he edited. From 1960 onwards, the Lishka organized a series of international conferences of European intellectuals on the plight of Soviet Jews. By 1963 their sympathisers across Europe were not only asking for cultural rights for Soviet Jews but also for family reunification, where appropriate. Unable to work through the representative British communal organization, the Board of Deputies, whose efforts were ineffective, the Israelis turned to the students. In 1964 under the leadership of Yakov Birnbaum students in the United States formed the Student Struggle for Soviet Jewry. The Israelis encouraged the establishment of a similar body in England two years later, the Universities Committee for Soviet Jewry. A number of student leaders organized the first public expression of disquiet, a march on the Soviet embassy from Hyde Park on 8 May 1966. Gordon Hausmann, who had similarly been approached by the Israelis, was the driving force behind this movement. He made contact with the Prime Minister, Harold Wilson, and helped to draft a non-partisan motion on Soviet Jewry in the House of Commons. The victory of Israel in the Six Day War in 1967 which reignited nationalist sentiment and pride among Soviet Jews also strongly motivated their co-religionists overseas, who started to campaign more vigorously.

The Soviet Jewry campaign in Britain was given a further fillip when Edward Kuznetsov and Mark Dymshits were given the death sentence after their trial in December 1970 for preparing to hijack an aircraft because their attempts to emigrate to Israel were frustrated by the authorities. The first World Conference on Soviet Jewry took place in Brussels in February 1971 with the demand that the right for Soviet Jews to emigrate be recognized more generally, not merely on grounds of family reunification. In Britain Ijo Rager, a counsellor at the Israeli embassy, encouraged the formation of a Women's Campaign for Soviet Jewry, also known as the 35's (see chapter three). An effective public relations campaign on behalf of a refusenik, Raiza Palatnik, was mounted by

Barbara Oberman. However, after a public relations disaster, in which a student leader left a briefcase containing correspondence with the Israeli embassy in the Soviet consulate office in London after a fracas, a diplomatic incident was narrowly avoided, and Barbara Oberman was asked to step down from the leadership of the 35's. This role was entrusted to Doreen Gainsford, who by a series of brilliant gimmicks in the protests which she organized secured the attention of the media and the wider British public. Although both the 35's and Barbara Oberman's new organization, the Committee for the Release of Soviet Jewish Prisoners, had their successes, the independent Committee for the Release of Valery and Galina Panov drew recruits from the world of ballet and left-wing Jewish activists, Equity and stars of stage and screen; and perhaps for a time overshadowed the other organizations.

Fearing loss of control of the Soviet Jewry campaign in Britain, the Board of Deputies set up the National Council for Soviet Jewry in December 1975 with tight regulation over its membership and finances; but it could never contain the activity of the students and women which was boisterous at times. Meanwhile, emigration rates of Soviet Jews climbed from a modest number in 1970 to 20,181 in 1974 because of the worldwide campaign, in which the movement in the United States and Britain played such an important role. This reached a peak in 1979 with 51,547 Jews leaving, but after this date numbers began to fall and dwindled to a trickle in the first half of the 1980s because of the Soviet invasion of Afghanistan in 1979.[7]

In chapter four I examine how thirty-five nations from the Eastern and Western blocs at a meeting of the Conference on Security and Cooperation in Europe (CSCE) signed the Helsinki Accords in 1975. This had momentous consequences for the religious and cultural freedom of Soviet Jews and for their right to emigrate. President Carter

---

[7] Pauline Peretz, Let My People Go. The Transnational Politics of Soviet Jewish Emigration during the Cold War (New Brunswick, 2015), p.344.

in 1977 put human rights at the forefront of his foreign policy. All of these Jewish organizations in Britain and the United States working for Soviet Jewry exploited the new legal framework to the full and started to emphasise the issue of human rights in their campaigning. David Owen, who was appointed as Foreign Secretary by the Labour Prime Minister James Callaghan, was very interested in the subject of human rights and followed the President's lead. But apart from allowing a parliamentary delegation sponsored by the Women's Campaign to see him about Anatoly Shcharansky's arrest, he held aloof from Jewish campaigners and was critical of what he deemed their narrowly focussed efforts. The Lishka's director, Nehemiah Levanon, asserted in 1978 that Britain should concentrate on individual cases and the cultural aspects of the campaign, leaving politics to the Americans. The Jackson-Vanik Amendment, which proposed limiting Soviet access to trade and credit according to their loosening controls on emigration, had been introduced by Senator Jackson on 4 October 1972 in the Senate and was signed into law by President Ford on 3 January 1975.[8] It was robustly supported by American Soviet Jewry campaigners; but after the signing of the Helsinki Accords, human rights gradually took over as the principal lever of the Americans for securing concessions from the Soviet government.

Looking back to the trials orchestrated by Stalin and later Khrushchev in the 1950s and 1960s, I show how these anti-Jewish trials were continued by Brezhnev in the 1970s under the influence of the Jewish or partly Jewish KGB chief Andropov (see chapter five). Likewise, the trials were based on fabricated and rigged evidence and sometimes fell apart. The defiance of the Prisoners of Zion when they were interrogated and in speeches at the end of their trials which became widely reported, boosted the morale of the refusenik community and drew admiration and growing support from diaspora communities.

---

[8] Henry L. Feingold, 'Silent No More' Saving the Jews of Russia: The American Jewish Effort, 1967-1989 (Syracuse,2007), p.109.

In the next chapter, I cover the early years of the dual leadership of Margaret Rigal and Rita Eker, who took over leadership of the Women's Campaign from Doreen Gainsford, who emigrated to Israel in 1978 (see chapter six). They built on the relationship developed by Doreen Gainsford with Margaret Thatcher, and in correspondence with her over many years tried to educate her in the realities of the changing Soviet Jewish scene and encourage her to take a firm stand on human rights. Margaret Thatcher was swept into office as Prime Minister after an election in May 1979. On 29 April 1981 Mrs Thatcher saw Avital Shcharansky accompanied by Lord Bethell, who told her about her husband's swiftly deteriorating health in prison. Mrs Thatcher entertained her to tea and agreed to be photographed with her on the steps of Downing Street to extend some protection to Anatoly while he endured horrendous conditions in prison. Mrs Rigal and Mrs Eker concentrated their efforts on trying to free Shcharansky, Ida Nudel and Alexander Paritsky, a Jewish cultural activist and Hebrew teacher from detention. But the Prime Minister's assistance was kept at a relatively low level, and she rarely breached safe Foreign Office guidelines, as priority was given to the reduction of missiles and conventional arms in Europe.

In December 1984 the Prime Minister invited Mikhail Gorbachev to visit Britain, as she wanted to make his acquaintance at first hand because he had been singled out as a man with a more flexible approach. She hailed the visit as a great success, and in March 1985 he succeeded his mentor Andropov as General Secretary and leader of the Soviet Union. In July 1985 Mrs Eker accompanied Avital Shcharansky on a visit to the Prime Minister, who presented a negative assessment of the efforts to free her husband and told her to reduce the scale of her campaign (see chapter seven). Everything on this issue continued to be left to the Americans, who suddenly secured his release in a spy swap in February 1986. Despite this, because of Margaret Thatcher's receptiveness to appeals from individuals to mediate with the Kremlin, her stature continued to grow among refuseniks as a figure personifying the good mother. Before her visit to Moscow in March 1987, she was briefed by the recently expelled Dr Orlov, whose view it was that Gorbachev was working with the KGB and releasing some well-known names to appease public opinion in the West, while detaining a multitude of less well-known names. Colin Shindler voiced a similar view, saying that Mrs Thatcher was confused between the small number of Jews granted exit visas and the 400,000 who had secured invitations from relatives in Israel but were detained in the Soviet Union. In addition, the insistence in a new law framed by the Soviet leadership on an invitation from a first degree relative, seemed to be an attempt to curb emigration. In other words, Gorbachev was regarded as somewhat of a sham as a reformer, an argument that Mrs Thatcher refused to accept. At the beginning of 1987 Gorbachev granted an amnesty to 140 political prisoners, who included Hebrew teachers. It was difficult to discern in which direction he was going. Before a December 1987 summit with President Reagan, when the Intermediate Forces Nuclear Treaty was signed, a few more prominent refuseniks were released. At this time Natan Shcharansky arranged the biggest ever mass Jewish rally on behalf of Soviet Jewry in Washington. Some analysts believe that this event lodged in Gorbachev's mind and persuaded him to allow the mass emigration of Soviet Jews. Others may conclude that it was the explosion in the nuclear reactor on 26 April 1986 at Chernobyl and the economic fall-out that finally induced Gorbachev to change his mind.

Even so, at a meeting between the Prime Minister and Edgar Bronfman of the World Jewish Congress, he relayed the message in July 1988 that though the Soviet Jewish emigration rate would be raised, it would still be less than 50,000 per annum. The surmise must be that Gorbachev was a reluctant convert to mass Jewish emigration from the USSR. No matter that Jewish scientists and engineers were discriminated against, he desperately wanted to retain these highly trained cadres, if the Soviet Union was to modernise rapidly (see chapter eight). More and more Jewish groups in the Soviet Union addressed appeals to Margaret Thatcher, as she was seen as the most sympathetic political leader in the West. The Women's Campaign insisted in a message to the Prime Minister that before a human rights conference was held in Moscow in 1991 the Kremlin would have to agree to changes in its emigration policy. France and increasingly the United States wavered about these pre-conditions. Thatcher took this up with the President and Shultz, the Secretary of State, negotiated specific criteria which had to be fulfilled by the Soviet Union before a conference could be held. The principal issues were the freeing of political prisoners and sane psychiatric detainees, who were falsely classified as mentally disturbed. Because of pressure from human rights and Jewish groups, particularly the Women's Campaign, on the Prime Minister, some measure of conditionality was introduced into the negotiations with Moscow by the State Department. By the spring of 1989, the Soviet economy was in difficulties because of the cost of cleaning up the Chernobyl nuclear disaster and the consequences of the explosion which exacerbated nationality tensions in the Ukraine. Seeking financial assistance from the West, Gorbachev opened the gates for much increased Jewish migration. Jewish emigration from the Soviet Union reached no more than 18,919 in 1988 and then climbed to 71,196 in 1989 before accelerating to 181,802 in 1990, reaching a peak in 1992 of 108,292 and 102,134 in 1993. By this date, the Soviet Union had disintegrated at the end of 1991 as it was enveloped in deepening economic and nationalities crises. Margaret Thatcher had stepped down as Prime Minister, the National Council was disbanded and the Women's Campaign gradually wound down its campaigning role and changed into a charitable organization.[9]

---

[9]Pauline Peretz, Let My People Go: The Transnational Politics of Soviet Jewish Emigration During the Cold War p.344.

Chapter 1 - Soviet Jewry Under Stalin
The Leninist Inheritance

In 1966 it was thought that there were some three million Jews in the USSR, though some experts believed that this was an underestimate. Of the fifteen nationalities designated as comprising the Soviet state, Jews formed the seventh largest population. Jews were predominantly an urban population as almost all of them lived in towns. By 1925, 1,120,000 Jews had been compelled by the authorities to close their small businesses, forcing half a million of them to leave their small shtetlach for new employment opportunities elsewhere and move to a cluster of big cities. Hence the Jewish population became concentrated even more heavily in a small number of major Soviet urban conglomerations.[10] Over one and a quarter million Jews lived in seven cities in 1963 – Moscow with 500,000, Leningrad with 325,000, Kiev with 154,000, Odessa with 118,000, Kharkov with 80,000, Kishinev with 42,000 and Minsk with 38,000. Because the Jews were so urbanized and the educational opportunities available in the larger cities were superior, their economic structure was rapidly transformed between the Revolution and the Second World War.

By 1939 Soviet Jewry included the following categories: 30 per cent were manual workers, 20 percent were artisans, 41 percent employees and members of the liberal professions, 6 percent farmers, and 3 percent filled miscellaneous professions. After the Second World War, about half the lawyers in Leningrad and Kharkov and about a third in Moscow were Jewish. There was also a proliferation of Jewish scientists and engineers and 10 per cent of the Soviet Academy of Science were Jewish. Jews

---

[10] S. Levenberg, 'Soviet Jewry: Some Problems and Perspectives', pp.29-37 and Chimen Abramsky, the Biro-Bidzhan Project,1927-59', p.63 both in Lionel Kochan ed., The Jews in Soviet Russia Since 1917 (London,1970).

could be found in large numbers in the film industry, 34 percent according to one estimate. During the early years of the Soviet regime, they were prominent in government, the Communist party, the diplomatic service and the higher ranks of the army, but in the 1930s Stalin started purging them from these positions. However, as the various nationalities comprising the USSR became better educated, there was greater competition for jobs and the prominent position of Jews in managerial positions in industry and their concentration in the sciences and the arts created resentment and sometimes antisemitism.[11]

From the first, the leaders of the Bolshevik Revolution of 1917 had an ambivalent attitude towards the Jews in the Soviet Union and left a tainted legacy. On the one hand, Vladimir Lenin made a declaration in 1918 denouncing antisemitism, but the Criminal Code of 1922 failed to make it an offence. Leon Trotsky denounced both the pogrom in Bialystok in 1906 and the staging of the blood libel trial of Mendel Beilis in 1913; but when Jews were massacred on an extensive scale in 1917 and 1918 in Ukraine and the Russian borderlands, at Lenin's request, he refrained from speaking out and refused to say anything about the closure of churches and attacks on clerics. It was estimated that 100,000 Jews, perhaps 150,000 or possibly as many as 200,000 Jews perished in these pogroms. Most of these were perpetrated by armies under the control of the Ukrainian nationalist leader Symon Petliura, though as many as ten or twelve percent of the victims fell at the hands of Red Army contingents. On the other hand, the revolutionaries saw Jews in racialised terms as outsiders, who were not part of the nation, and as being members of the bourgeoisie and therefore an obvious target for Communists involved in the class struggle. Trotsky refused to head the People's Commissariat of Internal Affairs and again rejected Lenin's plea to become his deputy in 1922; and only reluctantly assumed the position of People's Commissar for Military

---

[11] S. Levenberg, 'Soviet Jewry: Some Problems and Perspectives', pp.32-7.

Affairs in 1918, all because of his Jewish origins. Stalin's attitude towards the Jews was shaped by this ambivalent policy and perpetuated by his successors including Brezhnev and Khrushchev and perhaps even Gorbachev in a more subtle and less viscerally antisemitic way.[12]

At the outset of the Revolution ex-Bundists and former Zionists in the Jewish Commissariat, who had a lasting affinity to their Jewish family background, protested to the Bolshevik leaders at the centre about these antisemitic outrages, who failed to initiate an action plan to combat this hatred. So these Jewish leaders in the localities instituted educational courses to wean the revolutionaries off antisemitism. In the 1930s Jews were still protesting to the central government about this. By the late 1930s, Stalin briefly aligned himself with Hitler and intensified his policy of sacking Jews in important positions in the party and government. A decade later as Jews everywhere were removed from key posts, both local leaders and those at the centre ignored complaints about antisemitism.[13]

While condemning Zionism as a tool of the imperialists, Jewish Communist leaders hoped to appeal to the Jewish masses, by setting up the alternative of a Jewish colony in the Soviet Far East. The Biro-Bidzhan project, which started in 1928, was meant to absorb some of the impoverished Jews who had remained in the small towns. Soviet propagandists boasted that unlike the situation in Palestine they would not have to displace the indigenous inhabitants, as the area chosen was sparsely populated. However, an economic expert, Yuri Larin, warned that the soil was too infertile and the climate too harsh for mass colonization. His predictions proved to be correct. Jewish

---

[12] Brendan McGeever, lecture on 'Antisemitism in the Bolshevik Revolution' to the IJS 20 January 2021. Robert Service, Trotsky. A Biography (London, 2009), p.205.
[13] Brendan McGeever, lecture.

institutions were closed in 1948, emigration of Jews ceased, and in 1959 the 14,296 Jews comprised only 8.8 per cent of the population.[14]

When the Bolsheviks seized power, Zionism in its various strands was perhaps the dominant ideology in Jewish life. Its appeal continued because in the late 1920s three-quarters to half of Jewish youth in the areas with a dense Jewish population remained outside educational institutions and employment opportunities were lacking.[15] Although the Soviet government's policy was at first cautious and vacillating, the Jewish section of the Communist party, the Evsektsiya, were much more outspoken in their condemnation of Zionism as being 'counter-revolutionary... clerical and nationalist'. The Jewish subsidiary of the Communist party was filled with recruits from the Bund and Fareinikte, zealous opponents of the Zionists, whom they were determined to annihilate. In the Ukraine in 1919 the authorities ordered the closure of fifteen Zionist organizations and the Tarbut school system in Kiev with its emphasis on teaching in Hebrew, leaving enthusiasts with no choice other than emigration to Palestine. In St. Petersburg, the central Zionist office was shut and then allowed to re-open, while in Moscow seventy-five Zionist supporters were arrested and gradually released after the intervention of officials from the American Joint Distribution Committee. In 1922 the persecution of Zionists restarted with thirty-seven participants in a Tzeirei Zion conference in Kiev being tried by a military court which permitted twelve sentenced to two years' hard labour to leave for Palestine after they had completed thirteen months of their sentence. Their indictment claimed that 'To restore the Palestine state, these

---

14 Chimen Abramsky, 'The Biro-Bidzhan Project,1927,1959', pp.62-75. Salo W. Baron, The Russian Jews Under the Tsars and Soviets, pp.193-8.

15 Ziva Galili and Boris Morozov, Exiled to Palestine. The Emigration of Zionist Convicts from the Soviet Union 1924-1934 (London,2006), p.3.

representatives of the Jewish bourgeoisie rely on reactionary forces, ranging from Tiutiunik and Petliura to such rapacious imperialists as Poincare, Lloyd George, and the Pope'. In September 1922 more than 1,000 Zionists were arrested in Odessa, Kiev, Berdichev and elsewhere with further arrests in 1923. On 2 September 1924 several thousand Zionist activists were arrested, tried in secret and sent to prisons in the outlying regions of the USSR. The convicted Zionists were offered the choice of signing a statement agreeing that their activities were anti-Soviet or counter-revolutionary in return for which they were allowed to proceed to Palestine. Zionist training colonies were also broken up, their leadership languishing in prisons and labour camps. By this means the Soviet authorities rid themselves of the hard-core of Zionist devotees and impressed world Jewish opinion with their tolerance.[16]

According to Ziva Galili, in the decade 1924 to 1934 over 1,000 Zionists arrested for activities connected with their movement were given the choice of agreeing to deportation to Palestine, instead of serving a prison sentence or exile to the remotest parts of the Soviet Union. Other members of the Zionist youth movements and Hechalutz, an organization which trained youths in physical labour, stole across the border, escaping into Poland, Romania and Latvia, from where their transit to Palestine was arranged. The Soviet authorities also permitted trainees from farms run by the Legal Hechalutz and expelled members of Tel Chai to embark on boats for Palestine from Odessa. In all, approximately two and a half thousand active Zionists escaped from the Soviet Union and settled in Palestine in the years 1924 to 1934. In addition, some Jews from Central Asia and the Caucasus and families in towns with large savings were permitted entry into Palestine, avoiding the usual restrictions on

---

[16] J.B. Schechtman, 'The USSR, Zionism and Israel' in Lionel Kochan ed. The Jews in Soviet Russia Since 1917 pp.99-111. Nora Levin, The Jews in the Soviet Union Since 1917 vol. 1 (London,1988), pp.86-98. Salo W. Baron, The Russian Jew Under the Tsars and Soviets p.401 n.20.

immigrants. A group of Lubavitch Chasidim with money raised from sympathisers overseas also migrated to Palestine from the Soviet Union in this period.[17]

With the Zionist movement hamstrung and disintegrating, the Soviet authorities unleashed a vicious propaganda campaign between 1936 and 1939 against 'Zionist imperialist oppression of the Palestinian Arabs'. Before the dissolution of their organization in January 1930, the leadership of the Evsektsiya carried out a sustained campaign against the publication of Hebrew literature in favour of Yiddish and forced the shutting down of schools teaching Hebrew. At the same time, with the intensification of the anti-religious campaign in 1921-2, synagogues were requisitioned and religious classes, hadarim, were banned. Even so, it appears that as late as 1929, 12,000 children were still receiving a religious instruction in clandestine hadarim and that 800 were studying in yeshivot. The Soviet government led an intensive drive for Yiddish schools in 1925, a year of 'Ukrainization and Belorussification – and a time of vehement anti-Zionist and anti-clerical agitation'. Secular Yiddish schools reached their apogee in 1932-3, 'when about 160,000 children mainly in Belorussia and the Ukraine were attending elementary and secondary schools, factory schools, and institutions of higher learning'. From then onwards the Russification of the school system increased, while the socialist content of education began to be emphasized more rather than national and cultural traditions, so that Jewish children lost any connection with the past. But in 1939 the Soviet Union annexed eastern Poland and in 1940 the Romanian provinces of Bessarabia and Bukovina, besides absorbing Estonia, Latvia and Lithuania. In this way, they acquired a new two million-strong Jewish population with an intense Zionist affiliation which the Soviet state set out to destroy.[18]

---

[17] Ziva Galili and Boris Morozov, Exiled to Palestine, pp.1 and 80.
[18] J.B. Schechtman, 'The USSR, Zionism and Israel', pp.112-13. Nora Levin, The Jews in the Soviet Union Since 1917 vol.1 pp.68-86,98-116,177, and 182-7.

Stalin's Rule in the 1920s and 1930s

Stalin had a paranoid personality with little trust in people of all nationalities, but he had a heightened suspicion of Jews with their links to communities overseas. Under Lenin during the first years of the Soviet regime, Stalin hid behind the veneer of being an internationalist. During the 1930s it soon fell away, as he extirpated Jewish political rivals in show trials and scythed alleged opponents of his policies in their thousands and tens of thousands, including many Jews recruited from other political parties, eventually ruining the lives of millions of people. David Caute criticized Isaac Deutscher for underplaying the extent of the casualties inflicted in the purges by talking only of the men and women active in the Communist movement and the military officers caught up in them. 'So the tally remains thousands to their deaths and hundreds of thousands into prisons and concentration camps – rather than the millions who actually suffered and died in the Gulag'.[19] Once he allied himself between 1939 and the summer of 1941 with Hitler in the German-Soviet pact, Stalin saw that Jews were expendable and did little to warn the Jewish population of the Soviet Union that they were a special target of the Nazi war machine when the Germans invaded.[20] During the War years he was allied to the Western powers to defeat Hitler, but after the Second World War he viewed the Jews with their ties to Israel and the United States as a dangerous fifth column; and he revived and extended his pre-War hostility towards Jews, as a potentially traitorous element.

Nevertheless, Stalin's attitude towards the Jewish religious practice closely followed his existing policy towards the Russian Orthodox Church which in turn was based on Lenin's policy of nationalising Church property

---

[19] David Caute, Isaac and Isaiah (New Haven,2013), p.75.
[20] Stephane Courtois et alia eds., The Black Book of Communism. Crimes, Terror, Repression (Cambridge, Mass,1999), pp.302-3.

by a decree in 1918 and closing places of worship.[21] His anti-religious campaign of the 1920s and the early 1930s was relaxed because only 28 per cent of the houses of prayer of all the different faiths at the outset of the revolution were still open for worship and the Church was deemed to be sufficiently subdued not to mount a challenge to the Kremlin. But the functionaries in the principal areas, where Jewish population was concentrated in the Soviet Union, namely in the Ukraine and Belorussia, were particularly antisemitic, so that militant atheistic policies were more rigidly and harshly enforced in these areas. By 1936 and in the Ukraine only nine per cent of houses of prayer were still open, while in Belorussia there was a slightly better figure of eleven per cent of these venues still operating.[22]

Whereas there were only 40 to 50 legally functioning synagogues in the pre-Second World War USSR, there were a thousand additional synagogues in the newly annexed areas of Lithuania, Latvia, Estonia, Bukovina and Bessarabia which were incorporated between 1939 and 1940. However, in these new parts of the Soviet Union, there were also a number of clandestine minyanim in existence (small congregations with a quorum of ten adult males). In contrast to the older parts of the Soviet Union, where synagogue attendance was common only among the elderly, in the newly annexed areas the congregations included all age groups and Zionism was still strong among the youth.[23]

However, it was not only synagogues that were closed on an extensive scale under Stalin but also secular Yiddish spaces such as schools and theatres were also abolished and Jewish youth movements were disbanded. There were no longer social places for young Jews to meet. The knock-on effect of this attack on religious, Zionist and secular Yiddish cultural spaces, was a massive rise in

[21] Ruth Ellis, The Russian Orthodox Church. A Contemporary History (London,1986), pp.4-5.
[22] Mordechai Altshuler, Religion and Jewish Identity in the Soviet Union 1941-1964 (Lebanon NH,2012), pp.1-6.
[23] Mordechai Altshuler, Religion and Jewish Identity, pp.3,5.

intermarriage. Apart from this, under a 1918 decree only civil marriages were recognized as valid and had to be held in a registry office; and a religious ceremony, if held privately was tolerated, though increasingly looked on askance. Sarah Segev-Wobick estimated that the rate for men in Leningrad of exogamous unions in 1936 was 42.3 per cent and 36.8 per cent for women and Mordechai Altshuler adduced similar high rates of intermarriage. The intermarriage rates in the Soviet Union were vying with those of the Jewish community in Germany before 1933 and would soon overtake them, the Jews were assimilating so fast that the community appeared on the way to extinction. What happened to Jews during the Second World War and the foundation of Israel in 1948 would change all this. [24]

Soviet Jews in the Second World War

On 22 June 1941 Germany invaded the Soviet Union and Stalin, after a pause, aligned himself with the Western powers. But it was not until the Japanese attack on the American naval base at Pearl Harbour on 7 December 1941 that the United States entered the war. The leaders of the Russian Orthodox Church and parish priests out of a sense of patriotism called on their millions of followers to resist the German invasion, speaking to packed churches. Since Stalin required popular support for the War effort and as the Church could kindle such mass enthusiasm, after a surge of strong religious sentiment, he decided in 1943 to enter into a concordat with the Church. There was an easing of anti-religious restrictions with some monasteries reopening, theological education was allowed once more and the printing of some religious books resumed.[25]

---

[24] Sarah Wobick-Segev, Homes Away from Home. Jewish Belonging in the Twentieth-Century Paris, Berlin and St. Petersburg (Stanford, 2018), pp.47,69-71, 127,211 footnote 122; and Mordechai Altshuler, Soviet Jewry on the Eve of the Holocaust (Jerusalem,1998),p.270.
[25] Mordechai Altshuler, Religion and Jewish Identity pp.9-10. Jane Ellis, The Russian Orthodox Church. A Contemporary History (London,1986), pp.4-5.

Similarly, six weeks after the German invasion of the Soviet Union, an influential group of Jewish cultural figures including the poet Solomon Mikhoels and the novelist David Bergelson proposed holding a huge rally to elicit the support of Jews from Britain and the United States. On 24 August 1941 a huge rally took place in the Moscow Park of Culture which was addressed by prominent Soviet Jewish personalities. Mikhoels spoke of a war aimed at 'the total annihilation of the Jewish people'. The novelist Ilya Ehrenburg exclaimed that 'My mother tongue is Russian. I am a Russian writer. Like all Russians, I am now defending my homeland. But the Nazis reminded me of something else; my mother's name was Hannah. I am a Jew. I say this proudly. Hitler hates us more than anything, and this makes us proud'. Out of this group and out of a proposal of Henryk Erlich and Viktor Alter, the leaders of the Polish Bund, emerged the idea of a permanent organization, the Jewish Anti-Fascist Committee to rally support from Jews in the West for the Russian war effort. However, as part of a group of foreign socialists and Communists suspected of being disloyal, Erlich and Alter were placed under arrest and held in solitary confinement. Erlich committed suicide in prison in May 1942 and Alter was shot in February 1943.[26]

Likewise, as the German armies drew near to Moscow, on the High Holidays the synagogues were crowded with worshippers and there was a resurgence of religious feeling; many Jews from the forces appeared in uniform and members of the younger generation also returned. In cities in the Soviet Union absorbing countless refugees, Jews filled existing synagogues and newly created places of worship without encountering resistance from the local authorities. During the period 1941-48, there was a relative tolerance towards Jewish religious practice, though the attitude of the authorities became increasingly negative.[27]

---

[26] Joshua Rubenstein and Vladimir P. Naumov, pp.7-10.
[27] Mordechai Altshuler, Religion and Jewish Identity, pp.9-10, 16.

The Jewish Anti-Fascist Committee was established in the spring of 1942 under the direction of Solomon Lozovsky, the deputy chairman of the Soviet Information Bureau (Sovinformburo). One idea that appealed to him was for organizing 'a campaign for financial contributions especially in the United States, to bring medicine and warm clothing for the Red Army and people evacuated from regions occupied by the Germans'. He quickly realized that millions of dollars could be collected from wealthy American Jews with little effort. The Soviet regime had encouraged a group of Yiddish writers to create a secular Yiddish culture in the hope of Jews forgetting their religious and cultural traditions and assimilating. But the atrocities committed by the Germans revitalized their Jewish identities and they spoke out passionately about Jewish suffering and appealed to fellow Jews in the West for help. Ilya Vattenberg later explained that the war gave rise to 'nationalistic germs' because the 'cruel and bestial policy which Hitler carried out ...reminded many Jews that they were Jews'. A new Yiddish newspaper was launched on 17 June 1942 under the editorship of Shakhno Epshteyn which lasted for seven years. Mikhoels, Bergelson, Fefer and Kvitko were nominated as part of the editorial team. Knowledge of the deaths of Alter and Ehrlich leaked out in February 1943 which caused disquiet in the West. They had been executed 'as spies and subversive agents' bent on dissuading the Red Army from fighting the Germans.[28]

To repair the damage to the Soviet image, Mikhoels was allowed to go on an extended seven-month fund raising tour of the United States and Britain in 1943, accompanied by Itsik Fefer. He distrusted Fefer because he was a conformist and a lackey of the Soviet regime, probably sent to report on him. The biggest event Mikhoels and Fefer went to in the United States was a rally in the Polo Grounds in New York attended by 50,000, in which they made speeches in Yiddish urging support for the Red Army. B.Z. Goldberg, a left-leaning Yiddish journalist and

[28] Joshua Rubenstein and Vladimir P. Naumov, pp.11-15.

32

son-in-law of Sholem Aleichem, made a speech praising 'the great leader Marshal Stalin', while Sholem Asch made extravagant claims that the Soviet Union was the first nation to abolish antisemitism and Rabbi Stephen Wise shamefully denounced 'Jewish Trotskyites'. Not only were American and Soviet flags displayed but also blue and white flags in recognition of Jewish national aspirations – a dangerous symbol for Mikhoels and Fefer to be associated with.[29]

Stalin's Post-War Years

Meanwhile, Ilya Ehrenburg suggested the compilation of a Black Book enumerating the mass slaughter of Jews perpetrated by the Germans on Soviet territory, a proposal independently put forward by the American Committee of Jewish Writers, Artists, and Scientists. After their trip to the United States, Mikhoels and Fefer stated that Jews should be resettled in the Crimea, which would create a Jewish republic and solve once and for all the problem of Jewish cultural continuity in line with the nationalities policy of Lenin and Stalin. During the War, the Yiddish newspaper *Eynikayt* declared that 'no normal, thoughtful, and freedom-loving person could be opposed to the settlement and development of their home by Jews in Palestine...That is their absolute right as a collective'. As soon as the War was over, the political atmosphere in the Soviet Union darkened and attempts to publish a Black Book dealing with the fate of Jews under the Nazi occupation were condemned as being motivated by particularist Jewish concerns; and Suslov, an orthodox Marxist and Stalinist, was placed in charge of the Jewish Anti-Fascist Committee, a sign that boded ill for its continuation.[30]

Although the Soviet Union supported the creation of the state of Israel in May 1948, once it was clear that the new

---

[29] Joshua Rubenstein and Vladimir P. Naumov, pp.,16-17.

[30] Joshua Rubenstein and Vladimir P. Naumov, pp.17-32.

Jewish state was aligned with the West, Stalin shifted his support to their Arab rivals, as Cold War tensions mounted. When his daughter Svetlana married Grigory Morozov, a Jew, Stalin remarked that 'the Zionists put him over on you'. Stalin grew increasingly suspicious of what he perceived were the divided loyalties of the Jews in the Soviet Union and believed that Jewish support could not be relied upon in the event of a war with the United States. Mikhoels had freely voiced his opinion that monuments should be erected to the victims of fascism, becoming incensed that the site of the mass burial of over 30,000 Jews at Babi Yar near Kiev was left unmarked.[31] Nor was he deterred from expressing his enthusiasm for a Jewish state in Palestine. To soften Stalin's animosity towards Jews, Mikhoels approached Isaac Goldshtein, who was in contact with Stalin's relatives, in the hope that they could induce the Soviet leader to take not such a hard line. On learning of this, Viktor Abakumov, the Minister of State Security, had Goldshtein tortured and made to confess that Mikhoels had conspired with American and Zionist intelligence agents, making Stalin determined to eliminate him. The order was given to kill Mikhoels on a trip to Minsk in January 1948 but to make it appear as an accident.

There was a further upsurge of Jewish feeling in the Soviet Union with the foundation of Israel in May 1948 and large crowds greeted Golda Meyerson (Meyer) when she visited the Moscow synagogue in the autumn with shouts of 'Next year in Jerusalem'. Stalin explained to his daughter Svetlana that 'The entire older generation is contaminated with Zionism and now they're teaching the young people, too'. He decided that the time had come to close the Jewish Anti-Fascist Committee and to shut down the presses of *Eynikayt* and the Yiddish publishing house. While this was happening, the secret police pounced on the fifteen members of the Jewish Anti-Fascist Committee and one

---

[31] Lucy S. Dawidowicz, What is the Use of Jewish History? (New York,1992), pp.101-19.

other suspect, Zhemchuzhina, Molotov's wife, who had an indiscreet conversation with Golda Meyerson.[32]

On 28 January 1949 *Pravda* opened an anti-cosmopolitan campaign with headlines attacking a group of critics, nearly all of whom were Jews, who were said to be hostile to Soviet literature and drama. More articles and cartoons appeared attacking 'rootless cosmopolitans' and 'passport-less wanderers', who showed a lack of comprehension of Soviet culture. The cartoons displayed hook-nosed Jews and the newspaper accounts pointed to the Jewish origin of the targeted individuals, by giving their current names and their original surnames in brackets side by side. In 1950 the *American Jewish Yearbook* claimed that the leaders of the Jewish Anti-Fascist Committee had been arrested, which was true, and deported, which was a misconception. All the fifteen defendants were harshly interrogated with the exception of Fefer and beaten until they confessed. They were charged with four crimes: bourgeois nationalism; the creation of an anti-Soviet underground; treason against the Soviet Union; and spying on behalf of the United States. By more than coincidence with a number of high-profile trials in the offing, it was announced with impeccable timing at the beginning of 1950 that the death penalty had been restored for treason.[33]

A show trial had been planned against the leadership of the Jewish Anti-Fascist Committee, but the trial date of the Jewish Anti-Fascist Committee dragged on and, because a number of the defendants retracted their confessions, the trial did not start until 8 May 1952 and was not open to the public. Fefer, a sycophant of the regime was spared torture, and his confessions were used to implicate more than a hundred other persons, many of whom subsequently died.[34] All the defendants' wartime support for Yiddish culture or for the Jews in Palestine was resurrected and together with their appeals to world Jewry

---

[32] Joshua Rubenstein and Vladimir P. Naumov, pp.32- 47.

[33] Joshua Rubenstein and Vladimir P. Naumov, pp.48-53. Nora Levin, The Jews in the Soviet Union Since 1917 vol.1 pp. 504-5.

[34] Joshua Rubenstein and Vladimir P. Naumov, pp.52-4.

were now held against them. But the principal accusation concerned the Crimea project, in which it was alleged that Mikhoels and Fefer during their American visit had conspired with Zionists and imperialists to establish a base to demolish the Soviet Union. Boris Shimeliovich, a distinguished doctor and director of the Botkin Clinical Hospital, like Lozovsky, Markish and Bregman, refused to confess to any guilt. Even Fefer admitted at a closed session that he had been an informer and started to go back on his own earlier evidence. Lozovsky carried himself proudly and in his evidence started to dissect the prosecution case which started to fall apart.[35]

Alexander Cheptsov, the judge, who had presided over similar cases without demur, was somewhat bemused and grasped that the case had been fabricated and, unusually, made several attempts to halt it, but to no avail. When he appealed to Georgy Malenkov in the presence of the investigators Semyon Ignatiev and Mikhail Ryumin, he was rebuffed and told to carry out the Politburo's decision to impose the death penalty. Nevertheless, he kept on trying for some measure of reprieve and sent an appeal from Lozovsky to Stalin in a bid for clemency, again without a helpful response. Exceptionally, Lina Shtern, a physician and former professor at Geneva, received a sentence of five years in exile, while another of the accused, Solomon Bregman, died in his prison cell. All the other thirteen defendants were executed.[36]

Yet the trial had failed in its broader objective of inciting Soviet public opinion behind a nationwide antisemitic onslaught, which may well have been Stalin's original intention. Nevertheless, from this misconceived trial sprang an even more vicious vendetta, the so-called Doctors' Plot. Stalin, having disposed of numerous rivals in show trials, was growing ever more paranoid and

---

[35] Joshua Rubenstein and Vladimir P. Naumov, pp.51,54-5,58-9, and 59-60.

[36] Joshua Rubenstein and Vladimir P. Naumov, p.60.

unpredictable and Ryumin sought to win his favour by playing on his fears by questioning the treatment meted out to high-ranking politicians by doctors at the call of the Kremlin. Starting in the autumn of 1951, Ryumin and his team of security officials began assembling the evidence to charge a group of doctors with planning to murder the Kremlin's senior politicians. During the Middle Ages Jews had been accused of poisoning wells and, in the 1938 show trial of Nikolai Bukharin and other Soviet leaders, several doctors, at least one of whom, Dr Lev Levin, was Jewish, were charged with trying to murder prominent people associated with the regime; such antisemitic tropes were now utilised once again in manufacturing the Doctors' Plot. Ryumin and his team commenced by questioning Dr Shimeliovich about Yevgeniya Lifshitz, a top paediatrician, who treated the children and grandchildren of Kremlin officials; and Dr Miron Vovsi, the chief physician of the Red Army during the War and a relative of Mikhoels, which made him a suspect; and Stalin's personal doctor, Vladimir Vinogradov. All these doctors as well as others were arrested in 1952.[37]

Ignatiev claimed that Stalin ordered all the papers relating to the Doctors' Plot were in the first instance to be sent to him, after which he distributed specific documents to officials of his choice. In this way, he micromanaged the progress of the investigation. After extracting a confession out of Dr Etinger, a leading diagnostic physician, that he had shortened the life of Shcherbakov (1901-45), which was palpably untrue, Ryumin wrote to Stalin and so impressed him that his superior, Abukumov, the Minister of State Security, was dismissed and he was promoted.[38] Next Stalin saw this as a good opportunity to reveal the contents of Dr

---

[37]Jonathan Brent and Vladimir P. Naumov, Stalin's Last Crime. The Plot against the Jewish Doctors 1948-53 (New York,2003), p.4. Joshua Rubenstein and Vladimir P. Naumov, p.54.

[38] Jonathan Brent and Vladimir P. Naumov, Stalin's Last Crime pp.120-22 and 130.

Timashuk's letter, which was stored in his personal archive. She stated that on the basis of the electrocardiograms which she had seen, the illness of A.A. Zhdanov, a member of the Politburo, had been misdiagnosed and he had been given the wrong treatment, cutting short his life. What this revealed to the suspicious mind of Stalin was that there were medical saboteurs within the Kremlin hospital, who treated the political elite, and were deliberately killing their patients. There now followed the arrest of prominent doctors and a purge of the security service, the MGB, for failing to detect the machinations of the doctors. Between July 1951 and September 1952, 42,000 individuals were dismissed from their posts.[39] By the autumn of 1951, nearly all the Jewish officers had been removed from the state security service, after 'Stalin ordered the arrest of all Jewish colonels and generals in the Ministry of Security. A total of some fifty senior officers and generals were arrested'.[40]

A junior Jewish doctor, Dr Sophia Karpai, was the first to be arrested for incorrectly deciphering the electrocardiograms of A.A. Zhdanov. Despite brutal treatment, she courageously insisted that these tests gave an ambiguous result and that her reading of them was not misleading. Unable to break her stubborn will, the security service wanted to execute her, but Stalin ordered that she be kept in a cell, as he wanted Jewish doctors to be associated with the death of leading politicians. He could then say that they were acting on behalf of American and Zionist interests and that their conduct was treasonable. Karpai was lodged in a cold, damp cell, which exacerbated her asthmatic condition and she died shortly after her release in March 1953. [41]

---

[39] Jonathan Brent and Vladimir P. Naumov, Stalin's Last Crime, pp.154-7.

[40] Jonathan Brent and Vladimir P. Naumov, Stalin's Last Crime, pp.177-8.

[41] Jonathan Brent and Vladimir P. Naumov, Stalin's Last Crime pp.158-61.

During a discussion with his Minister of State Security, S.D. Ignatiev, in October 1951, Stalin railed at him, calling the MGB, 'nincompoops' and demanded that he 'expose the group of doctor-terrorists, of whose existence...he had long been convinced'. The Deputy Minister, Ryumin, an anti-Semite much more attuned to Stalin's way of thinking, noted that 'In Moscow there lived more than a million and a half Jews. They had seized the medical posts, the legal profession, the union of composers and the union of writers. I'm not even speaking of the trade networks. Meanwhile of these Jews only a handful are useful to the state; all the rest – are potential enemies'. He then hinted that 'he intended to put the question to the government about the expulsion of the Jews from Moscow'.[42]

In January 1952, Stalin again upbraided Ignatiev, telling him that 'If you do not expose the terrorists among the doctors, then you will be where ABAKUMOV now is [prison]'. They should be finding who murdered Dimitrov and who led comrade 'Andrey astray'. In March 1952, R.I. Ryzhikov, a deputy director of the Barvikha sanatorium, which was attached to the Kremlin hospital, was arrested. By August 1952, Stalin was telling Ignatiev that Ryumin was 'excellent' and that he should 'listen to him and take him closer to' himself.[43] A few months later, Stalin gave orders for the arrest of doctors associated with the Kremlin hospital: Yegorov its director, Vasilenko, Vinogradov, Borukh B. Kogan, Maiorov, and Miron Vovsi, a cousin of Mikhoels. As the investigation advanced, Stalin took a daily interest in its progress and ordered that the prisoners should be tortured to extract confessions.[44] However, Stalin tired of Ryumin's posturing and held him responsible for

[42] Jonathan Brent and Vladimir P. Naumov, Stalin's Last Crime, pp.171-2 and 182.
[43] Jonathan Brent and Vladimir P. Naumov, Stalin's Last Crime, pp.188 and 206-7.
[44] Jonathan Brent and Vladimir P. Naumov, Stalin's Last Crime, pp.212-13 and 217.

precipitating Dr Etinger's death which delayed the whole train of the investigation and dismissed him in November 1952.[45]

In the same month, Goglidze, who had been put in charge of the Doctors' plot investigation when Ignatiev went on sickness leave because of the pressure placed on him, wrote a memorandum to Stalin informing him of the up-to-date situation. 'During interrogation, VOVSI and KOGAN [B.B.] confessed that both of them, being Jewish nationalists, supported enemy ties with the leaders of the Jewish nationalist underground, operating under the cover of the Jewish Antifascist Committee'. Through documentation and these confessions, it has been established that a group of 'terrorist doctors' were active in the Kremlin hospital – YEGOROV, VINOGRADOV, VASILENKO, MAIOROV, FEDEDOROV, LANG and Jewish nationalists, ETINGER, VOVSI, KOGAN and KARPAI, who strove through medical treatment to cut short the life of leaders of the party and government... It is impossible to forget the crimes of those well-known doctors, committed not so long ago [in the 1930s], such as the crimes of Doctor Pletnev and Doctor Levin, who poisoned V.V. Kuibyshev and Maxim Gorky at the direction of foreign intelligence agencies. These villains confessed to their crimes at an open trial and Levin [Jewish by nationality] was shot, but Pletnev was sentenced to 25 years of prison'.[46] Stalin warned the Presidium of the Central Committee on 1 December 1952 that 'every Jew-nationalist is an agent of American intelligence', hinting ominously of their removal from any position of importance in the Soviet Union. Meanwhile, because of their sloppy handling of the doctors' investigation,

---

[45] Jonathan Brent and Vladimir P. Naumov, Stalin's Last Crime pp.222-3.

[46] Jonathan Brent and Vladimir P. Naumov, Stalin's Last Crime pp.265-6.

Goglidze advised Stalin that there needed to be a thorough purge of the intelligence agency.[47]

On 13 January 1953, *Pravda* announced in an article carefully edited by Stalin that 'The unmasking of the band of doctor-poisoners dealt a shattering blow to the American-English instigators of war... The bosses of the USA and their English "junior partners" know that success in ruling another country cannot be achieved by peaceful means. Feverishly preparing for a new world war, they urgently sent their spies into the rear of the USSR and into countries of the People's Democracy...' The article highlighted the names of a number of Jewish doctors, accusing them of being 'paid agents of American intelligence', who received directives from the American Joint Distribution Committee, a Jewish charity, and Mikhoels and Dr Shimeliovich of the Jewish Anti-Fascist Committee. The article ended by referring to the thoughtlessness in the ranks of our people which had to be corrected.[48]

Rumours started to abound among Jews that millions of them would voluntarily agree to be deported out of public view in the Soviet Union on a certain specified day in order to escape the indignation of the Russian people. A febrile atmosphere developed as people waited for the trial to commence with anxious Jewish parents keeping their children from school to escape bullying and meetings with an antisemitic edge being convened in offices and factories.[49] Four camps in Central Asia and the Soviet Far East started to be constructed, all suspiciously large for a relatively small number of political criminals arrested in the

---

[47] Jonathan Brent and Vladimir P. Naumov, Stalin's Last Crime, pp.267-70.

[48] Jonathan Brent and Vladimir P. Naumov, Stalin's Last Crime, pp.283,287-90.

[49] Jonathan Brent and Vladimir P. Naumov, Stalin's Last Crime, pp.283-4,293,300.

Soviet zones of Germany and Austria. According to one source, a professor of philosophy, Dmitri Chesnokov, had been asked by Stalin to prepare a Marxist-Leninist theoretical basis for the deportations, though there is no documentation to corroborate this. However, an unpublished letter due to be sent to *Pravda* and signed by fifty-five Jewish intellectuals has come to light in which it was stated that there were two groups among the Jewish population, 'the camp of the workers and the camp of the exploiters'. It went on to suggest that recently a spying group of doctor-murderers has been uncovered under the direction of the Zionist Joint-Distribution Committee which was affiliated to American intelligence. Using their medical skills, these doctors planned to cut short the life of Soviet leaders in government and the military. With the unpublished article was a letter from Ilya Ehrenburg, an apologist for the regime, dated 3 February 1953 to Stalin, stating that the only answer to the Jewish problem was their complete assimilation, but this might provoke an international outcry.[50] Nonetheless, the doctors refused to confess their links to the Joint, thus delaying the opening of the trial. Stalin fell ill on 1 March 1953 and died five days later. The new Soviet leadership tired of all the turmoil and released the doctors from prison on grounds that the evidence was fabricated.[51]

Stalin's attempt to shake-up the various cadres in the Soviet leadership and to return to the show trials and instability of the 1930s must be seen in the context of the Cold War. Stalin had been preparing his political and military advisers in 1951 for a possible war in Western Europe in 1953 and the *Pravda* article was highlighting the role of the Jews as the enemy within.[52] Despite their closely argued text, Jonathan Brent and Vladimir Naumov only

---

[50] Jonathan Brent and Vladimir P. Naumov, Stalin's Last Crime, pp. 287-90,294-5,297, and 300-6.

[51] Jonathan Brent and Vladimir P. Naumov, Stalin's Last Crime pp.308,312-22.

[52] The Black Book of Communism, pp.432-3.

assemble fragmentary evidence to prove that the Doctors' Plot was being utilized by Stalin to deport the whole of the Jewish population of the Soviet Union into labour camps rather than a small section of it. Moreover, there was a huge press campaign to target intellectuals, soldiers, industrial managers, party officials, and members of the security service as well as Jews.[53] Even so, the events of 1952 and 1953 for which Stalin bears prime responsibility marked a grave deterioration in the position of Soviet Jews.

At the same time, Stalin broadened his campaign against prominent Jewish Communists in Central Europe, especially those who had lived in Western Europe during the War or who had fought in the International Brigade in Spain. In Hungary the trial of Laszlo Rajk, who had campaigned in the International Brigade, in 1949 laid stress on his Jewishness and that of three other defendants. As Stalin switched his support to the Arab regimes after the birth of Israel in 1948 hard-line supporters of his previous policies were now branded as Zionists in a series of show trials. The Rudolf Slansky trial in Czechoslovakia, in which the Jewishness of eleven of the defendants was emphasised, focussed on American imperialism as the chief enemy in preparation for a forthcoming armed clash. Many of the defendants were executed, while their ashes were buried on a construction site near Prague. One of the few survivors, the Deputy Foreign Minister, Artur London, remarked later that one of his interrogators had praised Hitler's extermination programme, boasting that 'we will finish what he started'. When Stalin in 1951 was startled to learn that the agents of Titoism and Zionism in Romania had escaped prosecution and demanded action, the Finance Minister and the Interior Minister were arrested; the latter was executed and the former party official died in prison.[54] Ana Pauker, the Foreign Minister and a major figure in

---

[53] The Black Book of Communism, pp.242-9.

[54] The Black Book of Communism, pp.426-35. Jewish Chronicle, 3 January 2014, p.28.

Romanian politics, was arrested in 1953 and released in 1954. As a young girl, she had been close to her paternal grandfather, a charismatic rabbinic figure.[55] The trials of these secular Jewish internationalists, who identified almost completely with the nation to which they belonged or to the wider Communist community, continued into 1953 and 1954.[56]

An analysis of 56 Soviet newspapers and journals between 1948 and 1953, put the percentage of intellectuals denounced in the anti-cosmopolitan campaign who were Jewish as ninety per cent. In economics and sport, it was eighty per cent. In 1948 almost all the Jewish first-year students registered in physics and mechanics were expelled from the Leningrad Polytechnical Institute without explanation. From 1948 until 1959 not a single book was published in Yiddish in the Soviet Union. Between 1936 and 1940 there were about 800 Yiddish writers and journalists. Apart from the War when about forty of them died, hundreds perished in the prisons and labour camps in 1948-9, among them the novelist Der Nister. Jewish culture was stifled by Stalin, though it fared little better under his immediate successors.[57]

Nikita Khrushchev

From 1955 until October 1964 Nikita Khrushchev was the key figure in Soviet politics. He had been brought up in the Ukraine, where he acquired all the visceral anti-Jewish prejudices of his surroundings. Under his leadership, there was a relaxation of restraints on Russian and Ukrainian newspapers from 1957 onwards which published articles

---

[55] The Black Book of Communism, p.435. Robert Levy, Ana Pauker (Berkeley,2001), pp.15-17,28-9.

[56] The Black Book of Communism, pp.434-5.

[57] Nora Levin, The Jews in the Soviet Union Since 1917, vol.1 pp.504-11.

publicising antisemitic stereotypes of Jews, the Jew as an army dodger, lacking in moral scruples, and indulging in fraud to secure better housing and employment. On a visit to Poland in March 1956, Khrushchev exclaimed that 'in Poland, too, you are suffering from an abnormal composition of the leading cadres, as we once suffered from it... The percentage of high Jewish officials is now nil in my country, two or three per thousand...' With his eyes fixed on Roman Zambrowski, who was born Zukerman, he exploded, 'Yes, you have many leaders with names ending in 'ski' but an Abramovich remains an Abramovich. And you have too many Abramoviches in your leading cadres'. On a second visit six months later, he berated the Polish leadership, saying that the 'Red Army, shed its blood to liberate Poland and you want to deliver your country into the hands of the capitalists who are in league with the Zionists and Americans'.[58]

Nevertheless, at a closed session of the Communist party in 1956 Khrushchev denounced Stalin's crimes and the cult of personality, calling for a restoration of collective leadership and socialist legality, and boosting the general 'thaw' in society which had started a little earlier.[59] On 10 November 1954, the Central Committee of the party had passed a resolution stating the Church was loyal to the state and that nothing should be done to harm 'the sensibilities of the religious' by oppressive measures. A few months later another resolution was adopted, stating that the onus on closing a house of prayer no longer rested with the government of the USSR but resided with the governments of the republics of the Soviet Union. Crowds gathered around synagogues on High Holidays and in the relaxed atmosphere of these years between 1954 and 1959 Holiday minyans (a minimum of at least ten men assembling for

---

[58] Benjamin Pinkus, The Soviet Government and the Jews 1948-67 (Cambridge,1984), pp.91-2.
[59] Geoffrey Hosking, A History of the Soviet Union 1917-1991 (London, 1992), pp.334-7.

prayer) were set up in all the towns, where Jews resided, and permanent minyans resumed their activities.[60]

In 1959 Khrushchev changed tack and approved an anti-religious campaign which reached its zenith in 1961 with the closure of churches and synagogues below the low level left by Stalin's depredations but did not cease until his ouster from power in 1964.[61] He also sponsored the Society for the Spread of Political and Scientific Knowledge which spawned atheistic groups in towns and trained lecturers, their target being the suppression of unregistered religious organizations which in the Jewish case meant the closure of minyans. On 1 January 1953, the USSR had 133 registered congregations or synagogues which had dwindled to 90 by 1964, the largest number of closures of synagogues being in the Ukraine and Moldavia, where antisemitic sentiment was the strongest.[62] Again, in 1961 the press carried reports of nine trials involving economic crimes, eleven of the accused were sentenced to death, half of whom bore Jewish names. During the next few years over a hundred people were condemned to death for economic crimes, forty percent of whom were singled out as being Jewish.[63] Khrushchev also applauded his mentor for refusing to allow the establishment of a Jewish colony in Crimea because it could be used as an enemy base in time of war. [64] Despite his revival to some extent of Stalin's policies, his eldest son was married to a Jewish woman, and he did not quite share that streak of savage paranoia about all Jews which so vexed Stalin; and once assured of the loyalty of the Russian Orthodox Church, Stalin relied on a policy of

[60] Mordechai Altshuler, Religion and Jewish Identity, pp.90-1, 99-101.

[61] William Taubman, Khrushchev, pp.512-13.
[62] Mordechai Altshuler, Religion and Jewish Identity, pp.102-3, 112.

[63] Nora Levin, The Jews in the Soviet Union Since 1917 (New York,1990), vol.2 pp.616-17.

[64]Benjamin Pinkus, The Soviet Government and the Jews 1948-67, p.93.

stealth to suppress houses of worship rather than a blatant anti-religious propaganda campaign. Under Khrushchev the Soviet Union adopted a stronger line on the Middle East, becoming more pro-Arab and stridently anti-Zionist, recalling its ambassador to Israel for some months after the 1956 Sinai campaign.[65]

After the Second World War the last Jewish schools were closed and between 1946 and 1947 'the remaining... extensive pre-war publishing structure of the Jewish community was uprooted'. By destroying the intellectual elite of Soviet Jewry and crushing religious worship and secular Jewish culture, Stalin indicated that his aim was to obliterate Jewish life, it was nothing less than cultural genocide.[66] Despite promises, little had been done by his successors to rectify this parlous situation by 1966. Between 1964 and 1965, three Yiddish books were published, hardly a significant addition to Yiddish literature – extravagant promises about a greater number of such publications failed to materialize. Apart from this, *Sovietish Heimland*, a Yiddish magazine under the editorship of Aron Vergelis, a Soviet apologist and sycophant, was converted from a bi-monthly to a monthly. When an inter-faith mission of American clergymen visited Russia in February 1966, they found that Moscow only had two synagogues to serve half a million Jews and Leningrad had one synagogue, headed by an 85-year-old rabbi, to cater for 330,000 Jews. In 1962 the last rabbinical seminary was closed, and although promises were made in 1965 to open a new establishment, permits to allow students to reside in Moscow were withheld. No new prayer books were printed until 1958 when a limited edition of 5,000 was published. Unlike other faith communities, the Jews were not given permission to open a central religious organization and were forbidden to make contact with their co-religionists overseas.

[65] J.B. Schechtman, 'The USSR, Zionism and Israel' in Lionel Kochan ed., The Jews in Soviet Russia Since 1917, pp.118-19.
[66] William Korey, 'The Legal Position of Soviet Jewry: A Historical Enquiry' in Lionel Kochan ed., The Jews in Soviet Russia Since 1917 (Oxford, 1970), pp.85-7.

Consecrated space in the Moscow Jewish cemetery was in short supply, but requests for the allotment of space for a new burial ground were ignored. Outside Moscow and Leningrad, the state would not guarantee the supply of unleavened bread, matzah, on Passover. 'All religions in the Soviet Union face the future with confidence – except the Jews', for whom 'time is running out', an American mission's report ominously concluded. Overhanging everything was an 'atmosphere of fear and insecurity' among Jews intimidated by the long tradition of antisemitism in Russia.[67]

[67] Emanuel Litvinoff, 'Soviet Jewry after Khrushchev', Jews in Eastern Europe vol.111 (June 1966), pp.4-5 and 12-15.

Chapter 2 - The British Campaign Opens

The Birth of the Lishka

Isser Harel, the head of Mossad, and Shaul Avigur, who was in charge of Aliyah Bet, the secret organization to smuggle immigrants into Palestine when it was a British Mandate territory, were asked in 1952 to head a new body tasked with bringing immigrants from the Soviet Union and Eastern Europe into Israel and of providing Jews in the USSR with religious and cultural material. Their Arab neighbours portrayed Israel as a Crusader state with a small Jewish population which would quickly collapse under pressure just like their medieval, intruder Christian predecessor; and Israel's leaders knew that it was imperative for them to correct this imbalance of population. Israel's leadership was shocked at the Slansky show trial in Czechoslovakia in November 1952, when the defendants were charged with 'international cosmopolitanism, Trotskyism and Zionism' and wanted to help them to leave. The new organization was known in Israel as *Lishkat Kesher* (the Liason Bureau) or more popularly just as the Lishka (the Bureau). For the first few years of its existence, the new organization tried the well-tested methods of using smugglers and forged documents to surreptitiously remove Jews from the USSR and Eastern Europe with such poor results that Avigur decided that a long-term propaganda and educational programme was required among Soviet Jews. Israel's diplomats travelled throughout the Soviet Union, visiting synagogues, contacting members of Jewish communities and distributing literature. But the scope of the campaign was broadened even more in 1954, when the secretive organization focussed on stirring up opinion in the West and educating Jews about the fate of their Soviet brethren, calling its new policy *Nativ-Bar* (Hebrew for Open-Path). But the organization was popularly known as the Lishka to try and kept the target of its activity hidden. Avigur was appointed as an assistant to the defence minister and reported directly to Moshe Sharett, the Prime

Minister (1954-5). He recommended that every important embassy should have a representative of the Lishka. In 1955 a small permanent committee run by Avigur and Binyamin Eliav, of which Nahum Goldmann was a member, was created to organize the campaign in the Western world.[68]

Despite the outwardly bleak situation of Soviet Jewry, Mordechai Altshuler argued that the support enjoyed by legitimate religious institutions and hundreds of private minyans (small religious gatherings for prayer) showed that after the Second World War there had been a significant shift in attitudes as a result of the Holocaust. The Jews in towns, where religious traditions survived, felt alienated by the lack of support from the surrounding population, when members of existing communities were brutally and openly murdered with the participation of local people from a different nationality. Losing trust in the ideals of the brotherhood of man, the surviving Soviet Jews had a more positive attitude towards religion and an awakened national consciousness; and whether religious or not, were aghast at the discrimination displayed towards Jewish religious institutions and were determined to exploit their connections at the local level to restore them. Also, they were affronted at the failure to commemorate or memorialize the murder of so many Jews, particularly in Babi Yar. With the establishment of the state of Israel in 1948, many non-religious Jews visited synagogues or the spaces outside them on High Holidays to affirm their ties to the state. Jewish youths chose the synagogues and the adjacent areas outside them to stage a national demonstration on Simchat Torah (festival of the rejoicing in

---

[68] Nehemiah Levanon, 'Israel's Role in the Campaign', in Murray Friedman and Albert D. Chernin eds., A Second Exodus: The American Movement to Free Soviet Jewry, (Hanover, NH,1999), pp.71-3. Sam Lipski and Suzanne D. Rutland, Let My People Go: The Untold Story of Australia and the Soviet Jews 1959-1989 (Jerusalem, 2015), pp.20-1. Mordechai Altshuler, Religion and Jewish Identity, p.273.

the law). Members of the Israeli embassy, whether or not they were attached to the Lishka, started meeting local Jews in synagogues or private minyans in towns, where the bulk of Soviet Jewry was conveniently located, and distributed literature and esrogim (citrons) for the festival of Tabernacles and matzah for Passover. At times this led to tussles with rabbis and heads of the congregation, who were anxious not to offend the Soviet authorities with the ever-present risk of their congregation being disbanded. In addition, from the mid-1950s Western Jewish tourists also started visiting synagogues in increasing numbers, sometimes trying to contact relatives, and this acted as a brake on over-zealous Soviet officials.[69]

Emissaries in New York, London and Paris were ordered to approach individuals and activist groups in the West with information and the offer of financial assistance to promote the aim of expediting the emigration of Jews from the Soviet Union. It was found as necessary to educate the diaspora Jewish communities about the problems of Soviet Jewry as foreign governments. In New York, Dr Meir Rosenne and his assistant Moshe Decter aided the Student Struggle for Soviet Jewry established by Yaakov Birnbaum in April 1964 and another Cleveland group of activists. Further momentum was added to the movement in 1965 when Nehemiah Levanon was placed in charge of the Washington office of the Lishka; and a year later Elie Wiesel, already famous as a chronicler of the Shoah, published an account of his travels in the Soviet Union, *The Jews of Silence* (1966) which upbraided world Jewry for their passivity as regards the fate of their Russian brethren. Castigating their excuses for inaction, Wiesel observed that 'Our Jews have other problems on their minds ...' They say that 'It is exaggerated [the calamitous situation of Soviet Jewry]; or, we can do nothing about it; or, we must not do too much lest we be accused of interfering in the cold war...I believe with all my soul that despite the suffering, despite the hardship and the fear, the Jews of Russia will withstand

---

[69] Mordechai Altshuler, Religion and Jewish Identity, pp. 237-51,253-5.

the pressure and emerge victorious ...I returned from the Soviet Union disheartened and depressed. But what torments me most is not the Jews of silence I met in Russia, but the silence of the Jews I live among today'.[70]

The Lishka Wins the Support of the Western Intellectuals

The poet and novelist Emanuel Litvinoff (1915-2011) came to the attention of Eliav because of an article he was trying to publish in a Zionist publication about a trip he took to the Soviet Union in 1956. His father had been repatriated to Russia in 1917 to fight in the army and had disappeared without trace.[71] Litvinoff had already caused a stir in literary circles for an onslaught against T.S. Eliot for his antisemitism at the Institute of Contemporary Arts in 1951, referring to Eliot's 'snigger from behind the covers of history' and 'the sly words and cold heart'. His first wife, the model Cherry Marshall, took a British fashion show to the GUM department store in Moscow and Litvinoff, under the guise of managing the event, was able to secure a visa to enter the Soviet Union. As a youth, Litvinoff joined the Young Communist League before being expelled for Trotskyism and then flirted with Vladimir Jabotinsky's right-wing Zionist organisation. He was deeply troubled by the fate of the Jews, especially the sinking of the Struma crammed with refugees in February 1942 which left 791 dead, a tragedy which he blamed on the British authorities. This disaster prevented him from fully identifying himself as 'English' unlike other Anglo- Jewish writers. By 1956 he was regarded by the Israelis responsible for the Soviet Jewry campaign as a possible friend through the contact

---

[70] Gal Beckerman, When They Come for Us, We'll Be Gone. The Epic Struggle to Save Soviet Jewry (New York,2011), pp.51-2,140-7. Elie Wiesel, The Jews of Silence (New York,1966), pp.126-7.
[71] Emanuel Litvinoff, Journey Through A Small Planet (Harmondsworth, 1976), pp.22-4, 27-9. Barnet Litvinoff, A Very British Subject. Telling Tales (London,1996), pp.1-8.

they had with him, as he was then working for a Zionist publication. On his visit, he was entrusted with a letter from Nahum Goldmann to Shlomo Shlifer, the Chief Rabbi of Moscow. Despite being told by the British Embassy to deliver the letter through official Soviet channels, Litvinoff insisted on delivering it in person. When he went to the Central Moscow Synagogue, he found Rabbi Shlifer surrounded by surly bodyguards but he placed the letter down on the table and after three such visits the rabbi told him that Goldmann could visit Russia as a tourist – a significant rebuff, since Goldmann as both President of the World Zionist Organization and the World Jewish Congress was angling for an official invitation.[72] Probably Goldmann as an associate of the Lishka was trying to pave the way for negotiations with Soviet officials which would result in their agreeing to extend the religious and cultural rights of Soviet Jews.

On the Sabbath after the service, the Chief Rabbi 'delivered a quasi-political sermon in Yiddish clearly addressed to the foreign visitors', to which an American rabbi from a visiting delegation replied, 'It was an impassioned address that would have been embarrassingly rhetorical in English but was warm and sincere in Yiddish'.

"I want you all to know", the rabbi concluded, "that your brothers and sisters in America have not forgotten you." All over the synagogue people began to sob. The tears of the old summed up the poverty, separation and loneliness the Moscow congregation had experienced.

"As I began to leave", Litvinoff recalled, "hundreds of people surrounded me, or, rather, we went out to meet each other."

Shocked by the physical appearance of the elderly Jews, some of whom had returned from the Gulag, and their drab clothing, Litvinoff returned to the synagogue the next day.

---

[72] Interview with Maurice Samuelson 31 January 2018 based on notes of a conversation with Emanuel Litvinoff. Cherry Marshall, The Catwalk (London,1978), pp.77 and 87.

"I had noticed the day before how poorly they were clothed [as compared with the general population]: now I realised they were dressed in their best Sabbath clothes. The garments they wore now could have been picked up out of refuse bins. There were old women wearing men's ragged jackets with only a frayed vest underneath. One ancient had her feet wrapped in rags. There were bearded men in wretched, worn-out military tunics."

He discovered that "Many of them had spent long years in prison or labour camps. For what offences?"

Again, the expressive shoulder-shrugging: "For nothing at all – we are Jews," they replied'.

One gentleman, who looked prosperous and was wearing a business suit and happened to be an executive, took him aside, explaining that "Things are much better everywhere. But in the synagogues it is worse."

"What do you mean worse?" Litvinoff asked.

"People are afraid." Particularly around the Moscow Great Synagogue, Litvinoff sensed the pervasive atmosphere of fear, from the beadle constantly shushing him away to the congregants, whispering information in his ear, reminiscent of Nazi Germany in 1933. He visited the synagogue again and again, collecting money from his wife and some of the other models for distribution to the more wretched congregants. He returned to London via Paris, where he met Manes Sperber, a psychologist and later distinguished novelist, determined to do something for Soviet Jewry.[73]

Once in London, he resumed working at the *Jewish Observer and Middle East Review* and submitted an article to Jon Kimche, the editor, drawing attention to the abysmal condition of Russian Jewry. But he was called into the British Zionist offices by its leading officials, Schneier Levenberg and Lavy Bakstansky, who told him that the article could not be published, without saying why, though it was obvious that the Israeli authorities were moving very

---

[73] Emanuel Litvinoff, 'Visit to a Moscow Synagogue' Listener 3 April 1958. Interview with Maurice Samuelson 31 January 2018. Cherry Marshall, p.87.

cautiously fearful of upsetting the Russians. However, later Benjamin Eliav, a close associate of Avigur and a member of the Lishka, encouraged him to publish it elsewhere, seeming to contradict his own government's policy, and that is how 'A Visit to a Moscow Synagogue' came to be printed in the *Listener* in April 1958. Based on material supplied by the Israelis, Litvinoff started publishing a newsletter in the *Jewish Observer* drawing attention to the awakened nationalist sentiments of Soviet Jews in response to discrimination; and carefully dissected anti-Jewish articles in the Soviet press, noting their inaccuracies and mendaciousness. In April 1959, Litvinoff resigned from the *Jewish Observer* as assistant editor because an article was published on Soviet antisemitism in his absence in Scandinavia, without being properly checked for its accuracy. With the backing of the secret Israeli organization, Litvinoff formed a company, European Jewish Publications Ltd, to continue publishing the newsletter and to incorporate more considered pieces in a journal under the title of *Jews in Eastern Europe* and he also brought out an annual containing Soviet newspaper items on Jewish issues. Kimche introduced him to Israel Sieff, the British Zionist and World Jewish Congress leader but perhaps, more importantly, vice-chairman of Marks & Spencer, who put up £5,000 for the publications.[74] *Jews in Eastern Europe* was meticulously edited by Litvinoff, reaching the standard of an academic journal, and was eagerly studied by readers in Holland, Scandinavia, and America. Similarly in Paris Dr Meir Rosenne was encouraged by the Lishka to found the *Bibliotheque juive contemporaine*, again like Litvinoff operating under the auspices of the local World Jewish Congress office, while in New York Moshe Decter set up Jewish Minorities Research.[75]

[74] Interview with Maurice Samuelson, 31 January 2018.
[75] Nehemiah Levavon, 'Israel's Role in the Campaign' in Murray Friedman and Albert D. Chernin eds., A Second Exodus. The American Movement to Free Soviet Jewry (Brandeis University Press,1999), p.75.

Meanwhile, the Lishka orchestrated a growing international movement among unaffiliated left-wing intellectuals, but at first limited their openly stated objectives to demanding full cultural rights for the Jews as a national minority in the Soviet Union. On 15 September 1960, the first international conference of intellectuals on Soviet Jewry was held in Paris with the participation of about fifty professors, scientists, judges, writers, and religious leaders, including Martin Buber, Muriel Spark and Bishop Pike and others. It was organized by Dr Meir Rosenne and Dr Nahum Goldmann's assistant, Saul Friedlander, later the distinguished holocaust historian. Emanuel Litvinoff induced his English and Scandinavian friends to attend. Among those, who sent messages of support were Eleanor Roosevelt, Francois Mauriac, Dr Albert Schweitzer, M. Vincent Auriol, Richard Crossman and Bertrand Russell – the latter possibly a coup for Litvinoff, who subsequently corresponded with Russell and plied him with material about Soviet Jewry. Presided over by M. Daniel Mayer, a former French Cabinet Minister and Chairman of the League of Human Rights, it called on the 'Russian government to give her Jewish minority the same cultural and religious rights as those enjoyed by other minorities'; and secondly it asked that 'Russian Jews should be allowed to maintain contact with Jewish religious institutions in other countries, in the same way as did members of other faiths'. Dr Goldmann, the President of the World Zionist Organization and the WJC, advised the conference 'not to raise the problem of [Jewish] emigration from Russia, because emigration is considered contrary to Soviet ideology'. According to Nevanon, despite the bland speeches from Goldmann and Buber, 'the veteran ex-Communist Berger Barzilai, and a number of prominent personalities from England, Scandinavia, and other countries kept the conference on the right track'.[76]

Josef Berger-Barzilai (1904-1978) was a frequent Israeli representative at these international conferences of

---

[76] Nehemiah Levanon, 'Israel's Role in the Campaign', pp.76-7.
JewishChronicle, 23 September 1960, pp.1 and 48.

intellectuals, where he took a harder line than Goldmann more to the satisfaction of Levanon. He was born in Cracow and was brought up as an orthodox Jew and Zionist and at the age of fifteen emigrated to Palestine, where he joined a left-wing Zionist organization. In 1922 he helped found the Communist Party of Palestine and became its secretary, at the same time travelling throughout the Middle East to assist in the setting up of Communist parties in the Arab lands. Moscow then directed him to Berlin, where he served as secretary of the Anti-Imperialist League in 1931. A year later he was placed in charge of the Comintern's Near East department. By 1934, doubtful of some aspects of the Soviet regime, though still loyal, he was dismissed from his position and subsequently expelled from the Communist party. On 27 January 1935 he was arrested on the charge of being a Trotskyite and spent over 21 years in Soviet prisons and camps. Rehabilitated after Stalin's death and released from prison in 1956, his wife and son persuaded him to resume his former Polish nationality and to return to Poland. After a year in Warsaw serving as director of the Polish Institute of Foreign Affairs, he emigrated to Israel and became a lecturer at Bar-Ilan University. Disillusioned with Communism, he told an audience of intellectuals in 1965 that 'the Jewish problem in the Soviet Union could only be solved through the joint efforts of men of goodwill...He felt that unified protests from the world would change the position for Soviet Jews'.[77]

Isi Leibler, the Australian Soviet Jewry activist, had developed a close friendship with Emanuel Litvinoff, corresponding with him on a regular basis. In June 1965 Nahum Goldmann on the front page of the *New York Times* attacked Leibler for urging 'an intensification of the protest movement within the Free World'. Goldmann still placed emphasis on the religious and cultural rights of Soviet Jewry and 'quiet diplomacy', downplaying the issue of emigration. He claimed that 'Accusations are being made against Russia which are not justified, and which can only

---

[77] Josef Berger, Shipwreck of a Generation. Memoirs (London,1971), pp.7-10. Jewish Chronicle, 30 April 1965, p.18.

delay the solution of the problem, and even harm Soviet Jewry'. Emanuel Litvinoff advised Leibler to take up 'an outspoken position' against Goldmann, who was undermining the Soviet Jewry campaign. At a meeting of the World Jewish Congress in Strasbourg, Leibler asserted that ' *Shtadlonus* [intercession] and private diplomacy used since 1956 have been abysmal failures...The only approach...is a militant campaign to mobilise public opinion'. Leibler admitted that Goldmann is 'World Jewry's most outstanding spokesman... head and shoulders above all...he has a very sharp tongue and contempt for public opinion – so there is a cult of personality'. By the early 1970s, Leibler and adherents in Australia with the support of Maoz, the Israeli association for Soviet Jewry, had succeeded in marginalising Goldmann's agenda and the protest movement came to the fore.[78]

Nicholas Griffin, the editor of Bertrand Russell's correspondence, has asserted that his 'campaign for Soviet Jews was one of the most extensive... [Russell] undertook in the last decade of his life – comparable in extent only to those for nuclear disarmament and against the Vietnam War. In addition to general appeals on policy matters, he took up many individual cases, working both independently and in conjunction with Jewish organizations around the world. He wrote dozens of letters to persecuted Jews in the Soviet Union, to members of their families outside, and to the Soviet authorities on their behalf. He even sent parcels of clothing where he thought they were needed – and got his secretaries to write follow-up inquiries when it seemed the parcels might have been impounded by the authorities. In the nature of things, little of this work could be publicized'.[79] Influenced by his aides, Russell after 1967 argued for the right of Jews to emigrate from the USSR, though he did not advocate emigration to Israel. But it was primarily through the initial relationship

---

[78]Sam Lipski and Suzanne D. Rutland, Let My People Go, pp.73-8.

[79] Nicholas Griffin ed., The Selected Letters of Bertrand Russell. The Public Years,1914-1970 (London,2001), p.573.

that Litvinoff established with Russell that he was kept so involved with the campaign over so lengthy a period of time. Bertrand Russell at the time was the outstanding British public intellectual with enormous popular esteem, so that the causes endorsed by him often appealed to wide sections of opinion.

Early in 1962, Bertrand Russell, the novelist Francois Mauriac, and the philosopher of religion Martin Buber sent a telegram to Khrushchev about Soviet Jewry. Russell followed this up with a spate of letters and stated that he was 'deeply perturbed at the death sentences passed on Jews [for economic crimes]...and the official encouragement of antisemitism which apparently takes place'. In reply, Khrushchev upheld the right of the Soviet criminal system to punish culprits with the death penalty for economic crimes and denied that the large percentage of Jews charged indicated antisemitism.[80]

When *Izvestia*, the official organ of the Soviet government, refused to print a response addressed to it by Russell on 6 April 1963, he was furious and released its contents to the world press. He pleaded that 'Jews ... [should] be permitted full cultural lives, religious freedom and the rights of a national group, in practice as well as in law. During the last years of Stalin's life, Soviet Jews were totally deprived of their national culture and the means of expressing it. Leading intellectuals were imprisoned or executed by extra-legal practices which have since been condemned...I understand the objections to economic offences such as were expressed in the letter to me by Premier Khrushchev. I feel, however, that the death penalty upon citizens accused of the crimes harms the Soviet Union and allows those hostile to her to unjustly malign her. I consider the fact that sixty per cent of those executed are Jews to be gravely disturbing. I fervently hope that nothing will take place which obliges us to believe that Jews are receiving unjust treatment in contradiction to the law, and that those who break Soviet laws concerning economic

---

[80] Yaacov Ro'i, The Struggle for Soviet Jewish Emigration 1948-1967 (Cambridge,1991), pp.162-3.

offences will be rehabilitated'. Again in September, Russell wrote to Martin Buber soliciting his signature for an appeal to Khrushchev on behalf of Soviet Jews, as there had been an improvement in East-West relations since the treaty banning nuclear tests in the atmosphere was signed on 5 August. Since Stalin's death, 'there has certainly been some improvement in the status of Jews as individuals, but the meagre restitution of Jewish culture leaves the Jewish nationality more impoverished than any other national group in the USSR. They are also subjected to more harassment and deprivation than any other Soviet religious groups and are often the target of crudely offensive so-called atheistic propaganda. An additional matter of very grave concern is the preponderant number of Jews among those executed for economic offences and the tendency to report such cases in a way that reflects discredit upon the Jewish people as a whole'.[81]

Because Khrushchev's call for cultural rights for national minorities went unheeded in the case of Jews, the Israeli government believed that the Soviet leadership would prefer the easier option and let the Russian Jews go. So it floated the idea that Jewish families separated by the Second World War could be reunified, so long as those Jewish individuals who wished to emigrate, were allowed to do so, citing the permission granted to other minorities such as the Germans and Greeks. Resolutions on similar lines for family reunification were adopted by the World Jewish Congress and the British Board of Deputies. Couched in moderate terms, Nehemiah Levanon and Eliav thought that this appeal to unite broken families would gain the assent of Communists and left-wing personalities sympathetic to the Soviet Union. Through his contacts in London and Paris, Eliav sought the support of leading public intellectuals such as Bertrand Russell and Jean-Paul Sartre. Nehemiah Levanon was increasingly placed in charge of the campaign to mobilize Western opinion, as

---

[81] Ray Perkins Jr ed., Yours Faithfully, Bertrand Russell. A Lifelong Fight for Peace, Justice and Truth in Letters to the Editor (Chicago,2002), pp.318-19. Nicholas Griffin, p.573.

Avigur was ageing, and concentrated on enlisting the help of Jewish leaders and persuading Parliamentarians to support the campaign.[82] He had served as the agricultural attaché at the Israeli embassy in Moscow, as cover for his role in the Lishka, but he was caught visiting the apartment of a Jewish activist in 1955 and expelled with two other members of the Lishka from the Soviet Union.[83]

Across the world, Communist parties were put on the defensive by the pleas of the intellectuals sympathetic to the situation of the Jews in the Soviet Union. In 1957 Professor Hyman Levy, after investigating the condition of Jews in the Soviet Union, compared it to that existing in Tsarist times, for which he was promptly expelled from the Communist party in Britain. A resolution submitted by the British Communist party leadership in 1965 noted 'with concern criticisms made by prominent individuals in the international communist and general peace and progressive movements of the attitude of the Soviet Union to the religious and cultural requirements of the Jewish minority. Congress therefore calls on the national executive to approach the Soviet Government with a view to obtaining either a satisfactory rebuttal of such criticism or, where they may be valid, an assurance that their causes will be removed as speedily as possible'. The Australian Communist party went further, by stating in 1965 that 'antisemitism in the Soviet Union had not yet been eliminated'.[84]

By January 1963, there were faint indications of a new approach being tested, a demand that Soviet Jews, who had been separated by the Second World War, should be allowed to join their families living in Israel and elsewhere. At a United Nations sub-commission on the Prevention of Discrimination and the Protection of Minorities, the Co-ordinating Board of Jewish Organizations pointed out the

---

[82] Yaacov Ro'i, The Struggle for Soviet Jewish Emigration 1948-67, pp.122-24. Nehemiah Levanon, 'Israel's Role in the Campaign', p.75.
[83] Gal Beckerman, pp.140-1, and Mordechai Altshuler, Religion and Jewish Identity, pp.243-4.
[84] Jews in Eastern Europe, vol.111:4, pp.53-6.

barriers to Jewish emigration from Russia, provoking an outburst from the Soviet envoy.[85] At the conference of the Socialist International, the British Labour leader Harold Wilson raised the plight of Soviet Jewry, urging that the Soviet authorities should 'permit the reunification of individual Jewish families'. After Wilson visited Moscow in June, through his efforts at intercession, it was reported that four Russian families would be reunited in Britain, though they were not necessarily Jewish.[86] In a letter addressed to Khrushchev which became public in 1964 signed by Bertrand Russell together with Albert Schweitzer and Martin Buber expressing concern at the deprivation of Jewish religious and cultural facilities, there was also a plea that people separated for many years from their closest kin who had settled in Israel and elsewhere should be reunited.[87] By April 1965, Russell was reiterating the broader themes of the worldwide campaign for Soviet Jewry almost certainly cobbled together by the Israelis, demanding action in four areas. In a message sent to a conference of Scandinavian intellectuals held in Stockholm, he held that foremost was 'The reunification of families whose members have been separated either during the early years of the Soviet Union or during the invasion and massacres of the Second World War'. This was 'a matter of the greatest urgency. Many Soviet Jews are elderly and wish to join their relatives, from whom they have been separated for a long period. The USSR is now the only country where serious steps have not been taken to end this situation. Other Communist countries, such as Poland and Bulgaria, have allowed reunification on a generous scale and continued to permit Jews to rejoin members of their families in Israel and other countries. The Soviet Union has given official recognition to the principle of family reunification, but this has not been extended on a wide scale. It is not a question of the Soviet Union accepting a

[85] Jewish Chronicle, 25 January 1963, p.1.
[86] Report of the Foreign Affairs Committee, 7 October and 7 November 1963, LMA, BDBJ, ACC/3121/C11A/16.
[87] Jewish Chronicle, 21 February 1964, p.12.

new principle, but only of it implementing the existing one'.[88]

The Ineffectiveness of the Board of Deputies

Before proceeding with an account of the more robust student campaign on behalf of Soviet Jewry, it is necessary to assess the effectiveness of the Anglo-Jewish establishment's own campaigning in the 1960s and 1970s. All the evidence seems to point to the negative assessment of the Board of Deputies' capabilities already alluded to by previous historians and its poor record with regard to action on behalf of Soviet Jewry. Barnett Janner was a Labour MP and Vice-President of the Board of Deputies. When he asked in 1956 that a Jewish delegation be allowed to interview Nikita Khrushchev and Nikolai Bulganin, who came on a visit to Britain about Jewish religious and cultural rights in the Soviet Union, the Conservative Foreign Secretary turned down the request. Officials feared that the Soviet leaders would be 'too wily for Janner and his associates and would probably succeed in turning the argument to Russian advantage'.[89] Again, in January 1966 the Board wrote to Harold Wilson, the Labour Prime Minister, asking him to raise the issue of Soviet Jewry on his visit to Moscow in February 1966. The subject was broached, but this Dave Rich noted was due more to a letter from Levi Eshkol, the Israeli Prime Minister, than to the pleas of the Board.[90]

More generally, the Board succeeded in doing little for Soviet Jewry in the 1950s and the early 1960s until the advent of the student movement. When there were reports

---

[88] Jewish Chronicle 30 April 1965, p.18. Jews in Eastern Europe vol.111:4 (June 1966), pp.87-9.

[89] National Archives, FO 371/122810 Barnett Janner to Selwyn Lloyd, 6 January 1956, comments and reply, 27 January 1956.

[90] National Archives, PREM 13/2403. Dave Rich, 'The Activist Challenge: Women, Students, and the Board of Deputies of British Jews in the British Campaign for Soviet Jewry', vol.29, Jewish History (2015):163-85.

of isolated blood libel incidents in the Soviet Union in 1963, the Board 'agreed that it would not be appropriate at this stage to approach the Soviet Embassy in this matter'.[91] In October of the same year a letter addressed to the Soviet ambassador from the Board, requesting a meeting to air their concerns about their co-religionists, received no reply or acknowledgement, a clear snub; and a further letter to the ambassador in October 1965 on the anti-Zionist resolution at the United Nations-sponsored by the Soviet Union also went unanswered.[92] An attempt by the Chief Rabbi to call a meeting of communal organizations on 13 February 1964 to protest against the restrictions placed on the baking of matzah (unleavened bread for Passover) in the Soviet Union, was brushed aside by the Board. Its leadership was more concerned about a potential communal grab for power by the rabbinic authorities than the provision of matzah for Russian Jews. To end the dispute the Board contributed £250 towards the emergency despatch of matzah. But despite Janner's reference to 'confidential action which he had taken in order to exert pressure on the Soviet authorities to permit the bulk despatch of Matzot', the Soviet authorities refused to allow the major portion of these supplies to remain in the country.[93] All these actions by the Board, however well-meaning their intent, betrayed their essential weakness as an organization.

The 1968 Student Revolt in France and its Antecedents

Rabbi Abraham Heschel delivered a forceful sermon on 3 September 1963, noting that the American Jewish leaders claimed that there was little that they could do. But if Jews

---

[91] LMA, Board of Deputies of British Jews, Foreign Affairs Committee (hereafter BDBJ, FAC), ACC 3121/C11A/16, minutes of 6 June 1963.
[92] LMA, BDBJ, FAC, ACC 32121/C11A/16, minutes of 7 October and 7 November 1963; and minutes of 11 November 1965 and 3 January 1966.
[93] LMA, BDBJ, FAC, ACC 3121/C11A/16, minutes of 10 February, 2 March and 9 April 1964.

65

were prepared to go to prison to end racial bigotry in their own country, 'should ... [they] not be ready to go to jail in order to end the martyrdom of our Russian brethren? The six million are no more. Now three million face spiritual extinction. We have been guilty more than once of failure to be concerned, of a failure to cry out, and failure may have become our habit...discrimination against the political rights of the Negro in America and discrimination against the religious and cultural rights of the Jews in the Soviet Union are indivisible'. Heschel was able to convince Lewis Weinstein, the president of the Conference of Presidents of Major American Jewish Organizations, to set up a new body on 5-6 April 1964, the American Jewish Conference on Soviet Jewry.[94]

At the same time in the United States the civil rights movement took off in the mid-1950s, with widespread student participation in the early 1960s, and they also filled the ranks of the anti-Vietnam war protesters.[95] Young people, most of them white, went to the South in huge numbers in the Freedom Summer of 1964 to register black voters. Students for a Democratic Society was founded in the early 1960s and its offshoot sponsored community projects in the ghettos of Baltimore, Chicago, Philadelphia, Newark and elsewhere to help alleviate poverty. In 1967 200,000 people demonstrated in New York and 250,000 in San Francisco against the war in Vietnam and the drafting of young men.[96] Student numbers at the colleges swelled dramatically with a generational attitude gulf between them and the faculty, leading to the Berkeley Free Speech movement in 1964 and the general strike at Columbia in 1968. 'Universities attained unprecedented sizes, with

---

[94] Michael Vilenchuk, '"My Brother's Keeper". American Jewish Youth and the Making of the Soviet Jewry Movement'. Brandeis University Master's Thesis, 2017, pp.34-6.
[95] Norman F. Cantor, The Age of Protest. Dissent and Rebellion in the Twentieth Century (London, 1970), pp.281-99.

[96] Richard Vinen, The Long '68. Radical Protest and its Enemies (London, 2019), pp. 80-4,89-98.

student populations of tens of thousands, or even more than a hundred thousand'. In the past universities had trained the nation's small elites and scholars and had sometimes produced ideologues, but now when there was a political issue the student leaders could muster thousands of followers, causing chaos and violence not only in the United States but in Europe.[97]

Across the Atlantic, students smashing windows in Paris in an anti-Vietnam war demonstration led to the birth of the 'Movement of 22 March' in 1968, whose presiding genius was Daniel Cohn-Bendit (Danny the Red), a charismatic speaker. Quickly the students were joined by workers, peasants, and the lower ranks of the managerial class. For a short time it seemed as if the government of General de Gaulle would be toppled.[98] The insurrection in Paris in May 1968 sparked protest movements in the West, revitalizing the anger of American students. In West Germany, 70 per cent of the students were aged between 23 and 30, many of them pro-Palestinian intent on shocking their parents. Hence the formation of the Red Army Faction and the Baader-Meinhof gang. Consequently, a synagogue was fire-bombed on the anniversary of Kristallnacht. In Britain, the student revolt, dramatic at times, petered out during the vacation.[99] In Britain, student unrest in 1968 was on a smaller scale than in France, West Germany and the United States. The New Left gathered strength in 1960 when two earlier publications merged to form the *New Left Review* and there was a meeting place for sympathisers of the movement when the Partisan Coffee House was opened in Soho, London in 1956. In 1968 the biggest demonstration was against the Vietnam war, but other causes of the left were the struggle against apartheid in South Africa and the

[97]Joseph Ben-David, Centers of Learning. Britain, France, Germany (New York, 1977), p.129.

[98]Norman F. Cantor, The Age of Protest pp.316-23.

[99]Richard Vinen, The Long '68 pp.118-188.

civil rights campaign in Northern Ireland which started in 1967. The impact of the student revolt in Britain was less intense than elsewhere because so many universities were located a long distance from industrial cities, the general level of prosperity enjoyed by students, and university study here was more sharply demarcated from other phases of the lifecycle than elsewhere. It was only when the National Union of Students agreed to espouse political causes in 1972 that lifted student insurrection to new levels and encouraged more young recruits to join radical parties in the early 1970s.[100]

The British Jewish Students Federation dominated the European-based World Union of Jewish Students; and the WUJS Congress in 1967 'passed motions opposing apartheid and the Vietnam War, while the 1970 congress denounced imperialism and colonialism and expressed its support for the `liberation struggles in Africa, Latin America and Asia".[101] Young British Jews fully shared the radical sentiments of their fellow students and turned some of their anger at their parents for not taking enough action at the time of the Holocaust. They were determined not to allow it to happen again and formed organizations to assist Soviet Jewry in the United States and Britain before the student revolt here had exploded more generally.

The Lishka Stirs the Jewish Students in Britain to take up the Cause of Soviet Jewry

The generation born in the 1930s in Western Europe and the United States feared unemployment and poverty which had embittered the lives of their parents when they had started families. They wanted a regular life free from disruption and turmoil and were prepared to tolerate drudgery and order, so long as they could lead peaceful,

---

[100] Richard Vinen, The Long '1968 pp.193-6, 201-2, and 209-19.
[101]Dave Rich, 'The Activist Challenge: Women, Students and the Board of Deputies of British Jews in the British Campaign for Soviet Jewry', Vol. 29 Jewish History (2015), pp. 163-85.

uneventful lives. They were willing to accept a low position in the hierarchical societies in which they found themselves and were deferential to political leaders, judges and intellectual opinion makers. In the West, there was a post-war baby boom after 1945, when the younger generation who came of age in the 1960s, trashed the values of their parents and rebelled against capitalism, the military ascendancy of the United States and adopted rock music, different forms of dress and different ways of living. The restructuring of society continued into the 1970s, when there was a revolt within a revolt, and the women's liberation movement and gay liberation emerged, its adherents sometimes complaining about the slights they had suffered at the hands of the macho, heterosexual males, who had fuelled the youth revolt of 1968 and its antecedents.[102] It was no coincidence that a vast expansion of the effectiveness of the Soviet Jewry campaign occurred in the late 1960s and early 1970s, as this coincided with the youth revolt and the later women's movement. The Lishka quickly grasped the opportunities made available when Jewish youth and young women challenged their parents' generation with their failure to rescue enough Jews from the Holocaust; and were won over to saving the remnant of Soviet Jewry threatened with physical and cultural extinction.

Through the initiative of the Lishka and other Jewish organizations, the issue of Soviet Jewry was beginning to stir Jewish youth in the United States and later in Europe. In New York, a group of Jewish businessmen established the American League for Russian Jews, acting as a catalyst for the formation of the Student Struggle for Soviet Jewry set up by Yaakov Birnbaum on 27 April 1964, three weeks after the formation of the national body. On 1 May 1964, the SSSJ held its first demonstration outside the Soviet mission to the United Nations. Birnbaum was brought up in Hamburg, where he remembered some German boys invading his garden and stuffing mud into his mouth, but

---

[102] Richard Vinen, The Long '68 pp.14,35.

fortunately the family escaped to England. Later he informed David Dubinsky, the trade union leader, that his group had been formed to aid Soviet Jews and that it would not 'remain silent as did so many of our parents when the Nuremberg laws were promulgated'. In any case, he came from an activist family, his grandfather Nathan Birnbaum being a vocal exponent of Jewish cultural autonomy and a champion of the Yiddish language. Recruits poured into the SSSJ from the civil rights movement (28 percent of its members had formerly participated in civil rights protests), the anti-Vietnam war activists and later from student campus campaigners, but the primary motivation for many of the campaigners remained the suspected passivity of their parents during the Holocaust and their lingering inertia about Soviet Jewry now.[103]

During the summer of 1964, Khrushchev visited Scandinavia and was handed a letter from Scandinavian Jewish youth. In Norway in particular, Khrushchev became the target of appeals from the Norwegian Union of Socialist Youth in the form of an open letter which led to a discussion with officials from the Soviet embassy. The Norwegian Non-Violence Group also added their voice, speaking out against the 'mental strangulation' of the Jews.[104] On 4 April 1965, the SSSJ planned the Jericho march encompassing the Soviet mission to the United Nations in New York. Prior to the protest, the Jewish Student Club of Stockholm, which was affiliated to the World Union of Jewish Students, received a request to participate in what was intended to be a worldwide demonstration; and collected signatures which they handed to the Soviet embassy. In Europe, Jewish students took up the challenge more specifically a year later when Michael Hunter of the British Inter-University Jewish Federation helped found the Universities' Committee for Soviet Jewry and the World Union of Jewish Students organized a seminar in Brussels

---

[103] Marc Dollinger, Quest for Inclusion. Jews and Liberalism in Modern America (Princeton, 2000), p.221. Beckerman, pp.72-3 and 77-8. Ro'i, pp.209-10 and 229.
[104] Jewish Chronicle 3 July 1964, p.19 and Ro'i, pp.223-4.

from 28 April until 2 May 1965 on what action they could take on behalf of Soviet Jewry. It was the first gathering with a political focus as opposed to an educational one and presumably was held under the auspices of the Lishka. In all, seventy-five students from Western Europe were chosen to attend with a contingent of five from Britain and in addition some student representatives from Israel. Speakers included Emanuel Litvinoff, by now a veteran observer of Russian Jewish affairs, Elie Wiesel and an Israeli expert, Efraim Tari, who was the Soviet Jewry Officer of the Israeli embassy in London after 1967. At the closing session, resolutions were adopted calling for equality of culture for Soviet Jews, religious rights, a ban on anti-Jewish propaganda and family reunification.[105]

The leaders of the Lishka comprehended swiftly that the growing international student revolt and their own cause conveniently intersected and that the students' restlessness and propensity to agitate about many issues could be exploited, especially among Jewish students for them to be easily persuaded, after exposure to a short educational programme, to adopt the cause of Russian Jewry. Many adherents of the French radical left were Jewish and it has been estimated that over half of the members of the American New Left were secularised Jews.[106] Jewish students in Britain, as we have seen, often had leftist sympathies, and were more than willing to take up this new cause. Afterwards, it was announced that an exhibition covering all facets of Russian Jewish life had been displayed in Brussels, and that there were plans to take it to Holland, Denmark, Switzerland, France, Sweden and England. From its headquarters in Paris, the WUJS stated that Jews had been 'the target for a religious, cultural and educational discrimination exercised against no other religious or national minority in Soviet Russia... Only by bringing to the knowledge of all students the facts of this discrimination and by raising our voices in protest can we

---

[105] Michael Vilenchuk, pp.60-2 and 64-6. Jewish Chronicle 2 April 1965, p.59.
[106] Richard Vinen, The Long '68 pp.86,292.

hope that a responsive ear will hear our plea', foreshadowing a more activist approach by students and pressure from below on the Jewish establishment. In February 1966, the exhibition opened at the London School of Economics accompanied by a series of talks before moving to Oxford and various provincial centres.[107]

In Britain, student numbers jumped from 52,000 in 1945 to 100,000 in 1958 and continued to increase, reaching a planned target of 640,000 for the nineteen eighties.[108] Jews attending universities saw a similar expansion in numbers, rising from 3,000 in 1950 to six or seven thousand by the mid-1970s. At the end of the twentieth century, half of the Jews in the 18 to 19 age bracket had acquired a college education. Students were now an increasingly vocal and sophisticated voice in the Anglo-Jewish community, whose views commanded attention. But the student leadership was in a state of constant flux as they moved on to employment and the student societies waxed and waned until the incumbents were energetic enough to defy what was too often a timid communal leadership.[109]

The first public expression of opinion on behalf of Soviet Jewry in England was a march organized by Jewish students, who had formed the Universities Committee for Soviet Jewry in January 1966. The march on Sunday 8 May 1966 which stretched from Speaker's Corner Hyde Park to the Soviet embassy was according to one participant, Gordon Hausmann, attended by between 8,000 and 10,000 people, though others put it at a much smaller figure of one thousand; it was led by Hausmann, Ariel Whine, Allan Segal, and Michael Hunter. In addition to these Jewish

---

[107] Jewish Chronicle 28 January 1966, p.26 and 18 February 1966, p.31. Matthew Kalman, The Kids Are Alright. Chapters in the History of the World Union of Jewish Students (Jerusalem,1968), pp.39-42.
[108] Nicholas Timmins, The Five Giants. A Biography of the Welfare State (London, 2017), pp.157, 326.

[109] Todd M. Endelman, The Jews of Britain 1656 to 2000 (Berkeley, 2002), p.243.

students, according to Colin Shindler, 'there were also adherents of the New Left in the 1960s, who brought expertise from protests against the war in Vietnam... and against apartheid in South Africa'; and as Dave Rich noted, some of the students went on to adopt the campaigning methods of their contemporaries in the British New Left, some of whose leaders, such as Raphael Samuel, were Jewish. Hausmann, because of his family background, felt impelled to take action. Both his parents had escaped to England in 1939 only weeks before the outbreak of war, while one hundred and ninety relatives had perished in the Shoah, including his grandparents. Fearing the opposition of the Board of Deputies, he had been touring the country for months to encourage students to attend the rally; and he had written to the Prime Minister, Harold Wilson, drawing his attention to the forthcoming student protest and outlining their demands. At the head of the march was Henry Shaw, the director of Hillel House, the organization concerned with their welfare, and Bernard Kops, the playwright.[110]

The student leaders on arriving at the embassy presented a petition signed by 5,000 students and were admitted inside, where they held a two-hour debate with two second secretaries, P. Rogov and Y. Pavlov, on the situation of the Jews in Russia. This was the first time that any representatives of British Jewry had been admitted into the embassy, as previous efforts by the Board to establish relations had been rebuffed. The delegation complained about the restricted number of synagogues in Russia and the non-existence of a communal organization, only seven books printed in Yiddish since 1948, the lack of a permanent Yiddish theatre, and they asked for the repatriation of individuals to join their families overseas. Emigration, Rogov admitted, was up to the regional authorities. But the students clashed with the Soviet officials when the latter

---

[110]Jewish Chronicle 13 May 1966, p.1. Interview with Gordon Hausmann, 20 February 2018. J.C. 27 November 2015, pp.44-5 Colin Shindler 'The long march back home from Russia'.

claimed that Jews were not treated unfairly because there were a few in top positions and the embassy refused to accept the petition on grounds that it was anti-Soviet propaganda. A photograph of the leaders of the protest appeared in *The Times*, 'the first time that the subject of Soviet Jewry had been given such widespread publicity in the public arena'.[111] The demonstration was commended by the Board of Deputies as being 'a successful and well-conducted one'.[112]

Again, the students took the initiative when Harold Wilson met the Soviet Premier, Alexei Kosygin, briefly in the summer of 1966. Under their auspices, a letter was published in *The Times* on 27 June 1966 signed by over thirty prominent British intellectuals, including Kingsley Amis, Robert Bolt, Iris Murdoch, James Parkes, George Steiner and Herbert Read. It criticized the Soviet Union for denying Jews 'equal cultural and religious rights' and lagging 'far behind other East European countries in allowing Jews victimized by the Nazis to reunite with relatives abroad'.[113] Hausmann wrote on behalf of the Universities Committee for Soviet Jewry to Harold Wilson asking him 'to draw the attention of the Soviet Government to the deep-felt concern in this country for the welfare of the Jewish minority in the USSR'. Enclosed with the letter was a transcript of the students' dialogue with the Soviet embassy officials in May. In reply, the Prime Minister conveyed the message that he regretted that 'in the course of his short visit last weekend when there were many matters of great importance to discuss, it was not possible to raise with Mr. Kosygin the

---

[111] Jewish Chronicle 13 May 1966, p.1. Interview with Gordon Hausmann, 20 February 2018, transcript of the interview with Messrs. Rogov and Pavlov, and letter of Hausmann to the Jerusalem Post 29 October 1991. Gordon Hausmann, The Mermelstein Letters 1939-1947 (London,2014). National Archives, PREM 13/2403 Gordon Hausmann to Harold Wilson undated circa early May 1966 and reply from M.Palliser 4 May 1966. Daphne Gerlis, Those Wonderful Women in Black (London,1996), p.17.
[112] LMA,BDBJ,FAC,ACC 3121/C11A/17 minutes, 11 May 1966.
[113] The Times 27 June 1966.

question of the treatment of the Jewish community'.[114] To counter the student campaign, Aron Vergelis, the editor of *Sovietish Heimland*, was sent on a propaganda speaking tour of Britain on behalf of the Soviet government. Although the Board of Deputies had sponsored a boycott of his meetings, numerous venues were arranged for him to speak, where he was subjected to a bombardment of questions from Gordon Hausmann, Michael Hunter and Ariel Whine. Harry Landy, a prominent member of the Board, admitted that when S.Y. Agnon, a guest in his house, expressed a desire to meet Vergelis, he was unable to refuse the request of the Israeli Nobel Prize-winning novelist. The two men had subsequently met in his home, where they discussed Jewish literature.[115]

All this mounting pressure from the United States, Britain and elsewhere was having an effect on the Soviet leadership, and when Kosygin visited Paris in December 1966 he attempted to defuse it in an answer to a question about Jewish emigration at a press conference, which was printed verbatim in all the major Moscow newspapers. He declared that 'We shall do all that is possible for us if some families wish to reunite – and even if some among them would like to leave us – to open the road for them...' However, *Izvestia* the government mouthpiece later issued a statement 'intimidating the Soviet Jews from applying' and much the same attitude was adopted by regional authorities.[116]   Shortly afterwards in February 1967, Kosygin came on an eight-day visit to Britain, but he refused to receive a delegation from the Board of Deputies who wished to hand him a memorandum. Attempts were made by the Board through the Foreign Secretary and the Soviet ambassador to facilitate an interview but they were

[114] NA, PREM 13/2403 Gordon Hausmann to Harold Wilson undated circa July 1966 and reply of M. Reid to Hausmann, 19 July 1966.
[115] Matthew Kalman, The Kids Are Alright p.40. Interview with Gordon Hausmann. LMA,BDBJ FAC ACC/3121/C11A/17 minutes of 8 and 18 December 1966.
[116] JC 9 December 1966 p.1. LMA,BDBJ,FAC, ACC/3121/C11A/18 minutes of 23 January 1967.

also rebuffed.[117] Instead, the Board memorandum was delivered by the honorary officers to the Soviet embassy. Following this, on Sunday morning 12 February 1967, the Board held an emergency meeting of communal organizations at which the contents of the memorandum were read out, after which the audience rose silently to signify their approval of it. Barnett Janner's address was supposed to be a direct appeal to Kosygin, but the proceedings were kept in too low a key and were a somewhat futile gesture. In contrast, 2,200 students from universities all over Britain marched that same Sunday afternoon to the Soviet embassy. Banners carried by the students proclaimed their aims: 'Reunite Divided Families', 'Discrimination Stains Soviet Honour' and 'Reopen Jewish Schools'. A deputation of Gordon Hausmann, Michael Hunter and Helen Weinberg, flanked by several press photographers and television cameramen, walked to the embassy door, where they handed a memorandum to the third secretary. Because the demonstration was not intended to be anti-Soviet, the planned all-night vigil by the students outside the embassy was called off. 'It might have given the wrong impression', said Mr. Hausmann'. Sir Barnett admitted that he had been against the march lest it was misconstrued as being an anti-Soviet gesture, but 'it was orderly and dignified' and on reflection 'worthwhile'.[118]

In the course of Kosygin's visit to London, Bertrand Russell released the text of a moving appeal to the Soviet Premier solely concerned with the question of the reunion of families. He welcomed Kosygin's recent statement in Paris. He continued, 'Unfortunately, letters of appeal reaching me show that, despite your statement, applicants [for emigration] are encountering serious obstacles by officials. These obstructions, which have also been reported by the press, do a great disservice to the reputation of the Soviet Union as a country which keeps its promise'. He

[117] LMA,BDJB,FAC,ACC/3121/C11A/118 minutes of 23 January and 9 February 1967.
[118] JC 17 February 1967, p.11 and 24 February 1967 p.13.

enclosed an appeal by an Israeli woman Elka Kedari, whose immediate family had been annihilated by the Germans and whose remaining relatives in Moscow, the family of the Yiddish poet Joseph Kerler, had been unable to emigrate to Israel, even though they had been granted permission to leave in December 1965. Russell added: 'You can imagine, Premier Kosygin, the human happiness which you could create at one stroke of your pen'.[119]

Next Hausmann and his colleagues in the Universities Committee drafted a non-partisan motion on Soviet Jewry for both sides of the House of Commons to sign. He went to see Ted Short M.P., the chief Labour Whip, who recommended that he should seek Barnett Janner's help, but Hausmann told him that he was not inclined to do this because he wanted to win cross-party support. Ted Short was extremely helpful, even seeing Hausmann without a fixed appointment. When Hausmann asked him why he was so responsive, he explained that he was among the British troops that had liberated Belsen and that he had made a promise to himself to assist Jews whenever they were in need of help. On 9 June 1966, Janner informed the Foreign Affairs Committee of the Board that the students had been in touch with him about putting down an order paper in the Commons on Soviet Jewry.[120] In the end 340 M.P.s signed the motion denouncing Soviet discrimination against Jews, but the leader of the Commons Richard Crossman, although always known for his sympathy to the Jews, refused Janner a debate on the subject. At the Foreign Affairs Committee, Janner took full credit for inducing so many M.P.s to sign the motion, without fully acknowledging the students' role in this initiative.[121]

The momentous victory of Israel in the Six Day War which commenced on 5 June 1967 against the combined Arab armies not only caused a wave of euphoria to spread

---

[119] JC 17 February 1967, p.11.

[120] LMA,BDBJ,FAC,ACC/3121/C11A/179 June 1966.

[121] Interview with Gordon Hausmann. LMA,BDBJ,FAC, ACC/3121/C11A/18 minutes of 2 February 1967. JC 24 February 1967, p.13.

over the Jewish diaspora but also revitalized Soviet Jewry. During the war, the Soviet press claimed 'Israel was being crushed. That thousands of Israelis were dead. That Israel was being swept away in an Arab sea... But then the official news changed. Israel had won, but only as an aggressor, using overwhelming force against a defenceless foe.' "It was a clear lie against my people", said one trapped Soviet Jew.[122] Soviet Jews were once again proud to display their affiliation – there was a more defiant attitude shown by the younger generation, who had been discriminated against when they sought places in higher education commensurate with their qualifications and employment in good positions. A report compiled by anonymous writers declared that 'there are percentage quotas for Jews in higher education and occupations... The diplomatic service, foreign trade and the central party apparatus are practically barred to them'.[123] 'Suddenly, you saw young men and women openly wearing the Star of David around their necks. People began coming to OVIR [the Soviet office handling emigration applications] flaunting their Stars of David'.[124] So too, after Israel's overwhelming victory in 1967, when it was on the brink of a shattering catastrophe, induced a new feeling of optimism and a renewed determination among the students and younger women in the diaspora to campaign on behalf of Soviet Jews.

In October 1968, 'More than 1,000 British university students marched in a solemn torchlight procession to the Soviet Embassy in London', echoing the new mood stirring Russian Jewry. 'They were expressing solidarity with Jewish youth in the Soviet Union who, by celebrating Simchat Torah in the streets of Moscow the night before, courageously emphasised their refusal to abandon Judaism. A delegation of four students placed a letter protesting against the treatment of Jews in the Soviet Union into the letterbox of the Embassy. They blew the shofar, the

---

[122] Martin Gilbert, <u>The Jews of Hope</u> (Harmondsworth,1985), pp.108-9.
[123] JC 29 May 1970, p.15. JC 24 February 1967.
[124] Beckerman, p.222.

ram's horn, outside the building, returned to the rest of the marchers waiting outside the embassy gates, and blew the shofar again', before the demonstration dispersed. In contrast to previous occasions, Sir Barnett Janner M.P., president of the Zionist Federation, and Donald Silk its chairman, participated in the demonstration. The student leaders also made it clear that they intended to avoid any close alignment with right-wing groups and émigré circles, as this would only serve to alienate left-wingers and liberals sympathetic to their cause, whose views carried more weight in Moscow.[125] By 1969 the campaign for Soviet Jewry among students was intensifying, so that a demonstration in February attracted almost 10,000 marchers to the Soviet embassy, where a petition signed by 30,000 people and 800 university professors was handed to the First Secretary; and a section of the crowd went on to the Iraqi embassy because several Jews had been hanged in Baghdad a few days earlier. A follow-up demonstration in October attracted 1,500 people mainly students but this time there was an all-night vigil demanding the release of two Russian Jews, Boris Kochubievsky and Ilya Ripps. Poems were read by Danny Abse, Bernard Kops and Colin Lee.[126]

Public protests in collective letters by Soviet Jews against increasing signs of discrimination became a new feature of the campaign. In 1969, 18 Jewish families in Georgia addressed a petition to the UN Human Rights Commission with a copy for Golda Meir, the Prime Minister of Israel, demanding that they be allowed to emigrate.[127] 'In a dramatic gesture [almost] without precedent, 39 Moscow Jews, most of them doctors or engineers, have circulated to Western correspondents in the Soviet capital a statement demanding the right to emigrate to Israel and deploring the current campaign against Israel by the Soviet authorities', reported the *Jewish Chronicle* in March 1970. The statement ended that 'We believe that...

---

[125] JC 20 December 1968, p.8.
[126] JC 7 February 1969, p.18 and 10 October 1969, p.16.
[127] Beckerman, pp.147-8.

Jews will respond to the anti-Israel campaign not by abdicating, but that, on the contrary, their pride in their people will grow stronger and that they will declare: "Next year in Jerusalem'".[128] The letter of the Georgians in particular forced the Israeli government to come out into the open by demanding the right of Soviet Jews to emigrate rather than emphasising that this was a human rights issue.

Militant Jewish students under the name of the Front for the National Liberation of Soviet Jews failed to have a letter of protest accepted by the Soviet Ambassador in April 1970. A delegation from the World Union of Jewish Students, including Colin Shindler, was also rebuffed a few weeks later when they tried to hand over a 100-page report to the Ambassador. Instead, the report was sent through the post. A political attaché at the embassy complained that this campaign which had targeted more than twenty countries gave a false impression about the antisemitic atmosphere in the USSR – an indication that the Soviets were sensitive to this campaigning which was highly effective.[129] In September Dov Sperling, a young Russian Jew living in Israel who came on a short visit to Britain, reinforced these demands by advocating tougher campaigning by Western Jews which would permit a much greater number of Jews being allowed to emigrate to Israel. He was closely aligned to Menahem Begin's Gahal party, whose approach was harder than that of the Labour party and Levanon. [130] At the end of the year, Lord Janner, the chairman of the Board's foreign affairs committee, wrote to Edward Heath, the Conservative Prime Minister, asking him to convey to Andrei Gromyko, the Soviet Foreign Minister, a message about stopping the persecution of Russian Jews wishing to emigrate to Israel. Heath's contention was that some Soviet Jews were allowed to leave, but the number allowed to go was an internal matter of policy for the USSSR and their government was not to be dictated to as to what this number should be. Anatoli Dekatov, a civil engineer and

[128] JC 13 March, p.1 and 10 April 1970, p.16.
[129] JC 1 May, p.18 and 29 May 1970, p.15.
[130] JC 11 September 1970, p.18.

Hebrew teacher, was permitted to emigrate on payment of '900 roubles – 500 for forfeiture of Soviet citizenship; 400 for the exit visa to Israel'. If granted permission, he accurately predicted, that at least a million Soviet Jews would leave, maybe more, and that because these Jews were 'a continuous source of embarrassment and a nuisance...they will finally have to let the Jews go'. [131]

In 1971 the student campaign held several all-night vigils outside the Soviet embassy and a number of demonstrations, including one in Trafalgar Square. On 12 October 1971, 'More than 800 Jewish students and Zionist youth staged a series of impressive and non-violent demonstrations in London...in solidarity with Soviet Jewry and in protest against its treatment by the Russian authorities. While a well-designed exhibition was on display at the B'nai B'rith Hillel House, simultaneous torch processions were held outside the Soviet embassy, the Russian trade mission and the Tass news agency'. The exhibition was opened by Victor Fedoseyev, a non-Jewish Russian Zionist, who had emigrated to Israel with his Jewish wife, and who had been until recently editor of *Exodus*, the organ of the Russian-Jewish underground movement. He was writing a book on the Russian human rights movement. He believed that 'there was no such thing as Jewish rights, Russian rights or English rights. There was only human rights, to which Jews were also entitled'.[132] At this point in time, the issue of human rights was scarcely mentioned in the Soviet Jewry campaign in Britain, but when Kosygin arrived in Denmark in December 1971 he was greeted by student demonstrators at the airport with slogans proclaiming 'Human Rights for Soviet Jews' and 'Let My People Go'.[133] Barbara Oberman, who was hosting a meeting to be addressed by Rabbi Kahane, caused uproar when she criticised British Jewish students 'for engaging in an educational campaign instead of taking a more activist stand by going out to the streets to demonstrate'. Meir

---

[131] JC 13 November, p.9. and 20 November 1970, p.7.
[132] JC 15 October 1971, p.7.
[133] JC 10 December 1971, p.5.

Kahane was well-known as an advocate of taking violent action against Soviet diplomatic missions and emissaries. Young Herut members were stirred by Kahane's address with Ronnie Jacobs admitting even so that 'Our policy is activist, not violent'.[134] Throughout the 1970s, representatives of the Lishka continued to sponsor trips to the Soviet Union by interested students, particularly Americans, in the hope that they would take action on their return and engage more actively in the Soviet Jewry campaign.[135] But after a debacle in May 1971 in which a British student leader, Alan Freeman, lost a briefcase with correspondence implicating the Israeli embassy in a clash at the Soviet consulate in London, the Israelis lost confidence in the students and concentrated their resources on the more dependable women campaigners.[136] The Israelis were also upset with the British students, who in 1970 had become leaders of the World Union of Jewish Students, sponsoring a 'motion which linked Zionism logically with the right of Palestinian Arabs to national self-determination – a two-state solution'.[137]

---

[134] JC 19 November, p.8. and 10 December 1971, p.45.
[135] Deborah E. Lipstadt, Denial. Holocaust History on Trial (New York,2016), pp.10-15. Debbie Weissman, Memoirs of a Hopeful Pessimist. A Life of Activism Through Dialogue (Jerusalem,2017), pp.72-4.
[136] JC 21 May 1971, p.6.
[137]JC 27 April 2018, p.38.

Chapter 3 - The Women's Campaign

The Students Continue their Campaigning

Since the Six Day War and a new pride in being Jewish emerged, large sections of Russian Jewry felt their Jewish identity being revitalized and were ever more determined to emigrate because of their pariah status within the Soviet Union. This sense of urgency gripped a group of eleven people, most of whom were Jews, who planned to hijack an aircraft and fly it to safety outside the Soviet Union. But the group were ensnared by the KGB and after the first Leningrad trial in December 1970, Edward Kutznetsov and Mark Dymshits were sentenced to death, leading to campaigns by Jews in the West for the commutation of their harsh sentences. The first World Conference on Soviet Jewry which took place in Brussels between 23 and 25 February 1971 at the behest of the Lishka, demanded that the Soviet government 'recognize the right of Jews who so desire to return to their historic homeland in Israel', going beyond the plea for family reunion.[138]

Looking back, Colin Shindler pointed out that the first Leningrad trial 'hugely raised awareness of the Soviet Jewry issue both among Jews and non-Jews, especially as the death verdict came on Christmas eve 1970, bringing back memories of another Jew Jesus, who had gone to his death. The death sentences were reprieved a week later'. He also organised a meeting just after Christmas at the Chelsea Town Hall, which a large number of people attended addressed by Gideon Hausner, the Israeli attorney-general, who had prosecuted Eichmann; other speakers included Yosef Yankelevitch and Tina Brodetskaya and Lord Soper, a pastor and lively broadcaster. 'All this was done', recalled Colin Shindler, 'because the communal organisations were unable to gear up during the holiday period, it was left to the students. It was in essence the last major event

---

[138] Albert D. Chernin, 'Making Soviet Jews an Issue', in Friedman and Chernin eds., A Second Exodus, pp.59-61.

organised by the students before the real communal involvement from 1971 onwards'. This was followed by a meeting in Woburn House arranged by the Board of Deputies, but no doubt sponsored by the Lishka, in which Yosef Yankelevitch and Tina Brodetskaya emphasised that 'a sustained campaign of protest and pressure mounted outside the Soviet Union was the only effective way of ameliorating the plight of its Jewish community'. On 10 January 1971, there was a protest march from Speaker's Corner to the Soviet Embassy arranged by AJEX and the Association of Women's Organizations on behalf of Anglo-Jewry, with placards demanding human rights for Soviet Jews, the first intimation of women's potential as campaigners for this cause using human rights slogans.[139]

Help came from famous non-Jewish Soviet dissidents, such as Vladimir Bukovsky and Valery Chalidze, who were disgusted and shocked by the spontaneous applause from the specially selected audience in court which greeted the pronouncement of the death sentences on Kutznetsov and Dymshits. Equally appalled were the Pope and the West European Communist parties, including the British one. Dockers in Genoa refused to load Soviet vessels, while the Marxist President of Chile, Salvador Allende, pleaded for clemency. Behind this arousal of world opinion, was pressure exerted by Jewish activists and Israeli diplomats. Golda Meir requested the Spanish dictator, General Franco, to commute the death sentence on some Basque militants. As the United States needed him as an ally in the Cold War and he was anxious to rehabilitate his reputation, he agreed, thereby shaming the Soviet regime, who in turn reprieved Kutznetsov and Dymshits.[140]

---

[139] JC 8 January 1971, pp.3 and 5. Colin Shindler communication to the author, 23 December 2019.

[140] JewishChronicle 1 January 2021, pp.10-11. Colin Shindler, 'How the KGB laid the ground for the great Soviet exodus'.

Disillusion with the Students and the Women's Campaign Opens

The publication of *The Feminine Mystique* by Betty Friedan in 1963 kick-started the second-wave feminist movement in the United States and across the Atlantic in Britain. Friedan liked to present herself as a child of the consumer revolution, a woman ensconced in a comfortable suburban home, yet frustrated at being a full-time housewife and mother with contracting career horizons, a fate she shared with vast numbers of other college-educated housewives. She deftly side-stepped her role as a labour journalist and her own radical past.[141] The feminist revival in Britain was anticipated by the publication of Hannah Gavron's (1935-1965) *The Captive Wife* in 1966 to 'rave reviews' within months of her death. She was the daughter of the distinguished Zionist journalist and social critic T.R. Fyvel.[142] Gavron noted that young married couples of the 1950s were 'members of a new mass society where success has come increasingly to be measured in terms of money and consumption'. But 'in a work-orientated society [with full employment], those who do not work have a reduction in status, and housewives, no matter how arduous housework actually proves to be, do not feel themselves to be at work'.[143] Contraception became available to married British women in 1961 and to all women in 1967 through the invention of the pill, enhancing their sexual and general freedom. Another alienated Anglo-Jewish writer Eva Figes (1932-2012) brought out *Patriarchal Attitudes* in 1970 within months of the publication of Kate Millett's *Sexual Politics*(1969) and Germaine Greer's *The Feminist Eunuch*

---

[141]Daniel Horowitz, Betty Friedan and the Making of the Feminist Mystique (Amherst, Mass., 2000), pp.ix-xiii,1-15.

[142]New Statesman 12 November 2015 and Guardian 4 April 2009.

[143]Hannah Gavron, The Captive Wife (London, 1966), pp. x,xi,xii, 141-3, 146.

(1970) and immediately sprung to fame as a female polemicist. Whereas the women's movement in the United States was white, liberal, and middle class and strongly influenced by the civil rights campaigners, the women's liberation struggle in Britain emerged from the protests of the New Left and Socialist and Marxist groups, who campaigned against the bomb and the Vietnam war.[144]

As noted, there was a revolution within a revolution, and in the United States and elsewhere the second phase of the feminist movement was seen as a revolt against the lack of respect shown to women in the civil rights movement and other forms of protest in which they participated, where their views were often snubbed. Typical was the remark of Stokely Carmichael. When the Black Power leader was asked what would be the position of women in a revolution, he quipped 'prone'. Betty Frieden helped to found the National Organization for Women in the United States in 1966 to secure the legislation for some of the reform programmes which she espoused, while more radical Women's Liberation organizations were set up in the 1970s. Women were regarded in the macho culture which prevailed as easy prey to sexual conquest, though the more widespread usage of the pill in the late 1960s placed the sexes on more equal terms and led some men to rethink their sexual values. There was a huge enrolment of middle-class white women in colleges during the 1960s and gradually they moved in growing numbers into the professions of law and medicine and into business.[145] Likewise in the Board of Deputies and associated organizations in Britain during the 1960s, there were few female representatives and they tended, on the whole, to be deferential to the views of their male colleagues; and when their intervention was regarded as a departure from the

---

[144]Florence Binard, 'The British Women's Liberation Movement in the 1970s: Refining the Personal and Political', French Journal of British Studies (2017).

[145] Richard Vinen, The Long '68 pp.225-36.

usual norms, they were denounced as being hysterical and their view was given little credence.

These events, both the death sentences pronounced in the hijacking trial and the Women's liberation movement in Britain, also served as a catalyst for the formation of pressure groups of female activists intent on campaigning on behalf of Soviet Jewry. They stirred Barbara Oberman, who, having spoken to Pesach Mor while on holiday in Israel was told about a trip he had recently made to the USSR to see the situation for himself and about the numerous Jews, who 'want to get out'. Returning to Britain, Oberman approached the Board of Deputies and also had what she called a three-hour 'slugfest' with the Chief Rabbi Immanuel Jakobovits only to be rebuffed by both. She told the Chief Rabbi that they 'were heirs of those Diaspora Jews of a generation earlier who had failed to save the six million, and that he could change the course of history'. Everywhere she was told that public protests were out of the question and that she should rely on quiet diplomacy. Early in the spring of 1971, she attended a talk on Soviet Jewry at the Hampstead home of Joan Dale, given by Colin Shindler, a former Soviet Jewry student leader, who had been asked to stand in for Ijo Rager, the second secretary of the Israeli Embassy.[146] Here she heard about Raiza Palatnik, at 35 the same age as she was then, with whom she could identify completely, incarcerated in a dungeon because she wished to leave Russia. Had Barbara's own grandmother not left Russia, she felt that she would have shared a similar fate. Returning home, she made more than a hundred telephone calls that night to friends and mothers she was acquainted with from the Jewish schools her own children attended. Few answered the call to join her in a hunger strike outside the Soviet Embassy on May Day and the following night with a banner calling for the release of Raiza Palatnik. Among the dozen friends who responded were Sylvia Wallis, Zelda Harris and Zena Clayton. They were young and well groomed, and at the suggestion of

---

[146] Daphne Gerlis, Those Wonderful Women in Black (London,1996), p.28.

Joan Dale wore black, modelling themselves on the female anti-apartheid campaigners in South Africa.[147]

Clearly, the Lishka was cultivating likely Jewish women who would join their Soviet Jewry campaign and their aims overlapped with those of the women, who found it easy to identify with their trapped co-religionists overseas and were troubled by the notion that the older generation had not put enough effort into saving Jews in the 1930s and beyond. Once again, some members of the secretive Israeli organization were trying to tap into another section of Anglo- Jewish society, the women, who were in open revolt against the values of the preceding generation. They had the time, energy, enthusiasm and independence of spirit to accomplish something for themselves; and, as we shall soon see, the Israelis were becoming somewhat disappointed with the efforts of the students.

A letter was prepared by Barbara Oberman on behalf of Raiza Palatnik addressed to the Soviet Ambassador's wife, Madame Smirnovskaya, signed by the demonstrators on behalf of 'all 35-year old Jewish married women in Britain', asking her to use her good offices 'as a woman and mother' to stop the Soviet security police from torturing Raiza. When the note was delivered to the embassy on Sunday morning by a delegation of Myra Janner, Barbara Oberman and Sylvia Wallis, it was refused. However, 'following considerable publicity on the BBC [World at One Programme] and the national press, it was accepted on Monday morning'. When the BBC interviewed Barbara Oberman, a housewife and activist, they called her group the 35's and the name stuck, though their official designation was the Women's Campaign for Soviet Jewry. She explained to the press that if Miss Palatnik was not freed, her group would return to the Soviet embassy every day until she was released. If nothing happened by this Sunday, they would return with a much larger demonstration. 'The housewives, who squatted on the

---

[147] Barbara Oberman, 'Skirts Against the Kremlin', Jerusalem Post 25 July 2007.

pavement and on camp stools holding placards and banners, got a sympathetic reception from passers-by... During the night, there were many offers of food and drink – even of radio sets. One taxi-driver shot by without stopping, throwing out packets of cigarettes and shouting "Keep it up girls", as he disappeared. Several husbands gave moral support until 8 am.' Doreen Gainsford, who had been recruited by one of Barbara Oberman's friends as she worked in public relations, remarked that the police told them that theirs was 'the nicest and cleanest' demonstration they had witnessed. During the night Ijo Rager told them that Raiza was being moved to an ordinary prison in Odessa and put on trial. Out of that success, the 35's were born as a campaigning group. They had a flair for publicity. When *The Times* relied on official Soviet press accounts for news about the Leningrad trial involving Jewish dissidents, 300 women marched down Fleet Street and the editor and his deputy emerged to talk and pacify them.[148]

The 35's were a group of mostly middle-class housewives supported by their husbands, who by their political campaigning found a new purpose in life and a fresh sense of self-esteem. Even if they had not carefully read the new feminist writers, they were acquainted with their ideas and prepared to utilize their militant tactics but were careful not to overstep the boundaries of the law, even if they tested them to the limits. While most of these Jewish women campaigners did not identify closely with all the ideas of the Women's Liberation movement, they shared the belief that women had the right to be active in the political sphere; yet were sometimes willing to wear glamorous attire to attract attention in the media and achieve their aims.

The 35's continued to deliver letters on a daily basis to the wife of the Soviet ambassador on behalf of Raiza Palatnik for several weeks until they decided they would have to reduce this to a weekly delivery, and when this became impossible, the letters were despatched through the

---

[148] JC 7 May 1971, p.5. and 14 May 1971, p.48. Oberman, 'Skirts'. Daphne Gerlis, pp.32-4.

post. This activity continued for several years. At the same time, the 35's decided to hold a one-hour vigil outside the Soviet embassy on a Sunday morning in the middle of May 1971. Similar vigils were also arranged in provincial centres outside Soviet consular offices.[149] Raiza's father had been a political prisoner of Stalin in the early 1950s and the family was aware of its Jewish origins. Despite high qualifications as a librarian, she encountered great difficulties in finding employment because of antisemitism until she secured a position in a small library in Odessa. Here she came to the attention of the local office of the KGB as she took an increasing interest in Israel after the Six Day War, for which she was arrested and charged with slandering the Soviet Union and sentenced to two years in prison in June 1971.[150]

Early on, the Women's Campaign for Raiza was nearly derailed by a diplomatic incident at the Soviet consulate, when a group of fifty Jewish students and women plus Cyril Stein, a wealthy betting shop owner and philanthropist, visited it on Thursday 13 May 1971. They were ostensibly applying for visas for the Soviet Union to attend trials of Jewish dissidents in Leningrad and Riga, but they had come along with television cameramen with the purpose of publicizing the Leningrad trial. While in the consulate building, they found antisemitic and anti-Zionist literature which they held up in a window to show the camera crew posted outside. On seeing this, the consular staff asked for reinforcements from security men and there was a melee, in which Alan Freeman, a student leader, lost a briefcase with correspondence from the Israeli embassy. The next day the Russians called a hastily convened press conference, accusing Freeman of being in correspondence about his committee's actions with Ijo Rager, a political counsellor at the Israeli embassy, and asking for £644-48 to cover the expense of a proposed campaign. Further, they claimed that this state was trying to harm Anglo-Soviet relations, an accusation which was strongly denied by

---

[149] JC 14 May 1971, p.48. Gerlis, pp.30-1.
[150] Daphne Gerlis, pp.26-7.

Israeli officials. However, the British government issued a formal apology for the disturbance at the consulate.[151] During the night at 3am Rager visited Barbara Oberman, saying that her name had been found in the confiscated correspondence and that she should go into hiding. Doreen Gainsford and Zena Clayton called on Barbara Oberman, telling her that they wished to continue under the auspices of the Board of Deputies, which would mean eschewing any form of violence. Oberman was persuaded by Revd. Leslie Hardman, a liberator of the Belsen concentration camp and the minister of Hendon Synagogue, to step down from her position and found herself ousted from the organization she had founded; shortly afterwards, she set up a rival, more militant organization, the Committee for the Release of Soviet Jewish prisoners. With Joan Dale's support, Doreen Gainsford took over the direction of the Women's Campaign.[152]

Doreen Gainsford was the publicity officer of an offshoot of the Dior fashion house.[153] Her uncle was Phil Piratin, who was elected as a Communist M.P. in 1945, and her sympathies inclined towards the Labour party. A woman of tremendous energy and drive, she was not put off by outmoded condescending male attitudes and thought that women had every right to participate fully in all areas of politics, including the highest issues of foreign policy. Never before had Jewish women taken action without the approval of the Board of Deputies or the Israeli government. 'As a young child I heard about the Gestapo and the six million', she declared at the inception of the campaign, 'in my teens and twenties I openly criticised the older generation for sitting down and not fighting with everything they had for those six million. Now I find myself with nearly three million [Soviet Jews] – this time in another

---

[151] JC 21 May 1971 p.6, and Daphne Gerlis, p.34.
[152] JC 14 April 1978, p.24 and Daphne Gerlis, pp.34-5. Oberman, 'Skirts'.
[153] Mark Hurst, British Human Rights Organizations and Soviet Dissent,1965-1985 (London,2017), p.81.

country – but nevertheless in peril...Right now the Leningrad trials are on. Next is Riga, and so on and so on'. One of the Riga accused was Ruth Alexandrovich, a 23-year -old girl, who had already served a nine-month prison sentence for wanting to be openly Jewish and applying to emigrate to Israel. 'To those [who merely wish to be passive bystanders] I say if every Jew had actively worked for the six million, the criminal slaughter would never have happened'. Because of our campaign, Raiza has been moved from a dungeon to a prison. 'We shall not rest until she is free... and others like her'.[154] It was through their shared friendship with Michael Comay, the Israeli ambassador to Britain and Ijo Rager, that Doreen Gainsford and her husband became aware of the tribulations of Soviet Jewry; and that she became part of the movement to free them.[155] The whole campaign moved into higher gear with the professionalism of Doreen Gainsford, the active assistance of Ijo Rager from the Israeli embassy, and the telephone contacts made by Michael Sherbourne with Jews in the Soviet Union.

Every Monday morning Colin Shindler, a former student leader and campaigner, who was asked by the Israeli embassy to set up an information office, briefed the Women's Campaign with the latest news about Russian Jewry, highlighting the most alarming cases of maltreatment. He shared office accommodation with Emanuel Litvinoff in Percy Street in the West End. He also acquired information from letters arriving openly in the post and recruited Russian speakers, such as Michael Sherbourne and Mira Bornstein, to talk to Jews in the Soviet Union over the telephone. Between 1971 and 1975 Shindler briefed women on a regular basis.[156] According to Shindler, these housewives broke through the credibility gap which hampered the student protests of the 1960s. Students were tied to their lectures and studies and had limited time

---

[154] JC 21 May 1971, p.24. Doreen Gainsford telephone interview 5 June 2018.
[155] Doreen Gainsford telephone interview 5 June 2018.
[156] Colin Shindler interview 5 December 2017.

available for political activities, but housewives could make themselves available more readily in the day and at night, if need be. Ijo Rager, a counsellor at the Israeli embassy, realized that housewives were an under-utilized resource, who sometimes needed encouragement, which he gave them in defiance of the orders of his superiors in the diplomatic service in Israel; but who sometimes were prepared to go beyond the limits set by Rager himself. These housewives were better educated than their mothers and were in part a manifestation of the second-wave feminist movement which flourished on both sides of the Atlantic in the mid-1960s and 1970s. Whereas by 1972 the students could be safely marginalised, these women were not to be cowed by the male communal leadership nor by their male counterparts in the British government. By a mixture of gimmickry and innovative public relations techniques, they grabbed the attention of the press and the broadcasters. Government ministers were forced to listen to their views which had been formed so often in the shadow of the Holocaust.[157]

Michael Sherbourne (1920-2017), a schoolteacher who taught himself Russian, became a key figure in the Women's Campaign. As a youth in the 1930s, he had attended a meeting addressed by Sidney and Beatrice Webb, who despite its brutalities, regarded Soviet Communism as a new civilization, which had solved the problem of mass unemployment; and was angered by Bernard Shaw, who denied the existence of the Ukrainian famine. 'He wanted to fight in the Spanish civil war but was prevented by his family'.[158] To cap their infamy, the Soviet regime concluded a pact with the Nazis, which angered him even more. At a meeting in 1972, Sherbourne berated the Chief Rabbi Jakobovits for his inaction in failing to speak out about the dire situation of Russian Jewry and was

---

[157] Colin Shindler, 'Those Wonderful Women in Black' JC 25 July 1997; and 'Soviet Jewry Files' JC 17 January 2003.

[158] Colin Shindler communication to the author 23 December 2019.

alone applauded by Myra Janner, the wife of Greville Janner MP. A leading member of the 35's, she said you sound like one of us and invited him to meet Raiza Palatnik's sister, who was shortly coming to England to boost their ongoing campaign.[159]

During the 1970s and 1980s while holding his job as a teacher, he spent on average 35 hours a week making telephone calls to the Soviet Union to speak to activists, who had been refused emigration visas. He coined the word refusenik to describe their limbo status, a word that has been adopted into the English language. His telephone bills which included calls to the United States to exchange information were paid by the right-wing Zionist and founder of Ladbrokes, the biggest betting company in the world, the philanthropist Cyril Stein. Not only did Stein contribute lavishly himself, but he raised additional funds from wealthy friends.[160] Speaking in 1983, Sherbourne declared that 'until 2 or 3 years ago and even today, the occasional call does get through, although during the last year since Yuri Andropov has come to power, it has become almost impossible. However, during this telephone contact, we were able to gather a good deal of information about the plight of Jews in the USSR and one of the many contacts we had at that time, was with Anatoly Shcharansky. Sometimes he would talk with us for 40 minutes or an hour giving all the latest news – and I must stress here that none of the information he gave us was secret. We spoke on an open line. In those days before final refusals were given, the authorities used to give reasons for refusal. For example "no close relatives" or possessing [a] secret – this was often [the excuse] given to a private soldier who had played the balalaika in an army unit... or a soldier who had been digging ditches...' Again, Lev Blitshtein was not permitted to leave because as 'the manager of a sausage factory' he was said to be in possession of state secrets! Another important contact with whom Sherbourne started speaking

---

[159] Mark Hurst, pp.103-4. Daphne Gerlis, p.19
[160] Mark Hurst, pp.105-11. Doreen Gainsford telephone interview 5 June 2018.

in 1972 was Ida Nudel, who supplied him with news about the Jewish Prisoners of Conscience.[161] But it has since transpired that the KGB was bugging these telephone numbers which were passed on by prostitutes and other women to the refusenik network in return for abortions performed by a surgeon, who was a secret police informant.[162] All this information from many different sources was distributed by Sherbourne to the Women's Campaign, who gave them wider coverage in their circulars; and he also shared it with Fleet Street journalists, notably *The Times* columnist Bernard Levin, and activists from the Union of Councils in the United States.[163] Other important recipients of information were Greville Janner, who sometimes broadcasted on the Today programme and appeared on television, and the stellar historian and newspaper columnist Sir Martin Gilbert.

At the behest of Nativ, the First Brussels Conference on Soviet Jewry took place in February 1971 to coordinate Soviet Jewry activities on a worldwide scale. In March 1971 the Board of Deputies set up a separate Soviet Jewry Action Committee and a year later appointed Mike Whine, a young communal activist, who was a member of the anti-fascist 62 Group and the Jewish Aid Committee, as its officer; as usual, Stein stepped in and helped bankroll the position. It was felt that the Committee should be enlarged to include representatives of the 35's and the World Jewish Congress. Whine was keen on demonstrations and quickly grasped that the Women's Campaign was the most effective of the campaigning organizations. The new policy of cooperation between the Board, the 35's and the students was first seen on 18 April 1972, when a convoy of fifty cars encircled the Soviet trade mission in Highgate for ninety minutes, displaying banners critical of Soviet repression, while their drivers threw out leaflets, and later in May

---

[161] Southampton, MS 254/A980/I/3/2 Sherbourne draft of a 1983 talk.
[162] Interview with Jerry Lewis 22 May 2018.
[163] Mark Hurst, pp.106-9. Daphne Gerlis, p.20.

when there was a combined demonstration for Raiza Palatnik.[164]

Under Doreen Gainsford's leadership, the campaign for Raiza Palatnik to be released from prison and for her to be allowed to emigrate to Israel continued with unabated vigour and slowly expanded in new directions by the formation of branches of the 35's in Britain and overseas. From agitating on behalf of one individual, the Women's Campaign took Sylva Zalmanson under their wing and extended their help to other refuseniks. Whatever reservations the Jewish establishment had, the 35's stated that they with their 'allies in women's organizations, in Ajex [the Association of Jewish Ex-Servicemen], in the student bodies and the Board of Deputies – will continue our work. And we shall not stop until every Soviet Jew who wishes to make Israel his home is able to do so, and, above all, until Ruth Alexandrovich, Raiza Palatnik and their brave brethren are released from Soviet gaols and prison camps'.[165]

In July 1971 a table was laid in front of the Soviet embassy with the meagre rations typical of a prisoner's meal. In September, the Women's Campaign picketed the Royal Albert Hall during concerts of the Leningrad Philharmonic Orchestra in protest against the persecution of Jews in the Soviet Union. In addition, Liverpool housewives demonstrated outside an International Congress of Librarians to show their displeasure at the continued detention of Raiza Palatnik. At the end of the month, after the dismissal of Raiza's appeal against her sentence, the Women's Campaign dressed in black staged a demonstration outside the Soviet embassy.[166] Katia Palatnik undertook a five-day hunger strike in Moscow to protest against the conditions in the Dnieprodzerjensk

[164] Dave Rich, 'The Activist Challenge: Women, Students, and the Board of Deputies of British Jews in the British Campaign for Soviet Jewry', Jewish History vol.29 (2015):163-85.
LMA,BDBJ,FAC,ACC/3121/C11A/2227 March 1972 and 13 April 1972.
[165] JC 6 August 1971, p.17.
[166] JC 1 October 1971, p.6. Daphne Gerlis, p.223.

labour camp, to which her sister Raiza had been consigned. Here she suffered from dysentery with continuous headaches and developed a heart condition. On the third night of the festival of Hanukah in December, more than 1,000 people congregated on the Bayswater Road outside the Soviet embassy in London. 'The feeling of being at one with the Jews in the Soviet prison cells was heightened by the appearance of twelve members of the 35's Committee of Women wearing red striped smocks over their dresses, representing the garb worn by the prisoners. Each carried a placard bearing the names of the incarcerated prisoners'. The Chief Rabbi lit three Hanukah candles, indicating how well the 35's were working with sections of the Anglo-Jewish establishment. On being granted permission to leave for Israel in January 1972, Katia Palatnik vowed to campaign for her sister to be given the right to join her and came to Britain under the auspices of the Women's Campaign to meet the press, religious figures and activists. Although the 35's supported by the Chief Rabbi wanted her to talk to children in Jewish secondary schools about her sister, this was rejected by the Board, as they 'did not approve of involving children in this sort of [political] action'. Nonetheless, the campaigning continued until Raiza was eventually permitted to emigrate in 1973; and the exit of both sisters from the Soviet Union convinced the leadership of the Women's Campaign that their tactics of confrontation and pressure were bearing fruit.[167]

At the end of 1972, the Women's Campaign intruded into the Festival of Russian Music, which was launched in Britain, making Russian diplomats very uncomfortable, giving the Foreign Office a diplomatic headache and making the Jewish impresario, who arranged the tour, so uneasy that he wished to deny any connection to it; but above all, it thrust the issue of Soviet Jewish emigration into the public spotlight. On the night of 7 November, slogans and Stars of David were painted on the Soviet consular building and the embassy's living quarters in London. At

---

[167] JC 17 December 1971, pp.7 and 8, and 3 March 1972, p.8. Daphne Gerlis, p.7 and Mark Hurst, p.86. Dave Rich, 'The Activist Challenge'.

the opening of the festival women stood silently with torches and banners 'calling for the release of Jews from Russian labour camps' at the entrance to the Festival Hall and confronted Mr Smirnovsky, the ambassador. Leaflets and fake programmes about Valery Panov were handed to concertgoers. Having decided not to disrupt the concert itself, the 35's permitted a lone protestor to appeal to the audience during the interval, and a British official was 'frankly relieved that there had been no serious incidents at the concerts'. During the concerts at the Fairfield Hall Croydon and in Harlow, Victor Hochhauser, the impresario, told officials that 'There were peaceful pickets of Jewish ladies with placards, etc., who behaved responsibly'. On 14 November, the Russian State Choir performed at the Queen Elizabeth Hall. 'At the entrance a silent and dignified group of torch-holding Jews handed out leaflets to the accompaniment of a lone cello player... In addition, after each of the first three items a pair of demonstrators scampered across the stage for a few seconds trying unsuccessfully to unfurl their small banners at the same time'. They were quickly removed by officials.[168] To Foreign Office chagrin, the Russian diplomats complained about the event and Julian Bullard telephoned Lord Janner, begging him 'to use his influence with the Group of 35 or whatever Jewish organisation had been responsible to restrain them'. At the premiere on 20 November of Shostakovich's 15 Symphony with the violinist David Oistrakh performing a 'group of 10 young demonstrators chanted for 15 minutes, before the concert, lining the main staircase, before they chained themselves to the stairs and were removed amicably by the police. Outside the building a few people gave away leaflets'.[169]

On 26 November, women outside the Albert Hall 'carried torches, shouted slogans and distributed leaflets in

[168] NA, FCO 34/148 report of E.V. Vines 9 November 1972; and G.H.H. Walden 15 November 1972.
[169] NA, FCO 34/148 J.L. Bullard to G.H.H. Walden 21 November 1972. E.V. Vines to Mr Kirby 21 November 1972.

the form of mock programmes'. Between the overture and the concert 'demonstrators had shouted slogans, including one against Mr Hochhauser, and leaflets had been scattered from the balconies'. At a lunch given on 27 November, a woman, Sylvia Wallis, lay down on the forecourt when the Soviet ambassador arrived in his car and flowers were tossed into it, while other members of the 35's shouted slogans. He left his car and 'looked visibly shaken'. All the demonstrators asked to be arrested but only their leader Doreen Gainsford was reported by the police, though she was not convicted of any offence.[170]

Victor Hochhauser came under unrelenting pressure from the Jewish community, of which he was a prominent member, to have nothing to do with the concerts; and soon found the use of the term festival in the promotional material embarrassing. To placate him, the government agreed to a suggestion that the concerts carried a publicity label, stating that they were promoted 'In accordance with the Anglo-Soviet cultural Agreement'. Officials found that 'Dealing with Hochhauser's changes of mood was time-consuming', but after the conclusion of the festival, an official from the Foreign Office wrote a polite letter of thanks to Victor Hochhauser to mollify him.[171]

The Committee for the Release of the Panovs

Next, the Women's Campaign threw its weight behind the Committee for the Release of Valery and Galina Panov which was set up in 1972 to assist Valery Panov and his wife Galina to leave the Soviet Union. The group consisted of members of the theatrical profession, its leaders being Rosemary Winckley and her sister Patricia Barnes, and Pamela Manson, an actress and left-wing Jewish activist,

---

[170] NA, FCO 34/148 J.L. Bullard to G.G.H. Walden 27 November 1972. J.W. Forbes-Meyler to E.V. Vines 27 November 1972.
[171] NA, FCO 34/148 E.V. Vines to Sir John Killick Moscow 19 December 1972; and E.V. Vines to Victor Hochhauser 18 December 1972 and G.F.N. Reddaway to Hochhauser 20 December 1972.

and the main thrust of the campaigning came from them; but it was independent and was not by any means a front organization for the 35's. Valery Panov was the principal dancer of the Kirov Ballet Company of Leningrad until he and his wife applied to emigrate to Israel in March 1972. Clive Barnes, the dance critic of the *New York Times* and the husband of Patricia Barnes, after watching Valery over a series of performances, hailed him 'as one of the most remarkable male dancers of our day. His Harlequin, quirky, airborne and with a kind of supernatural cheekiness, was not only outstanding as a dance performance, but, much more, remarkable as a piece of dance acting'. Rudolf Nureyev, also a member of the Kirov Ballet, had defected to the West a decade earlier; and the Soviets were extremely suspicious of the loyalties of their dancers. For some reason, suspicion had fallen on Panov in 1959 during a tour of the United States, when he was ordered to return home on the pretext that both his parents had been killed in a car accident -- a summons that turned out to be based on deliberately false information. To his increasing frustration, he was never allowed to travel overseas with the company again, although his colleagues were. In early 1972 Valery was dismissed from the Kirov Ballet after a session at which some fellow dancers denounced him as a traitor; others said that he deserved to be sent to Siberia or shot, while his wife was demoted to the corps-de-ballet. Galina was also a star performer, having won a gold medal in an international dancing competition at the age of eighteen. When the authorities put pressure on her to divorce her husband, Galina resigned from the Kirov Ballet. Valery's father, a loyal Communist party stooge, came from an Orthodox Jewish family, while his mother was the product of 'an unblessed union' between a minor member of the gentry and an illiterate peasant, so that according to the strict interpretation of rabbinic law Valery was not Jewish; and nor was his wife.[172] At first, Galina's mother, to whom she

---

[172] NA, FCO 28/2603 Memorandum on Valery and Galina Panov circa 1974. Valery Panov with George Feifer, To Dance (London,1978), pp.52-3.

was not particularly close, was willing to give permission for her daughter to leave the Soviet Union, though she subsequently withdrew it. This was after the KGB facilitated the granting of a pension to her as compensation for wartime injuries which had previously been withheld. An attempt was made to put Valery on trial on a trumped-up charge of assaulting his mother-in-law, though this was put aside for lack of evidence. During a visit by the American President Nixon to Moscow in the summer of 1972, Valery was arrested for allegedly spitting at a policeman and given a ten-day prison sentence for hooliganism. 'He spent the first three days of this sentence in an unheated cell infested with bugs in a cell filled with cripples and amputees intended as a grim warning to him' that he would never dance again.[173]

Reflecting on why he was not permitted to travel abroad like other members of the Kirov Ballet, Valery thought that it was because he was infatuated with America in a similar fashion to any adolescent; and that the final proof of his disloyalty was when he purchased a 16-mm camera from his advance earnings, which the KGB regarded as a payment for espionage. But he was never told the reason for his ban on foreign travel, nor were members of his company. He was just stuck in limbo as a warning to the others for being over-enthusiastic about the benefits of capitalism and life in the West.[174] Valery was immensely aided by Fedya Medina, a cellist and ballet fan from Bogota, who relayed what was happening to him to Western correspondents based in Moscow and to the American and British consulates. More important, he acted as an interpreter in telephone conversations with John Cranko and the twin sisters Rosemary Winckley and Patricia Barnes, the wife of Clive Barnes, who made this information more widely known in the West.[175]

---

[173] NA, FCO 28/2603 Memorandum on Valery and Galina Panov circa 1974. Colin Shindler, 'How the Panovs Got their Visas', Jewish Observer and Middle East Review 14 June 1974.
[174] Julie Kavanagh, Rudolf Nureyev (London,2007), p.133.
[175] Valery Panov and George Feifer, To Dance p.313.

Under the prompting of the ladies in the Committee for the Release of the Panovs, two thousand members of the acting profession in Britain and the United States signed a petition in November 1972, including Laurence Olivier, Richard Attenborough, Vanessa Redgrave and Woody Allen for the Panovs to be permitted to leave. Their cause attracted the attention of Bernard Levin, who wrote a piece in *The Times* in December 1972 asking again: 'why? Why in this case are talented people forbidden to follow their art in one country, forbidden also to leave a place in which they are not wanted, and in which they do not want to be?'[176] In March 1973, stage and film stars mustered by the Committee tried unsuccessfully to deliver a petition to the Soviet embassy on behalf of the Panovs. Leading the demonstration were Fenella Fielding, Robert Stephens and Anton Dolin and they were joined by Janet Suzman and the director Lindsay Anderson. The petition was signed by the cast of more than twenty West End shows as well as by Paul Scofield, Sir Frederick Ashton and Tennessee Williams; opera singers Joan Sutherland and Sir Geraint Evans; the actors Deborah Kerr, Roger Moore, Peggy Ashcroft, Maggie Smith and Diana Rigg; and some ballet dancers and choreographers. Telegrams of support were received from Lord Olivier, Lauren Bacall, Paul Newman, Clive Barnes and the Stuttgart Ballet. A dancer wearing the costume of Petrouchka, Valery Panov's favourite role, stood outside the embassy.[177]

Despite the pleas of the Council of Manchester and Salford Jews and the petition of the theatrical profession, the Lord Mayor refused to cancel the visit of the Kirov Ballet Company to the city because of his wish not to impair trade relations with the Soviet Union.[178] On 21 May 1973 there were protests by young Liberals and members of the local branch of the 35's outside Manchester Opera House at the opening night of the Kirov Ballet. An actor, Tutte

---

[176] Colin Shindler, 'How the Panovs Got their Visas', and JC 25 May 1973 p.12.
[177] JC 16 March 1973 p.12.
[178] JC 25 May 1973 p.12.

Lemkow, dressed as Petrouchka in honour of Valery, danced outside, and leaflets were handed to those entering the theatre. Members of the Women's Campaign had also booked 40 seats in the fourth, fifth and sixth rows. As the Russian national anthem was being played, they held up placards spelling out Panov's name, after which they filed out. Fifteen members of Herut rushed onto the stage, chanting 'SS, KGB, let the Jews in Russia free'. Police chased them around the auditorium before escorting them from the theatre, without making any arrests. Non-Jews resented the heckling in the Opera House, so much so that some uttered antisemitic comments and there was clearly a need to repair community relations.[179] Added pressure was put on Moscow by the protests arranged by the Women's Campaign against the Georgian Dancers for a season at the Coliseum by ladies from the 35's standing in the theatre with umbrellas proclaiming 'USSR FREE JEWS'.[180]

Expelled from his union, Valery was barred from practising daily in a dance studio, without which his dancing technique would deteriorate; so he and his wife were forced to practise instead on a barre in the inadequate confined space of his small flat. Because of this situation, Valery on 2 November 1973 started a hunger strike demanding the right to emigrate to Israel, in which Galina joined him for five days. On 11 November, their applications for a visa to emigrate were accepted for the first time. But Valery persisted with his hunger strike until a doctor friend urged him to abandon it because it could do permanent damage to his health. In November 1973, Valery ended a 21-day hunger strike, when little progress had been made with his application, but threatened to renew it unless the couple was granted exit visas.[181] Meanwhile, a journalist from the *Daily Express* was present at Panov's home when a police officer asked him: 'Why have you done no work for so many months? How did you get your money? Do you

---

[179] JC 25 May 1973 p.7 and 8 June 1973, p.40.
[180] Colin Shindler, 'How the Panovs Got their Visas'.
[181] NA, FCO 28/2603 memorandum on Valery and Galina Panov circa 1974.

want to go to prison for parasitism?[182] Valery was offered the right to leave the Soviet Union but refused to do so unless accompanied by his wife. His wife Galina wrote to Mr Kosygin, the Soviet Prime Minister, complaining of the clumsy attempts made to separate her from her husband.[183]

On 22 January 1974, an official from the Foreign Office met Parastaev, the Soviet cultural attaché, at a reception in the Czech embassy and the attaché told him that they 'were most anxious for the tour [of the Bolshoi Ballet Company for the summer season] to be successful and [hoped] that all steps within the law would be taken to prevent unfortunate incidents.' The British official tried to reassure his Soviet counterpart and emphasised that there was a right to peaceful protest in his country. What disturbed the Soviet side the most were 'the incidents at the Coliseum with the Georgian Dancers where he said interruptions on the stage would have led to physical danger to the performers if they had been a classical ballet company'.[184]

Since February 1973, Equity, the actors' union, at the behest of members prompted by the Committee for the Release of the Panovs, had been making representations on behalf of these two dancers without a satisfactory response. Peter Plouviez, the secretary of the union, informed the Conservative Home Secretary, Robert Carr, in January 1974 that it was 'a matter of grave concern that two fellow artists have been... denied the right to work and deprived, too, of the right even to attend class (an absolute necessity in the case of ballet dancers)'. A growing section of his members was pressing his council to take action and he urged him to consider withholding permits for visits by Soviet artists and companies to this country. Like the Soviet cultural attaché, he pointed to the real possibility that a tour by Soviet companies or individual artists would become the target of protests with the danger of the disruption of

[182] JC 14 December 1973, p.6.
[183] JC 28 December 1973, p.32.
[184] NA, FCO 28/2602 E.V. Vines to Mr Hull 23 January 1974.

performances.[185] A civil servant, E.A. Grant, replied on behalf of the Home Secretary, noting that it was not consistent to urge the Soviet authorities to allow greater freedom of movement to those such as the Panovs, while at the same time denying Soviet citizens the right to enter Britain. He also put forward a fresh concern about the Conference on Security and Cooperation in Europe, the second stage of which was currently taking place in Geneva. 'The Government attach particular importance to the third item of the Agenda of this Conference which provides... for a thorough examination of such questions as travel for personal and professional reasons. The latter, in our view, includes the right to leave one's country. The United Kingdom are [is] pursuing this item energetically: you will understand that such action as you propose would cut the ground from beneath their feet'.[186]

A similar letter was addressed on 21 January 1974 by Equity to Sir Alec Douglas-Home, the Foreign Secretary, followed by another one on 8 February. But not receiving a prompt reply to the earlier letter, a telegram signed by among others, Sir John Gielgud, Rex Harrison, Susan Hampshire, Cat Stevens and Twiggy was sent to the Minister of State as well as with a message for the British ambassador in Moscow. They asked Julian Amery, the Minister, to pass on to the Soviet authorities their profound concern at their continual refusal to grant the Panovs exit visas, stating that it was indefensible to try and separate wives from their husbands.[187] As Amery was busy in his constituency electioneering, his private secretary M.I. Goulding answered on his behalf.[188] Sir Alec, the Foreign Secretary, replied to the Equity letter in almost identical

---

[185] NA, FCO 28/2602 Peter Plouviez to Robert Carr 23 January 1974.
[186] NA, FCO 28/2602 E.A. Grant to Peter Plouviez 13 February 1974.
[187] NA, FCO 28/2602 telegrams from Sir John Gielgud and others to Julian Amery 5 February 1974; and Peter Plouviez to the British ambassador Moscow 9 February 1974. Peter Plouviez to Sir Alec Douglas-Home 8 February 1974.
[188] NA, FCO 28/2602 M.I. Goulding to Sir John Gielgud 19 February 1974.

terms that the British government had 'no standing to represent citizens of the USSR, and there are definite limits to our ability to influence the Soviet authorities in a more liberal direction'. But we do make representations that 'their internal policies can have an adverse effect abroad. I have made this point myself both to the Soviet Foreign Minister in Moscow and to the Soviet Ambassador in London on several occasions'. He repeated the point that in the talks taking place in Geneva, they would emphasise the freer movement in Europe for everyone including Soviet artists.[189] Scribbled on a letter to an official instructing him to draft the reply for Sir Alec was a comment from the permanent secretary, Sir John Killick, stating that 'a visit by the Bolshoi would impose many unwanted strains on our relation[s] with the USSR'.[190]

Sir Alec's reply to the secretary of Equity was disingenuous, as he had already made clear to the M.P.s All-Party Committee for Soviet Jewry that he was not prepared to raise the specific issue of Jewish emigration from the Soviet Union at the CSCE talks proceeding in Geneva. A correspondent claimed that his position that 'the right of Jews to leave Russia cannot be divorced from the right of any other Soviet citizen to leave his country – is a virtual invitation to the Soviet delegation to reject any concrete discussion on the subject of emigration'. Further, Sir Alec claimed that 'to raise in Geneva the specific problems of Soviet Jews would be unlikely to promote through the conference a lessening of the restrictions on movement between East and West for all Soviet citizens, including Jews'. The British government's stance, however, failed to take into account the factors which impelled Jews to emigrate in large numbers, the denial of their religious, educational and cultural rights, which were granted to other minorities.[191]

---

[189] NA, FCO 28/2602 Sir Alec Douglas-Home to Peter Plouviez 15 February 1974.
[190] NA, FCO 28/2602 C.J.R. Meyer to Mr Holt 15 February 1974.
[191] JC 21 September 1973, p.13.

Victor Hochhauser, the London-based Jewish impresario, signed a contract with Goskoncert for the engagement of the Bolshoi Ballet for a six-week season in London opening on 12 June 1974. To protect himself as far as the Jewish community was concerned, he had assigned his rights under the contract with the Soviet cultural organization to the manager of the Coliseum, Lord Harewood and others, he informed the British ambassador in Moscow; but he was still ultimately responsible as the financial guarantor of the tour and would be heavily in debt if it failed. This was the least factor that worried him and then a snide remark from the British ambassador with antisemitic undertones: 'I don't believe this for one minute'. Hochhauser told him that he did not, however, expect much trouble from the Jewish community over the tour, a misreading of the situation. 'What, in Hochhauser's submission, bothered him most was the likelihood, as he saw it, of a frontal clash between the Bolshoi and Equity. There were some big names behind the Equity agitation...and, demonstrations apart, Equity could bring the show to a standstill by pulling out the Musicians' Union and the stagehands' union...in sympathy. Moreover, although British Jewry might not be involved, the techniques used to disrupt the Georgians were well established. Apart from creating a rumpus outside the theatre, demonstrators bought tickets, got inside, jumped on the stage and shouted. Britain, unlike America, was weak in these circumstances and the police never did any good'. Hochhauser advised officials at the Soviet Ministry of Culture that while he would always fulfil his side of the contract, it might be best to withdraw or postpone the visit of the Bolshoi, but he saw no enthusiasm from his counterparts to this suggestion.[192]

Meanwhile, C.J.R. Meyer of the East European and Soviet Department of the Foreign Office advised the British cultural attaché in Moscow that 'Lord Harewood of the Sadler's Wells Trust, who are organising the Bolshoi

---

[192] NA, FCO 28/2602 Terence Garvey to J.L. Bullard 19 February 1974.

season, has not unnaturally sought our advice on whether he should go ahead and sign contracts for the season. He knows of course that the decision must be his'; and this was the approach they were inclined to adhere to. But the Foreign Office was also waiting for a new government to be formed after the parliamentary elections on 28 February 1974, when they would advise the incoming administration as to whether or not to go ahead with the tour. At this stage, their recommendation was that 'the threat of demonstrations is not in itself sufficient to justify calling off the Bolshoi season (the developments on the Panov and Solzhenitsyn fronts may change all that)'.[193]

On 21 February 1974, Eleanor Fazan on behalf of the British Committee for the Release of the Panovs wrote to Julian Amery, the Minister of State at the Foreign and Commonwealth Office, with some enclosures indicating the current state of play in the campaign for the Panovs' right to emigrate. First, they had written to the International Federation of Artists based in Stockholm, appealing to them to set up similar committees for the Panovs in Europe as had been set up in Britain and the United States. 'The late John Cranko and the Stuttgart Company, and the Royal Danish and the Swedish Ballet Companies, have all been actively concerned and involved... Valery and Galina Panov are being held as prestige symbols and as a deterrent to other Russian artists who may wish to emigrate to the West'. It was planned to hold a gathering of solidarity of well-wishers on 12 March next, the anniversary of Valery Panov's birthday. Secondly, there was a long letter written by Pamela Manson of the British Committee to the current issue of *The Stage and Television Today*, declaring that 20,000 actors here and in the United States had signed a petition asking for the release of the former Kirov dancers, Valery and Galina Panov. An Equity delegation told the Soviet cultural attaché, Parastaev, that while fellow artists like the Panovs languished, Soviet companies would not be welcomed in England. She hoped that the Arts Council and

---

[193] NA, FCO 28/2602 C.J.R. Meyer to H.J. Spence Moscow 15 February 1974.

the governors of Sadler's Wells would discourage any proposed visit of the Bolshoi Ballet. In the meantime, she asked members of the Prospect Theatre Company to decline to go on their proposed tour of the Soviet Union, although they had signed the petition which was forwarded to the Soviet embassy.[194]

Lunkov, the Soviet ambassador in London, had sounded out both Hochhauser and the British-Soviet Friendship Society, a Communist-dominated body, about the ability of Equity to disrupt the proposed Bolshoi Ballet tour; and seems to have passed on some poor advice of the Friendship Society that Equity had little influence over other trade unions, so that the visit should go ahead. On 4 March 1974, the British cultural attaché in Moscow informed London that the other night he had had a conversation with Golovin of the cultural section of the Soviet Foreign Ministry and had warned him about the possibility of collective action being taken by British trade unions. 'Equity had strong views about the Panovs' case and had it in its power to take action against the Bolshoi visit which could have the effect of ruining the visit and would have put a strain on Anglo-Soviet relations instead of improving these relations, as cultural exchanges... were supposed to do'. Parastaev, the Soviet cultural attaché in London, then questioned a Foreign Office official, Christopher Meyer, in the same terms about the ability of Equity to interfere with the progress of the tour and was told bluntly that they could do so.[195]

On 5 March 1974 the *Daily Mail*, despite attempts by the Foreign Office to squash it, ran a story that that there could be little enthusiasm even among 'the most dedicated balletomane for the ambitions of the Earl of Harewood to bring the Bolshoi to Britain this summer', while there was

---

[194] NA, FCO 28/2602 Eleanor Fazan to Julian Amery 21 February 1974; and Eleanor Fazan to the International Federation of Artists 20 February 1974 and The Stage and Television Today 21 February 1974.
[195] NA, FCO 28/2602 Llewellyn Smith to C.C.J. Meyer 4 March 1974 and minute of C.C.J. Meyer 7 March 1974; and C.C. J. Meyer to Lewellyn Smith 8 March 1974.

still no satisfactory outcome of the Panovs' emigration application.' But Lord Harewood, chief of the Sadler's Wells Opera Company, is pressing ahead with negotiations – despite the fact that America has cancelled a proposed visit by the Kirov over the Panov situation', as the stevedores had threatened industrial action over this issue. 'If the Russians have any sense of delicacy', the newspaper warned, 'they will not expose their beloved Bolshoi to the inevitable demonstrations that would accompany their arrival here, in the eventuality of further persecution of the Panovs'. On 2 April, the *Daily Mail* referred to the 'propaganda roasting' suffered 'by the Soviets over their abysmal treatment of the Panovs; and noted not only how attempts to provide cut-price tours of the Moscow Classical Ballet had been rebuffed by New York and Paris but also that London should do the same'.[196] Apart from this, the *Daily Mirror* was running a campaign against the Bolshoi season in London, while the *Spectator* ran an item on 23 February questioning the wisdom of Lord Harewood's invitation.[197]

To mark Valery Panov's thirty-sixth birthday on 12 March 1974, a group of leading actors and dancers orchestrated by the Committee for the Release of the Panovs, including Sir John Gielgud, Alan Bates, Malcolm McDowell, Anton Dolin and Wayne Sleep, marched from Speakers' Corner in Hyde Park to the Soviet embassy. Here they drank a toast to the Panovs and sang 'Happy Birthday' outside the embassy. A similar birthday vigil was held by the American Committee outside the Plaza Hotel in New York, where there were the same celebrations of Valery's birthday. Among the large crowd, who participated were Lotte Lenya, Hal Prince and Carol Channing. A statement was read from the legendary Martha Graham:

---

[196] Daily Mail 5 Marchand 2 April 1974, and NA, FCO 28/2602 Julian Bullard to C.J.R. Meyer 6 March 1974.
[197] NA, FCO 28/2602 Brief prepared by C.J.R. Meyer for Sir John Killick for Lunkov's visit.

'Dancers are a shining thing. They give delight and rekindle memories, and to a certain extent are gods and goddesses'.

'I have always thought that the Soviet Union had understood this, but evidently this is not so'.

'I appeal to the Soviet Union, as an older dancer, to let the Panovs choose their own lives'.

'Not shame but only honour will be reaped by Russia for this gesture'.[198]

Julian Bullard prepared a submission as to what official advice the incoming Labour party administration of Harold Wilson should offer as regards the prospective Bolshoi tour of Britain, which was seen by Roy Hattersley, the new Minister of State at the Foreign Office. 'From the departmental point of view', Bullard advised, ' it would be best to take a middle line: neither washing our hands of the affair entirely, nor giving the Russians and Lord Harewood firm advice, but drawing their attention to the difficulties and leaving them to draw whatever conclusions they wish'. The police would deal with demonstrations and the Russians might insist on enhanced protection, but the most serious problem would be Equity's threat of action.[199] It was arranged that Bullard would speak to Mr Caulton, Lord Harewood's deputy, as he was away in Vienna along the lines indicated in his memorandum. Caulton said that they would put off confirming the contract with the Russians until the situation became more clarified. While Equity had it in their power to disrupt performances, he thought that they would not utilize it, but others disagreed with him.[200] What also was apparent was that Soviet diplomats were becoming increasingly worried about the ability of Equity to spoil the smooth running of the Bolshoi tour. In fact, Madame Furtseva, the Soviet Minister of Culture, told a Canadian impresario that 'the Panov case would be "solved" favourably by mid-March', though this was

---

[198] Valery Panov with George Feifer, To Dance (London,1978), p.374; and JC 15 March 1974, pp.1 and 3.

[199] FCO, NA 28/2603 Julian Bullard to Sir John Killick 8 March 1974.

[200] NA, FCO 28/2602 Julian Bullard to Sir John Killick 18 March 1974.

discounted by the Foreign Office.[201] Perhaps their scepticism was misjudged but perhaps it was not. During a conversation with Sir Fitzroy Maclean in May she 'took the line that Panov was a poor dancer and really too old', dismissing his importance and that of the problem.[202]

As Lunkov, the Soviet ambassador, was not available, Lord Harewood and Kenneth Robinson, the chairman of the Sadler's Wells Trust, called on Semenov, the charge d'affaires and Parastaev, the cultural attaché, who simply reiterated that Panov was no longer a problem and that the tour should go ahead.[203] Unsatisfied with the advice offered by officials, Lord Harewood insisted on seeing a member of the government and a meeting was set up for him on 4 April 1974 with Roy Hattersley, the Labour Minister of State, which he attended with Kenneth Robinson. Lord Harewood told Bullard that 'he would be relieved if the Russians themselves were to call off the tour. It now seems there is little chance of that'. Instead, they were propagating the fiction that Panov 'had been dancing again in Riga'.[204] Hattersley stated that the decision to proceed with the tour or cancel it was a matter for them to decide. From the government's point of view, the danger was that Equity could bring the performances to an end, but he did not anticipate 'a major demonstration or catastrophe'. To this, Robinson replied that the Bolshoi would be bringing over their own stage staff, so that unless they could involve the other two theatrical unions, the Musicians' Union or NATKE (National Association of Theatrical television and Kine Employees) there was little risk of performances being cancelled. For the government's information, Mr Robinson declared that the Sadler's Wells Board were split on the issue with Lord Goodman, the solicitor and fixer for the

---

[201] NA, FCO 28/2602 Harry Spence Moscow to C.J.R. Meyer 13 March 1974, and Julian Bullard to Sir John Killick 18 March 1974.

[202] NA, FCO 28/2604 John Forbes-Meyler to C.J.R. Meyer 29 May 1974.

[203] NA, FCO 28/2603 C.J.R. Meyer to B.G. Cartledge Moscow 19 April 1974.

[204] NA, FCO 28/2603 Julian Bullard to Mr Goulding 3 April 1974.

Wilson government, and Mr Rothschild vehemently opposing the visit of the Bolshoi.[205]

Meanwhile, on 6 March Pamela Manson of the Committee for the Release of the Panovs wrote to the new Prime Minister Harold Wilson, pleading with him to discuss the solution of the Panov visa problem with Lunkov, the Soviet ambassador. She added your colleague Tom Williams had been very helpful in the past with dealing with Conservative Ministers; 'but naturally we hope for better results with you in office!' A reply was sent by Lord Bridges, Wilson's private secretary, on the usual lines drafted by Foreign Office officials and following the precedents established by Conservative Ministers in the former administration.[206]

On 26 March 1974, Pamela Manson again wrote to the Prime Minister, thanking him for the prompt reply to her previous letter. She referred to an answer from the former Conservative Home Secretary, in which he stated that the government was 'keeping an `open door policy' '; and that they were requesting the Russians to do the same. She now asked why, when the Russians were not allowing the Panovs out, was the government keeping the door open for visiting Soviet companies and permitting the Prospect Theatre Company to travel to the USSR? 'I am asking whether your Government can stop both these visits, or, alternatively whether their taking place can be dependent on the Soviet authorities releasing the Panovs?' Harold Wilson's response was to say that he was fully aware of the strength of feeling in the country about the Panovs' situation. However, he believed that it would be a retrograde step 'to sever cultural contacts built-up by non-governmental organizations here'. It should be left to the government 'to decide on what sorts of visits should take place'. Only by meeting Soviet representatives could he impress on them the strength of public feeling about the

---

[205] NA, FCO 28/2603 Summary record of a conversation between Roy Hattersley and Lord Harewood and Kenneth Robinson 4 April 1974.
[206] NA, FCO 28/2603 Pamela Manson to Harold Wilson 6 March 1974; and Lord Bridges to Pamela Manson 19 March 1974.

treatment of the Panovs and the other dissidents.[207] Steps in this direction were precisely what, as we shall see, Wilson decided to take, as he continued to be troubled by the issue. This was made clear in his meeting with Academician Kirillin on 20 May 1974.

In the first week of May, Equity wrote to Michael Foot, the Secretary of State for Employment, that the Sadler's Wells Trust had applied to the department for permission for the Bolshoi Ballet to appear at the Coliseum for a six-week season starting on 12 June 1974; and as usual they had been asked to give their views on the validity of the application. Until Equity had made private approaches to the Soviet Union of Performers, the Minister of Culture and the cultural attaché in London, they had made minimal comments about the situation of the Panovs which had in fact worsened. 'We believe that the Department should refuse permission for the Bolshoi Ballet Company to enter now because we are convinced that Governmental approval for a visit of the Russian Ballet Company at this time will be taken by the Soviet authorities as showing approval of the treatment of Valery and Galina Panov'. If the government take a different view to our own, we would not encourage the organization of demonstrations against the Bolshoi but many of our members as well as the general public feel so strongly about the fate of the Panovs that they will demonstrate. We share the views of the government about the need for detente and want the maximum measure of cultural exchange between our nations. We do not wish to indulge in political demonstrations against other countries, but see the issue of the Panovs as 'simply one of common humanity... To support the entry of the Bolshoi Ballet at this time will be seen as an act designed to give comfort to those within the Soviet Union who stand against individual and artistic freedom'; and for this reason they should not be allowed to come to Britain. In a covering letter, Equity warned that they would be informing the

---

[207] NA, FCO 28/2603 Pamela Manson to Harold Wilson 26 March 1974; and Lord Bridges to Mrs Manson 23 April 1974.

press of their approach to him and of the union's attitude towards the proposed visit of the Bolshoi.[208]

On 22 April, the *Daily Mail* announced that Lord Harewood had made public that the Bolshoi Ballet was coming to London for a six-week season starting on 12 June 1974. Although the plight of the Panovs weighed on their minds, when coming to a decision about the tour, Lord Harewood said, as he was a great admirer of Russian performers and felt sorry for them, the tour would go ahead. Commenting on this, Pamela Manson of the Committee for the Release of the Panovs intimated that the Bolshoi would be met by 'demonstrations and petitions when the dancers arrive...I feel Lord Harewood is undermining us. It will be made very clear to the dancers that they are not welcome'.[209]

Pressure was kept up on the government by the theatrical profession by the playwrights Tom Stoppard and Robert Bolt, writing to James Callaghan, the Foreign Secretary. Stoppard maintained that thousands of people in Britain would say that the invitation by the trustees of the Coliseum to the Bolshoi was inappropriate and that the government should say so. Bolt declared that the Panovs were being held against their will in the Soviet Union and that he was 'concerned for the creative freedom' of such persons.[210] Claire Bloom and Constance Cummings, actresses at the top of their profession, added their voices of protest.[211] Other luminaries of the British theatre, such as Peggy Ashcroft, Olivier, Peter Hall, Harold Pinter, Frederick Ashton, Jonathan Miller, and Marie Rambert,

---

[208] NA, FCO 28/2603 Peter Plouviez to Michael Foot 7 May 1974; and the same to the same 7 May 1974.

[209] Daily Mail 22 April 1974.

[210] NA, FCO 28/2603 Tom Stoppard to James Callaghan 9 May 1974; and Robert Bolt to James Callaghan 10 May 1974.

[211] NA, FCO 28/2605 Claire Bloom and Hillard Elkins to James Callaghan 24 May 1974; and C.J. R. Meyer to the same 31 May 1974. FCO 28/2604 Constance Cummings to James Callaghan 14 May 1974; and Roy Hattersley to Constance Cummings 21 May 1974.

wrote a joint appeal in *The Times* , while a separate letter was sent by Sybil Thorndike Casson and Diana Cooper.[212] Concurrently the Women's Campaign for Soviet Jewry started protesting more vociferously and sponsored a petition to the Sadler's Wells Trust against the coming Bolshoi tour of Britain because of the deterioration in the position of Soviet Jews.

Doreen Gainsford contacted the Prime Minister pointing out the persecution of the Jews in the Soviet Union, such as the Panovs and the dismissal of most Jewish members of the Leningrad Symphony Orchestra when some members had applied to emigrate to Israel. The Women's Campaign had always been proud of Wilson's humanitarian views and could not understand 'how he could condemn the sports visit to South Africa, whilst on the other hand ... [encouraging] the Soviet Union to continue their persecution of innocent Jews'. Similar appeals were addressed by Gainsford to a number of M.P.s and the Foreign Secretary, James Callaghan.[213] This contradictory policy of the government was also emphasised in letters to the Prime Minister by Zelda Harris, another prominent member of the 35's, and David Hamburger, an influential figure in Labour party politics in Manchester.[214] A member of the Women's Campaign in the guise of a British Lion paraded outside 10 Downing Street with a vest emblazoned with the slogan, 'Ban the Bolshoi whilst the USSR persecutes Jews', as a letter was handed in.[215] A question was asked in Parliament by Piers Dixon, the Conservative member for Truro, on 15 May 1974, eliciting a reply from James Callaghan, who repeated his previous answer of 27 March: 'I have made personal representations to ambassadors of countries where we

---

[212] The Times 7 June 1974.
[213] NA, FCO 28/2604 Doreen Gainsford to Harold Wilson 13 May 1974; and to George Younger M.P. 13 May 1974, Roderick MacFarquhar 13 May 1974 and James Callaghan 13 May 1974.
[214] NA, FCO 28/2604 Zelda Harris to Harold Wilson 15 May 1974 and David Hamburger to Harold Wilson 15 May 1974.
[215] Daily Telegraph 16 May 1974.

thought that human rights were being suppressed, irrespective of the nature of the regime'.[216]

When the Secretary of State for Employment replied to Equity that he doubted whether refusal of entry to the Bolshoi Company would be of any help to the Panovs, Peter Plouviez informed the Prime Minister that he did not share this pessimistic assessment. Without wishing to minimise the value of individual or unofficial protests or demonstrations, the most effective means would be for the government on behalf of the Panovs telling the Soviet Union that a visit by the Bolshoi would be unwelcome. 'It would seem to us that this action which we are now asking you to take would not be inconsistent with the views of your Government as expressed in relation to visits of South African teams to this country and British teams to South Africa'. Whatever the intentions of the British government, allowing entry of the Bolshoi will seem to be an endorsement of the views of those in the Soviet government, who wish to curb 'individual and artistic freedom'.[217]

With pressure bubbling up from this and various other quarters, the Prime Minister, Harold Wilson, suddenly grasped that he had a nasty political problem on his hands which required his immediate attention. A man with acute political antennae, he had discussed the situation with his private secretary, Lord Bridges, who was advised by Foreign Office officials to suggest two courses of action: one was to write to the Soviet ambassador, Lunkov, asking the Soviet authorities whether or not they had had time to consider the point he had made to Academician Kirillin about the impact of their actions concerning the Panovs on British public opinion; the other was to instruct Sir Terence Garvey, the British ambassador in Moscow, to speak to Gromyko in the same terms.[218] In

---

[216] NA, FCO 28/2604 Piers Dixon to James Callaghan 15 May 1974 and Callaghan's reply.
[217] NA, FCO 28/2605 Peter Plouviez to Harold Wilson 17 May 1974.
[218] NA, FCO 28/2605 minute with illegible signature to C.J.R. Meyer about a conversation with Lord Bridges 3 June 1974.

answering Equity, the Prime Minister underlined that he had followed the case of the Panovs closely and shared their concern, he was aware of the feelings aroused in the country by this issue and was opposed to the violation of human rights wherever this occurred. He denied that the attitude of the government to the plight of the Panovs and British sporting teams touring South Africa was inconsistent, claiming that the government's attitude towards the deprivation of human rights was the same everywhere. 'There was no double standard'.[219]

A day later Wilson on 4 June wrote to the Soviet ambassador reminding him of the dinner he had given in honour of Academician Kirillin on 20 May, when he had occasion to refer to the Panov case. 'I spoke about the Government's desire to improve relations with the Soviet Union, and to avoid anything which might impair the forthcoming visit of the Bolshoi Ballet: and asked for my remarks to be communicated to the Soviet leadership'. The opening night of the Bolshoi was only a week or so away, and that he was personally interested in the matter of the Panovs, so that if there were any fresh developments, he wished to be kept informed.[220]

As we have indicated, Lord Goodman was used by the Wilson government to fix intractable problems. A man of some girth and known as two dinner Goodman because of his colossal appetite, his zest for work matched that for food; and after a busy day at his law firm, once a week or at fortnightly intervals, he would descend on the Prime Minister's office, where his skills as a negotiator and legal knowledge would be exploited to put at rest current political problems. [221]

Doubtless his intervention in the Panov affair at this point was another move by the Wilson government to facilitate exit visas for the Panovs and a tour of Britain by

---

[219] NA, FCO 28/2605 Tom Bridges to Peter Plouviez 3 June 1974.
[220] NA, FCO 28/2605 Harold Wilson to Lunkov 4 June 1974.
[221] Arnold Goodman, Tell Them I am on My Way (London,1993), pp.208-218. Brian Brivati, Lord Goodman (London,1999), pp.75-91,269.

the Bolshoi Ballet free from disturbance. After Lord Goodman promised the trustees of Sadler's Wells that he would make an attempt to persuade the Soviet authorities to change their attitude to the release of the Panovs, he wrote a letter to the Soviet ambassador and received an invitation to meet him. He called on Lunkov on 29 May 1974 accompanied by Lord Olivier and Lord Drogheda, the chairman of Covent Garden. The Russians regarded the linkage made by the United Kingdom between the Panov case and the visit of the Bolshoi as artificial. Galina was the only child of an elderly mother and Soviet law stipulated that no one could leave the Soviet Union without making adequate provision for elderly relatives. Indeed, Australia had a similar law.[222] But this was a blatant falsehood, as her mother had recently come into receipt of a state pension for war injuries, for which she had been applying for many years.[223] Not knowing this, Lord Goodman offered to arrange bountiful provision for Galina's mother for life, an offer which the Soviet ambassador implied put 'a different complexion on it'. The ambassador promised to communicate this offer to his government.[224]

Victor Hochhauser was upset by an article in *The Times* from the columnist Bernard Levin accusing him of pretending to have nothing to do with the Bolshoi tour. According to Hochhauser, 'he planned to bring the Bolshoi to Britain in 1972; that this was cancelled by the Russians after September 1971; that Goskoncert had offered the Bolshoi for 1973, later postponed until 1974; but when the agitation over the Panovs developed, Hochhauser saw clearly that he could not take the lead in presenting the season, and therefore agreed in writing with Lord Harewood that the Sadler's Wells Trust should negotiate the contract, handle the publicity and act as `presenter' in

---

[222] NA, FCO 28/2605 Lord Bridges to M.O'D. B. Alexander 5 June 1974. Arnold Goodman, Tell Them (London,1993),pp.308-10.
[223] NA, FCO 28/2603 memorandum on Valery and Galina Panov circa 1974.
[224] Lord Goodman, Tell Them p.210.

the technical sense'.[225] In fact, Victor showed a *Jewish Chronicle* reporter a 'copy of a letter dated April 19, 1974, to Mr Rupert Rhymes of the London Coliseum. In this he stated that "we have now completely withdrawn from this particular presentation of the Bolshoi Ballet"'. This meant that he had waived his right to any share of the profits of the tour and only wanted to be compensated for any disbursements incurred before his letter of waiver. Until the story became public in June 1974, Victor concealed his personal involvement in the presentation of the Bolshoi.[226] Jewish groups had strongly criticised him previously in 1973 for arranging the tour of Soviet musicians to Britain; and because he did not wish to be subjected to such opprobrium again, at what some might consider to be a late stage, he waived his right to any share of the profits made on the tour.

Having been invited by Semenov of the Soviet embassy to attend the Bolshoi opening night, the Prime Minister, Harold Wilson, made it clear that he would not attend unless the situation of the Panovs 'radically improved'. On 5 June, the Prime Minister was interviewed for the radio programme 'Analysis', when he claimed that he was unexpectedly asked a question about the Panovs and felt unable to conceal his own views on the question. 'I personally take the view, and I have informed the Soviet Government of this, that the visit of the Ballet would be more acceptable to all of our people, including myself, because I would like to see it, if for example the Panovs were allowed their freedom and allowed to go'. So far there has been no response from the Soviet government, though he hoped there would be one. 'I have had long experience dealing with applications for Soviet citizens to be released and many have been successful, and it doesn't help to say too much in public'. He still hoped that the Bolshoi visit would increase the understanding of our peoples and the ballet-loving public if there was the right gesture. This was a clear message from one head of government to another.

---

[225] NA, FCO 28/2606J.L. Bullard to Sir John Killick 25 July 1974.
[226] JC 14 June 1976, p.6.

In instructions to his private secretary, Wilson wanted him to convey to the Soviet embassy the contents of his remarks on the radio before they were broadcast on Thursday evening 6 June.[227]

On 7 June 1974, the *Daily Mail* ran a story that the Prime Minister had made a personal appeal to the Soviet Prime Minister, Alexei Kosygin, to free the Russian ballet dancers, Valery and Galina Panov; and there was a misleading passage that this personal message had been sent through the British embassy in Moscow a few days ago; and the report went on correctly to quote the broadcast which confirmed that indeed a clear message had been despatched.[228] Although draft instructions to the British ambassador in Moscow to deliver such a message through Gromyko, the Soviet Foreign Minister, had been prepared, Harold Wilson at the same time gave his interview to the BBC; but meanwhile, James Callaghan, the Secretary of State, without consulting the Prime Minister, decided not to send the telegram. Callaghan was keener for unimpeded trade and cultural relations with the Kremlin than Wilson. At this point, the broadcast was not beyond recall, but Wilson after reading the transcript of the interview ordered that it should be broadcast in full. Wilson was a master of political manoeuvre and acted with great guile, telling the Soviet ambassador later that he had been asked the question about the Panovs 'unexpectedly' and had then given them advance warning of his answer; but he pretended to have been caught off guard, as the broadcast was not despatched until a day later and he could easily have asked for the offending passage to be omitted. This was his way of sending a message to the Soviet leadership about the Panovs, but he never sent a personal letter to Kosygin as some accounts seem to infer.[229] Most Ministers took a decision not to attend the opening night of the Bolshoi, either using the excuse of having a prior

---

[227] NA, FCO 28/2605 Lord Bridges to M.O'D. B. Alexander 5 June 1974.
[228] Daily Mail 7 June 1974.
[229] NA, FCO 28/2605 record of a conversation between Harold Wilson and Lunkov 10 June 1974.

engagement or for some other reason being unable to attend; apart from this, there was the additional consideration that the government was facing a Three Line Whip on that evening, when every vote was vital.[230]

On 6 June, Semenov, the charge d'affaires at the embassy, arranged a meeting in the afternoon with Christopher Meyer of the Soviet department at the Foreign Office, to seek an assurance that the Bolshoi season would proceed 'under "normal" circumstances'. In addition, he handed him copies of anonymous threatening letters from the Jewish Defence League which seem to have unnerved the Russians before the Bolshoi visit.[231] On April 22 1971, the Jewish Defence League in New York had left bombs on the nineteenth and twentieth floors of a building containing the offices of Amtorg, the organization dealing with Soviet American trade. Despite a blast which brought down a ceiling, blew out doors and windows and damaged a concrete stairwell, miraculously no one was hurt. Since then the Soviets treated such warnings from this organization seriously.[232] The next day Meyer, after consulting higher, telephoned Semenov and confirmed 'the Government's intention to do everything possible to ensure the maintenance of the law and the safety of the performers'. He advised his permanent secretary that Special Branch anticipated demonstrations in the vicinity of the Coliseum on the nights of 12 to 15 of June, again on 28 June and on the last night 20 July 1974. A rally organised by the Board of Deputies was planned on the opening night and Jewish picket groups would operate on the pavement opposite the theatre, where they and perhaps some Ukrainians would distribute leaflets. One of the Jewish groups planned to make a peaceful protest on the stage before the opening performance. 'For the initial

---

[230] NA, FCO, 28/2605 C.J.R. Meyer to B.G. Cartledge Moscow 7 June 1974.
[231] NA, FCO 28/2605 C.J.R. Meyer to Sir John Killick 7 June 1974; and Jewish Defence League to Lunkov 23 April 1974 and 28 May 1974.
[232] Gal Beckerman, When They Come for Us pp.232-3.

performance at least, two Special Branch officers will be in the theatre and extra police will be on duty'.[233]

From Valery and Galina's point of view, the campaign for their freedom was intensifying in the West with protests against the Kirov Ballet when it appeared in Manchester in 1973 and with the cancellation of Kirov's tour of the United States. Meanwhile, the Bolshoi was due to visit Britain in June 1974 and Equity, the actors' union, demanded that the tour be postponed until both of the Panovs were allowed to leave and the electricians' union were threatening to switch off all lights in the theatre, where the company was due to perform. The cultural isolation of the Soviet Union was growing and Clive Barnes rebuked the regime in a fierce press attack. 'Just how stupid can the Russian bureaucracy be?', he railed.[234]

But the KGB's harassment of the couple continued until they were allowed to leave the Soviet Union. Valery and his brother were served poisoned tea on a Vilnius-Moscow train on 30 May 1974; perhaps it was a bungled attempt to kill them or cripple Valery, so that he would be unable to dance anymore; and Galina because of the unrelenting pressure put on her miscarried their first child a few days before their departure had been agreed to by the Soviet authorities. Five minutes after sipping some of the tea on the train, Valery started sweating and felt the most acute nausea he had ever experienced, compelling him to vomit into the basin of his sleeping compartment, while at the same time he had an attack of diarrhoea and rushed to the toilet at the end of the carriage. His brother Alec had also been poisoned and rushed to the toilet at the other end of the carriage. Valery emerged from the toilet with his mind in a haze and his heart pumping violently. The two of them called for help; fortunately, an acquaintance of Alec was on the train and they were told to drink water incessantly, which proved to be useless; they could scarcely breathe. When the train stopped at Minsk, they were taken by ambulance to a hospital, where doctors treated them and

---

[233] NA, FCO 28/2605 C.J. R. Meyer to Sir John Killick 7 June 1974.
[234] Valery Panov with George Feifer, To Dance pp. 376-7.

saved their lives.[235] If Brezhnev wanted to salvage his policy of detente with the West, Valery reasoned they would have to grant exit visas to him and his wife; and this is what happened. At Vilnius the KGB telephoned Valery on 7 June and he was told that permission had been granted both for him and Galina to leave the country. This was a story picked up quickly by Reuters and was conveyed to London by the British embassy in Moscow on 8 June 1974.[236]

A meeting was set up by the Soviet ambassador Lunkov with the Prime Minister Harold Wilson on 10 June 1974, two days before the Bolshoi's opening performance, to deliver a message from Brezhnev, the Soviet leader. Lunkov said the ballet company were worried about threats to their safety which might upset their performance and the artistes had encountered unpleasant vocal demonstrations when they had entered the theatre that day for a rehearsal. The Prime Minister 'did not think that there would be serious demonstrations now [that the Panovs had received exit visas]; although they might be organised, the persons undertaking them represented a small minority of the British population. He thought that the Soviet decision over the Panovs would help very much'. The ambassador delivered a message from Brezhnev that affairs in Geneva were proceeding slowly as they were becoming bogged down in trivialities and the basic mission of the conference was being lost sight of: 'the consolidation of detente in Europe and beyond its borders, the securing of peace and reliable security, the organisation of broad cooperation between states in various fields'.[237]

On 12 June 1974, analysing the reasons why the Soviet leadership had relented and allowed the Panovs to leave,

---

[235] JC 14 June, p.5 and 21 June, p.44 1974. Valery Panov with George Feifer, To Dance pp.377-8.

[236] Valery Panov with George Feifer, To Dance pp.378-80. Julie Kavanagh, Rudolf Nureyev p.472. NA, FCO 28/2605 Terence Garvey to London Telegram 634, 8 June 1974.

[237] NA, FCO 28/2605 record of a conversation between Harold Wilson and Lunkov 10 June 1974.

Terence Garvey, the British ambassador, admitted he had been wrong, as he had never expected the leadership to grant them exit visas. Why did the Russians change course so late in the day? 'Though I should like to think otherwise, I fear that it is less than probable that they did so in response to Mr Wilson's broadcast interview. All else apart ... there was hardly time between Thursday afternoon and Friday evening. The decision must have been made some days previously! It may well be that the Prime Minister's well-chosen words to Kirillin on 20 May played a part, reinforced by Kirillin's and Kotelnikov's own experiences in Britain and by the mounting evidence that the Bolshoi tour faced trouble... I suspect that this gesture was directed also to President Nixon, who will be in Moscow in a fortnight and from whom Brezhnev certainly wishes to get agreement to a CSCE Stage 3 summit'.[238] In addition, it should be pointed out that the Prime Minister reinforced the significance of his message to Kirillin by sending Lunkov a follow-up letter on 4 June 1974 highlighting the significance of his conversation about the Panovs and by allowing the broadcast to be made with the offending passage.

This analysis omits the meeting of the 29 May between Lord Goodman and the Soviet ambassador which by offering Galina's mother a munificent pension for life called the bluff of the Soviet government and undermined its case for detaining Valery's wife any longer. There was also the failure of the KGB plot to poison Valery, life-threatening as it was. This meant that other options had to be tried because of the adverse publicity the bungled operation was attracting. Nor was enough weight given in this analysis by the British ambassador to the firepower of the international campaign mounted by the Committee for the Release of Valery and Galina Panov which drew in the glitzy theatrical world of the theatre, ballet and Hollywood superstars. At its centre were the twin sisters Patricia Barnes and Rosemary Winckley, who ran the Committee in

---

[238] NA, FCO 28/2695 Terence Garvey to Sir John Killick 12 June 1974.

Britain. Patricia, a ballerina, was married to Clive Barnes, the influential theatre and ballet critic of the *New York Times* and that is how the Committee in Britain was able to coordinate its demonstrations with those happening in the United States. Behind the mobilization of Equity, the actors' union was the Committee for the Release of the Panovs which in turn was directed by Rosemary Winckley and won the support of Pamela Manson, a Jewish left-wing activist and actress, entrenched within the inner counsels of the union; and once one union was involved, other trade unionists offered assistance. Lord Olivier, according to his biographer, 'was genuinely put out when the newspapers made too much of his contribution and said nothing of Rosemary Winckley and others who had devoted far more time and effort' to the Panov campaign. He apologized to Rosemary, who replied that they were 'indebted' to him. 'It is a wonderful thing to know that someone you've profoundly admired for years is as great a human'.[239] It is interesting as well to note how many leading Jewish figures in the world of the theatre, such as Clare Bloom, Jonathan Miller and Tom Stoppard, who usually held aloof from anything to do with Anglo-Jewry or Israel, threw themselves into the cause. Even Vanessa Redgrave and Cat Stevens, who were known later for their Israel bashing, joined the campaign. Additional support was offered by the 35's and the M.P.s' Inter-Parliamentary Committee for Soviet Jewry, but the Women's Campaign had little, if anything, to do with the Committee for the release of the Panovs which was fully independent.

The Bolshoi Visit to Britain

Because the police had forbidden any demonstration at the airport on the arrival of the Ballet Company, the Women's Campaign set up an elaborate plan to surprise the company, when it arrived at the Royal Horseguards Hotel in Whitehall. As the Women's Campaign knew the time of

---

[239] Philip Ziegler, Olivier (London,2013), p.369.

the flight, a young man connected with the 35's raced ahead of the coaches from the airport containing the ballet dancers and their support staff and when the vehicles approached the hotel sounded his horn. Members of the Women's Campaign parked around the corner from the hotel in their cars or waiting on the pavement with concealed placards now assembled near the hotel.[240] More than 50 demonstrators chanting and waving banners met the Bolshoi company, as it dismounted from four coaches. Using loud hailers, they informed the company in English and Russian: 'You represent the Soviet Government which is persecuting Jews, so we are going to persecute you'. A woman representing the group told reporters that 'From Wednesday night demonstrators will wait outside the Coliseum stage door and will offer leaflets to the audience as they go into the theatre... [their] aim will be to make the audience feel as guilty as possible'.[241] Every night a minicab driver also stood outside the theatre dressed as a ballet dancer in a tutu and plimsolls, as his feet were too big for ballet shoes.[242]

A Communist front organization, the Ad Hoc Committee to Welcome the Bolshoi Ballet, accused Zionist elements of harassing the Bolshoi artists by hiding behind 'humanitarian' slogans in line with Soviet propaganda. They further claimed that disrupters were linked to the Zionist leadership in Israel and to the Middle East conflict, and to the role played by the Soviet Union in support of the Arab peoples to liberate land seized by the Zionists in 1967. 'To apply pressure on the Soviet Union, and to secure manpower to settle the stolen land and to staff the Israeli army, the Zionists are conducting a vicious campaign of anti-Soviet provocation such as the persecution of the Bolshoi artists'. They went on this vigil to welcome the ballet company and to offer them traditional British

---

[240] Daphne Gerlis, p.78.
[241] Guardian and Daily Express 10 June 1974.
[242] Daphne Gerlis, p.78.

hospitality.[243] Solly Sachs, a well-known fellow traveller, who had lived in the Soviet Union, wrote an open letter praising the existing educational opportunities open to Jews and the lack of racial discrimination in the USSR, both falsehoods; and stating that the Zionists were at the forefront of international reaction, having 'a diabolical plan to try to kindle antisemitism in the Soviet Union so that the three million Jews will be forced to emigrate to Israel'.[244]

During the tour of the Bolshoi Ballet Company to Britain on 27 June 1974 demonstrators affiliated to Herut, right-wing Zionists, interrupted a performance at the Coliseum theatre, by 'throwing nails and bolts on to the stage and releasing white mice among the audience' – behaviour condemned by the Anglo-Jewish establishment. In contrast, members of the Women's Campaign demonstrated peacefully outside the theatre, but Doreen Gainsford their chairwoman said that while she could not approve of interrupting a performance of the ballet 'she could fully understand it in the light of the humiliation and persecution of the Jews wishing to leave Russia'.[245] Amplifying her position on the question of violence in a letter to Greville Janner, she confessed that while she deplored 'persecution, I deplore even more those who turn a blind eye to it and I don't think that I am prepared in public to criticise rather anyone's actions, be they a little wider than my own. I would not tolerate violence but I don't believe anyone has practised any form of violence on the Soviet Jews scene, even the wildest members of Herut and one or two or ten or fifteen letters that you have received, I think could have been answered with this very point explained'.[246] In contrast Barbara Oberman, defending the action of the militants, claimed that 'The British public, including leading stage personalities, trade

---

[243] NA, FCO 28/2605 Ad Hoc Committee to Welcome the Bolshoi Ballet circa June 1974.
[244] NA, FCO 28/2605 Solly Sachs to Equity 28 May 1974.
[245] JC 5 July 1974, p.1.
[246] Southampton, MS254/A980/1/1/45 Doreen Gainsford to Greville Janner 14 November 1974.

unionists and most of the press, were more sympathetic to the cause of Soviet Jewry during the time of the Bolshoi Ballet visit than at any time before...' Yet during this visit the Soviet authorities had incarcerated 50 Jews, cut off the telephone lines of the Jewish activists, Uri and Anna Berkovsky were sent to Soviet prison camps, and Hillel, already serving a term of ten years in a labour camp for wishing to emigrate to Israel, was sentenced to five months in solitary confinement.[247]

The Soviet leadership and embassy took strong exception to an incident at the Coliseum which affected the Ballet Company. Mr Rogov, a counsellor at the Soviet embassy, accompanied by his second secretary, called on Julian Bullard at the Foreign Office the next day to vent their anger. Rogov complained that a 'group of rowdies threw nails, screws and other sharp-edged objects on to the stage of the theatre during a performance...By way of supplementary points Mr Rogov said that eggs had been thrown on to the stage, making it slippery and adding to the hazards for the dancers. Mice had been released in the auditorium, and it was only fortuitous that nobody had screamed, which could easily have started a stampede, given the risk of bombs'. Their patience was wearing thin and they would be taking a definite decision as to whether or not to continue the tour, depending on the response to their representations. To this onslaught, Bullard replied that the United Kingdom regretted what had happened and wanted a successful British tour of the Bolshoi to contribute to Anglo-Soviet relations. The British authorities would do all in their power to ensure that the law was not broken and 'the lives of the performers are protected'. He added his own personal regrets, saying that the authorities were in touch with the police. While the decision as to whether or not to continue the tour was one for the Soviet authorities, he 'was sure that its premature termination would be a matter of great regret to very many people in this country'; and that the British Council were planning to hold a

---

[247] JC 26 July 1974, p.19.

reception in honour of the Bolshoi at the end of their season.[248] Five men were asked to leave the theatre because of the incident, though the existing law made it difficult to prosecute them. One man was arrested outside the theatre for a breach of the peace, unrelated to his action inside.[249] On 19 July, Rogov again accompanied by Gventsadze called on Julian Bullard with a series of minor complaints, such as letters being pushed under the doors of the performers and approaches to them to seek political asylum.[250] So too, after Moscow radio warned that after the hooliganism of Zionist elements their government would have to consider the continuance of the Bolshoi tour, Callaghan sent a soothing message through the British embassy for Suslov and the Soviet leadership.[251]

Throughout their visit the Ballet Company and the British public were not allowed to forget the dire situation of Russian Jewry by the Women's Campaign; it was very effective psychological warfare. Members of the Essex branch of the 35's waved banners calling for the freedom of Russian Jews and followed members of the Bolshoi through the town when they visited Greenwich Observatory.[252] One morning while they were having breakfast, demonstrators from the Women's Campaign dressed in prison garb surprised the company and presented them with plates displaying the meagre daily intake of Jewish political prisoners – a photograph of this scene appeared in the *Guardian*. In addition, a group calling itself 'Vulgar Display' booked a suite of rooms on the ground floor opposite the entrance to the hotel for an exhibition of photographs,

---

[248] NA, FCO 28/2606 J.L. Bullard to Sir John Killick 28 June 1974.
NA, FCO 28/2606 J.L. Bullard to Sir John Killick 28 June 1974.

[249] NA, FCO 28/2606 R.C.C. Cook to J.L. Bullard 28 June 1974; N.K.J. Witney to J.L. Bullard 10 July 1974.
[250] NA, FCO 28/2606 J.L. Bullard to N.K.J. Winey 22 July 1974.
[251] NA, FCO, 28/2606 Dobbs Moscow to Foreign Office telegram 2 July 1974, Moscow radio transcript of broadcast 3 July, James Callaghan to Dobbs Moscow 4 July 1974, and Dobbs Moscow to Callaghan telegram 5 July 1974.
[252] JC 19 July 1974, p.8.

showing the plight of Soviet Jewry. After complaints from the Bolshoi, the management of the hotel agreed to keep the doors to the exhibition shut.[253] On 21 July 1974, when the Ballet Company left for the airport, they had to pass a group of women and children, some attired in ballet costume, waving protest banners. Six members of Herut were dressed as mice to remind them of their recent unhappy experience.[254]

Victor Hochhauser and his wife confirmed the Foreign Office 'impression that the season at the Coliseum had been tense and unhappy. The dancers were very nervous, and after the defection of Barishnikov in Canada they had been forbidden to have any dealings with private citizens in the UK, except in groups. The Hochhausers were shocked at the lengths to which some of the demonstrators had gone. They thought that the Jewish lobby was more demonstrative in London even than in New York...Goskoncert were not likely to send a Soviet ballet or opera company to Britain again in the near future, nor would Hochhauser himself be willing to handle one'.[255] The Hochhausers 'thought the release of the Panovs on the eve of the opening night knocked quite a lot of stuffing out of the hostile groups; but that if they had not been released, the demonstrations would have been so bad that the tour would have been broken off in the middle'.[256] These contemporary accounts show how Victor Hochhauser was trying to distance himself from the campaign to boycott the Bolshoi - a curiously ambivalent position, considering his position in Anglo-Jewry. Sudden diplomatic storms in the past had caused the impresario problems. Because of the Soviet invasion of Prague, plans to bring over the Red Army Choir in 1969 had foundered and Hochhauser had lost £5,000; in 1971 the tour of David Oistrakh had been cancelled because of a diplomatic contretemps.[257] 'But he

[253] NA, FCO 28/2606 19 July 1974.
[254] JC 26 July 1974, p.5.
[255] NA, FCO 28/2606 J.L. Bullard to Sir John Killick 25 July 1974.
[256] NA, FCO 28/2606 J.L. Bullard to Sir John Killick 29 July 1974.
[257] The Times 25 March 2019

would continue to represent Richter, Oistrakh and other Soviet soloists who were his personal friends as well as long-standing artistic associates'. He added that Rostropovich was preparing to spend several years in the West on the international concert circuit, so long as he could bring his family over.[258] Relations with Moscow froze when Hochhauser gave Rostropovich, the celebrated cellist, shelter in his own home, after the latter spoke out in favour of Solzhenitsyn. Victor refused to boycott individual Soviet performers, many of whom, he claimed, were sympathetic towards Jews.[259] Eric Graus of Herut conceded that Victor Hochhauser had given 'substantial assistance to Jews emigrating from Russia to Israel', which just shows the communal minefields he was trying to navigate. Victor's wife Lilian recalled smuggling religious books into the Soviet Union and visiting ' the relatives of people who had lost touch with their families'. The Hochhausers were also keen Zionists, who bought a house in Israel, but the Soviet authorities chose to overlook this when it suited them to do so.[260] Victor had a masterly touch and will be remembered as one of the most influential figures in popularising live classical music in this country.

Valery and Galina Panov settled in Israel, dancing with the Bathsheva and Bat-Dor dance companies between 1974 and 1977. 'They visited London after their release. A reception was held on the lawn of the Israeli Ambassador's home. Lawrence Olivier gave a magnificent address to all those gathered there'.[261] Valery was a choreographer and principal dancer with the Berlin Opera Ballet between 1977 and 1983 and later the artistic director of the Royal Ballet of Flanders, while Galina danced in London and New York. From 1992 until 1997 Valery was the director of a ballet

[258] NA, FCO28/2606 J.L. Bullard to Sir John Killick 25 July 1974.
[259] The Times 25 March 2019.
[260] JC 14 June 1974, p.6. Sunday Times 21 July 2019 Brian Appleyard, 'To think, I knew Shostakovich'.
[261] Colin Shindler communication to the author 23 December 2019.

company in Bonn.[262] Unhappily, their careers pulled them apart and he and Galina divorced. Galina continued her career, dancing with many different companies in France, Britain, Canada and the United States. Valery settled in Ashdod in Israel, where he founded the Ashdod Art Centre, a ballet troupe and in 1998 with Ilana Yellin-Panov, the Panov Ballet Theatre. Here Valery and Ilana ran a ballet company and school together. But since the birth of their son and an operation to repair a heart valve, Ilana suffered from severe depression and in December 2009 she committed suicide by jumping from their penthouse apartment.[263]

The Committee for the Release of Soviet Jewish Prisoners

Barbara Oberman, after she decided to quit the Women's Campaign, founded a new organization – the Committee for the Release of Soviet Jewish Prisoners which was affiliated to Herut, the right-wing Zionist organization; and was prepared to utilize more robust confrontational tactics. Of one matter she was certain, that she did not want to be under the control of the Board of Deputies. She hired, a veteran news photographer, Sydney Harris, to accompany her companions when they demonstrated and he always made certain that there was a glamorous young woman in the photograph, as the picture editors were invariably happy to publish them. When the Russians displayed a car on a stand at the Ideal Home Exhibition, a group of five women from Barbara Oberman's organization attended wearing shirts emblazoned with a prisoner's name and sat on the car. Oberman wore an outfit with Sylva Zalmanson's name. A *Daily Express* photographer captured a shot of her ejection from the exhibition. At 3.30 a.m. the next day, Oberman was telephoned by a reporter from the newspaper to say that Sylva Zalmanson was displayed on their front page and that she looks remarkably like you. On another occasion, her organization led a goat down Bond

---

[262] Website of the Panov Ballet Theatre.
[263] Haaretz 14 January 2010.

Street with the women again wearing prisoners' names on their sweaters, but the goat which Barbara was holding suddenly bolted with her desperately holding on to it. Her photograph with this scene appeared in the press across the world. Bernard Levin wrote a feature on the pregnant Jewish prisoner Ludmilla Prussakova, enabling Oberman's committee to invite the pregnant actress Hayley Mills to a demonstration outside the Soviet embassy.[264]

At Christmas 1972 Barbara and two friends dressed in Father Christmas outfits distributed imitation roubles to passers-by outside the Moscow Narodny Bank in London, brandishing the slogan 'Russia Roubles for Ransom of Soviet Jews', drawing attention to the punitive fees paid for exit visas.[265] Barbara Oberman's committee assisted Irina Markish when she staged a three-day fast outside the Soviet embassy for her husband, the writer David Markish, who was trapped in the USSR, and collected signatures from prominent literary figures on his behalf which she presented to the ambassador at the end of the fast. Barbara also arranged radio and television interviews for Mrs. Markish while she was in London. She also at her own expense took Mrs. Markish on a tour of the United States, but when her husband, David Markish, and his mother were released, Barbara was not invited to an Anglo-Jewish communal reception, nor was her group invited to a communal seminar on the problems of Soviet Jewry.[266] The male communal leadership wanted to show their distaste for the innovative tactics of the women which broke sexual and other boundaries.

During 1974, the persecution of Jewish dissidents intensified. In the summer Jewish scientists came up with an innovative idea and announced an international seminar on 'Collective Phenomena and the Application of Physics to other Fields of Science' to be held in Moscow starting on 1 July 1974. The conference enjoyed the sponsorship of

[264] Barbara Oberman, 'Skirts against the Kremlin'.
[265] JC 15 December 1972 p.7.
[266] JC 16 June 1972, p.6, 22 December 1972, p.38, and 7 September 1973, p.7. Interview with Barbara Oberman 6 June 2018.

seven Nobel prize winners from the United States, Britain and France. After a Soviet press campaign maligning the conference and stating that it was a cover for Israeli spying, ten Soviet Jewish scientists, who constituted the planning committee, issued a careful rebuttal. Professor Alexander Voronel was seized in the street by the militia and warned that he could face prosecution for inciting national enmity, which he rejected. The KGB threw the organizers, outstanding scientists such as Mark Abzel, Victor Brailovsky, Alexander Lunts, Dmitry Ramm and Alexander Voronel, into prison. The wives of the organizers, who evaded arrest, were warned that their husbands could receive a fifteen-year sentence for treason; but if their husbands renounced their participation in the conference, they would be given exit visas for Israel. All the participant scientists and their families were placed under house arrest until ten in the evening on 5 July, when the conference was due to finish. The harsh treatment and harassment of the Jewish scientists caused uproar generally among scientists overseas, so much so that the Soviet Union had to cancel celebrations to mark the 250th anniversary of the founding of the Academy of Sciences somewhat abruptly.[267]

After the announcement of a visit to Britain in March 1975 by Alexander Shelepin, the former KGB chief, who was regarded as mainly responsible for instigating the policy of persecuting Russian Jewish dissidents, the Women's Campaign threatened widespread demonstrations and hunger strikes in retaliation. Shelepin was leading a delegation of Russian trade unionists to Britain. Barbara Oberman claimed her group would haunt him and on one occasion pursued him dressed as ghosts, but it rained and the dye on the red inscription on the sheets that they were wearing ran and appeared like blood. Likewise, Doreen Gainsford warned that 'wherever Shelepin goes, we shall go after him'.[268] The Women's

---

[267] Emanuel Litvinoff, Insight: Soviet Jews (November,1987), pp.201.
[268] Interviews with Doreen Gainsford 5 June 2018 and Barbara Oberman 6 June 2018. JC 21 March 1975, p.56.

Campaign pressed the Board of Deputies to hold a mass demonstration during his visit and the Board arranged a march on Friday 4 April from the West London Synagogue to the Soviet embassy, in which about two hundred persons participated. It was noted in the minutes of the Soviet Jewry Action Committee that 'There had been [`very little' suspiciously crossed out] some TV and press coverage of the demonstration'. So the protest was somewhat a damp squib. A spokesman for the Board remarked rather lamely that 'We are demonstrating against the treatment of Jewish activists in the Soviet Union and not against Shelepin in particular, though his visit here is most unwelcome'. This reflected the thinking of the Foreign Affairs Committee which 'was against a public Jewish demonstration but approaches should be made to Trade Union leaders requesting their cooperation by raising the issue of Soviet Jewry privately with Mr. Shelepin' – a forlorn hope.[269]

The Women's Campaign organized a midnight 'Seder Service' in Trafalgar Square conducted by the Revd. Leslie Hardman and Greville Janner M.P. with massed banners proclaiming 'USSR Release Innocent Jewish Prisoners NOW', while only one placard demanded human rights for Soviet Jews. At all the preceding rallies, the emphasis had been on freeing Prisoners of Zion and the demand for human rights was a relatively new issue gradually coming to the fore in the campaign, though Barbara Oberman's group carefully steered clear of this issue. Two fifteen-year-old girls fasted for fifty hours outside the Soviet embassy, after which the Women's Campaign and other communal and Zionist groups held a demonstration to coincide with the ex-KGB chief's arrival. With the two girls for part of their vigil, were Mrs Batia Orlov-Tsitlionok and Mrs Ida Nashpits, the mothers of two prominent Prisoners of Zion, who had specially flown in from Israel. Their sons had just been sentenced to five years internal exile for demonstrating outside the Lenin library in

---

[269] JC 28 March 1975, p.18 and JTA 3 April 1975.
LMA,BDJB,ACC/3121/C1/10 minutes of Soviet Jewry Action Committee 13 March 1975.

Moscow for the right to emigrate to Israel. But following the instructions of the Soviet Jewry Action Committee, this protest was kept separate from the campaign against Shelepin.[270]

The biggest and noisiest demonstration against Shelepin was held outside the TUC headquarters by a large crowd of Ukrainians and Lithuanians, denouncing him as a murderer. Only a small group of Jewish women were available to participate in protests because it was the Passover holiday period and they held placards urging the release of 'Prisoners of Zion'. One of the male demonstrators seized Barbara Oberman's megaphone and took up her cry of 'Shelepin, Schelp [carry] him out' in a booming voice. But Barbara Oberman remembered that the British press attributed the liveliness of the demonstration to supporters of the cause of Soviet Jewry, thus turning it into a public relations triumph. At a press conference, Shelepin, stung by the opposition he had encountered, alleged that the protest had been called by a small group of Zionists, all of whom had each been paid £5 for shouting slogans. Shelepin, a hard-line member of the Politburo, ignominiously cut short his visit after two days and slunk out of the country almost surreptitiously.[271] His visit to Britain was ultimately a fiasco, so much so that his manoeuvring in the Soviet Union as the leading contender to succeed Brezhnev was thwarted.

The Intensification of the Women's Campaign and the Re-organization of the Board of Deputies

An early objective of the Women's Campaign was to demand the release of prisoners of Zion, Soviet Jewish activists, who had been imprisoned and to reiterate their right to emigrate to Israel. Among the captives was Sylva

---

[270] JC 4 April 1975, p.1. and JTA 3 April 1975.
LMA,BDBJ,ACC/3121/C1/10 minutes of the Soviet Jewry Action Committee 13 March 1975.
[271] Barbara Oberman interview 6 June 2018. JC 4 April 1975, p.1 and JTA 3 April 1975.

Zalmanson, the wife of Edward Kuznetsov, who had participated in the scheme to borrow an aircraft and fly to freedom in Sweden. Her role in the plot was to erect a flimsy shelter over the captured pilots. The defendants' lawyers argued that the charge of treason should be reduced to the lesser one of trying to facilitate their own illegal departure abroad. Instead of a light sentence, as some predicted, Sylva was given a ten-year prison term and transferred to the women's section of the Dubrovlag complex of strict camps at Potma, where she was forced to sew mittens. Despite ill-health brought on by the arduous conditions, her optimistic spirit was indomitable and she continued to write letters to international leaders and went on periodic hunger strikes.[272]

In November 1971, the wives of Jewish and gentile M.P.s staged a short vigil outside the Soviet embassy on behalf of Sylva Zalmanson, later forming the All-Party Wives Group for the Release of Soviet Jewry. The 35's developed a tactic of preparing and publicising 'a prisoner's banquet' to highlight the fate of imprisoned Jewish prisoners of conscience. To celebrate the formation of the All-Party Parliamentary Committee for the Release of Soviet Jewry, whose driving force was Greville Janner M.P., one such unappetising meal was served in the House of Commons on 23 February 1972 by the 35's. The eminent nutritionist Professor John Yudkin commented that the daily diet 'will not sustain an inactive child of three years'.[273] Just over a year later in March 1973 the film star Ingrid Bergman was the guest of honour at a lunch organized by the Women's campaign to launch a national sale of medallions to secure the release of Sylva Zalmanson. She was served a meal which consisted of black bread, salt herring and a bowl of watery cabbage soup, representing half the daily intake of Sylva Zalmanson. Bergman

---

[272] Colin Shindler, The Jewish Observer and Middle East Review 30 August 1974.

[273] Daphne Gerlis, p.116. Central Archives of the History of the Jewish People. Women's campaign for Soviet Jewry, Zelda Harris Papers, brochure of the All-Party Parliamentary Committee.

139

described the meal as 'terrible', 'just [enough]to keep you alive. It is figured out so exactly that though you might rather die, it forces you to stay on'.[274]

Another tactic developed by the Women's campaign in this ongoing struggle on behalf of Sylva Zalmanson, was to disrupt theatrical and sporting events featuring Russian dignitaries and sporting stars, as the Soviet government attached great importance to cultural and sporting exchanges. A bouquet with a message about Sylva was handed to the Russian tennis champion Olga Morozova at Beckenham in June 1972. Six months later, women campaigners wearing football jerseys surged onto the pitch at a Crystal Palace match against a Soviet team, their spokeswoman remarking that Sylva Zalmanson's only 'crime was her wish to go to Israel'. Mrs June Kenton, later famous as a purveyor of underwear to the Queen, fell flat on her back in front of Russian skaters in October 1973, when she raced across the ice rink in Streatham with colleagues from the 35's, as she attempted to disrupt the international ice dancing championships. The *Daily Express* featured a photograph of this mishap on its front page. Nonetheless, the unruffled campaigners presented their Sylva Zalmanson medallions to the bewildered Soviet skaters.[275] At the end of January 1974, the second secretary at the Soviet embassy in London assured an interdenominational delegation of clergymen that he would pass on to the appropriate Soviet authorities their request for Sylva's sentence to be reviewed. Through a spy swap arranged between the Soviet Union and Israel, the Bulgarians freed Heinrich Shefter, a Jew, and Sylva was released from internment on 22 August 1974 and both were exchanged for a convicted Russian spy Yuri Linov. Although she was informed that she could leave for Israel, Sylva insisted that before she left the Soviet Union she

---

[274] Evening Standard 24 March 1973 and Telegraph 29 March 1973. Mark Hurst, pp.82-3.
[275] Daily Express 5 October 1973. JC 1 September 2006, p.29.

should be allowed to visit her husband, who was still in prison and the authorities had to bow to her wish.[276]

Following the more widespread campaigning by Jewish organizations in the United States, Europe, Australia and Canada and the more militant posture adopted by the Women's Campaign for Soviet Jewry and the vigorous campaigning of the women's group established by Barbara Oberman which had a knock-on effect on the somewhat supine posture of the Anglo-Jewish establishment, Kosygin, the Soviet Prime Minister on a visit to Canada in October 1971 was forced to deny repeatedly that there was a Jewish problem in the Soviet Union. By the end of 1971, a year since the Leningrad trial of a group of Jews charged with the alleged hijacking of an aircraft, the number of Jews leaving the Soviet Union surged from a modest 1,046 in 1970 to 14,300 a year later, 31,478 in 1972 and 20,181 in 1974. Most of the emigrants to Israel in the first half of the 1970s came from the more traditional Jewish areas of the Soviet Union, the Baltic states, Moldova, and parts of the Ukraine and Belarus, and were inspired by Zionist and religious motives.[277] An additional and perhaps overriding reason for this relaxation of the Soviet Union's attitude towards the emigration of some of its Jewish citizens was that Brezhnev was seeking detente with the West at the sessions of the Conference on Security and Cooperation in Europe.

In March 1971, Soviet Jewry concerns were removed from the Foreign Affairs Committee of the Board of Deputies and handed to a new body, the Soviet Action Committee, which because of its lethargic approach was dubbed 'The Inaction Committee'.[278] However, there was so much friction within the Board generated by the clash of powerful personalities between its President Michael Fidler, a Conservative MP, and Barnett Janner and his son

---

[276] JC 5 July 1974, p.1.
[277] Robert J. Brym, The Jews of Moscow, Kiev, and Minsk: Identity, Antisemitism, Emigration (New York,1994), p15.

[278] Daphne Gerlis, p.52 and Dave Rich.

Greville, who were Labour supporters, and the difficulty of dealing with the more militant posture of the women, that Mike Whine found his own position as the Soviet Jewry officer untenable, and he resigned after holding the position for two years.[279]

The international protests on human rights staged by the Women's Campaign were subjected to scathing criticism by some members of the Soviet Jewry Action Committee. 'Dr Roth [of the WJC] expressed his opposition to the proposed action in Geneva [in March 1975] and Mrs Mitchell said that efforts should be made to prevent what she regarded as irresponsible action'. A resolution was then adopted stating that the 35's 'proposed delegation to the Conference on Security and Cooperation in Europe at this juncture was inopportune and undesirable and asked that it be cancelled'. While expressing regret that it was arranged without prior consultation of the Board, it left the way open for Doreen Gainsford to discuss the matter with Dr Roth; and in spite of the resolution, the Women's Campaign sent their delegation to Geneva to join like-minded women from other countries.[280] President Nixon made a speech in Annapolis which seemed to confirm that the policy of non-interference in Soviet internal affairs would continue, and this paved the way for a successful outcome of the Conference in Geneva.[281] Michael Fidler condemned a demonstration by the 35's at an international athletics meeting in Crystal Palace in the summer of 1975, saying that it drew adverse comments from non-Jews; but Doreen Gainsford retorted that she was accustomed to booing on such occasions and that 'the Levich brothers had advised her that sport was an extremely sensitive area within the USSR'.[282]

---

[279] Dave Rich, 'The Activist Challenge'.
[280] LMA,BDBJ,ACC/3121/C1/10, Soviet Jewry Action Committee 6 and 13 March 1975.
[281] NA, FCO, 28/2605 Terence Garvey to Sir John Killick 12 June 1974.
[282] LMA,BDJB,3121/C1/10 minutes Soviet Jewry Action Committee 22 July 1975.

In the summer of 1975, the Board responding to the challenge of the Women's movement nationally and internationally appointed a sub-committee of Greville Janner, QC, MP, Dr S.J. Roth of the British section of the World Jewish Congress and Eric Nabarro 'to consider how best to organise, coordinate and direct Soviet Jewry activities in the United Kingdom nationally under the board's continuing authority'. Plans were put into effect for the calling of a national Soviet Jewry conference at the end of the year which would include 'the leadership of all the organisations involved in Soviet Jewry work'. Since 1971, the students had been floating the idea of the formation of a national council for Soviet Jewry to represent Anglo-Jewry. Doreen Gainsford told the Jewish press that she favoured such a conference 'completely independent of the Board of Deputies'; and privately advised Greville Janner that 'she had not seen but only been told about what the proposals say and I am totally against them. It appears to me that what is suggested is an identical set-up to the present one under a different name'.[283]

In December 1975, a conference was held at which the National Council for Soviet Jewry was established; though ostensibly independent, it was financially and constitutionally in thrall to the Board of Deputies. Marcus Einfeld, an Australian barrister with a mollifying touch, explained that 'the setting up of the [National] Council had been a long and complex operation, and he would like to thank the members of his Steering Committee as well as many people from around the country who had helped to bring the negotiations to a successful conclusion'. At the time Marcus Einfeld was working 'in London for the World Jewish Congress in a diplomatic capacity'.[284] Under his scheme, the President of the Board was ex-officio, also President of the new National Council, and the Treasurer of

[283] Dapne Gerlis, p.22 and JC 18 July 1975, p.1; and Southampton, MS254/A980/1/1/45 Doreen Gainsford to Greville Janner 3 October 1975.
[284] JC 22 January 1971, p.6 and 29 August 1975. LMA, BDBJ,ACC/3087/001 8 February 1976.

143

the Board became co-Treasurer of the Council. Forty members of the Council represented organisations, synagogues and public bodies in Anglo-Jewry, while the other twenty members were appointed by the Board. Moreover, the honorary officers of the Board were to vet the selection of the Chairman and Vice-Chairman of the Council before they were elected to office. No delegation on behalf of the Council was to make representations to the government without the agreement of the President of the Board.[285] The essential funds for the upkeep of the Council came from Israel after Yehoshua Pratt, the representative at the Israeli embassy, spoke to Nehemiah Levanon of Nativ, who in turn passed on their request to Leon Dulzin, and the funds were then channelled through the Jewish Agency. This subvention in turn gave the Israelis a discreet but nevertheless enforceable control over activities of the National Council and ultimately of what the Board of Deputies undertook on behalf of Soviet Jewry. Initially, an annual budget of £40,000 was proposed, though this was deemed 'to be considerably below the Council's requirements'; and the grant from Israel was supplemented by subscriptions paid by the organisations affiliated to the Council and by gifts from donors.[286] It was a stratagem designed to keep a measure of control over the boisterous activities of the Women's Campaign and the students but was never completely successful.

Marcus Einfeld returned to Australia where he became a judge sitting in the Federal Court. Foolishly, in retirement he appealed against a ticket for speeding, claiming that someone else was driving his car at the time which was found to be untrue. For giving perjured evidence, he was sentenced a three-year prison term and stripped of his honours.[287]

[285] JC 26 December 1975, p.6; and LMA,BDBJ,ACC/3087/001 press release 28 September 1981.
[286] LMA,BDBJ,ACC,308711 honorary officers minutes 15 November 1977 and 4 January 1978.
[287] Wikipedia Marcus Richard Einfeld.

Both the Women's Campaign for Soviet Jewry and Barbara Oberman's Committee for the Release of Soviet Jewry had their escapades featured in the national press and both also had their successes in that individual Prisoners of Zion were allowed to emigrate. Yet in certain respects the most successful of the women's pressure groups was the Committee for the Release of Valery and Galina Panov, staffed by the twin sisters Rosemary Winckley and Patricia Barnes, associated with the world of the ballet, which won the support of Equity, the actors' union, and attracted the most attention in the national press and the concern of the government at the highest levels. By gathering the support of a powerful trade union, Equity, and stars of stage and screen with an international reputation, it achieved enviable levels of publicity which outshone the efforts of the Women's Campaign and Barbara Oberman's group. Although the persecuted Jews in Russia demanded full exposure of their plight, Foreign Office Officials continued to draw the opposite conclusion: the worst excesses of the protesters alienated the dancers and disinterested neutrals, so that the Soviets 'will conclude that the release of the Panovs was a mistaken display of weakness'.[288] Any intervention on behalf of Soviet citizens should continue to be made on a government to government basis behind closed doors. On the other hand, the worldwide campaign for the release of Soviet Jewry was garnering support not only from Jews in Britain and the United States but from neutral opinion, the stars of stage and screen and the ballet world and from scientists everywhere.

Around this time, when the Western and Eastern blocs were negotiating at the Conference on Security and Cooperation in Europe, the Prime Minister and Callaghan, the Foreign Secretary, started speaking about human rights in connection with Soviet Jews but it is doubtful whether at this point they were mouthing more than platitudes. For when it was pointed out to them on a number of occasions

---

[288] NA, FCO28/2606 N.K.J. Whitney to B.G. Cartledge 26 July 1974.

of the contradiction between denouncing the visit of British sports teams to South Africa, while saying nothing about the persecution of Jews in the USSR, the government denied this was the case. At the same time, under the urging of the Lishka, the Women's Campaign shifted some of its activities to continental Europe, where it staged demonstrations in connection with meetings of the Conference on Security and Cooperation in Europe; and we now turn to an exploration of the wider international arena.

Chapter 4 - CSCE and Human Rights

Human Rights and the Helsinki Accords

By the late 1970s, the whole nature of the British Campaign for Soviet Jewry was changing. Nehemiah Levananon in an address to the National Council for Soviet Jewry suggested that the British and other European Soviet Jewry organizations should concentrate and taking up individual cases and the cultural aspects of the campaign, leaving major political issues to the movement in the United States; and that is what seemed to have happened.[289] At the same time, the Women's Campaign, both in the process leading up to the Helsinki Accords and in the years afterwards with follow-up meetings, reframed their pleas for Soviet Jewry in terms of human rights. While the adoption of families, sustained campaigning for individuals and enhancing Soviet Jewish Culture became the mainstay of the work of British organizations, the National Council was not altogether satisfied with the flow of information from Israel. In particular, they needed more details about activist families left behind in the Soviet Union. Even if Doreen Gainsford was refused a visa to enter the Soviet Union, Zelda Harris, Jane Moonman, and Rita Eker went on trips there and the Women's Campaign organized a regular stream of visitors to all parts of the USSR with briefing sessions before the trip and de-briefing afterwards. More importance was attached to sending letters and parcels to refusenik families and vain attempts were made to remove the impediments put in place by the Kremlin to impede their arrival in Israel.

What was important was that Soviet Jewry organizations in Britain shifted their focus to a new dialogue on human rights with successive Labour administrations from 1975 onwards, which started to respond to their pressure, however inadequately. During the 1970s, there was a proliferation of human rights

---

[289] LMA, ACC3087/11 National Council honorary officers minutes 12 January 1978.

associations in Britain in response to the Helsinki meetings; and the Soviet Jewish organizations with their new emphasis on human rights became indistinguishable from other human rights groups. Before Western governments bothered to make human rights an essential part of the Helsinki Accords, there had to be the birth of a human rights body with a new approach, Amnesty International, and a place for it on the international scene after the failure of the post-war Marxist and nationalist anti-colonialist utopias. The goals of Amnesty International were relatively modest, with their aim of freeing individuals from imprisonment because of their political convictions or religious beliefs. Human rights did not appear as a threat to either capitalist or Communist regimes, because they were largely ignored, despite the Declaration of Universal Human Rights, and that was why Western and Eastern bloc governments had been willing to sign the Helsinki Accords. Whereas the Labour administrations in the past tended to say little in public about human rights, the about turn by President Carter in 1977, when he made human rights a central feature of his administration, caused the Labour Foreign Secretary, David Owen, to align himself with Carter's more positive attitude.

Amnesty International was founded in 1961 by Peter Benenson, a barrister and Jewish convert to the Catholic universal Church, as an organization to save individuals from imprisonment without a fair trial for their political and religious views. Against the viewpoint of Samuel Moyn, James Loeffler has argued that Benenson was sceptical of Catholic thinkers in the mould of Thomas Aquinas like Jacques Maritain, who treated human rights as a vehicle for the re-assertion of natural law; however, at the same time Benenson played down the influence of the Jewish quest for justice on the evolution of his own ideas. Yet the first person he contacted, when he was thinking of establishing a new organization, was Rabbi Maurice Perlzweig, who had taught him at Eton and worked for the World Jewish Congress. Recently, on the tenth anniversary of the Universal Declaration of Human Rights, Perlzweig claimed that if their implementation was to progress, a new approach was necessary.[290] Benenson deemed people imprisoned for their beliefs to be prisoners of conscience, so long as they did not advocate violence and conspire with foreign governments. Such individuals were assigned by Benenson to local chapters, who would adopt a prisoner and start a letter-writing campaign for their release – a model of activism seized on by other organizations, including Soviet Jewry ones. So too, these Jewish campaigners invented the phrase 'Prisoners of Zion' to describe individuals unfairly detained by the state and serving a term in prison before they could be released and be permitted to travel to Israel. By the 1970s, Amnesty International grew into an international human rights organization and by the mid-1970s had 100,000 members in two thousand chapters spread across the world.[291]

One of Amnesty's first big cases was that of Gedalia Pechersky, a Soviet citizen from Leningrad, a religious Jew and Hebrew teacher, who wanted to emigrate to Israel and was accused of cavorting with foreign agents and sentenced to twelve years in a Siberian prison camp, after which he was permitted to leave for Israel. Initially, relations between Amnesty and Jews involved in the human rights movement and the government of Israel were excellent but soured after the Six Day War and Israel's conquest of the West Bank and Gaza and worsened after Benenson's early death. [292]

Throughout the 1970s, under the impact of a detente between East and West and the growing human rights obligations undertaken by parties to the Helsinki Accords, human rights organizations mushroomed in Britain and the

---

[290] James Loeffler, Rooted Cosmopolitans. Jews and Human Rights in the Twentieth Century (New Haven,2018), pp.211-17. Whereas Moyne attributed the new evolution of human rights to Catholic philosophers, James Loeffler attributed much of it to Zionist lawyers.
[291] James Loeffler, Rooted Cosmopolitans, pp.217-19,262.

[292] James Loeffler, Rooted Cosmopolitans, pp.221-3.

United States. In the early 1970s, the Working Group on the Internment of Dissenters in Mental Hospitals and the Medical and Scientific Committee for Soviet Jewry were set up in Britain, followed later by the Royal College of Psychiatrists' Special Committee on the Political Abuse of Psychiatry which all took up such cases of unfairly detained individuals with the Soviet authorities. Apart from this, Michael Bordeaux established Keston College in Kent in 1970 to document and challenge religious persecution in the Soviet Union. So too, the Women's Campaign for Soviet Jewry under the evolving international relations between the superpowers in the 1970s which favoured détente, morphed into a like-minded human rights organization.[293]

At the annual Dartmouth Conference which in the summer of 1971 took place in Kiev, there was an informal exchange of views between influential American and Soviet opinion makers and there seemed to be some movement in the Soviet response. Among the American delegates, was Dr Samuel Pisar, a survivor of Auschwitz and a death march, an international lawyer with doctorates from Harvard and the Sorbonne, who published a book on *Coexistence and Commerce* to critical acclaim in 1970. He was one of the intellectual architects of detente. After sterile opening sessions with the denunciation of the United States for being the agent of a sinister Zionist plot and the events unfolding in Vietnam, Dr Pisar in his reply noted that it was unnecessary to put the word Jew on identity cards in the Soviet Union when there was no Jewish nation among the Soviet republics. There had been a long history of antisemitism in Russia, and if Jews felt uncomfortable remaining in the Soviet Union for religious or cultural reasons, they should be permitted to leave. He informed the Soviet delegates that yesterday we accompanied you to the memorials marking your Great Patriotic War against the Nazis, but later today it might be worth paying a visit to Babi Yar, a site where tens of thousands of Jews were buried

---

[293]Mark Hurst, British Human Rights Organizations and Soviet Dissent (London,2017), pp.6-8.

without a memorial and which at that time went unrecognised by the Soviet state as a place of mass murder. The Soviets provided a bus for their American visitors to go to the site, where a state guide explained the circumstances of the mass burial, and when to everyone's surprise the Soviet delegation later joined them.[294] Samuel Pisar later became a doughty campaigner for Soviet Jewry and for the restrictions on the novelist Solzhenitsyn and the eminent scientist Dr Sakharov to be lifted.

The relationship between East and West became more constructive with the signing of the 1963 Nuclear Test Ban Treaty and the 1968 Nuclear Non-Proliferation Agreement, following the death of Stalin in 1953. Between 1971 and 1974 some 25 bilateral agreements were concluded between the United States and the Soviet Union; and they engaged in talks on arms limitation, exchanging data in connection with this.[295] In November 1972, thirty-five nations from the Western and Eastern blocs attended a meeting in Helsinki, Finland, to set up the Conference on Security and Cooperation in Europe (CSCE). It was a Soviet initiative to secure guarantees as to the inviolability of the new frontiers in Eastern Europe. Further preliminary drafting sessions were held in Geneva in July and September 1973 and January 1974. In return for mutual security guarantees, Western nations pressed for a greater flow of information and more cultural and educational exchanges between the two blocs, for family reunification and speedier emigration procedures. The Helsinki Final Act was signed on 1 August 1975 by thirty-two European nations on both sides of the Iron Curtain together with Canada, the United States and the Soviet Union, and contained three baskets. Basket one conferred guaranteed borders. Basket two outlined areas of cooperation in the fields of trade, science, technology and environment. The contents of basket three were what chiefly interested Jewish groups because they incorporated human rights

---

[294] Samuel Pisar, Of Blood and Hope (London,1980), pp.192-3, and 201-12.

[295]David Owen, Human Rights (London,1978), pp.35-6.

provisions, such as the stipulation that applications for family reunification had to be dealt with by states 'in a positive and humanitarian spirit' and 'expeditiously'; and the clause stating that participating states will respect fundamental freedoms, 'including freedom of thought, conscience, religion or belief for all without distinction as to race, sex, language or religion'. At three-yearly intervals each signatory was obliged to participate in regular reviews of its compliance with the terms of the agreement, opening the way for human rights organizations to make representations.[296]

Yuri Andropov, the secret police chief, persuaded the ailing Soviet leader Leonid Brezhnev to sign the Helsinki Accords, even though Basket three pledged participating states to uphold human rights and political freedoms. Andropov confided to the diplomat Anatoly Kovalev that 'In 15 to 20 years we'll be able to allow ourselves what the West allows itself now, freedom of opinion and information, diversity in society and in art. But only in 15 to 20 years, after we're able to raise the population's living standards'.[297] Andrei Gromyko, the Foreign Minister, added his support, having been re-assured by Nixon's Annapolis speech, in which he endorsed the view that there would be 'no interference in the internal affairs' of other states.[298]

Washington remained sceptical. Henry Kissinger dismissed Helsinki as 'a meaningless psychological exercise'. Robert Gates, the CIA director, remembered that 'The Soviets desperately wanted CSCE. They got it and it laid the foundations for the end of their empire. We resisted for years... only to discover years later that CSCE has yielded benefits to us beyond our wildest imagination. Go

[296] Elliott Abrams, 'Lessons of the Soviet Jewish Exodus', Jewish Review of Books (Spring 2019). Wendy Eisen, Count Us In pp.60-2. Gal Beckerman, When They Come for Us pp.352-6. Colin Shindler, Exit Visa. Detente, Human Rights and the Jewish Emigration Movement in the USSR (London,1978), p.120.
[297] William Taubman, Gorbachev pp.142 and 144.
[298] NA, FCO 28/2605 Terence Garvey to Sir John Killick 12 June 1974.

figure'.[299] Quite apart from this, Kissinger told Golda Meir, the Israeli Prime Minister, in 1973 that 'if they put the Jews in gas chambers in the Soviet Union, it is not an American concern. Maybe a humanitarian concern'. Both Nixon and Kissinger shared the view that international harmony and detente could not be jeopardized for the sake of Soviet Jewry.[300]

Harold Wilson as Prime Minister

Harold Wilson, the British Prime Minister, was always much more optimistic than other Western leaders that he could wring concessions out of the Soviet Union in relation to CSCE. Summing up European opinion, he stated that 'Detente means very little if it is not reflected in the daily lives of our people. There is no reason why, in 1975, Europeans should not be allowed to marry whom they want, hear and read what they want and meet whom they want'. In his speech at the opening of the summit conference on 30 July 1975, he referred to the 'freedom of movement for individuals and families who wish to start a new life outside Europe, whether in the Middle East or elsewhere'.[301] Even earlier in 1975 while the final form of the treaty had not been entirely settled, Wilson expressed confidence that the provisions in Basket three could be utilised to assist the emigration of Soviet Jews. When the British Prime Minister met one of the Soviet leaders, Mr Kosygin, at lunch in the British embassy in Moscow on 17 February 1975, he casually mentioned a list of cases of persons seeking exit visas which the Foreign Secretary had handed to Mr Gromyko during their trip. It appears that the list included the names of known dissidents and Jews. Far from taking this amiss, Kosygin assured him that 'whenever he had raised individual cases in the past, the Russians for their part had always tried to help. On the

---

[299] TLS 21 & 28 December 2018 Benjamin Nathans.
[300] Elliott Abrams, "Lessons of the Soviet Jewry Exodus", (Spring, 2019) *Jewish Review of Books.*
[301] NA, PREM 16/1463 P.R.H. Wright to P.J. Weston 4 August 1975.

specific question of Soviet Jews, Mr. Kosygin concurred with the Prime Minister's comment that the Panovs and Ruth Alessandrovich had been released primarily because of Mr. Wilson's personal intervention'.[302] Wilson seemed to share the confidence and optimism of Benenson, the Amnesty leader, that progress could continue to be made on a one to one basis.

Wilson told Martin Gilbert, who assisted him in his literary efforts, that 'since 1964 he had been active in trying to get Jews out of Russia...' On one visit 'he deliberately left his papers lying around on the table of the *dacha* which had been put at his disposal by the Russian government so as to ensure that the fact of his knowledge and concern got back to the authorities. This oblique approach seemed to work best. When he raised certain cases directly with Kosygin, the latter affected to fly into a rage. He later told Wilson privately that it was unwise to refer to such questions in front of subordinates; he would do what he could, he promised'.[303]

On his return from Moscow, Wilson happened to meet Greville Janner MP the day after he was back in London and told him that a list of names had been handed to the Soviet leaders, giving Greville momentarily the impression that one of his lists with Jewish names had reached the Russians. Greville was the son of Barnett Janner and succeeded his father as a Labour MP, rising to become President of the Board of Deputies 1979-85. Quick to take umbrage at the confusion and muddle as to which list had been handed over, Greville muttered to Roy Hattersley, the Minister of State, that this would cause 'a "blazing row" if true', since the Board of Deputies was under the same impression. The Prime Minister commented that the Board had always been much more understanding of his predicament than Greville, whom he had found to be

---

[302] NA, PREM 16/1463 record of conversation between Harold Wilson and Andrei Kosygin on 17 February 1975. Kenneth O. Morgan, Callaghan. A Life. (Oxford,1997), p.453.

[303] Philip Ziegler, Wilson, The Authorised Life of Lord Wilson of Rievaulx (London,1993), p.388.

unhelpful.[304] To calm the situation, it was proposed that Hattersley should meet the younger Janner from the All-Party Committee for Soviet Jewry in July to explain that there had been three lists, two provided by Greville which had been sent to the Prime Minister and Foreign Secretary and a third list compiled by the department. 'This last list... consisted of cases of family reunification and so on which formed the subject of part of Basket 3 at the CSCE' and had been handed to the Soviet authorities. 'Whether coincidentally or by design this list had included some of the names on Mr Janner's list'.[305] Incidentally, one of the lists had been compiled by the Women's Campaign and handed over at a confidential meeting with Wilson on 5 February.[306]

On 24 July 1975, Hattersley met Greville and Timothy Sainsbury of the All-Party Committee to sort out the confusion and to suggest that 'the list which Mr. Janner had sent to the Prime Minister might be up-dated and taken by...[him] to the CSCE summit in Helsinki', to which Greville agreed. Hattersley emphasised that the Prime Minister would take the new list to Helsinki with him and would then decide on the spot whether or not there was a suitable occasion for passing it to the Russians. Greville agreed to compile a shorter list of about a dozen names consisting of 'ordinary people' as well as 'better-known... academics'. Hattersley said this made good sense, as 'the Soviet authorities were more receptive to releasing one or two unknown people than publicity mongers who would spend all their time in the West criticizing the Soviet Union and its actions' – an attitude which shows a distinct lack of sympathy for the dissidents. Greville raised the case of the imprisoned Dr Shtern, saying that including his name in the list might offer him some protection. Hattersley repeated that 'it was better to keep to the simple issue of human

---

[304] NA, PREM 16,1463 Harold Wilson to James Callaghan 4 July 1975.

[305] NA, PREM 16/1463 record of call of Greville Janner and Timothy Sainsbury on Roy Hattersley 24 July 1975.

[306] NA, PREM 16/1463 Doreen Gainsford's list of refuseniks 5 February 1975.

rights and civil liberties in which the participation of ourselves and the Russians in CSCE gave us some standing'. However, he sensed that 'the Russians were worried about the aftermath of the CSCE. They felt that the final document might be used as blackmail in cases such as that of Dr Shtern'.[307] The Foreign and Commonwealth Office (FCO) preferred not to disclose to the public that Greville's updated list of names was handed over to Gromyko at the Helsinki summit. 'There seems to be every advantage in sticking to the line that the Prime Minister has himself taken in the past that these matters are best dealt with in private discussion rather than in public declaration'.[308]

Nonetheless, the FCO conceded that all the participants at the meeting, when the Helsinki Final Act was signed, recognized that 'the principle of human rights is an integral part of detente and a legitimate cause for public and governmental concern'. Hence it was necessary to insert a new paragraph in the model answer to members of the public and MPs when they pressed ministers about what action they were taking to assist a particular dissident or Jewish victim of Soviet oppression. These model answer sheets were relied on by civil servants when they drafted an appropriate reply for the approval of members of the government. The relevant new section ran as follows: 'The successful conclusion of the Conference represents a renewed affirmation of the principle of respect for human rights and fundamental freedoms and the Final act of the Conference also contains practical recommendations on ways to facilitate freer movement. We hope that these will lead to more liberal administrative practices in future'. But the Prime Minister's private secretary, Patrick Wright, agreed with his Foreign Office counterpart that the basic point in these letters that 'HMG have no formal standing to

[307] NA, PREM 16/1463 record of call of Greville Janner and Timothy Sainsbury on Roy Hattersley24 July 1975.
[308] NA, PREM 16/1463 P.J. Weston to P.R.H. Wright 4 August 1975, and same to same 7 August 1975.

intercede with the Soviet authorities on behalf of any Soviet citizen' had not changed.[309]

Wilson was upset, when Margaret Thatcher, the new Conservative Leader of the Opposition, reprimanded him in the House of Commons for the difficulties encountered over the granting of exit visas by the Soviet authorities to their citizens. He wrote to his old political friend Lord Sammy Fisher, the President of the Board of Deputies, telling him 'As you know, I hate saying anything publicly about this, since every statement made can be counterproductive for the future. Nevertheless I feel entitled to say what I did say, because as you know, exit visas have been granted to between 70 or 80 Jews alone, irrespective of non-Jewish Soviet citizens, most of whose names were supplied by me to you and your organisation. Dayan at the marriage of Ruth Alessandrovich, said that she and her fiancé had been let out only because of my strong pressure'. What he wanted him to do was to write to the Leader of the Opposition because he feared that great harm had been inflicted for party political purposes, even going so far as to send Fisher a draft statement which he desired him to issue on behalf of the Board. 'I personally, since 1954 with my colleagues, have been in touch with Mr. Wilson even before he was elected Leader of the Opposition in 1963 about the release of Soviet Jews and he has secured the release of very many controversial cases of which usually only private, rarely public, acknowledgement has been made'. I feel that such matters should not become the subject of political controversy, as the Board represents people of all political affiliation.[310] In turn, Fisher had every confidence in Wilson, whom he hailed as 'one of the best friends our community ever had'.[311] Colin Shindler compiled 'lists and details about refuseniks which eventually reached Wilson. He presented such demands every time he met Soviet leaders. Gerry Wootliff, a prominent Jewish dentist with links to

[309] NA, PREM 16/1463 P.J. Weston to P.R.H. Wright 7 August 1975 with text of new model reply.
[310] NA, PREM 16/1463 Harold Wilson to Lord Fisher 26 February 1976.
[311] JC 30 April 1976 p.21.

Wilson, also passed material to the Prime Minister'.[312] Wilson felt very strongly about keeping his actions on behalf of Soviet Jewry out of the public domain, especially as an old political crony on the left of the Labour party, Ian Mikardo, was of the same opinion. Mikardo also felt that 'undue weight had been given to the question of Jews in the Soviet Union and insufficient attention had been paid to the general question of the treatment of dissidents there'[313]. To put this in context, Mikardo had a daughter living in Israel and had transacted considerable business with East Germany.[314]

The Soviet Dissidents Utilise the Helsinki Accords

Anatoly Shcharansky proposed to the physicist Yuri Orlov and the writer Andrei Amalrik that something needed to be done to make it difficult for the Soviet Union to ignore the Helsinki Accords. After prolonged discussions, Orlov decided that they should set up a Helsinki Watch Group in Moscow in May 1976 to monitor Soviet compliance with the agreement. Orlov, a founder member of the Moscow chapter of Amnesty International, later shifted the date for the annual silent demonstration in Pushkin Square from Constitution Day to International Human Rights Day. Small groups of dissidents first in the Soviet capital and then in other parts of the Soviet Union began to 'assist in the fulfilment of the Helsinki Accords', by collecting information about 'human rights violations and transmitting it to the West'.

---

[312] Colin Shindler communication to the author 23 December 2019.

[313] NA, PREM 16/1463 notes of call by Ian Mikardo on Harold Wilson 15 July 1975.

[314] Colin Shindler communication to the author 23 December 2019.

Similar groups were established in the Ukraine, Lithuania, and Georgia.[315] By this means, a transnational network of human rights pressure groups was built up in which Soviet Jewry campaigners played a prominent role. In the West, organisations protesting on behalf of imprisoned Christians, Jews and dissidents incarcerated in prisons, labour camps and sometimes in mental hospitals, moved their governments to put pressure on the Kremlin. In the USSR the defiance and bravado of dissidents and the subsequent publicity in the West for their courageous acts slowly eroded the confidence of the Soviet authorities in the hard-line course that they were pursuing was beneficial in the long run. But because of the immediate failures as regard to human rights, particularly the massive crackdown on dissidents, public opinion in the West tended to be sceptical about the benefits of the Helsinki Final Act and by extension towards the follow-up meetings in Belgrade, Madrid, and elsewhere.[316]

Whereas the Universal Declaration of Human Rights was virtually unknown in the Soviet Union, being published only on a single occasion and in a small edition, the provisions of the Helsinki Final Act received wide coverage in the Soviet press and had 'an explosive effect' according to Ludmilla Alexeyeva. Shortly after her enforced departure from the Soviet Union, she described the activities of the Moscow Helsinki Group in great detail. Some information was relayed to the Moscow Helsinki Group over the telephone, other informants contacted Orlov and his team in person, still more information came through the post. A petition of the Pentecostals, a Christian sect, had been signed by 7,500 persons, who wished to emigrate. One-third of the visits or approaches to the Orlov group concerned the right to hold and practise religious beliefs. Vitaly Rubin, a sinologist, and Shchransky both

---

[315] Natan Sharansky, Fear No Evil (London,1988), pp.xxi-xxii. TLS 21 & 28 December 2018 Benjamin Nathans. Robert Horvath, The Legacy of Soviet Dissent. Dissidents, Democratisation and Radical Nationalism in Russia (London,2005),p.94.
[316] David Owen, Human Rights pp.36-7.

refuseniks dealt with Jewish emigration, while Mnyekh and Meimann concerned themselves with not just German emigration but that of Ukrainian political prisoners, whose only means of freedom was to be allowed to travel overseas. There was also the case of the worker who wished to emigrate to secure a better standard of living for his family, instead of a life of perpetual drudgery. Nineteen reports had been produced by the Moscow Group on different aspects of the human rights situation in the USSR; and additional items of information, often on individual cases concerning arrests on political, religious or national grounds were also passed on to the British and American embassies, foreign correspondents in Moscow, Amnesty, and four Western radio stations broadcasting to the Soviet Union. All three Helsinki Groups in the Soviet republics had connections with the original Moscow Group from the beginning.[317] Later Alexeyeva was to note the constant infighting in the Jewish refusenik movement between the politicals like Slepak and Shcharansky, who advocated emigration, and those who thought that more attention should be paid to the revival of Jewish culture in the USSR, though there were other divisive factions too.[318]

The KGB planted spies in the ranks of the Jewish movement and suborned others to become informants, creating an atmosphere overcast with suspicion and dissension. Of all the foreign missions in Moscow, only the United States embassy appointed a member of their diplomatic staff specifically for the purpose of keeping in regular contact with dissidents and Jews wishing to emigrate and the incumbent of this office was usually Jewish. On 28 February 1977, two refuseniks, Professor Benjamin Fain and Iosif Begun, tried to enter the American embassy, when militiamen prevented them from entering the embassy in the company of a member of its staff. On 2 March Fain made another attempt to gain access to the

---

[317] NA, FCO 28/3094 record of conversation between Bryan Cartledge and Mrs Lyudmilla Alexeyeva on 10 March 1977.
[318] Ludmilla Alexeyeva and Paul Goldberg, The Thaw Generation. Coming of Age in the Post-Stalin Era (Boston,1990), p.292.

embassy with another refusenik Vladimir Prestin, but both were seized before they met the diplomat outside the embassy. Contact was made again with Fain and the diplomat concerned, Larry Napper, invited Fain to his flat. He arrived at Napper's home without a 150-page report on the last December abortive Jewish cultural symposium which was the purpose of their meeting. Nonetheless, 'The Americans still have an open mind on whether Fain's activities are genuine or a provocation under KGB control'- they were, in fact, completely genuine.[319] Another Jewish State Department official, Mel Levitsky, was accused by *Izvestia* of being 'a CIA link to Jewish dissidents'.[320]

The British contacts with prominent dissidents were 'limited to occasional meetings hosted by others', as diplomats believed that Western newspaper correspondents were well informed about what the dissidents were saying and doing, so that there was no need to keep in direct touch. 'We have been inhibited from frequent contact with dissidents', remarked C.L.G Mallaby in a report to London, 'by the belief that the Soviet authorities might more readily react against us than against the Americans, e.g. by press articles, attempts to cut down our contact with Russians, or even expulsions'. The one dissident he hoped to meet was Orlov 'because of his CSCE activity', by talking to him on a social occasion in the home of an American colleague or newspaper correspondent.[321] Britain was in the league of secondary powers and the government was wary of upsetting the USSR, a superpower, who would find it relatively easy to retaliate against them; and was prepared to sacrifice dissidents rather than see detente disintegrate.

---

[319] NA, FCO 28/3094 L.R. Kay Moscow to Roderic Lyne EESD 9 March 1977.
[320] NA, FCO 28/3094 J.E. Cornish, British embassy Washington to Roderic Lyne 4 March 1977 with minute of 9 March 1977.
[321] NA, FCO 28/3094 C.L.G. Mallaby Moscow to B. Cartledge EESD 4 February 1977.

The Soviet Jewry Campaign Shifts to Human Rights Issues

The Women's Campaign Goes International on Human Rights

At some point in the early 1970s, the Women's Campaign shifted some of its focus to the international arena, probably at the behest of the Lishka, after there seemed to be new opportunities arising out of the discussions in Geneva because of a new international concern for human rights to facilitate the emigration of Soviet Jews. The fact that some of the women's flights to the European capitals were subsidised by the Israelis seems to point to the involvement of Nativ in this change of policy. As early as 27 September 1973, at one of the preliminary meetings held at Geneva, G.H.H. Walden wrote to a fellow Foreign Office official, warning him about Doreen Gainsford, who 'never slow to capitalise on any contact has now asked me to put you in touch with her when she visits Geneva... I do not see how you could refuse to have a word with her: I was forced to see her because she had a tenuous line to the Minister of

163

State. I am therefore telling her to contact you on arrival...You will no doubt wish to avoid giving her ammunition'.[322] In January 1975 she informed British diplomats that 'She planned to circularize every delegation to the CSCE at Geneva calling for better treatment of Soviet Jews'. But colleagues warned Mr Tickell to dissuade her from pursuing what they regarded as a 'limited objective'. In fact, the West was 'using all its negotiating advantages at CSCE to secure good texts in a variety of fields, but particularly in Basket 111'.[323]

'When we first received information about the Helsinki conference, everybody said it was not going to get off the ground', Doreen Gainsford recalled. Then came the meeting in Geneva, [Nehemiah] Levanon [of the Lishka] enabled us to bring women from ... [a number] countries to stand on the streets. We had access and handed over material to the delegations, regarding the `third basket'. The Secretary General of CSCE also received materials from us'.[324] In March 1975 Sylvia Sheff, the leader of the Manchester branch of the 35's, informed the Soviet Jewry Action Committee of the Board of Deputies that twenty-seven people, representing women from eleven countries, had formed the International Women's Committee for Soviet Jewry and agreed to send a delegation to Geneva in the summer. 'Approaches [were made] to ambassadors of the countries attending the European Conference on Security and Cooperation in the summer. They were received by all except the Soviet Union and the Eastern European Bloc countries... The Committee was warmly received by the Swiss Ambassador who was completely sympathetic and keen to lend his support to future approaches by the Women's Committee on behalf of Soviet Jewry. There was a similar reaction from the Swedish Ambassador... the majority of ambassadors to the

[322] Barak Levy-Shilat, 'Nice Jewish Girls Don't Do That: the Housewives Campaign for Soviet Jewry'.
[323] NA, FCO 28/2669 A. St. J.H. Figgis to Burns and Tickell 17 January 1975.
[324] Barak Levy-Shilat, 'Nice Jewish Girls Don't Do That'.

Conference were at least sympathetic and at best very encouraging in their support. They were keen to know the very latest news on the plight of Soviet Jewry'. But this was an over-optimistic assessment, as France would not despatch their ambassador to parley with the women's delegation and the United Kingdom's diplomats remained somewhat aloof.[325]

At a preparatory CSCE meeting in Belgrade in June 1975, Doreen Gainsford and Linda Isaacs and other women belonging to the 35's were arrested in the entrance hall of their hotel and taken to the rear of the building where they were threatened with deportation to prevent a demonstration. On refusing to move unless they saw representatives from their embassy, they were beaten and carried into police vans. They were transported to the airport, where they were kept waiting for seven hours and then had their passports stamped with a ban against returning to Yugoslavia for one year.[326]

A month later Gainsford with eight other activists demonstrated outside the American embassy in Helsinki, where President Ford and the Soviet leader Leonid Brezhnev were conferring before a European security summit. They wanted world leaders at the final session of the CSCE before the signing of the agreement to deal with the perilous situation of Soviet Jewry. As they were unfurling banners urging the 'USSR Honour the Agreement – Give Human Rights to Soviet Jews', the Finnish police whisked the women away. But this was not before Doreen Gainsford shouted at Brezhnev: 'You are signing—and persecuting Soviet Jews'. It was part of the International Campaign for Soviet Jewry, an umbrella organization of women's groups from ten European countries, the United States and Canada. Later in the day, they staged a further protest in the harbour opposite a moored Soviet ship which was serving as Brezhnev's temporary headquarters during his trip. Gainsford sent the

[325] LMA,BDBJ,ACC/3121/C1/10 minutes of the Soviet Jewry Action Committee 13 March 1975.
[326] Daphne Gerlis, p.177.

Finnish President, the chairman of the conference at which the Helsinki Accords were signed, a bouquet of flowers. The Women's Campaign apologized to him for the demonstrations, explaining that they were protesting against the imprisonment on false charges of Dr Shtern and Sender Levinson and the recent arrest of three other persons, whose only crime was the wish to emigrate to Israel. But the women's detention by the police gave them widespread press and television coverage, the BBC reporting that 'the summit conference is the highlight of Brezhnev's career, only marred by a demonstration for Soviet Jewry rights'. Gainsford sent the British Prime Minister, Harold Wilson, a single rose with a note saying how proud she was of British democracy. The demonstrations were based on a new twofold campaigning theme, the old one of demanding the easing of the restrictions placed on the emigration of Soviet Jews and their release from prison on trumped-up charges when they applied for an exit visa, and the new one of emphasising the human rights side of this protest.[327]

Harold Wilson, the Labour Prime Minister, though sympathetic to the cause of Soviet Jewry and sometimes prepared to act, as in the case of the Panovs, was often restrained by Foreign Office officials. A briefing paper prepared by them in 1974 demonstrated their concerns over the tactics of the Women's Campaign. 'Candidates at the last general election, including the Prime Minister' had been approached to sign an appeal to the USSR 'for the release of prisoners of conscience'. The Prime Minister had also been invited to a meeting in the Commons to be addressed by a prominent refusenik, Silva Zalmanson. The memorandum continued that 'The Jewish lobby should be told that it would not be in keeping with HMG's position if the Prime Minister or members of the government lent their names to petitions, attended the House of Commons meeting or received Miss Zalmanson'. By way of a conciliatory gesture, they suggested that Mr Wilson could

---

[327] JTA 31 July and 4 August 1975 and JC 1 August 1975, p.1. Daphne Gerlis, pp.52 and 177.

'go over the ground with her'. Britain's position was that 'while we have every sympathy with Soviet Jews, we have no formal standing to intervene on behalf of Soviet citizens with the Soviet government'.[328] But now the international political situation had changed, after the signing of the Helsinki Final Act by the Soviet Union, and the campaign for Soviet Jewry was able to enlist more support from the British government and this was given added impetus by their being able to emphasise the issue of human rights. This gave them legitimate grounds for intervening more frequently with the British government at ministerial level and also with Foreign Office officials.

When the crew of the Soviet guided missile destroyer Obraztsovy made a call at the Portsmouth naval base on 28 May 1976, the Russians forgot to put their clocks forward to British Summer Time and became marooned for a time, as the ship missed the tide. Supporters of the 35's held banners on the cliff tops and sailed around and around the vessel in little boats with banners in Russian and English calling for 'Human Rights for Soviet Jews' for almost an hour. The Soviet crew stood to attention on the ship while this was happening. 'Everywhere the [town's] dignitaries went, the demonstrators [from the Women's Campaign] followed – on the ramparts as the Obraztsovy sailed in, outside the Queen's Hotel, outside the Guildhall', a reporter from a local newspaper observed. As the Soviet seamen came out of the Portsmouth Guildhall, they were met by women from the 35's dressed in prison garb with the name of imprisoned Prisoners of Zion on their chests.[329] Letters to Lt-Captain Bognanov and Vice-Admiral Leonenkov, who was in charge of the goodwill mission, pointed out the Soviet violation of the Helsinki agreement, referring to the case of Captain Mikhail Edelman, an ex-naval officer. He had been refused a visa to join his daughter in Israel since 1971 and in the meantime had been harassed and

---

[328] JC 25 February 2005, p. 9.
[329] Daphne Gerlis, pp.79-80. The News Portsmouth 28 May 1976. Daily Mail 29 May 1976.

persecuted. Wide coverage of these events in the media marked it as a notable publicity coup.[330]

In 1976, Zelda Harris, an important member of the Women's Campaign, started a correspondence with Harold Wilson, who had recently retired as Prime Minister and returned to the backbenches, about the plight of Vladimir Prestin, a prominent cultural activist. Through a personal intervention, Wilson had secured a visit to Moscow by members of the City Livery Club; and Zelda wondered whether this was a good opportunity to raise the issue of Prestin. His private secretary wrote to Mrs. Harris that 'As Sir Harold said to you in his letter, of the 17th of June, and as Lord Murray reassured you, Sir Harold does have his own way of raising these matters. He has only very recently been in touch with the Soviet authorities on certain cases - including this one as well. But I do not think the City Livery Club visit would be a correct vehicle'.[331]

Throughout 1976 and 1977, there were several more demonstrations in which the human rights aspect of the Soviet Jewry movement was emphasised by the Women's Campaign - at the Camden Arts Centre in December 1976 in front of the Soviet ambassador, at the Soviet embassy in February 1977, to which a huge petition was wheeled in a supermarket trolley, and at a wreath-laying ceremony by representatives of the Soviet army in Westminster Abbey, when women carried placards demanding, 'Human Rights for Soviet Jews' in March 1977. There were also demonstrations outside the Aeroflot office in Piccadilly, and several more protests against the visit of Boris Ponomarev, the secretary of the Central Committee of the Soviet Communist party.[332]

---

[330] JC 4 June 1976, p.10.
[331] Central Archives for the History of the Jewish People, Women's Campaign for Soviet Jewry, Zelda Harris Papers, Arthur Murray to Mrs. Harris 21 June 1976 and Marcia Falkender to Mrs. Harris 15 September 1976.
[332] Daphne Gerlis, pp.228-230.

Callaghan as Prime Minister: a Step Backwards on Human Rights

Having retired through ill health, Wilson was replaced as Prime Minister by James Callaghan on 5 April 1976. At the end of October, there was a confidential meeting between Boris Ponomarev, a member of the Politburo, and Callaghan. When Greville Janner tried to present him with a copy of Magna Carta emphasising British concern for freedom and a Jewish prayer book, his efforts were brushed aside and treated with disdain. Later Ponomarev went on a visit to the Highgate Cemetery with a delegation from his embassy to pay his respects at the grave of Karl Marx, where he was confronted with a group of women from the 35's attired as ghosts. They shouted that they were 'the ghosts of Karl Marx carrying the spirit of the Helsinki Agreement that you have murdered by persecuting Soviet Jewry' -- a newsworthy incident.[333] 'Greville [Janner] believed that Callaghan was much less sympathetic to the cause compared to Wilson'.[334]

At his meeting with the Prime Minister, Ponomarev stressed that the Soviet leadership wanted to make detente irreversible and favoured a development of Anglo-Soviet relations in all fields. Since the visits of Senators Javits and Ribicoff and a delegation of United States Congressmen, including some Zionists, Ponomarev claimed that there had been no complaints about the situation of Russian Jewry.

Callaghan wished to express his concern because this issue was an irritant in their bilateral relations and gave opponents an opportunity to make difficulties. Human rights were covered by the Helsinki Final Act and gave each side the chance to express their views, as they both had on Chile, and the Soviet Union was not slow to do so on Northern Ireland. 'He had himself handed a list of personal [family reunification] cases to Mr Gromyko during his visit to Moscow and was very glad that nine of these cases had

---

[333] Hurst, p.85.
[334] Colin Shindler communication to the author 23 December 2019.

been met. He hoped that these would be a first instalment, and that others would follow. There were three cases which were at present causing particular interest in this country, namely Vladimir Bukovsky, Mrs Nudel and Georgi Vins', the Russian Baptist leader. In reply Ponomarev noted that of the 2.4 million Jews in the Soviet Union, 50,000 had been granted exit visas between 1971 and 1975; and that only 9,000 requests had been made for exit visas, a gross under-estimate, while there were several thousand applications from Jews wishing to return. When Ron Hayward, the Labour party general secretary, visited the Soviet Union he had handed Suslov a list of names and all had been allowed to leave apart from 'two people who were working in [the]

defence establishment...About 95 to 97 per cent of all [exit] visa applications had been granted'.[335]
Callaghan did not challenge him on this highly inflated figure of successful visa applications. The exchange between the two men signified how much easier it had become to raise the question of Soviet Jewry since Helsinki, though only one of the three individuals mentioned by the Prime Minister was Jewish, Ida Nudel. Nevertheless, the Prime Minister was able to assure Greville Janner that he had borne in mind his recent letter at the meeting with Ponomarev.[336]

In June 1963, the Soviet dissident Vladimir Bukovsky was arrested for making photocopies of anti-Soviet literature, namely the 'New Class' by Milovan Djilas and was convicted of insanity under Article 70.1 of the Russian criminal code. He was found to be mentally ill by Soviet psychiatrists and sent to the Special Psychiatric Hospital in Leningrad for treatment. In all, he spent eleven and a half of the next fourteen years in hospitals, prisons and labour

---

[335] Samuel Moyn, The Last Utopia. Human Rights in History (Cambridge, Mass., 2010), pp.45,124, and 148-57.
NA, PREM 16/1463 record of a meeting between the Prime Minister James Callaghan and Boris Ponomarev on 28 October 1976.
[336] NA, PREM 16/1463 James Callaghan to Greville Janner 28 October 1976.

camps before he was released in December 1976, after a strong campaign for his freedom mounted in the West. He was opposed to the West dealing with Brezhnev and took a pessimistic view of Helsinki. When Callaghan was asked in the Commons on 13 January 1977 whether he would see Bukovsky, he said 'No' because he preferred to deal with the Soviet leaders privately than through propaganda. Thatcher, the Leader of the Opposition, responded 'That is one of the most disgraceful and undignified replies ever given by a Prime Minister in this House'.[337] Margaret Thatcher was already laying down a distinct marker between her policy on human rights and that of the Labour government.

Human Rights Come Into Their Own Around 1977 and is Followed by Repression

According to Samuel Moyn, the human rights movement arose when the misguided 'utopias' of nationalistic anti-colonialism and revolutionary Communism revealed their internal flaws. In the revolutions in the eighteenth century and the latter half of the nineteenth century, it was common for states to announce declarations of rights but these only applied to their own citizens. The post-Second World War saw the establishment of non-governmental organizations dealing with human rights which only did so as part of their programme and were bounded 'by the borders of religion, ethnicity, or gender on whose behalf they lobbied'.

Around 1977, a series of seemingly accidental events coalesced together, giving rise to the internationalist conception of individual human rights as being more important than state sovereignty. First, although Amnesty International had been founded in 1961-2 with its new agenda on human rights, proclaiming that human rights existed in individuals from birth and that these could not be limited or subtracted by states, the organization only came into prominence in 1977, when it was awarded the Nobel Prize. Secondly, at the same time, dissidents in Warsaw Pact countries and in authoritarian South

---

[337] Nicholas Bethell, Spies pp.78-80.

American states rejected a purely political response to repression in favour of moral opposition in this way attracting a wider coalition of supporters. Thirdly, the Soviet Union signed the 1966 International Covenant on Civil and Political Rights and the International Covenant on Economic and Social Rights, though they did not come into force until a decade later, expecting many of the provisions to remain unenforceable. Finally, international lawyers, who were affected by the more congenial political climate, particularly in the United States, where President Carter was outspoken on the issue, breathed fresh life into the hollow phrases of the Helsinki Accords, after being subjected to relentless lobbying by human rights organizations. In embracing human rights, Soviet Jewry groups moved from supporting family reunification and the right of a few individuals to leave the USSR to upholding the legitimacy of mass emigration according to the 'general principle of freedom of movement and emigration'.[338]

In contrast to Britain, the subject of human rights gained new traction in the United States when Jimmy Carter gave an interview to 'Playboy' magazine in the autumn of 1976 in which he spoke about human rights and later when he was inaugurated as President in January 1977. In his speech on that occasion, he proclaimed that 'Because we are free, we can never be indifferent to the fate of freedom elsewhere'; and in answering a letter from Sakharov, the Soviet physicist and dissident, Carter declared that America would 'continue our firm commitment to promote respect for human rights, not only in our country but also abroad'. To Dobrynin, the Soviet ambassador in Washington, this reply was an impermissible interference in the internal affairs of the USSR in breach of Principle VI of the Helsinki Agreement.[339] Cyrus Vance, the Secretary of State, tried to ease the tension between the superpowers, by playing down President Carter's remarks in a speech at the

---

[338] Samuel Moyn, The Last Utopia pp.60,124,148-57.
[339] Nicholas Bethell, Spies pp.84-5.

University of Georgia. In it he stated that 'In pursuing a human rights policy, we must always keep in mind the limits of our power and wisdom'.[340]

By January 1977, the KGB had concluded that the benefits of a crackdown on dissidents outweighed the damage it would do to their international reputation. Utilising the Christmas break, when foreign correspondents would be out of the capital, three days after the New Year secret policemen swooped on the apartment of Ludmilla Alexeyeva, a key member of the Moscow Helsinki Group, and removed linen bags stuffed with samizdat and Helsinki Group documents. On 1 February, Ludmilla was told that she and her family had three weeks to leave the country. On 3 February, the prominent dissident Alexander Ginzburg was arrested. That night police came to arrest Professor Orlov but he eluded them. On 9 February, he suddenly appeared in the afternoon at Ludmilla's apartment before her departure and beckoned to her not to speak but to converse by writing everything on a notepad, after which he instructed her to contact Shcharansky, as he wished to hold a press conference. At six in the evening, Shcharansky returned with Robert Toth of the *Los Angeles Times* and David Mason, the Associated Press correspondent. Orlov pleaded with the Helsinki Final Act signatories to declassify information hitherto marked as secret. By now the KGB had become aware of Orlov's presence in the apartment and surrounded it, arresting him the next day. Before his arrest, Orlov instructed Ludmilla to represent their group in the West.[341]

In Georgia, Merab Kostava and Zviad Gamsakhurdia, a future president of the country, were arrested and the Ukrainian Helsinki Group was broken up, by the KGB planting evidence of criminal behaviour on the part of the leadership, so that they could be detained

[340] Colin Shindler, Detente, Human Rights and the Jewish Emigration Movement in the USSR (London,1978), p.226.

[341] Ludmilla Alexeyeva and Paul Goldberg, The Thaw Generation, pp. 289-91.

later.[342] On 15 March 1977, Anatoly Shcharansky was arrested and charged with treason, a charge which could result in the death penalty and was much more serious than the charges facing the other Soviet dissidents. More than any other group, the Jewish refuseniks seemed to be the KGB's prime target.

James Callaghan remarked to Lord Fisher, the President of the Board of Deputies, that he had received a considerable number of letters from British Jews on the current difficulties faced by their co-religionists in the Soviet Union which were 'a cause for legitimate and serious concern...The Foreign and Commonwealth Secretary is paying the closest attention to the latest developments concerning Jews and other human rights campaigners in the Soviet Union, including the arrest of Anatoly Shcharansky. They have obvious relevance to the Final Act of the Conference on Security and Cooperation in Europe which is to be discussed at Review Meetings in Belgrade later this year'.[343] Even so, a circular letter from close relatives of Shcharansky, Masha Slepak, Professor Lerner and Ida Nudel to heads of government was not answered by Callaghan but by a Foreign Office official so as not to upset the Russians. He stated that human rights were an integral part of government policy and they hoped for progress at Belgrade.[344]

The preparatory talks for the Belgrade review conference were held in mid-June 1977 when it was agreed to have a full review of the implementation by all sides of the provisions of the Helsinki Final Act. At this preparatory meeting which was attended by professional diplomats on all sides, who had worked so well together at Geneva, they settled the agenda of the main meeting in October and

[342] Nicholas Bethell, Spies and Other Secrets (London,1994), pp.92 and 94.

[343] NA, PREM 16/1463 James Callaghan to Lord Fisher 20 February 1977.

[344] NA, PREM 16/1463 Avital Shcharansky and others to James Callaghan 6 June 1977; W.K. Prendergast to B.G. Cartledge 8 July 1977 and his draft reply.

decided that it would fix the date and location of a second follow-up conference. Moreover, delegates from certain Eastern European countries were told privately that if they did not improve their performance on humanitarian questions, they would encounter considerable flack at the main October meeting.[345] Arthur Goldberg, a former Supreme Court Justice and permanent United Nations representative, was appointed to lead a large American delegation of 140 members to the main follow-up meeting of the conference which opened in Belgrade on 4 October 1977. He had been involved in the Soviet Jewry movement from the 1960s and had tried to convince President Kennedy to take action. By contrast, the British and French delegations had a dozen members, while even the Soviet delegation was half the size of the American one. Some of the discussions were overshadowed by the sentencing of 'Charter 77' human rights campaigners in Prague, a bad omen from which the conference never properly recovered. Ambassador Goldberg adopted what more cautious diplomats described as a 'forthright and publicity-orientated approach to human rights', causing much resentment in other delegations and within his own delegation from professional diplomats. But he was only following the lead of President Carter and was fully supported by the White House.[346] One official described his 'imperious and sometimes insensitive manner' as incensing neutral and non-aligned diplomats.[347] On 15 October, Goldberg criticized a country which misused an opt-out on classified information, allowing some to emigrate when others doing the same job were prevented from leaving because they possessed state secrets. Even worse, potential emigrants lost their jobs when they applied for exit visas and were then imprisoned as parasites for not working. And was 'it consistent with the humanitarian provisions of

---

[345] NA, FCO 28/3979 Carroll Sherer, 'Breakdown at Belgrade' Washington Quarterly (Autumn 1978).

[346] NA, FCO 28/3660 report on the CSCE Follow-Up Meeting 4 October 1977 to 9 March 1978.

[347] NA, FCO 28/3660 R.E. Parsons to David Owen 13 March 1978.

the Final Act to harass or imprison people for peaceful, non-violent political dissent or religious belief?' He also criticized the fact that four Czech dissidents members of 'Charter 77' had been put on trial for campaigning for human rights, a lead in which he was followed by other Western delegations. By November 7, Goldberg started naming individual names and condemned the arrest of Ginzburg, Orlov and Shcharansky, infuriating the Soviets.[348] Ambassador Goldberg annoyed some NATO members by briefing the press as to private discussions at the conference, while at the same time blaming the Europeans 'for any softening of his stance'.[349]

David Owen Does an About Turn on Human Rights as Dissent is Repressed

At first, Britain like other West European states wanted to adopt a slow evolutionary policy with regard to the implementation of human rights and supported a non-polemical stance at the talks. In fact, the Minister of State, Lord Goronwy-Roberts's speech at the opening of the conference was so anodyne that it drew criticism in the press. He was in any case reluctant to raise the issue of Soviet Jews at Belgrade. He had advised that when the Foreign Secretary, David Owen, met Lunkov, the Soviet ambassador in London, for lunch he should express his general concern about the plight of refuseniks and offer to send details; and that if Lunkov proved to be unresponsive about receiving a list of names, the matter should be dropped. In any case, they should prepare their own list of names, not pass on Mr Begin's list, and omit people with no British connection and 'counter-productive cases like hijackers'.[350] If anything, the Secretary of State, David Owen, wished to be at the front of the movement for human

---

[348] Colin Shindler, Detente, Human Rights, p.240. Gal Beckerman, p.367.
[349] NA, FCO 28/3660 report on the Follow-Up Meeting.
[350] NA, FCO 28/3531 P.J. Bacon to Mr Stephen 6 January 1978.

rights; and was displeased at the 'relative invisibility' of British participation in the talks in Belgrade. So after a meeting with Ambassador Goldberg, he changed the British position to one of 'close and fairly visible support'. Owen's 'approach was influenced not only by his personal and political commitment to a high profile for human rights issues but by his growing belief in late autumn 1978/early 1979 that, as a result of a combination of circumstances (Soviet `opportunism' in Africa/ the build-up of Soviet military expenditure/ the detentions and prospective trials of dissidents, etc.) public opinion in the UK was losing faith in... the detente process... His endorsement of greater pressure on the Soviet Union at Belgrade was therefore specifically aimed at keeping public support for the Government's detente policy, which he continued to pursue'.[351]

Carroll Sherer, an American whose husband's policy of quiet and patient diplomacy had been scotched by Goldberg, denounced the Belgrade review meeting as a disaster, the end of detente. British diplomats did not agree, stating that the concluding document had certain merits. It included a reaffirmation by all governments 'to implement fully all the provisions of the Final Act (including by implication the human rights aspect)...Finally it fixes a precise date in the autumn of 1980 for the next type of Belgrade meeting in Madrid'. If it could be said that the Final Act was 'a blue-print for Utopia', a Europe governed by its provisions would be 'an earthly paradise'. Belgrade was part of a process and the whole process possessed value, especially in the long-term 'human dimension of detente'. Certain Eastern European countries, such as Poland, Hungary and Romania, sought more freedom of manoeuvre, while even the hard-line members of the bloc, including the Soviet Union itself, had some 'people within the official hierarchy who are prepared to see some loosening up of the system and correspondingly greater toleration for individuals'. This optimistic viewpoint

---

[351] NA, FCO 28/3979 C.A.J. Fergusson to Bullard 2 April 1979.

existed in the Foreign Office establishment years before Thatcher's courtship of Gorbachev.[352]

As the proceedings in Belgrade gradually slithered to what seemed an inconclusive end on 9 March 1978, the Soviet Union stepped up its harassment and oppression of dissidents and refuseniks. When Vladimir Klebanov tried to form a trade union, he was incarcerated in a psychiatric institution. In Georgia, Grigory Goldshtein, a member of the local Helsinki Watch Group, was charged with parasitism and sentenced to one year's imprisonment in a labour camp. The same sentence was meted out to Pavel Abramovich for teaching Hebrew. The well-known Hebrew teacher Iosif Begun was released from prison but was not allowed to live with his family in Moscow. Dissidents resident in the West, such as General Pyotr Grigorenko, Mstislav Rostropovich and the artist Oscar Rabin, were all stripped of Soviet citizenship. In May 1978, Dr Orlov was tried for criminal activity in connection with his leadership role in the Moscow Helsinki Group, being sentenced to seven years in prison followed by five years in internal exile. During the trial, the *Daily Telegraph* and Reuters correspondents were harangued with the warning 'You Zionists, you Israelis, we will shoot you'. The Kremlin first targeted the leadership of the Jewish dissident movement, particularly those with links to the Helsinki Watch Committees, and the political activists as opposed to those who placed an emphasis on reviving Jewish culture. The trials of Vladimir Slepak and Ida Nudel opened on 21 June 1978, followed by the trials of Shcharansky and Ginzburg on 10 July 1978.[353]

---

[352] NA, FCO 28/6660 R.E. Parson to David Owen 13 March 1978.
[353] Colin Shindler, Human Rights and Jewish Emigration Movement pp.245-59.

The Women's Campaign Step Up Action on Behalf of Jewish Dissidents

The draconian measures undertaken by the Soviet authorities boosted the human rights campaigners in the West and reinvigorated the movement for Soviet Jewry. In December 1976 the Medical and Scientific Committee for Soviet Jewry petitioned the Soviet authorities 'to adhere to the spirit of the Helsinki Accords coinciding with the Review Meeting in Belgrade', as the Goldshtein brothers had been 'deprived of basic human rights'.[354] In addition, the Women's Campaign informed the Foreign Office of the arrest of Grigory Goldshtein, who with his brother Isai, was a member of the Georgian Helsinki Monitoring Group; and on 26 January Sylvia Becker called on R.M.J. Lyne at the Foreign Office to hand over a dossier of documents about the case, only the next day to telephone with the message that he had been released from detention, though this proved to be a temporary reprieve. Her purpose was to make certain that the government was kept fully up to date with the case to ensure that its relevance was utilised at the closing session in Belgrade.[355] The same official told his superior that Doreen Gainsford had telephoned to complain that 'not surprisingly' she had been refused a visa by the Russians; she intended to take this up with the Soviet ambassador and should this fail she would publicise the refusal of her application. Llewellyn Smith minuted that 'refusal of visas to critics such as Mrs Gainsford is in Soviet interests is probably right: letting her in would do them more harm in adding fuel to the WCSJ campaign/ encouraging dissidents etc. than keeping her out does them in terms of publicity'.[356]

In May 1977, Zelda Harris and Jane Moonman took an Intourist trip to Moscow to investigate the current situation facing the refusenik community and to ascertain

---

[354] NA, FCO 28/3532 petition of the Medical and Scientific Committee for Soviet Jewry to Brezhnev December 1977.
[355] NA, FCO 28/3532 R.M.J. Lyne to Lewellyn Smith 30 January 1978.
[356] NA, FCO 28/3532 R.M.J. Lyne to Lewellyn Smith 30 January 1978.

the latest news about Anatoly Shcharansky after his arrest. They visited the Slepak's flat which was nearby and the centre of Jewish activity. Vladimir Slepak 'is a lovely lion of a man, handsome and bearded, warm and affectionate' with very good English, Jane Moonman recalled. Ida Nudel arrived. She is tiny and has 'large brown eyes which shine with intelligence. She is full of energy, aggression and passion – `indomitable' is the word but in a large gathering she stays in the background, letting others do the talking'. The next day, which was a Saturday, they went to the Prestin's home which was in the suburbs for a Sabbath lunch, prepared by his wife Elena. Zelda had befriended Vladimir Prestin, who by profession was a computer engineer and a teacher of Hebrew in his spare time, but he regarded himself as fortunate for having a job as an operator of lifts. Here they were joined by Pavel Abramovich, another electronics engineer, and his wife. Pavel Abramovich was the brother-in-law of Vladimir Prestin and a fellow teacher of Hebrew, part of the cultural renaissance of Russian Jewry. Also in attendance at the lunch were Professor Benjamin Fain and his wife Shoshana and Leo Elbert from Kiev. He was involved with a cultural symposium, only to have his wife Hannah, a cardiologist, beaten up by unknown assailants outside the hospital where she worked. Zelda Harris was busily engaged in talking to the wife and son of Iosif Begun. He was awaiting trial for parasitism, but he was insisting on speaking Hebrew at the trial and on wearing a yarmulke (skullcap), all part of the Jewish cultural re-birth.[357]

On Sunday they were collected by Josif Beilin, the husband of Dina Beilin, who worked with Shcharansky, and escorted to the home of Professor Lerner to meet Anatoly's mother Mrs. Milgrom and brother Leonid. Two reporters from the *Daily Mirror*, John Pilger and Eric Piper, also came to hear the latest news. Mrs Milgrom reiterated that she was certain that Anatoly would withstand the pressure in prison, as he was not guilty of any crime.

---

[357] Jewish Observer and Middle East Review 2 June 1977.

Western support would 'result in his freedom in the end'. Ida Nudel collected Jane Moonman to take her to the apartment block, where she lived. She explained that 'We were not allowed to learn Jewish history or practise our rituals for so many years and it is only recently that people have begun to defy the rules and a Jewish identity has started to emerge again'. But when Ida spoke to Jane Moonman about her work with Jewish prisoners, she took her to a playground area so that the conversation could not be overheard. We stood 'there in our macs and headscarves in the pouring rain and I feel, more than at any other time, the desolation of the conditions in which our friends live'. Zelda came back to the hotel with gifts from the Prestins and his friends for us and people in England. On Monday, which was the day of their departure, Josif Beilin came to the hotel with messages and to make arrangements for telephone calls.[358] What Jane Moonman's diary revealed was the meeting of two British activists with both wings of the refusenik movement, the political and cultural, at a time when persecution was stoking Jewish pride and defiance and causing a reaffirmation of Jewish identity. The British campaigners' protests now broadened to encompass the fate of those engaged in the struggle for Jewish cultural revival in the Soviet Union -- Vladimir Prestin, Pavel Abramovich and Iosif Begun.

When Professor Alexander Voronel left for Israel in December 1974, the leadership of those who wanted to ensure the resurrection of Jewish culture in Russia was entrusted to Vladimir Prestin. Voronel was a key figure in the Jewish renaissance in the USSR. He had also started regular scientific seminars for scientists, who had been dismissed from their positions for applying to emigrate to Israel to enable them to keep up with the latest research; and his organization not only enlisted outstanding local names among refusenik scientists but also the support of high calibre foreign scientists. As a young man, Prestin shared a room with his scholarly grandfather Felix Shapiro,

---

[358] Jewish Observer and Middle East Review 10 June 1977.

who published a Hebrew-Russian dictionary sponsored by the government in the 1950s. He found someone who shared his ideas in Professor Benjamin Fain, a scientist based at the Institute of Chemical Physics in 1975. This group among refuseniks believed that unless an enthusiasm for all aspects of Jewish culture and Hebrew flourished once again in the Soviet Union, the number of immigrants who saw their final destination as Israel would continue to fall; and that the number of the so-called dropouts (noshrim) destined for other locations would continue to increase. Together Prestin and Fain established a new samizdat journal, *Jews in the USSR*, with a more popular appeal than Voronel's earlier publication, by including features on Jewish holidays and recipes. They also planned to hold an international seminar on the state of Jewish culture in the Soviet Union and its future prospects, but on 21 December 1976, the day of the symposium, Fain and Prestin were arrested as well as other speakers. At ten o'clock in the morning, about a hundred participants gathered at the synagogue, where the conference was due to be held, but none of the conference organizers were there, and it was obvious that they had been detained. Natasha Rosenstein, an activist, offered her home for the conference. Under the chairmanship of Professor Naum Meiman, who was associated with the Helsinki Watch Committee in Moscow, the conference took place there. About sixty persons attended the symposium, when seven papers were read. Among the participants were Sakharov and his wife Elena Bonner, whose mother was Jewish. Gal Beckerman pointed out that from this the whole refusenik community drew the conclusion that the Soviet authorities were not going to allow the smallest glimmer of Jewish cultural expression; it was as much a threat to the regime as political action.[359]

As we have seen, Zelda Harris, another frontline member of the Women Campaign's team, had taken a

---

[359] JTA new bulletin 30 December 1974. Gal Beckerman, pp.335-9. Mark. Y. Azbel, Refusenik. Trapped in the Soviet Union (Boston,1981), pp.448-9.

particular interest in the case of Vladimir Prestin and his wife and called on 3 January 1978 on Mr Lyne, an official in the Eastern European and Soviet Department of the Foreign Office(EESD). 'She has been in frequent touch with EESD about this case, and has always been most reasonable and sympathetic towards the Government's approach to human rights in the Soviet Union', he observed. She was worried, as Mrs. Prestin was having a nervous breakdown. Vladimir was an electronics engineer of no importance without access to classified information and she could not understand why he had been waiting since 1969 for an exit visa. She asked the government to 'take exceptional action on behalf of the Prestins... She has since written to say that she hopes that Dr Owen and the UK delegation at Belgrade will be made aware of the case'. Action on behalf of the Prestins and a number of other dissidents was under consideration in a proposed meeting between an official from their department and the Soviet ambassador, Lunkov; it was a government tactic for not naming names in the closing sessions at Belgrade and avoiding confrontation with the Russians.[360] Nonetheless, Mrs. Harris persisted and asked Harold Wilson whether he had been in touch with the Foreign Office about Prestin. Wilson obviously sympathetic observed that 'I am afraid that all of us must just continue to do what we can in our own way to persuade the Soviet Government to take action, in particular, on this sad case. I shall certainly do so'.[361]

In mid-March 1978, the Duke of Devonshire called on Llewellyn Smith of the EESD to say that his interest in the cause of Soviet Jewry had been rekindled, especially in the case of Vladimir Prestin about whom he had asked a question in the House of Lords on 14 June 1977. 'His Jewish contacts in this country, including Mrs. June Jacobs [of the National Council for Soviet Jewry], were trying to persuade him to take action designed to secure the emigration of

---

[360] NA, FCO,28/3532 Roderic Lyne to Llewellyn Smith and Scott 6 January 1978.
[361] Central Archives for the History of the Jewish People, WCSJ, Zelda Harris Papers, Harold Wilson to Mrs Harris 7 February 1978.

Prestin, e.g. by taking a visit to the Soviet Union and while there making representations'. While this was out of the question, he was prepared to see Lunkov, the Soviet ambassador, with whom he had been in contact after he had arranged a visit for him to the art collection at Chatsworth. The Duke was advised by his interlocutor that M.P.s and others had made representations to the Soviet embassy, only to be rebuffed by junior officials, who said it was tantamount to interference in Soviet affairs. In these circumstances, the Duke decided that his best course was to write to Lunkov about Prestin.[362]

At the same time, Mrs. Harris informed Lyne that Prestin's brother-in-law Abramovich had been warned by the District Procurator that he would be indicted for parasitism, while Prestin had been told that 'his request to emigrate would not be considered for a very long time'.[363] In May she announced that Dr Victor Polsky would be visiting Britain to promote the cases of Prestin and Abramovich, both of whom were his personal friends. She requested a meeting between him and Dr Owen, the Foreign Secretary, but was not put off when it was explained that 'Dr Owen did not normally meet such people'. Instead, she requested a meeting between Dr Polsky and an official from the East European and Soviet Department which was acceptable, though later she announced that he would not be calling.[364]

On 21 June 1978, Mrs Harris brought a refusenik, Leonid Kochevoi, to meet Mr Lyne at the Foreign Office. He spent an hour and a half discussing the present situation of Soviet Jews and pressing the case of Vladimir Prestin and Pavel Abramovich, whom he knew. Like Prestin, Kochevoi was a 'simple engineer' rather than a high calibre scientist and was on a three-week visit mainly to the North of England to draw attention to the cases of Prestin and

---

[362] NA, FCO 28/3532 M.J. Llewellyn Smith to Mr Hull 14 March 1978.
[363] NA, FCO 28/3532 Roderic Lyne to Mr Roland 6 March 1978.
[364] NA, FCO 28/3532 to Mr Roland 6 May 1978; and note of L.A. Dean Soviet Section Research Department 14 June 1978 with attached comment.

Abramovich by addressing meetings of trade unionists and academics. Neither man 'had been engaged in particularly sensitive or secret work'. He saw a danger that in concentrating on Shcharansky, Ginzburg and Orlov 'the West would forget about the equally deserving and potentially more easily soluble cases, such as those of Prestin and Abramovich. He even speculated that the Soviet authorities were deliberately drawing attention towards Shcharansky's case and away from others'. Lyne emphasised that Ministers 'were alive to the need to approach human rights on a broad front rather than concentrate on a few well-publicised cases'. Their best hope was to continue with their persistent moderately phrased campaign. What the 35's want minuted, Llewellyn Smith, 'is for Ministers to approach human rights on a broad front but including specific & named representations across the whole of that front. What Ministers want is to approach human r[igh]ts on a broad front so as not to incur the disadvantages of naming names'.[365]

Despite these setbacks, Zelda Harris wrote to Sir Harold Wilson again at the beginning of July 1978. Again, he answered her in a sympathetic tone. 'As you know', he remarked, 'I have been doing what I can about this case and I shall continue so to do, but it is a very difficult one, as I am sure you are aware'.[366] Because of the contentious issue of their being in possession of state secrets and their active roles in reviving Jewish cultural expression, Prestin and Abramovich, only reached Israel in March 1988.[367]

During February 1978, Alexander Slepak, the son of Vladimir and Masha Slepak, came to Britain for a three-week stay to publicise his parents' case. His father was one of the best known Jewish refuseniks, a member of the Moscow Helsinki Monitoring Group and an associate of Shcharansky. Greville Janner MP of the All-Party Parliamentary Committee for Soviet Jewry sponsored his

---

[365] NA, FCO, 28/3532 Roderic Lyne to Llewellyn Smith 22 June 1978.
[366] Central Archives for the History of the Jewish People, WCSJ, Zelda Harris Papers, Harold Wilson to Zelda Harris 14 July 1978.
[367] JTA, 17 March 1988.

visit and asked Dr Owen to meet Alexander Slepak. In a submission, K.B.A. Scott of the FCO advised against Owen personally seeing former dissidents, as the innumerable meetings would be a burden and 'a publicised meeting between a former dissident and a Minister would annoy the Soviet Government without achieving any benefit for the dissidents and `refuseniks".[368] The Women's Campaign had already set up a meeting at the EESD section of the Foreign Office on 10 February for Alexander to meet Mr Lyne. In the event, Mrs Becker and Mrs Rigal arrived at the appointment without him in some embarrassment. They explained that Alexander Slepak, whom they described as somewhat 'arrogant and humourless' had decided not to keep the appointment, as it would prejudice his chances of meeting the Prime Minister or Dr Owen. But perhaps this was nothing more than youthful naivety and an expression of his pain at being separated from his parents for so long an interval. Civil servants detected some rivalry between the Parliamentary Committee and the Women's group and there was a fear that Greville Janner would approach Dr Owen directly to try and fix a meeting.[369] June Jacobs of the National Council for Soviet Jewry in April asked Dr Owen to meet Alexander Slepak, who was depressed, as he had not seen his parents for eight years and this would encourage him. She promised to keep the meeting secret. Again Dr Owen's answer was still 'No'.[370] In June Mrs Jacobs made a third request for a meeting between Alexander Slepak and Mrs Fridman, the sister of Ida Nudel on the one side, and Dr Owen on the other which was similarly rejected. It appears that Dr Owen had met Mrs Jacobs and Mrs Fridman briefly during the Labour party conference in Brighton in October 1977. But a publicised meeting would 'provoke a sharp response from the Soviet side' and make them 'less responsive to British government

---

[368] NA, FCO 28/3531 K.B.A. Scott to Mr Sutherland 9 February 1978.
[369] NA, FCO 28/3531 Margaret Turner to K.B.A. Scott; and the same to Lord Goronwy Roberts 10 February 1978.
[370] NA, FCO 28/3531 W.K. Prendergast to K.B.A. Scott 10 April 1978; and note by Prendergast 11 May 1978.

representations on human rights cases'; and the stunning conclusion: 'it would make it more difficult for Dr Owen to turn down requests that he should receive the relatives of those involved in more serious cases (eg Mrs Shcharansky)' – a myopic misjudgement which was reversed by Mrs Thatcher when she became Prime Minister.[371] On the other hand, it could be argued that these persistent requests for meetings on the same matter from different sections of an ill-coordinated campaign on behalf of Soviet Jewry did little to ingratiate the organizations either with officials or ministers.

Stanley Clinton Davis, a junior Minister in the Labour government, asked on 9 December 1976 whether he could attend a Hanukah Service at the Southgate Progressive Synagogue for Soviet Jewry only to be dissuaded. A similar request in April 1978 to attend a symbolic Passover Service outside the Soviet embassy in support of Jewish students was also rebuffed. He was advised that attending even in a private capacity would be a breach of the ministerial code and 'be damaging to the Government's overall policy on human rights in the Soviet Union'. It was claimed that some progress had been made in 'developing a dialogue with the Soviet Union on human rights' over the past two years, a grotesque exaggeration. Soviet receptiveness to British representations would be reduced if Ministers 'participate in the public activities of pressure groups' in what they would deem to be 'a provocative demonstration'.[372]

Accompanied by Mrs Jean Carlsberg of the Women's Campaign, Mr Tzvi Essas visited another member of the Eastern European and Soviet Department of the FCO, Stephen Wordsworth, on the morning of 23 May 1978. He was the father of Ilya Essas, a physicist and mathematician, who had been denied an exit visa to join his parents in Israel. He was worried that because his son had lost his job, he was vulnerable to a charge of parasitism. His son's wife

---

[371] NA, FCO 28/3531 K.B.A. Scott to Mr Fergusson 23 June 1978.
[372] NA, FCO 28/3531 K.B.A. Scott to Mr Fergusson 18 April 1978 with draft reply of Goronwy Roberts to Stanley Clinton Davis; and private secretary of David Owen to Jonathan Arkush circa April 1978.

was alleged to have been exposed to secrets while working in the design department of a construction company. However, she had left this job in 1971 and other co-workers with similar access to secrets had been allowed to leave. Mr Essas became emotional several times during the interview, exclaiming 'help me'. With the assistance of Lord Janner, it had been arranged that Mr Essas would also be meeting various peers and MP.s to press the case on behalf of his son. This meant that at least he had the political weight of the Board of Deputies behind him.[373] The South Florida Conference on Soviet Jewry was also working on Ilya's behalf, circularising members to write to Col. General Shchelokov to protest against the confiscation of 'personal letters and books on Jewish culture' and denial of an exit visa. These acts were 'violations of the Helsinki Final Act which calls for the respect of human rights and the reunification of family members'.[374]

On 19 May 1978, the Women's Campaign sent a circular to all adopters about the well-known refusenik Iosif Begun, who had been arrested outside the court while waiting to hear the sentence pronounced on Dr Orlov. He was charged under Article 198 of the Criminal Code for violation of passport regulations, as he did not have permission to live in Moscow with his family. Those interested in his case were urged to send cables of protest to Major Zotov at Police Station 52 Moscow and letters of support to his family.[375] On 27 June, the Women's Campaign arranged for Professor Benjamin Fain accompanied by Mrs Simone Goldfarb and Mr Glass, a solicitor, to meet Roderic Lyne at the Foreign Office. Begun had tried to place an advertisement in a Moscow evening newspaper as a teacher of oriental languages but the newspaper had refused to accept his advertisement. He had given private lessons and tried to pay the taxes for doing

[373] NA, FCO 28/3532 S.J. Wordsworth to Llewellyn Smith 23 May 1978.
[374] NA, FCO 28/3532 circular of South Florida Conference on Soviet Jewry circa May 1978.
[375] NA, FCO 28/3532 Barbara Lyons of WCSJ to all adopters of Iosif Begun 19 May 1978.

so, which was a perfectly legitimate activity and taking place all the time. For this, he was charged with parasitism and sentenced to two-years internal exile. His re-arrest had serious implications for human rights, as the authorities appeared bent on making a concerted effort to stamp out the teaching of Hebrew within the Jewish community. They all made a strong plea for the British government to make private representations on Begun's behalf. The Minister of State agreed and minuted that if 'low-key representations' were made to the Soviet ambassador, the case of Iosif Begun might be mentioned.[376] While awaiting trial, Begun, who had a stubborn personality, went on hunger strike, in protest. His trial opened on 28 June and he was given a sentence of three years in internal exile to keep him out of circulation for a longer period than stipulated in law which was one year's imprisonment.[377]

A month later, on 9 June, Roderic Lyne had a lengthy meeting with Dr Alexander Lunts, who was accompanied by Rita Eker and Barbara Lyons, and described him as 'one of the most impressive and intelligent Soviet émigrés I have met'. Lunts had held a senior position in a Moscow Institute specialising in computers before securing an academic post in Israel. The meeting was timed to mark the end of the extended period of Anatoly Shcharansky's detention when he would either be tried for treason or permitted to go abroad, and to brief the FCO on the current situation. 'Dr Lunts was encouraged that human rights were now an acknowledged item on the agenda of East/West relations, but disappointed that President Carter had ceased to speak out strongly as in the first months of his administration. He said that Western Governments should be prepared to take risks in the course of human rights, and to be more bold in speaking out'. Lyne countered that the government did not favour taking 'risks in East/West relations which might jeopardise peace and security'. To this, Dr Lunts replied that the Soviet Union needed Strategic Arms Limitation

[376] NA, FCO 28/3532 Roderic Lyne note on call of Professor Benjamin Fain 28 June 1978 with minute of 30 June.
[377] NA, FCO 28/3532 L.A. Dean to Roderic Lyne 30 June 1978.

agreements far more desperately than the West and that they should build a new generation of nuclear weapons. He also 'complained that American political leaders gave too much weight to the emigration figures, and not enough to specific cases'. His hard-line approach was common in Soviet dissident circles and the refusenik community.[378]

Moreover, Dr Lunts was disinclined to believe the 'rumours that Shcharansky would be expelled from the Soviet Union without trial, perhaps in exchange for a Chilean Communist or a Soviet spy'. The recent arrests of Mr and Mrs Slepak and Ida Nudel had nothing to do with the Shcharansky case. 'He said that for internal reasons the Soviet authorities wished to be seen taking a hard line against a certain number of Jews: and that there was a `quota' of Jewish prisoners of conscience to be maintained (Dr Lunts said that a study of the total number of prisoners over several years had shown that the figures were more or less constant)'. People in Moscow had informed him that the trials of the Slepaks and Nudel were being arranged hastily, but he doubted whether Shcharansky would be released, given that this had been denied by so authoritative a source as Victor Louis, a Soviet journalist used by Western media outlets in Moscow, who was known to have close connections with the KGB. When asked his opinion of Professor and Mrs Levich, 'He said Levich would never be allowed to emigrate', as 'he had held too senior a position, and had access to too much information. Dr Lunts compared this case to that of Professor Lerner, who left last year having always taken great care to avoid receiving classified material, even to the extent of sending envelopes back unopened'.[379]

In a vain attempt to rebut a welter of adverse criticism, a group of Russian lawyers led by the Vice-President of the Soviet Bar Association, Samuel Zivs, a Jew, spoke in a committee room in the House of Commons in

---

[378] NA, FCO 28/3532 Roderic Lyne to M.J. Llewellyn Smith and Mr Scott 12 June 1978.
[379] NA, FCO 28/3532 Roderic Lyne to M.J. Llewellyn Smith and Mr Scott 12 June 1978.

defence of the sentence imposed on Dr Orlov. 'We appreciate that you in Britain would not want such a law. But we in the Soviet Union have this law [Article 70 of the Russian Criminal Code] and it must be enforced'. But these spokesmen only succeeded in outraging MP.s.[380] In contrast the FCO adopted a somewhat supine attitude as regards the trials of Vladimir Slepak and Nudel, not bothering to try and send representatives to the hearings, unlike their American colleagues.[381] When Slepak and Nudel were sentenced, the Communist *Morning Star* newspaper had a headline proclaiming, 'Hooligan dissidents exiled'. The *Guardian* reported that 'Several Western diplomatic sources, while saying that they saw in the lighter sentences no change in the Kremlin's campaign of repression against political and religious dissenters, nevertheless thought that Moscow might be trying to soften its image after the world outcry over the trial and maximum sentence of seven years in prison and five of internal exile against Dr Yuri Orlov'. The *Financial Times* made the point that Slepak 'had been a major figure in the Helsinki Group and the Jewish movement since the arrest last year of Mr Anatoly Shcharansky, Dr Yuri Orlov and Mr. Alexander Ginzburg'.[382]

After a request from Mrs Jane Moonman, the editor of the Zionist Yearbook and a well-known campaigner, to Dr Owen to receive her, it was decided that Mr Stephen, the private secretary of the Minister of State would meet her in his place. She wanted to discuss ways in which members of the public could express their views on the Soviet government's attitude to human rights. 'Dr Owen had previously met leaders of responsible Jewish organizations informally – he met Doreen Gainsford and members of the Women's Campaign for Soviet Jewry during the Labour Party's Conference last year', though as a rule other

---

[380] Nicholas Bethell, Spies and Other Secrets p.98. NA, FCO 28/3532 Sylva Becker to Roderic Lyne 14 June 1978.

[381] NA, FCO 28/3532 Keeble Moscow embassy to FCO 21 June 1978.

[382] NA, FCO 28/3532 Morning Star, Guardian and Financial Times all 22 June 1978.

members of the Foreign Office team usually fielded any questions from ministers.[383] Mrs Moonman explained to Mr Stephen that she was frustrated at the increasingly hardening of the Soviet authorities attitude towards dissent. She handed over an appeal from a group of Moscow refuseniks, listing all the recent tribulations suffered by Jewish activists including the 'trumped up accusation of "treason" against Shcharansky. Their activism had attracted the attention of the international community to the 'many...instances of the violations of human rights, especially in regard to emigration from the USSR'. She added a request for the government to intervene on behalf of Ida Nudel, a courageous woman 'suffering from stomach ulcers'.[384]

Her pleas were reinforced by Mrs Dina Beilina, who accompanied her and had taken over the task of caring for the Prisoners of Zion when Ida Nudel had been sent into exile. Mrs Beilina believed that the Central Committee of the Communist party had taken a decision 'to clear all the major dissidents out of Moscow before the Olympic Games...The Russians could be faced with a choice between continued repression and the loss of the Olympic Games, and some measure of liberalisation as the price of keeping the Games'. To this, Mr Stephen retorted that the government had taken a series of measures, such as the cancellation of Mr Bratchenko's visit and so forth, to show their displeasure; but in parenthesis, it may be observed that it is doubtful whether these actions amounted to more than a series of pinpricks. He also promised that a British observer would attend the trial of Mrs Slepak. Mrs Beilina referred to the forthcoming Congress of Geneticists, an area referred to in the Shcharansky trial as involving secret information. British specialists in the field should think twice before attending. There was also a Congress of

---

[383] NA, FCO 28/3532 Llewellyn Smith to Mr Fergusson 13 July 1978.
[384] NA, FCO 28/3532 note of call of Mrs Jane Moonman and Mrs Dina Beilina on Mr Stephen 26 July 1978; and transcript of message received from Moscow on 4 July 1978 compiled by Michael Sherbourne.

Mathematicians on the horizon, where again action could be taken on behalf of Shcharansky. Mrs Moonman said they could not accept the Soviet definition of detente, where they were free to do what they liked with human rights campaigners. Mr Stephen declared that Dr Owen insisted that 'detente must include respect for human rights and freedoms'.[385]

The only gain from this interview with Mr Stephen was that the government reversed its policy of not trying to send a member of the Moscow embassy to the trial of Soviet dissidents. A member of Chancery tried to gain admission to Mrs Slepak's trial, only to be told by a militia officer that there was no trial, that it was open, and that the courtroom was full.[386]

David Owen's Ambivalence on Human Rights Issues

Although he was deeply interested in the whole area of human rights and was the first Foreign Secretary to publish a book on the subject in 1978, Dr David Owen was curiously ambivalent when speaking about the Soviet Jewry campaign and the general movement for human rights. Owen seemed to lack an in-depth understanding of the changing place of Jews within the structure of society in the USSR or knowledge of their wartime history. In May 1977, despite the intimidation of Soviet Jews and the concocted evidence on which many of them were tried, Dr Owen issued the following statement: 'After a careful assessment, I do not believe that the present evidence justifies assertions that the Soviet Government are mounting a deliberate and broad antisemitic campaign, which some have compared with the events of the 1930s. The individuals against whom action has been taken have taken a strong and courageous stance on a matter of great sensitivity, but the moves which have been taken against them do not, so far, appear to

---

[385] NA, FCO 28/3532 note of call of Mrs Jane Moonman and Mrs Dina Beilina on Mr Stephen 26 July 1978.
[386] NA, FCO 28/3532 Mr Wade-Gery Moscow to FCO 25 July and 26 July 1978.

constitute a campaign on a mass scale directed by the Government against the Jews'. For this assertion, he was rebuked by a fellow Labour MP Millie Miller, who raised the case of an elderly gentleman who was preparing to leave for Israel and had sold everything but was now told his permission to emigrate had been withdrawn. A Conservative member of the House, Lynda Chalker, referred to the reduced number of exit visas being issued by the Soviet authorities to the Jews currently living there, who wished to live and worship freely; and another MP, Richard Luce, claimed that there were still 280,000 Jewish applicants waiting to have their requests for exit visas processed.[387]

Dr David Owen made a speech to the Zionist Federation at the Cafe Royal on 1 February 1978 with Eric Moonman, another Labour MP presiding, attacking Jewish organizations for concerning themselves exclusively with the human rights of Soviet Jews. 'It is, of course,... understandable that in fighting for human rights, Jewish groups should concern themselves mainly with Jews in Communist countries, and we all respect the determination, persistence and the ability to operate on an international scale that they show in making their views felt. But, the fact that this concern is displayed so conspicuously and at times almost exclusively in the cause of Soviet Jewry does, in my view, tend to limit the effectiveness of the groups concerned. It may even cause some resentment among those who are competing for public sympathy and support on behalf of equally deserving cases and [which] do not involve Jews'. He suggested that the 'force of Jewish lobbying' would have greater impact, if they extended their campaign to cover other ethnic and religious groups in the Soviet Union and elsewhere.[388] After a public outcry at his remarks, Dr Owen issued a statement by way of apology, saying that 'The Jewish lobby on Soviet Jewry was the most effective and the strongest in Britain because it naturally stemmed from a

---

[387] JC 27 May 1977, p.6.
[388] JC 3 February 1978, p.40.

commitment which was itself based on identification'; and
sent a letter to the Zionist Federation, saying that his speech
was not meant as a 'rebuke'.[389]

Owen Briefed on Anatoly Shcharansky by Doreen Gainsford

June Jacobs of the National Council for Soviet Jewry
was flabbergasted by Dr Owen's remarks, requesting an
urgent consultation with him, which he avoided, by
suggesting that she should speak to one of his officials or
have a word with him at Doreen Gainsford's farewell party,
to which she demurred. In contrast Doreen Gainsford tried

---

[389] JC 10 February 1978 ,p.4. NA, FCO28/3531,W.K. Prendergast to
EESD 15 February 1978.

a more sophisticated approach, by suggesting that though they differed in their views, his words had been taken out of context by the *Telegraph* and *Jewish Chronicle*.[390] She had tried to cultivate a working relationship with the Foreign Secretary from the time they first met informally at the Labour Party conference in 1977. She followed this up with a deputation to David Owen on December 15 in pursuance of the 35's campaign to secure the release of Anatoly Shcharansky from prison. Among the members of the small delegation were Jeremy Thorpe MP, the Liberal leader, and Lord Foot. Owen said the Soviet detention of Shcharansky 'placed a `black cloud' over the Belgrade review of the Helsinki Agreement'. Helene Hayman MP and Lord Foot also had a conversation with an embassy official about Shcharansky but he refused to accept a petition. There was also a two-hour protest staged by the Women's Campaign outside the embassy.[391]

Later, Doreen Gainsford informed Owen that she was emigrating to Israel and invited him to her farewell party in the House of Commons sponsored by the Committee for the Release of Nudel and the International Committee for Shchransky's Release. She told Owen that her successors in the Women's Campaign would be Rita Eker, Linda Isaacs and Margaret Rigal. Margaret and Rita had just returned from Moscow where they met many refuseniks. These people were all of the opinion that the more severe charge of treason against Shcharansky, who had done exactly the same thing as Ginzburg and Orlov, was unquestionably because he was a Jew; and she and he differed on this point. [392] A few weeks ago she held a clandestine meeting with a senior Soviet official, who encouraged her group to continue their campaign; and claimed that a cursory glance at the Soviet national and provincial press revealed the extent of antisemitism. The imprisonment of Shcharansky

---

[390] NA, FCO28/3531 Doreen Gainsford to David Owen 15 February 1978.
[391] JC 23 December 1977, p.6.
[392] NA, FCO28/3531 Doreen Gainsford to David Owen 8 February 1978 with invitation.

was not only designed to test the will of the Jewish people across the world but the strength of their support. Owen popped into the farewell party, though there was no time for him to chat to Doreen. However, she continued to cultivate his friendship and hoped to be of assistance to him when he visited Israel.[393] Gainsford also invited Lord Goronwy Roberts, the Minister of State, to her party and thanked him for the assistance shown to her by many members of his department through the years.[394]

As Colin Shindler and Greville Janner both pointed out, for Jewish groups to fight for internal changes in the USSR would place the refusenik movement in a dangerous position. If they adopted this position, Jews would no longer be allowed out of the Soviet Union; and that was why it was imperative that Jews kept themselves separate from the general human rights movement.[395] On the other hand, it should be pointed out that in the United States Raphael Lemkin and some Jewish organizations participated with Ukrainian and other émigré groups in the campaign for a Genocide Convention, although there was accumulating evidence that certain ethnic groups in Eastern and Central Europe cooperated with the Nazis in the slaughter of Jews.[396] Shindler, however, castigated the Jewish leadership of this country as well for ignoring non-Jews, whom Soviet Jews supported. In 1972 Slepak and four other Jews demonstrated outside the courthouse when Vladimir Bukovsky, a prominent campaigner against the incarceration of political prisoners in psychiatric institutions and advocate of Jewish emigration, was tried,

---

[393] NA, FCO 28/3531 Doreen Gainsford to David Owen 15 February 1978.

[394] NA, FCO 28/3531 Doreen Gainsford to Lord Goronwy Roberts 8 February 1978.

[395] JC 10 February 1978, pp.4 and 16.

[396] John Cooper, Raphael Lemkin and the Struggle for the Genocide Convention (London,2008), p.213. David Cesarani, Final Solution. The Fate of the Jews 1933-1949 (New York,2016), pp.401-5. Omer Bartov, Anatomy of a Genocide: The Life and Death of a Town Called Buczacz (New York, 2019).

but there was no response from the leaders of Anglo-Jewry; and when Bukovsky was freed and came to Britain, a reception organised for him by the Women's Campaign was boycotted by the same communal leadership. Again, the communal leadership was silent when Sakharov was awarded the Nobel Prize, though he bravely intervened on behalf of Soviet Jews on a number of occasions. On the other hand, two non-Jews, Federov and Murzhenko, participated in the plot to escape on an aircraft and their release was also campaigned for by the 35's. In addition, Shindler also asserted that the Moscow Helsinki Committee played an effective 'role in the life of the Jewish emigration movement between 1976 and 1978' and that 'a probable majority of members of the activist Exodus movement' supported it rather than a few isolated individuals. 'Moreover, it is important to note that those Jewish activists associated with the committee were not nonentities on the periphery of the movement, but very prominent activists such as Vladimir Slepak, Ida Nudel [Shcharansky] and Professor Alexander Lerner'. Nonetheless, there was an informal alliance between the two protest movements, the Jewish and the more general community of dissidents;[397] and it could be argued that the international vitality of the movement for Soviet Jewry reinvigorated the activism of the Soviet dissidents generally and was an important reason for their eventual success. Apart from this, Jewish assistance to the campaign against the abuse of psychiatry for political reasons in the Soviet Union gave additional backbone to the whole movement. Names such as Dr Semyon Guzman, Victor Fainberg, Dr Marina Voikhanskaya in the USSR, and Sidney Bloch, Dr Harold Merskey, and Dr G.A. Low-Beer in this country attest to this.[398]

---

[397] JC 26 January 1979.
[398] NA, FCO 28/2932 the case of Misha Voikhansky circa December 1975, Victor Fainberg to James Callaghan 21 March 1976, Lord Bethell to Yuri Andropov 1 May 1976. FCO 28/3094 Dr G.A. Low-Beer to David Owen 5 March 1977. Mark Hurst, British Human Rights Organizations and Soviet Dissent, 1965-1985 pp.11-78.

In September 1978, Mrs Glenda Woolf called on Stephen Wordsworth at the FCO to plead the case of Yosif Mendelevich, one of the participants in the plan to divert an aircraft from the Soviet Union to Sweden. She had previously taken up the case in April with Joel Barnett MP, who had written to David Owen and had received a rather negative reply. Owen made it clear that the government could not possibly intervene on behalf of someone involved in a hijacking. It was distressing nevertheless to read of the suffering of Mendelevich on account of his religious observances. The government, however, as a general rule was 'right to concentrate in discussions with the Soviet Union on improvements in human rights on a broad basis, and to concentrate on categories of cases and the achievements of agreed standards of behaviour, rather than persistently to confront the Soviet Union over individual cases. There are cases where individual names can and should be mentioned, in private representations. But these must be few if these representations are to be effective and the ground must be chosen with great care'.[399] Here was the clearest exposition of the government's policy with regard to human rights. A similar response was sent to the Labour MP, Frederick Willey, with regard to Kaljn Matik, an Estonian, who was imprisoned in the Soviet Union, showing that this was the general government response to pleas for individuals from all ethnic groups.[400] When in September Mrs Woolf asked the government to assist in sending a prayer-book to Mendelevich, Wordsworth said that the Soviets would interpret any intervention as an official representation on his behalf and that this would have no effect – a very weak response.[401]

To the British government's surprise, Professor Levich and his wife were given permission to leave the Soviet Union at the end of October 1978. He was a world-

[399] NA, FCO 28/3532 David Owen to Joel Barnett 24 April 1978. David Owen, Human Rights (London,1978), p.44.
[400] NA, FCO 28/3453 David Owen to Frederick Willey 29 March 1978.
[401] NA, FCO 28/3532 note of call of Mrs Glenda Woolf and Mrs Bridgeman on S.J. Wordsworth 25 September 1978.

renowned expert on physiochemical hydrodynamics with access to classified information. An invitation had been extended to him by University College Oxford to accept a visiting fellowship in the previous year but when an approach was made to the Soviet embassy by the Foreign Office, the approach was snubbed; and it was then decided that when Dr Owen had lunch with the Soviet ambassador on 23 January, he would renew the request and informally mention Levich's invitation and say that they might take another look at their file because of his wife's worsening heart condition.[402] Professor Brian Spalding had collected the signatures of 5,000 scientists from across the world to put pressure on the Kremlin on Levich's behalf. But the decisive intervention came when Senator Edward Kennedy visited Moscow and presented a list of eighteen cases, of which Levich's was the best-known name. Llewellyn Smith minuted that this was 'Brezhnev's personal decision, based on a desire not to complicate US/Soviet relations, & to be helpful to Kennedy, at a critical period in the SALT negotiations'.[403] Sakharov had forecast as early as June 1977 that Levich, a figure of much international attention, would be allowed to leave when the Soviet authorities decided that the gesture of his release would be most effective. Arriving in Israel in December, Levich and his wife were welcomed at the airport by cabinet ministers and the Soviet Immigrants Union.[404]

The European Parliament adopted a resolution on the situation of the Jewish community in the Soviet Union in its November session which its President forwarded to David Owen.[405] The resolution deplored the resurgence of antisemitism in certain circles in the Soviet Union and mentioned the 'parodies of justice' which resulted in heavy

---

[402] NA, FCO 28/3531 K.B.A. Scott to Mr Sutherland 3 January 1978.
[403] NA, FCO 28/3531 minute of Llewellyn Smith 26 October 1978.
[404] Daily Telegraph 25 October and 9 December 1978; NA, FCO 28/3096 C.L.G. Mallaby Moscow to A. St. J.H. Figgis London 28 June 1977.
[405] NA, FCO 28/3532 Emilio Colombo to David Owen 30 November 1978.

sentences being imposed on Shcharansky, Ginzburg, Vladimir Slepak, Begun, and Goldshtein. It reiterated that the Soviet Union was one of the signatories of the Helsinki Accords and had ratified the International Covenant on Civil and Political Rights. It went on to deplore 'the constant violation of human rights and basic freedoms of the Jewish community in the Soviet Union – particularly as regards the right to emigrate, the exercise of national, religious, cultural and educational rights and freedoms – and the parody of justice which serves as a pretext for repression and antisemitic propaganda'. It called on their Foreign Ministers, the Council and Commission to persuade the Soviet authorities to release the men and women from prison who had been convicted for trying to exercise the rights laid down in the Helsinki Final Act. It appealed to member states' governments in the context of preparing for the Madrid Review meeting which would take place in November 1980 to insist on the Soviet Union fulfilling its obligations under the Final Act. The government acknowledged receipt of the resolution and said it would be brought to the attention of the department concerned.[406]

By the late 1970s, under the leadership of Eker and Rigal the Women's Campaign came to appreciate that demonstrations were 'no longer considered newsworthy'.[407] Although protests continued from time to time, the National Council claimed it was becoming increasingly difficult to attract large crowds to such communal gatherings. A demonstration outside the Soviet embassy during the visit of Gromyko in 1976 only attracted 'disappointing' numbers and a mass rally in Trafalgar Square two years later 'was not considered appropriate at the present time in view of the small numbers of people

---

[406] NA, FCO 28/3532 resolution of the European Parliament on the Jewish community in the Soviet Union 14 November 1978; and G.G.H. Walden to Emilio Colombo 5 December 1978.
[407] Mark Hurst, Human Rights p.95.

who appeared willing to join rallies, marches, etc'.[408]
Occasionally, such demonstrations were judged to be a
success. 'The Students and Academics Committee held a
successful protest march and Seder' outside the Soviet
embassy in March 1979 and an International Day of protest
for Ida Nudel on 21 June 1979, an idea which originated
within the National Council, attracted much attention
across the world.[409] Increasingly, the Women's Campaign
relied on gimmicks to attract the attention of the national
press, but from time to time mini-demonstrations were
staged outside the Soviet embassy, travel agencies or at
sporting events, when the Soviet violation of the human
rights of their Jewish community was highlighted.[410]

Looking back on his period in office, Owen was of the
opinion that Jimmy Carter wanted extensive cuts in
strategic weapons, but when this was proposed in 1977
many of the elderly politicians in the Kremlin thought that
the President was trying to trick them; and consequently,
Cyrus Vance was rebuffed by the Soviet Foreign Minister,
Andrei Gromyko, in the Strategic Arms Limitation Talks 11
when he first approached him about this. In the end,
Gromyko accepted that 'Jimmy Carter's intentions towards
arms control were... genuine' but was 'perplexed' by the
emphasis put on human rights. Although the United
Kingdom wanted substantive progress in arms control and
genuine advancement in the implementation of human
rights, there was implicitly a difficult choice between these
two objectives. If there was a choice, Owen decided that
arms control must have priority. He was concerned about
nuclear weapons, his principal fear being their
proliferation, particularly in Pakistan and South Africa. He
admitted as well that he was more suspicious of the goals
of Soviet foreign policy than his Prime Minister or the

---

[408] LMA, ACC 3087/001 minutes of executive of National Council 9
May 1976 and 17 July 1978.
[409] LMA, ACC3087/001 minutes of executive of National Council
chairman's report 1 July 1979.
[410] Southampton, MS 254/A980, 1/3/2 history of the Women's
campaign circa 1989.

mainstream Labour party.[411] 'Unless the relaxation of tensions brings greater enjoyment of human rights, detente has no meaning or purpose beyond our immediate survival', he wrote in 1978. 'Detente should not be just about the absence of war and the avoidance of crises: it should tell us something about conditions of peace'. However, 'The emphasis must be on the discussions between the United States and the Soviet Union about further limitation of strategic arms, and on the talks between the military alliances at Vienna about balanced force reductions in Europe'.[412]

Reflecting on the past, he thought that Gromyko's attitude to human rights was as niggardly and dour as ever, as he resented the West's intervention in what he considered were the internal affairs of the Soviet Union. He listened to Owen's 'representations on Sakharov and others and promised to look at the list of people we wanted them to release so that they could travel to the West, but he left me in no doubt that any concessions would be made from pure cynicism, merely as a device for improving British press comment and public attitudes to the USSR...'[413] Owen flayed the organizations taking part in the Soviet Jewry campaign for not bothering enough with 'equally deserving' human rights cases within the Soviet Union and elsewhere 'which do not involve Jews'.[414] But we have seen that some of this criticism was misplaced, as Jews played a prominent role in the Helsinki Monitoring Groups and this was to minimise the participatory role of neighbours from other ethnic groups in the murder of Jews during the Holocaust and the ongoing mistrust which this engendered.

The somewhat timid, flawed human rights policy of the Callaghan government was gradually reversed by Margaret Thatcher. Even the political asylum extended to Polish Jews by Callaghan first as Home Secretary and later

---

[411] David Owen, Time to Declare (London,1992), p.336.
[412] David Owen, Human Rights pp.43,51.
[413] David Owen, Time to Declare p.337
[414] David Owen, Human Rights p.45.

as Prime Minister, especially after the 1968 anti-Zionist campaign, was of a much more limited character than that offered by Sweden and Denmark. Dave Rich exaggerated the effectiveness of the Board of Deputies as a pressure group on human rights issues in this respect. As Dr Leopold Sobel explained, Britain took in a small number of refugees, who were mostly academics. 'In comparison a minute country like Denmark opened its doors to more than 3,000 [Polish] refugees and Sweden to more than 2,500'.[415]

Amnesty and the Women's Campaign: an Unhappy Relationship

Before she departed for Israel, Doreen Gainsford had tried to enlist the support of Amnesty International, the leading human rights organization, for the cause of Soviet Jewish women. At a conference on Women Against Torture held under the auspices of Amnesty International in 1975, she successfully proposed a series of resolutions for the Soviet government 'to cease harassment of Soviet Jewish women, to release Jewish prisoners of conscience and to allow them to emigrate to Israel'.[416] Again, in the same year an Amnesty report entitled 'Prisoners of Conscience in the USSR' stated that among the 10,000 political and religious prisoners Jews were singled out for special hardship. From material smuggled out of the Perm labour camp, it was apparent that 'The administration utilises informers and spies and uses false witnesses in order to be able to impose additional punishment upon the Jews'. Jews were forbidden from practising their religion or congregating together for a few minutes, while conversations in Hebrew and Yiddish merited punishment.[417] Another example of cooperation between the two organizations was that on Kol Nidre night

---

[415] JC 19 January 2018, pp.10 and 11 and 26 January 2018 letter of Dr Leopold Sobel.
[416] JC 14 November 1975, p.6.

[417] JC 21 November 1975, p.4.

in 1978, marking the beginning of the fast of the Day of Atonement, members of the Liverpool branch of Amnesty International paraded outside a concert hall where the Leningrad Philharmonic Orchestra was performing, as the local branch of the Women's Campaign had mounted a protest earlier in the day. Demonstrators bearing placards including the Right Rev. David Shepherd, the Bishop of Liverpool and a test cricketer, stood outside the concert hall and distributed leaflets denouncing the treatment of Jews and Christians in the Soviet Union .[418]

After the 1967 Six Day War and the Israeli occupation of Arab territories, relations between Jews and Amnesty International became strained. To supporters of Israel, the authorities there had an agonizing choice between security and the suppression of civil liberties in the interest of combating terror. Amnesty leaders regarded Israel as being steeped in an atavistic tribal nationalism, so their concerns were given short shrift. Benenson had dismissed Israeli anxiety about security on the same day as three buses were blown up in Jerusalem and Martin Ennals, his successor, had angered them with his easy acceptance of vague accusations of torture in prisons by the Palestinians. While the plight of Individual Prisoners of Zion was sometimes taken up by Amnesty International, they were not prepared to recognize the Soviet Jews, a large number of whom had been refused the right to emigrate, as a specific category all of whom were entitled to be accepted as prisoners of conscience.[419] Thus in 1987, for example, the Ducorum branch of Amnesty International was writing letters to the well-known refusenik Iosif Begun and his wife, but Rita Eker informed them that though their letters were not arriving, the Beguns wanted them to continue writing. Their message was: 'Please tell our friends to continue writing as this makes the Soviet authorities aware of our situation'. She promised, however, that if they addressed a

---

[418] JC 20 October 1978, p.10.

[419] James Loeffler, Rooted Cosmopolitans pp.276-88.

letter to our dear friends, she would ensure that it reached them through someone who travelled to the Soviet Union. [420]

Nonetheless, relations between the Women's Campaign and Amnesty International deteriorated still further. Joyce Simson of the 35's wrote to Ian Martin, the Secretary-General of Amnesty International, a few years later that 'For many years since our organizations have been campaigning for Human Rights, we have enjoyed a very fruitful working relationship. The most pressing cases are those of Felix and Roman Bodner of Tashkent and Mr Yuri Massover of Moscow...There is also the troublesome case of Dmitri Berman... who is at present holed up in the Canadian Embassy. EVERYONE OF THE PRISONERS HAS BEEN CLEARED OF ANY CRIMINAL CHARGES AND EVERYONE HAS BEEN LANDED IN PRISON BECAUSE OF PROVED ANTISEMITISM – the criteria by which you judge a case worthy of adoption'. Dr Andrei Sakharov intervened on behalf of Yuri Massover and Dmitri Berman. 'Please could you kindly tell us and the families of these prisoners why Amnesty International refuses to take up these cases and why in the past few years, you have only been interested in one Jewish prisoner, Mikhail Holos who refused to be conscripted [?]...But please could you tell us by what yardstick you judge these Jewish cases'.[421]

In her reply, Anne Burley, the head of the European region research department, claimed that Amnesty International was 'aware of the cases of Jewish prisoners mentioned in your letter... As you may be aware our organization has in the past taken up cases of persons charged with or convicted of criminal offences, provided we have received sufficient evidence to indicate

[420] Southampton, MS254/A980 1/3/73 Rita Eker to Stefanie Logie 6 April 1987.

[421] Southampton, MS254 A980 1/3/73 Joyce Simson to Ian Martin 11 December 1991.

convincingly both that the charge has been false, and that the reason for bringing it was to punish a person's conscientiously-held beliefs or solely because of their ethnic origin, religion, sex, colour or language. In the cases you raise we have at present no information to indicate that antisemitism constituted the sole grounds for their arrest'. We are monitoring the situation and actively seeking further information.[422] This exchange of views supports James Loeffler's proposition that 'Soviet Jewish emigration took place at a time when Jews were becoming marginalized in the international human rights movement'.[423]

Yet the leaders of the Women's Campaign persisted and took up the cause of many of the outstanding Jewish political dissidents in the USSR, including Anatoly Shcharansky, who was also deeply involved in the Soviet human rights movement; and this was when the Lishka offered little encouragement to his wife's efforts on his behalf because the Israelis did not want to be seen as interfering in the internal affairs of the Soviet Union. The leadership of the National Council and that of the 35's also took up the cause of those involved in the cultural and purely scientific education of the Soviet Jews, as the persecution of dissidents of all kinds intensified. We now turn in the next chapter to an account of the trials of the refuseniks in the political and human rights wings of the Soviet Jewry movement and those who straddled the divide and were also interested in Jewish culture, whose sentences inflamed opinion in the West.

---

[422] Southampton, MS254 A980 1/3/73 Anne Burley to Joyce Simson 13 March 1992.

[423] James Loeffler, Rooted Cosmopolitans p.292.

Chapter 5 - The Refusenik Trials

The Growth of Dissent Among Jews

By 1979 the Soviet Union was becoming a much more educated society than it was before the Second World War and the influx of these qualified individuals meant that it was stratified in new ways. Whereas in 1939 11% of the population had received secondary education and 1.3% higher education, four decades later these figures had leapt to 70.5% for secondary schools and 10% for higher education. At the same time as graduates were finding it increasingly difficult to find employment commensurate with their qualifications, Jews were gradually being squeezed out of positions of influence in the elite – the party, the security services, and the Foreign Ministry, though they were still concentrated in large numbers in the arts and sciences.[424] By 1959, the proportion of university graduates among Jews already mounted to 11.4 per cent as compared to 1.8 per cent for the Russians.[425] As Geoffrey Hosking pointed out 'a few intellectuals – the so-called dissenters – became the most discontented and `de-ideologized' of all Soviet citizens. There were good reasons for this: in their outlook, expectations and lifestyle, many of them were members of what we in the West would call the `free professions', dependent on the nomenklatura for their appointment, but free of direct party interference in their daily working life. Two groups tended to develop openly dissenting views: scientists and writers', among whom there were many Soviet Jews.[426]

During the 1930s, Stalin instituted a system of territorial-ethnic recruitment. Regional elites were purged

---

[424] Geoffrey Hosking, A History of the Soviet Union 1917-1991 (London,1992), p.402. Walter Laqueur, The Long Road to Freedom. Russia and Glasnost (London,1989), p.127.

[425] Antony Polonsky, The Jews in Poland and Russia 1914 to 2008 (London,2019), p.657.

[426] Geoffrey Hosking, A History of the Soviet Union 1917-1991 p.404.

and replaced with local party loyalists. He also made it compulsory for each person to carry an internal passport with details of their nationality, and this became the administrative means by which a scheme of ethnic recruitment was imposed. Jews and ethnic Germans without a designated homeland were disadvantaged in this system of recruitment. At first, because of the lack of sufficiently educated persons, Jews who were preponderantly urban residents still found attractive employment positions available. Robert J. Brym pointed out that 'In 1973, when Jews only represented about 1 per cent of the population, they comprised nearly 2 per cent of university students in the USSR, over 6 per cent of all scientific workers, nearly 9 per cent of all scientists, and 14 per cent of all Doctors of Science (the equivalent of a full professorship in North America)'. Within two generations of the Russian Revolution, Jews had been transformed from a destitute and marginalized minority, especially in the Ukraine and Belarus, into the country's most educated ethnic group. Between 1967 and 1971 the position of Jews began to deteriorate, despite their good academic qualifications, when they applied for university admission, giving an impetus to their desire to emigrate. Ethnic quotas became pronounced. For example, 'In 1979 there were 47 non-Jewish and 40 Jewish student applicants to the Mechanics and Mathematics Department of the Moscow State University. The non-Jews had won 26 Mathematics Olympiads, the Jews 48, yet 40 non-Jews and only six Jews were accepted into the Department. These and similar circumstances were repeated countless times, especially in the better schools and institutes'. [427]

Moreover, Antony Polansky stated that the younger generation of Jews felt that they had become 'effectively second-class citizens' as compared to their parents' generation. Jewish resentment was well expressed by Mikhail Agursky: 'The Jews had been converted into an

---

[427] Robert J. Brym, The Jews of Moscow, Kiev, and Minsk: Identity, Antisemitism and Emigration (New York, 1994), pp.11-14.

estate of slaves. Could one really expect that a nation that had given the Soviet state political leaders, diplomats, generals and top economic managers would agree to become an estate whose boldest dream would be a position as head of a lab at the Experimental Machine-Tool Research Institute or senior researcher at the Automatics and Telemechanics Institute. The Jews were oppressed and humiliated to a much greater degree than the rest of the population'.[428]

Because antisemitism was officially condemned in the 1920s and early 1930s, Jews in the localities could at least complain to the central authority.[429] With the gradual disappearance of Jews from positions of influence and their replacement by native elites, particularly Russians and Ukrainians, strong antipathy to Jews developed among the Communist party leadership after 1945. By 1976, the Central Committee was 82% Slav and the Politburo consisted almost entirely of Russians and Ukrainians.[430] Russian nationalists regarded Jews as having too close ties to their co-religionists overseas, as being part of an international community, and as being a 'ferment of decomposition' more open to Western influence than any other section of Soviet society. Jews could not be denounced openly but were criticised using coded language such as 'cosmopolitans' and 'Zionists'. In the early years of the twentieth century, the Russian far right in the person of Pavel Krushevan in Kishinev developed the idea of a Judaeo-Masonic conspiracy which would subvert the international order, undermine Christianity, provoke a gigantic conflict and lead to Jewish world domination. What provoked this dire warning was the sudden rise of Zionism with its promise to regain possession of the Holy

---

[428] Antony Polonsky, The Jews in Poland and Russia 1914 to 2008 (London,2019), p.658.

[429] Brenda McGeever public lecture 20 January 2021.

[430]Walter Laqueur, The Long Road to Freedom p.128 and Geoffrey Hosking, A History of the Soviet Union 1917-1991 p.430.

Land and take over the Christian holy places.[431] During the 1960s and 1970s a new anti-Zionist literature appeared which invoked the same themes as those reiterated in the 'Protocols of the Elders of Zion'. Writers attempted to justify the anti-Jewish pogroms in Tsarist Russia and claimed that the Zionists manipulated the Nazis into unleashing the Second World War, Eichmann was a mere tool in their hands.[432] Soviet leaders after Stalin made concessions to the multifarious nationalities comprising the USSR, thus enabling a cultural revival among many different groups during the 1960s and 1970s, but Jews were excluded from this dispensation. The only options open to them were to assimilate or emigrate. In this period, too, under Khrushchev's anti-religious campaign of 1959-64, churches were closed in large numbers, but then the position eased and the Russian Orthodox Church could still count many millions of members.[433]

The Soviet dissident movement sprung from a group of intellectuals who were alienated by the Leninist tradition of revolutionary violence, and insisted on the rule of law and human rights.[434] They absorbed the idea of human rights and popular sovereignty from the French revolutionary tradition, but accorded primacy to 'a higher moral authority... by using the word conscience'.[435] The first public protest by these dissidents was in 1965 when a group of two hundred demonstrated in Pushkin Square, Moscow, in support of the writers Andrei Sinyavsky and Yuli Daniel, who were facing trial for trying to undermine the Soviet system in their publications. Sinyavsky was not Jewish but wrote under the pseudonym of Abraham Tertz to indicate

---

[431] Steven J. Zipperstein, Pogrom. Kishinev and the Tilt of History (New York,2018), pp.146 and 174.

[432] Walter Laqueur, The Long Road to Freedom pp.128-31.

[433] Geoffrey Hosking, A History of the Soviet Union 1917-1991 pp.431-6 and 438-43. Jane Ellis, The Russian Orthodox Church p.5.

[434] Robert Horvath, The Legacy of Soviet Dissent, pp.6,81.

[435] Philip Boobbyer, Conscience, Dissent and Reform in Soviet Russia (London,2005), pp.228-9.

his sympathy for Jews.[436] The KGB put Sinyavsky and Daniel on trial in February 1966 for works they had written and smuggled abroad for publication. Sinyavsky received a sentence of seven years in a labour camp, Daniel was given five years. In January 1968 four dissidents, among whom was Alexander Ginzburg, were tried and sentenced for publishing a transcript of the Sinyavsky-Daniel trial.[437]

Within the Central Committee, Yuri Andropov, who became KGB chairman in 1967, took the strongest line against dissidents. He had participated in crushing the Hungarian uprising and was deeply discomforted by the Prague Spring of 1968. Influenced by this, he overhauled the security service, setting up the KGB Fifth Directorate with specialized departments to monitor intellectuals, students, nationalists, religious believers and Jews.[438] Among these groups his particular bugbear was the Jews. Because, it was claimed, he was himself in fact wholly or partly Jewish, he had to prove that he was ultra-loyal, for some of his colleagues on the Politburo were Russian nationalists and racist antisemites.[439] 'The KGB and politburo heads saw the Zionist and Jewish movements as a clear, immediate and real danger which is only second to the main enemy, the United States'. When a demonstration took place by dissidents against the invasion of forces from the Warsaw Pact into Czechoslovakia in August 1968, police attacked the protesters, claiming 'they are all Jews'.[440] Andropov was convinced that Western ideological subversion was the greatest threat to the Soviet Union. He was obsessed by the damage writers and poets could inflict

---

[436] Colin Shindler communication to the author 23 December 2019.

[437] Christopher Andrew and Vasili Mitrokhin, The Mitrokhin Archive pp.403-4.

[438] Christopher Andrew and Vasili Mitrokhin, The Mitrokhin Archive: KGB in Europe and the West (London,1999), pp.400,405-6.

[439] Ronen Bergman, 'The KGB's Middle East Files: the Fight against Zionism and World Jewry'.

[440] Colin Shindler communication to the author 23 December 2019.

and regarded Solzhenitsyn as a dangerous opponent of the Soviet state and social system, not resting until he drove him into exile.[441] So too, in the spring of 1968 a privately produced samizdat journal, *The Chronicle of Current Events,* started publication and continued appearing until 1984 with a break between 1972 and 1974. National, religious, and human rights groups aired their grievances in this forum and there were full reports of the trials of dissidents, instead of the garbled official versions. Jews as well started writing to *The Chronicle of Current Events* and contacting foreign journalists. Even a Jewish samizdat journal commenced publication in 1970 under the title of *Exodus.*[442]

As part of a growing clamour among Soviet Jews for exit visas after the 1967 Israeli victory, Golda Meir, the Prime Minister, received another appeal from Georgian Jews as did the Israeli ambassador to the United Nations. On 10 November 1969, Golda Meir broadcast the contents of the letter which was addressed to her on Kol Yisroel and the message was relayed by Radio Liberty, the Voice of America and the BBC. Everything seemed to point to a shift in stance by the Israelis to a more activist policy. But the Soviet Union denied that there was a demand for exit visas and continued with its policy of repression.[443]

The Three Leningrad Trials

I focus on the trials of prominent Jewish dissidents, partly because the death sentences passed on two of the alleged plotters stirred the conscience of world Jewry and gave an enormous fillip to the establishment of vigorous campaigning organizations in Britain and the United States, partly because their defiant speeches at their trials made

---

[441] Christopher Andrew and Vasili Mitrokhin, The Mitrokhin Archive pp.405-6. Ronen Bergman, 'The KGB's Middle East Files: the Fight against Zionism and World Jewry'.
[442] Geoffrey Hosking, A History of the Soviet Union 1917-1991 pp.418-19 and 436-7.
[443] Wendy Eisen, Count Us In (Toronto,1995), pp.30-1.

these refuseniks into household names, with whom Jews and public-spirited individuals across the world could identify, and partly because accounts of the trials appeared in *Jews in Eastern Europe*, a journal sponsored by the Lishka and published in Britain and disseminated among opinion makers. Some of these trials in the early 1970s have already been mentioned tangentially in the chapters dealing with the student and Women's Campaign for Soviet Jewry, but my main focus in this chapter is on the trials of persons belonging to the political and cultural wings of the refusenik movement in the second half of the decade, after the clamp-down on dissent by the KGB.

Again, on 14 June 1970 thirty-seven Leningrad Jews signed an appeal to U Thant, the Secretary-General of the UN, asking him to intercede with the Soviet authorities about Jewish emigration when he visited Moscow. Frustrated at the lack of progress, Mark Dymshits, an experienced pilot unable to obtain employment on a civil airline, conceived of a plan to seize an aircraft on a scheduled flight and fly it to Sweden in an attempt to gain worldwide publicity for the plight of would-be emigrants. He had been introduced by Grigory Butman, the leader of the Leningrad Zionist group, to some activists in Riga. Some of the plotters intended to be passengers on the first flight out of Smolny airport which was in the vicinity of Leningrad. Meanwhile, another smaller group would be waiting at Priozersk, where it was due to make a stop and tie up the pilot when he stepped out of the aircraft. Meanwhile, Mendelevich and the Zalmanson brothers, who were on board the flight, would deal with the co-pilot. Before the plan could be activated, on the morning of 15 June 1970, the police, who had prior knowledge of the scheme, arrested twelve people as they left the terminal at Smolny and walked across the tarmac to board the flight; and another four were picked up earlier by the police in the forest around Priozersk. A few hours later the police raided Jewish homes in Kharkov, Leningrad, Moscow, and Riga, detaining a few individuals for questioning, and making further raids over a widening area.[444]

Among those arrested near Priozersk were Leib and Meri Khnokh, Silva Zalmanson and Boris Penson. The larger group caught at Smolny included Edward Kuznetsov (the husband of Silva Zalmanson), her two brothers Israel and Wulf Zalmanson, Yosif Mendelevitch, Anatoly Altman, Mendel Bodnya, Mark Dymshits, his wife Alevtina and their two daughters, and two non-Jews Yury Federov and Alexei Murzhenko. The escapees were a motley band. Edward Kuznetsov, who was brought up by his Russian mother, was editor of *Phoenix-61*, a daring underground poetry journal and for his activism was given a seven-year term in the gulag. After his release, he embraced the Jewish identity of his father as a means of fleeing from Communism to Israel. The two non-Jews were recruited by him. Anatoly Altman was a Buddhist, while the rest were mostly Zionist idealists. Mrs Khnokh, who was pregnant and Mrs Dymshits and her daughters were released and not charged. Wulf Zalmanson, who was an army officer, was tried in a separate military court. The others known as the 'Leningrad Eleven' were charged under article 64-A which carried the death sentence for treason and betrayal of the fatherland; under article 15 for the preparation of a crime and under article 93(1) for misappropriating state property on a large scale.[445]

In the trial which opened in Leningrad on 15 December 1970, the prosecution denied there was a Jewish question in the Soviet Union, dwelling instead on the machinations of international Zionism. Apart from Bodyna, who recanted, all the defendants supported each other in court. Death by firing squad was decreed for Dymshits and Kuznetsov, fifteen years for Mendelevich, ten years for Sylva Zalmanson, and fifteen to ten years for the rest of the

---

[444] Gal Beckerman, When They Come for Us, We'll Be Gone (New York,2011), pp.172-99. Nora Levin, The Jews in the Soviet Union Since 1917 vol.2 (New York,1990), pp.672-3 and 676.

[445] Beckerman, When They Come for Us pp.173, 195, 203, 205. Nora Levin, The Jews in the Soviet Union Since 1917 pp.673, 677.

accused, apart from Bodyna, who received a reduced sentence of five years. The harshness of the sentences electrified not only the Jewish world but also was condemned by international opinion. 'Franco in fascist Spain had sentenced Basque terrorists to death in a trial in Burgos. The Israelis quietly intervened. The Basques were reprieved by Franco and this put extra pressure on the Kremlin to do the same with Dymshits and Kuznetsov'.[446] As a result of concerned international diplomatic opinion and a new spirit of activism in world Jewry, the death penalty decreed for them was commuted to fifteen years imprisonment, while some of the other defendants now had their sentences reduced. Above all, it aroused the Jewish world from its slumber to set up organizations – the National Council and the National Conference for Soviet Jewry, and the British Women's movement -- to campaign for the right of Soviet Jews to emigrate.[447]

Sylva Zalmanson gave a stirring and defiant speech in her own defence. She proudly proclaimed that 'We shall never abandon the dream of being reunited with our people in our ancient homeland. Some of us did not believe in the success of escape or believed it very slightly.... we noticed that we were being followed, but we could no longer go back... go back to our past, to the senseless waiting, to life with our luggage packed. Our dream of living in Israel was incomparably stronger than fear of the suffering we might be made to endure. I wanted to live over there with my family, work there. I would not have bothered about politics – all my interest in politics has been confined to the simple wish to leave. Even now I do not doubt for a minute that some time I will live in Israel... This dream, illuminated by two thousand years of hope, will never leave me. Next year in Jerusalem! And now I repeat, "If I forget thee, O Jerusalem, may my right hand wither"'.[448]

---

[446] Colin Shindler communication to the author 23 December 2019.

[447] Gal Beckerman, <u>When They Come for Us</u> pp.205-7 and pp.216-17.
[448] Gal Beckerman, <u>When They Come for Us</u> p.206.

To distract the attention of Western opinion, the Soviet authorities delayed the trial of the second group of those arrested, who were members of the Leningrad Zionist Society, until May 1971 and did little to publicise it. During a period of eleven months, the accused who were scientists, engineers and doctors with a thorough grounding in Hebrew and Jewish culture, were interrogated in order to make them confess. The Soviet authorities linked them all to the hijacking plot, although they had all repudiated it well before it was put into motion. They were charged with stealing a duplicating machine and distributing anti-Soviet Zionist literature, such as Leon Uris's novel, *Exodus* and a collection of slanderous letters from the samizdat journal *Exodus*. Their organization was said to have slandered Soviet domestic and foreign policy by encouraging people of Jewish nationality to emigrate to Israel. Zionists were depicted as being responsible for the Hungarian uprising in 1956 and were connected with the 'counter-revolutionary forces in Poland and Czechoslovakia in 1968'.[449]

At the trial, Grigory Butman, one of the principal persons to be accused admitted discussing plans for hijacking an aircraft with Dymshits, who was sentenced in the first Leningrad trial, but declared that he had abandoned such plans since 10 April 1970 and was not guilty of this particular charge. He admitted participating in an organization and distributing literature on Israeli or Jewish themes, entering a qualified plea of guilty. He confessed to teaching Hebrew and creating a Zionist organization to combat assimilation and to obtain permission to go to Israel. While he could not see how this activity could be described as being anti-Soviet, he acknowledged that he had been persuaded that it might be understood as such. Another one of the accused, Mikhail Korenblit, admitted that he had given up the idea of participating in the hijacking after talking to Mogilever, Chernoglaz and Kaminsky and that the fact that Jews with

---

[449] Gal Beckerman, When They Come for Us p.217. Nora Levin, The Jews in the Soviet Union Since 1917 p.685. 'The Second Leningrad Trial' in Jews in Eastern Europe vol.iv:7 (November 1971), pp.30,51.

a higher education were on trial proved that there was no antisemitism in the USSR – a point made by several of the defendants and probably extracted from them by their interrogators. Victor Shtilbans repented of his willingness to assist with the hijacking by giving the pilots drugs to make them drowsy, and denounced Zionism, for which he received a relatively light sentence of one year's imprisonment. Vladimir Mogilever and the other defendants were not charged with participating in the hijacking but with the other offences and stood their ground. Korenblit claimed to be 'profoundly surprised that some of my comrades admit that they were guilty of taking part in an anti-Soviet, Zionist organization. Our organization was interested only in matters that concerned the Jewish people and the Jewish state'. Lassal Kaminsky admitted that he was one of the leaders of the Leningrad Zionist organization, though he did not consider this to be 'anti-Soviet... Under Zionism we understand the movement for the unification of Jews in their historical homeland, Israel'. All he would concede was that the Soviet Union was trying 'to restrain the most extremist Arab leaders' and that he might have made 'mistakes during the production of literature', inserting the odd 'anti-Soviet utterances'.[450]

Some of those accused in the first Leningrad trial were brought as state witnesses to the more peripheral second trial but stood firm when they gave evidence. Dymshits testified that when he had put the plan to Butman, he said that 'his friends were against it and it was decided to ask Israel if such an action made sense. I was angry. It was clear to me that the answer from Israel could only be negative. We separated on cool terms and I said I'd handle the idea myself'. Kuznetsov added that 'they had put together a group in Riga for illegal flight abroad. He had considered it essential to do this and saw no reason why they should seek the blessing of `any government'. Silva Zalmanson asserted that 'after finding out that the Leningradites were categorically against the idea of

---

[450] 'The Second Leningrad Trial', pp.51-9.

crossing the border illegally, we carefully concealed our preparations from them. We told them that we too had given up the project because we were afraid that they might cause our plan to fail'. Mendelevich confirmed that 'he had known "precisely" that the Leningrad defendants had categorically rejected the plane hijacking project as far back as April'. 'Witness after witness called by the prosecution gave evidence of the accused's innocence, according to the unofficial report [of the trial]...'[451]

The final statements of the defendants according to the unofficial reports appear to show that they all curiously seem to have capitulated under pressure from the prosecution in return for more lenient sentences or threats to their families. Mikhail Korenblit said that 'I admit my guilt, I repent...I understand the attitude of the courtroom to our enemies'. L. Korenblit admitted his guilt and was 'ready to accept his punishment'. Lassal Kaminsky claimed that he understood that 'I am tried as a Jew, and not because I had applied for emigration to Israel, not for my convictions, but for concrete crimes. But why did the prosecution ask for me a measure of punishment that is at least one and a half times greater than for my comrades in the dock? I was not one of the founders of the organization and entered the committee only in the last days. I wrote and helped transmit abroad a few letters, but I never wished to cause harm to the Soviet State'. On 11 April, when everyone had gone home, he stayed with Butman into the early hours of the morning to dissuade him from participating in the madcap hijacking scheme. Butman, too, acknowledged his 'guilt before the State and before my comrades. I am ready to answer for the fact that at one time I intended to commit a terrible crime according to the laws of all countries. But I ask the court to take into account that under the influence of my comrades and my own reflections, I voluntarily renounced plans for the hijacking of a plane in order to leave the USSR. I had no desire to exchange socialism for capitalism. I value the achievements of the revolution but

---

[451] 'The Second Leningrad Trial', pp.59-64.

in order to live with my people, and in order to raise the question of the emigration to Israel of those who wish it, I was ready to take the terrible risk for myself and for my family. I understood that I had been wrong. Now I see the Soviet Government is going halfway to meet those Jews who wish to settle by allowing emigration to Israel'. Taking into account the 'sincere repentance' of the accused, they all received more lenient sentences Tass claimed, but the sentences still ranged from ten years to one.[452]

The third trial of those tenuously linked by the authorities to the Leningrad hijacking plot was held in Riga between 24 and 27 May 1971. There were four defendants, Ruth Alexandrovich, a twenty-three-year-old nurse, Mikhail Shepshelovich, a physicist, Arkady Shpilberg, a design engineer and Boris Maftser, a young engineer. Although there was a strong Jewish nationalist tradition in Latvia, the courtroom was packed with hostile government supporters, while only close family members of the accused were allowed to attend the trial. Two eminent foreign lawyers, Professor Henry McGee, the counsel for Angela Davis, who was currently on trial in the United States, and Maitre Lallmond, acting for Regis Debray, were barred from the courtroom. Colin Shindler 'was involved in briefing McGee and sending him to Riga'.[453] Emanuel Litvinoff noted that 'The theme of hijacking was placed in the forefront of Chief Prosecutor's Dmitry Chibisov's final speech... Constant emphasis on this theme, despite its irrelevance to the substance of the Riga trial was intended to legitimise the fact that the 'hijack plot' – with its obscure involvement with the secret police – had given the KGB an excuse to round up Jews in various parts of the Soviet Union who had been connected, however remotely, with defendants in the first Leningrad trial. In each of the trials, therefore, the prosecution played on the theme of the hijack to suggest in some degree or other every defendant was

---

[452] 'The Second Leningrad Trial' pp.67-8. Nora Levin, The Jews in the Soviet Union Since 1917 p.685.
[453] Colin Shindler communication to the author 23 December 2019.

guilty of treasonable complicity in the hijacking'. All four of the accused in the Riga trial were charged with fabricating and disseminating literature, including a Zionist underground journal *Iton*, allegedly slandering the Soviet Union by means of a clandestine press which some of them set up.[454]

Under the pressure of being held incommunicado for ten months which was in itself illegal, Boris Maftser broke under interrogation, incriminating the other accused. Added to this were his further concerns, when his younger brother was beaten up by thugs, his wife lost her employment and his mother died. Maftser admitted in court that 'The literature distributed by us gave a one-sided view of the situation in the Near East, defamed the nationalities policy of the Soviet State. This literature, in essence, was anti-Soviet...Yes, I conducted Zionist, anti-Soviet activity. I am guilty of this'. He deeply regretted 'the damage caused by' his 'actions', begging 'to earn forgiveness' from the Soviet people.[455] But none of the other defendants would fully admit any guilt. At the most Ruth Alexandrovich conceded 'the facts presented against her by the prosecution, but at the same time she stated that she did not have the aim of undermining or weakening the Soviet regime'. Mikhail Shepshelovich's defence lawyer argued that his client 'did not engage in the distribution of literature. He carried out a purely technical task at Maftser's request', while the stoutest defence was mounted by Arkady Shpilberg's lawyer. He asserted that his client 'never had anti-Soviet feelings. This can be seen even from the testimony of Mogilever, when he says that `Shpilberg talked me out of anti-Soviet activity'... he has become passionately devoted to the idea of emigrating to Israel, of living there, of teaching his children the Jewish language and Jewish culture. We can disagree with his ideas, but for this one is not put in prison'. Prosecution witnesses were called from the previous Leningrad trials to weave the story

---

[454] 'Riga—the Unofficial Version' in <u>Jews in Eastern Europe</u> vol.iv:7 (November 1971), pp.91-8.
[455] 'Riga—the Unofficial Version', pp.83, 105-6.

of a conspiracy. Shpilberg was given a sentence of three years in a corrective labour camp with a strict regime, Shepshelovich two years and Alexandrovich and Mafster both one year.[456]

The last prosecution linked to the hijacking plot opened in Kishinev on 21 June 1971, when nine young men between the ages of 24 and 35 with Zionist sympathies stood in the dock of a hostile courtroom. To prove collusion between Jewish groups in the two cities, David Chernoglaz, Anatoly Goldfeld and Hillel Shur, all from Leningrad, were also indicted. It was alleged that Mikhail Korenblit flew to Kishinev, where he met Alexander Galperin and asked him for volunteers to purchase tickets for the flight. Dymshits was called to give evidence, claiming that he 'needed 54 companions to buy all the tickets'.[457] One of the leaders of the Leningrad group, David Chernoglaz, it was alleged, came to Kishinev to pay Galperin, Voloshin, and David Rabinovich money for a duplicating machine stolen from a design institute. All the defendants were also charged with the production of slanderous Zionist anti-Soviet literature. Hillel Shur refused to testify in the open court hearing, while four out of five witnesses, who were friends of the accused, refused to give evidence which could have incriminated them.[458]

Towards the end of the trial, the accused under immense pressure from their legal advisers and barracked by a hostile crowd in the courtroom were persuaded to enter guilty pleas to secure lighter sentences. Defence lawyers were supposed to provide some balance to the proceedings but often indulged in a more strident denunciation of Zionism than the prosecution. David Chernoglaz admitted that he 'violated the laws of the state, committed crimes that I repent and I am ready for the punishment I deserve'. Anatoly Goldfeld, named with Chernoglaz as a principal defendant, 'regretted his

---

[456] 'Riga--- the Unofficial Version', pp.152, 154, 158-9.
[457] 'The Kishinev Trial' in Jews in Eastern Europe (November 1971), pp.160 and 167.
[458] ' The Kishinev Trial', pp.168-9 and 171.

involvement in bandit plans and theft that inflicted damage to the Soviet state... Never again shall I permit violation of Soviet laws'.[459] Emanuel Litvinoff added that 'Like all defendants', Lazar Trakhtenberg '... got a higher education and well-paid job'. He confessed that 'I am ashamed in front of my family and relatives who always tried to develop in me a feeling of respect for the motherland and society... Such a finale to my activities had not occurred to me even in a nightmare. I concealed crimes-- the stealing of state-owned property, the property of the state which has brought me up and to which I owe everything good in me. I will redeem my guilt'. According to Tass, the news agency report, 'Arkady Voloshin, Alexander Galperin and Harry Kirshner asked the court to take into account their repentance and frank confession'. A poignant plea of repentance was uttered by Semyon Levitt. 'I and I alone am guilty for the present pain of my parents and wife, who need me and from whom I myself have torn myself away. I will never again commit anything against the law and will stop anyone who dares encroach on the laws of my Soviet motherland'. David Rabinovich confessed that the theft of the copying machine was 'a black, terrible time... I felt greatly relieved when I told the inquiry officer frankly about everything. A heavy burden was lifted from my shoulders'. David Chernoglaz received a sentence of five years, despite his abasement; Anatoly Goldfeld four; Alexander Galperin two and a half years; and David Rabinovich one year; all the other defendants were sent to prison for two years.[460]

Although Sverdlovsk, a city in the Urals, had a Jewish population of 30,000, it had no synagogue or Jewish cultural facilities. Headed by Valery Kukuy, a senior planning engineer at a design centre for agricultural machinery, ten Jews from Sverdlovsk wrote to President Podgorny in December 1970, protesting against the death sentences imposed on Dymshits and Kuznetsov and the severe punishment imposed on the others at the first

[459] 'The Kishinev Trial', pp.173-4.
[460] 'The Kishinev Trial', pp.174-5 and 177.

Leningrad trial. An article in *Uralsky Rabochy* targeting Kukuy and one of the signatories of the appeal, Yury Kosharovsky, whipped up a febrile antisemitic atmosphere with allegations of Zionist spies. Written materials including a famous story of 'A Dog's Heart' by Bulgakov were confiscated from Kukuy, after a search of his home. His defence counsel asked that he be given a year's forced labour for verbal slander. Kukuy defended himself in court, denying that he had committed any offence. He continued, 'I love the Russian language and literature and I am grateful to those who have taught them to me. But I have my own homeland, Israel, and nothing in the world, not even this court, can prevent me from reaching my goal and living in my country with my people'.[461]

The Trial of Raiza Palatnik

On 1 December 1970, Raiza Palatnik, a 34-year-old librarian, was arrested in Odessa as part of the more general KGB crack-down on Jewish activists. In October her home had been searched but all the police found were Russian literary magazines, typed copies of Jewish and Russian poetry, the Universal Declaration of Human Rights and some books on Israel. In response Raiza penned an angry protest, asking why when Stalin had been condemned was not antisemitism equally targeted? 'Why did they not reopen Jewish schools, theatres, publish Jewish newspapers and magazines?' After her arrest in December, she was despatched to an insane asylum but as the doctor there considered that she was of sound mind, she was returned to the authorities and incarcerated in a prison to await trial. At first, she was made to share accommodation with prostitutes and later placed in a cell with bedbugs, where the sanitary conditions were deplorable and the food

[461] 'Valery Kukuy, Sverdlovsk' in Jews in Eastern Europe (November 1971), pp.196-205.

inadequate.[462] News of her treatment filtered through to Israel and embassies overseas were alerted. That is how some determined housewives in London heard of Raiza Palatnik's plight and staged a demonstration on her behalf outside the Soviet embassy on 1 May 1971, resulting in the formation of the Women's Campaign for Soviet Jewry, better known as the 35's.

Raiza Palatnik's trial started in Odessa on 22 June 1971, when she was charged with keeping and distributing material containing anti-Soviet slander. Among the items were a protest by Moscow Jews against the anti-Zionist press conference of prominent Jews held on 4 March 1970, in which they denounced Israel as a bloodthirsty heir of the Nazis, an article on Einstein and Zionism and a poem by the Soviet poet Korzhavin. The head of the library, where Raiza worked, Svetlich, said that she 'sometimes expressed herself in a disloyal manner'. After working at the library for five years, Raiza was passed over for promotion, despite a good work record, and the job was given to a Russian girl, who was a newcomer. When Raiza referred to this and said it was because she was Jewish, Svetlich said nothing. Two of Raiza's neighbours under cross-examination by her defence counsel, admitted that Raiza had said nothing against Russia, contradicting their signed statements extracted under pressure. Three colleagues from the library also gave evidence in her defence. When Raiza was asked by the prosecutor why she had refused to work on an exhibition of Soviet books in 1962, she retorted that surely she could remember the year. 'There was Khrushchev and there was nothing to buy in the shops', drawing laughter from the court. The prosecutor ignored the evidence given in court, relying instead on the pre-trial statements of witnesses collected under pressure by the KGB. She was given a sentence of two-years imprisonment to the disgust of her family, who shouted 'We are with you, Raiza! The whole Jewish people is with you. We will meet in Israel!'[463]

---

[462] 'Raiza Palatnik, Odessa' in Jews in Eastern Europe (November 1971), pp.185-9.
[463] 'Raiza Palatnik, Odessa', pp.188-90.

In a statement in her own defence Raiza Palatnik read to the court, she defiantly set out her own vision and proclaimed that henceforth she was a citizen of Israel. She opened by asking, 'Why am I on trial? I am being tried because all my life I have deeply felt my Jewishness, because I dared to participate in the rebirth of national consciousness of the Jews in the USSR who wish to emigrate to Israel. I know that in recent months, the months of my arrest, quite a large number of Jews, including some of my friends, have gone to Israel... I think that the generally observed decrease of the Jewish population in the USSR is connected with the increasing emigration to Israel. I dare to hope that the day will come when I too shall be able to realise my constant dream and go to the country whose achievements have all been created by the hands of my people, the country I consider as my only Homeland. Eight months ago, during the searches of my home and my arrest, the situation was entirely different. Permission for emigration had then been granted to only a few individuals and the authorities were frightened by the growing lava of applications for emigration, demands that became more and more insistent from day to day'.[464]

The authorities tried 'the age-old' method of intimidating the Jews. 'My arrest is one of the links in this chain'. The prosecution witnesses were subjected to the 'same working over' as I endured, but in court 'changed their testimonies or refuted completely the testimony they had given previously... The charge scarcely dwells on the contents of the incriminating literature, calling it `illegal' and `slanderous' only because it is printed not by typography but on a typewriter. I am, however, profoundly certain that neither Galich's songs, nor Korzhavin's poems contain any slander. They are talented authors... writing about things they themselves have gone through and what they know well. They write about the lawlessness, the cruelty and the camps that existed in the epoch of the personality cult... We, librarians, know very well what

---

[464] 'Raiza Palatnik, Odessa', pp.190-1.

harsh conditions of censorship exist in the Soviet Union, and how often works that cannot be published for years because of their ideological impurity, suddenly become the most popular and widely read. I can give as example the poems of Akhamatova, the books of Platonov and Mikhail Bulgakov, published in the Sixties... Or, let us say, the works of the Jewish writer David Bergelson, shot in 1952 for `Anti-Soviet Activity', and rehabilitated four years later, in 1956!... I have not admitted and do not admit myself guilty of the crime of which I am accused... Seeing around me, and experiencing on my own skin, the absence of rights and legality, and realising it is impossible to restore the trampled justice, I have decided to give up Soviet citizenship and have written a statement to this effect to the Praesidium of the Supreme Soviet of the USSR. From this day I consider myself a citizen of Israel'.[465]

The KGB Increases Repression and Unleashes a Political Response from the United States

In the summer of 1973, the KGB for the first time staged the successful show trial of Pyotr Yakir and Victor Krasin, after breaking the resistance of Victor Krasin, who revealed the names of sixty dissidents. Yakir's father was the Jewish General Yona Yakir executed on Stalin's orders during the purges of the army in 1937.[466] At the trial Yakir and Krasin incriminated themselves, thereby demoralizing the whole dissident movement. Dissidents named by the two defendants were interrogated by the KGB, most of whom admitted their errors or promised to remain silent. Unable to trammel Solzhenitsyn, the KGB forced him into exile first in Switzerland and then into the United States. Three prominent physicists Andrei Sakharov, Valery Chalidize, and Andrei Tverdokhlebov, who was Jewish, founded the

---

[465]'Raiza Palatnik, Odessa', pp.191, 193-6. Nora Levin, The Jews in the Soviet Union Since 1917 pp.692-3.
[466] Colin Shindler communication to the author 23 December 2019.

Committee for Human Rights in November 1970. The KGB left Sakharov alone because of Western concern for him which gave him a measure of protection.[467] At the same time, the KGB decimated the Jewish cultural and Zionist organizations in the Soviet Union by imprisoning many of its leaders and by allowing others to emigrate to Israel. More generally they reduced the whole momentum of the movement by issuing more exit permits between 1971 and 1973 to Jews wishing to leave the USSR.[468] Soviet trade negotiators did their utmost to obtain most favoured nation terms for trade and credit from the United States with the negotiations progressing well. At this point on 3 August 1972, the Soviet politicians blundered by introducing the diploma tax which introduced a sliding scale of payments from departing emigrants, in addition to the existing payments. These additional fees 'ranged from the equivalent of £2,250 for an arts graduate to £9,700 for one holding a doctorate of science'. Legislators in the United States were convinced that if the Soviet Union really wanted this trade bill, they would have to make concessions on human rights which would be written into the bill. The education tax swung opinion in favour of this position. On 16 March 1973, the Soviet leadership suspended the education tax as an interim measure but this was not a sufficient concession.[469] Here for the first time Western powers began to utilise human rights as a lever to influence the Kremlin. On 3 January 1975, Congress passed the Jackson-Vanik amendment to the trade bill, making adequate emigration a condition for improved trade relations between the United States and the USSR. As a riposte, the Soviet Union engineered the passing of a UN resolution in 1975 equating Zionism with racism. Throughout 1974 and succeeding

---

[467] Christopher Andrew and Vasili Mitrokhin, The Mitrokhin Archive pp.408-13.
[468] Nora Levin, The Jews in the Soviet Union Since 1917 p.690.
[469] Southampton, MS254/A980/1/3/82 Insight: Soviet Jews November 1987.

years emigration rates declined and Jewish protestors were harassed, as the KGB tightened their campaign against activists. In 1974, the number of those allowed to emigrate shrunk to 20,994, thirty per cent less than the previous year.[470]

On 1 August 1975, leaders of 35 nations gathered to sign the Final Act of the Conference on Security and Cooperation in Europe (CSCE). In return for recognizing the post-Second World War boundaries in Europe, the Soviet Union pledged to honour human rights. Dissidents in the USSR founded Helsinki Watch Groups to monitor the progress of human rights within the Soviet Union and to record their violations. Information collected by these groups was transmitted to Western newspaper correspondents in Moscow and other cities and passed on to Jewish visitors. The response of the Russian security apparatus was to arrest some of these informants and to disrupt their telephone and postal links. Roy Medvedev was of the opinion that the Politburo had taken a crucial decision in the autumn of 1976 'to heighten dramatically the pressure on the activists and to cut off their contacts in the West, from which they draw moral support'.[471]

So Yuri Orlov and Alexander Ginzburg were arrested in February 1977. Strangely Dr Mikhail Shtern was released from prison on 15 March 1977 because of Western pressure. A Jewish physician from the Ukraine, he had been arrested in 1974 on concocted charges and sentenced to eight years in labour camps. His sons Victor and August were allowed to emigrate to the West in 1975 and started a campaign for his freedom, mainly backed by the Paris-based *Comite pour la Liberation du Docteur Stern*. More than fifty Nobel laureates signed petitions for Dr Shtern's conviction to be squashed and for him to be released from detention. In April 1976 a panel of legal experts presided over by Sir John

---

[470] Nora Levin, The Jews in the Soviet Union Since 1917 pp.709,703-8 and 725. Southampton, MS254/A980/1/3/82 Insight: Soviet Jews November 1987.
[471] Nora Levin, The Jews in the Soviet Union Since 1917 pp.723, 725-29.

Foster QC concluded that 'the verdict against Dr Shtern was perverse and could not have been arrived at by any reasonable tribunal'. Later his sons started organizing the International Stern Tribunal composed of Western authorities on Soviet and human rights law which was to be convened in Amsterdam in March 1977. Jean-Paul Sartre and Simone de Beauvoir promised to attend. By happy coincidence, one week before it was due to meet Dr Shtern was released 'on grounds of Soviet humanitarianism'.[472] As recently as 4 March, Anatoly Shcharansky had been organizing a press conference for Dr Shtern's wife to demand his freedom. But now the KGB agents, who had been following him for many days were closing in on him, his own arrest seemed imminent and the release of Dr Shtern was a public relations ruse to distract attention from an alarming accusatory article in *Izvestia* against Jews and Zionists.[473]

Dr Mikhail Shtern was born in 1918 and after qualifying as a physician worked in many medical institutions before being appointed as director of the Outpatient Clinic of the Vinnytsia Provincial Endocrinological Health Centre in the Ukraine in 1963. During the time of the alleged Doctors' Plot, he was dismissed from his position in Vinnytsia but reinstated in 1954.[474] When his younger son August applied to emigrate from the Soviet Union, Dr Shtern was again dismissed from his position at the hospital and his other son Victor, a physicist, was forced to find work as a telegraph-boy. Meanwhile, the permission granted to August Shtern and his wife to emigrate was withdrawn. On 29 May 1974, Dr Shtern was arrested on charges of extortion and accepting bribes from patients and was kept in custody until the trial

---

[472] Christopher Andrew and Vasili Mitrokhin, The Mitrokhin Archive p.427. Natan Sharansky, Fear No Evil pp.4-5. August Stern ed. The USSR versus Dr. Mikhail Stern (New York,1977), William B. Simons, Introduction, pp.5-8. Independent 24 June 2005.
[473] Natan Sharansky, Fear No Evil pp.5-6.
[474] Independent 24 June 2005.

opened on 2 January 1974.[475] At the trial, Dr Shtern observed that his family's desire to leave the USSR did not violate Soviet law and was in accordance with the United Nations Declaration of Human Rights which was adopted by the Soviet Union. Further, he asserted that the evidence against him was fabricated on the model of the infamous 1952 Doctors' Plot under Stalin. While the court would not allow many witnesses who wanted to testify on Dr Shtern's behalf, of the thirty-nine witnesses called by the prosecution practically all of them with the exception of Huzhva 'retracted their accusations; and many of them simply thanked Dr Shtern for treating them'. Dr Shtern became alienated from Huzhva, whose wife Maria was his patient, because he was a drunkard and thief, who stole a wristwatch belonging to the doctor. Here Dr Shtern's testimony was corroborated by the evidence of a nurse at the dispensary, while the Huzhvas' evidence was shown to be mendacious by other witnesses and the hospital records.[476] Despite this, Dr Shtern was given a sentence of eight years in a labour camp.

The Trial of Anatoly Shcharansky

Anatoly Shcharansky's (later Natan Sharansky) only connection with the Zionist movement was an uncle called Shamai, who had emigrated from Odessa to Palestine in 1924. Caught as they were between an oppressive heavily antisemitic atmosphere in the Soviet Union and the elation at Israel's victory in the 1967 War, some Russian Jews began thinking of emigrating to Israel. In Moscow, Shcharansky was introduced to Vladimir Slepak, whose home was a meeting place for Jewish activists and those with a renewed sense of Jewish identity.[477] During the summer of 1972, Shcharansky finished his mathematics course at the prestigious Moscow Physical-Technical Institute. There he

---

[475] The USSR versus Dr. Mikhail Stern pp.28-30 and 229.
[476] The USSR versus Dr. Mikhail Stern pp.232-5.
[477] Martin Gilbert, Shcharansky (1987), pp.21-2 and 30-1.

excelled in the English class at the Institute, picking up the finer nuances of the language. Shortly before graduation, as an independent-minded spirit Shcharansky applied for an exit visa to Israel. He also decided to participate in Professor Alexander Lerner's mathematics seminar for excluded mathematicians, who were not allowed to attend the International Congress on Mathematics in April 1973 held in Moscow. As the Yom Kippur War continued into the second week of October 1973, Shcharansky demonstrated outside the Moscow Synagogue in a display of solidarity and met Natalia (Avital) Shtiglits, with whom he soon formed a friendship. He was studying Hebrew in a class in preparation for his move to Israel and he invited her to join him in learning the language. In November 1973, Shcharansky was informed that he was refused an exit permit because he had been given access to classified material – a falsehood. Unexpectedly, he had become a refusenik. Nevertheless, he was given employment at the Moscow Research Institute for Oil and Gas in automation computing, though the work was not designated as being secret.[478] On 15 May 1974, Shcharansky in a show of leadership encouraged his friends to try to walk through a line of militiamen outside the Lebanese embassy in Moscow in protest at a terrorist attack in Israel. Here in Ma'a lot, twenty children had been murdered. He and Avital married in Moscow on 4 July 1974, the day before she left the Soviet Union for Israel, as he was still waiting for his exit visa.[479]

Because of his facility in English, Shcharansky became a spokesman for refuseniks in meetings with journalists and Western politicians. He was a founder of the Moscow Helsinki Group monitoring the Soviet Union's human rights record and acted as Professor Sakharov's secretary, when the latter had to communicate with the English speaking world. As a key figure in the Moscow human rights organization, he acted as the linkman joining

---

[478] Martin Gilbert, Shcharansky pp.28-31.
[479] Martin Gilbert, Shcharansky pp.42-3 and 46.

together Jewish campaigners and other dissidents, liberals, nationalists of all varieties, and Pentecostal Christians.[480] Like Professor Alexander Lunts, Shcharansky believed in public protest and communicating these activities to the outside world. Here again, his English language skills were essential as he struck up a deep and lasting friendship with Michael Sherbourne in London over the telephone from the time when they first spoke in January 1974, thus leading to him telling the Jewish world what was happening in the daily life of individual refuseniks.[481]

As part of the general clamp-down, an article was published in *Izvestia* on 4 March 1977 denouncing Jewish activists, in particular David Abzel, Vitaly Rubin, Alexander Lerner and Shcharansky, and accusing them of carrying out acts of espionage for the CIA, while Lipavsky exposed himself as an informer, who had infiltrated refusenik circles. He accused the activists of being 'enemies of socialism' and of 'deliberately exploiting the so-called question of human rights in the interests of imperialism and world reaction'.[482]

Coinciding with the appearance of Lipavsky's letter in *Izvestia*, the apartments of Lerner, Slepak, Shcharansky, Boris Chernobilsky, Dina Beilin and Michael Kremen were searched. On the following day, the refusenik leaders telephoned through to Michael Sherbourne a response to Lipavsky's letter. It opened by saying that the accusations were 'reminiscent of the anti-Jewish trials of the 1950s', particularly the alleged 'Doctors' Plot' of January 1953. 'We have always informed Western public opinion and the Western press about our conditions and sufferings in open letters and declarations and in open telephone calls. We have never hidden from the Soviet authorities that we have kept the Western world aware of what we have been trying to achieve, in open conversations and letters through the post. What we have been doing quite openly not only has

---

[480] Martin Gilbert, Shcharansky pp.88-9 and 190.
[481] Martin Gilbert, Shcharansky pp.39 and 68.
[482] Martin Gilbert, Shcharansky pp.167-72.

been in the interests of those Jews who wish to emigrate and go to Israel but has been in the interests of the Soviet people as a whole, and in the interests of improving relations between the Soviet peoples and Government, and the government and peoples of the Western world'. Their response ended by stating that 'With this new prospect of fresh anti-Jewish trials, based on completely false evidence, or, in fact, on no evidence at all except lies, we can only regret that the Soviet Union is returning to the worst excesses of Stalin's time'. Professor Lerner also issued an additional response, denying that he was ever in touch with any intelligence authorities or foreign organisations, nor had he received any reward from them for his activities.[483]

Lerner, Slepak, and Shcharansky, who most feared arrest, issued a new appeal to the Israeli Parliament. They claimed that 'the Soviet authorities [will] ... go to almost any extreme lengths in order to suppress the growing national renaissance of the Jews of Russia. They are now continuing the campaign of anti-Jewish trials of Beilis, Dreyfus and the so-called `doctor-poisoners' of 1953'. Although he had five-and-a-half years of an eight-year labour camp sentence to finish, Dr Mikhail Shtern was suddenly released from prison on 15 March 1977. Hearing this, Shcharansky asked his friends who was going to be arrested in his place? He was soon to know the answer. He was arrested later that day'.[484]

After the Helsinki Accords, the issue of human rights came to the fore and there were growing protests by Soviet Jews and their international supporters. Because the refuseniks were the most feared segment of the dissident movement, Shcharansky believed that the Jewish activists had been singled out and treated as traitors unlike the others in the Helsinki Watch Group, such as Orlov and Ginzburg; the latter was merely charged as being anti-Soviet, but the Jewish movement had to be completely

[483] Martin Gilbert, Shcharansky pp.172-4.

[484] Martin Gilbert, Shcharansky pp.184-7.

broken and 'crushed more forcibly'. Moreover, Shcharansky with hindsight thought that the case against him was rapidly improvised four days before his arrest, so that the KGB did not have the time and opportunity to use Dr Lipavsky's services to the full, by enabling him to plant incriminating evidence; and as a consequence, other witnesses had to be selected to prove his alleged plotting. As he enjoyed the most extensive contacts with the foreign press, Shcharansky was chosen as the victim of the secret police. In the end, the trial and detention of Shcharansky for treason became a momentous duel to the death between him and Andropov, its instigator, played out in the international media arena.[485]

As we have seen, the first occasion when the 35's, the Women's Campaign, made direct contact with the Foreign Secretary was through its delegation to protest at the continued detention of Anatoly Shcharansky in December 1977. The Israeli government was reluctant 'to classify him as a Zionist prisoner because he had been involved in the Helsinki Committee'.[486] He was arrested on 15 March 1977 and held in prison for a prosecution case to be built against him until 10 July 1978, when his trial opened in Moscow.

Avital Shcharansky and Hyde Park Demonstration of the NationalCouncil for Soviet Jewry

---

[485] Natan Sharansky, Fear No Evil pp.163-4.

[486] Colin Shindler communication to the author 23 December 2019.

Women's Campaign Demonstration before Shchransky Trial

Women's Campaign Demonstrators issue a
Distress Signal for Shchransky

Originally held by the Moscow KGB office, Andropov personally signed an order transferring the case to the national office. Shcharansky was charged with 'espionage' and 'helping a foreign government to carry out hostile activities against the USSR' under article 64-A of the Russian criminal code – a charge of treason which could invite a sentence of 'Rasstrel: death by gunfire'. As far as the charge of espionage was concerned, Shcharansky was accused of sending information to the West about 1,300 people who possessed state or military secrets and who wished to emigrate. It was alleged that disclosure of this information also provided details of 200 enterprises in towns and the identity of important state officials. It was further alleged that Shcharansky gave the information to Robert Toth, who was a journalist and an operative of the Central Intelligence Agency and took orders from Vitaly Rubin another intelligence agent of the Americans, who had emigrated to Israel. Dr Lipavsky, who in the past had helped many refuseniks, had become a Soviet agent; and in his evidence before the court, he told them about a letter from Rubin to Shcharansky which was delivered to Moscow in an American diplomatic bag and which was handed by him to the KGB. There was also a questionnaire composed by Rubin's wife again delivered in a diplomatic bag.[487]

According to the prosecution, Shcharansky helped to arrange conspiratorial meetings between Toth and Soviet scientists. Zapylyaeva, a typist, was called to prove the lists of individuals refused exit visas and a caretaker Zakharov likewise had to give evidence about a photocopy of a partially complete list of refuseniks found by him in Toth's dustbin. It was also alleged that Shcharansky fabricated material to denigrate the Soviet system, sending it overseas by means of journalists and Zionist emissaries as well as through his many telephone conversations with Michael

---

[487] The Trial of Shcharansky pp.42-5 in A Chronicle of Current Events Nr. 50 (London,1979). Natan Sharansky, Fear No Evil. (London,1988),pp.12-13 and 21. Martin Gilbert, Shcharansky, pp.168-72.

Sherbourne. Shcharansky was said to have been the author of letters, telegrams, and memoranda which discredited the Soviet regime and which he utilised to advise outside powers to put pressure on the USSR to change its policies. It was alleged that his activities led Congress to adopt the Jackson-Vanik Amendment which undermined the attempt by the Soviet Union to acquire the most favoured nation trade status. Among the foreign visitors with whom Shcharansky was said to have conspired was Richard Pipes, an eminent American historian of Russia, and Senator Brooke. Vladimir Riabsky was called as a prosecution witness to prove this point.[488]

Among the other prosecution witnesses called to give secret evidence was Leonid Tsypin, who had been refused an exit visa to Israel in 1972 and hung around refusenik circles until he was revealed as a spy. A few months after Dr Lipavsky came out as a government informer, the Moscow evening newspaper of 17 May 1977 disclosed that there was another agent of the authorities in refusenik circles, Leonid Tsypin. He denounced foreign anti-Soviet organizations, including Zionist ones, which he claimed had instructed him to collect evidence of the absence of rights for Jews in the Soviet Union and the infringement of human rights.' 'International Zionism like any manifestation of racism, like Nazism', he declared, 'is alien and hostile to all Soviet people, including Soviet Jews'. Although the evidence was given in secret because of the importance which it was invested with, Tsypin spoke only in general terms and the secrecy was a sham.[489]

The second charge against Shcharansky was under article 70 of the Russian criminal code that of preparing and sending material abroad which defamed the Soviet political and social system. Reactionary circles abroad utilised this material to undermine Soviet foreign policy initiatives and to put pressure on the USSR to change its internal policies. He was accused of having acted as the link between the Zionists and foreign journalists. His activities with the

[488] The Trial of Shcharansky in A Chronicle of Events, pp.42-7.
[489] Martin Gilbert, Shcharansky pp.196-7 and 241.

Moscow Helsinki group were condemned because of the documents he signed and sent overseas to generate publicity. Hostile publishing houses and radio stations overseas were said to have disseminated the material which Shcharansky provided. Two British television documentaries, 'A Calculated Risk' and 'The Man Who Went Too Far', with which Shcharansky was associated, were included in the indictment under this section.[490]

Dr Lipavsky played a pivotal role in the attempt by the Soviet authorities to ensnare Shcharanksy. As a physician, he became deeply involved with evaluating the medical condition of refuseniks, who went on hunger-strike, and wheedled his way into a friendship with Professor Vitaly Rubin, a refusenik leader until he emigrated to Israel. He was frequently invited to the Rubins' home, where he met foreign visitors and made Shcharansky's acquaintance. Robert Toth speculated that Lipavsky became an informant in 1973 to secure the release of his father from prison, others thought this change of allegiance might have come about later. According to his own account, he applied to emigrate to Israel in 1974. In January 1977 he suggested to Shcharansky that they find a room together in the middle of Moscow and helped him move his belongings there. At this juncture Shcharansky was heavily engaged with his work for the Moscow Helsinki Group which was under siege by the authorities, so he rarely slept at home, preferring to spend the night with friends. At the end of February 1977, Lipavsky disappeared without warning, before resurfacing in the *Izvestia* article on 4 March 1977, revealing that he was a KGB agent. A few months later President Carter confirmed that Shcharansky had never had any relationship with the Central Intelligence Agency. On 7 March 1978, Washington announced that after offering his services, Lipavsky had been recruited as a CIA agent for nine months in 1975; evidently, we now know that he was a double agent, while Shcharansky had never been on the agency's books.

---

[490] The Trial of Shcharansky, pp.47-9.

However, becoming suspicious of Lipavsky, the CIA rapidly dispensed with his services.[491]

Unable to gain permission to visit her son in prison, Shcharansky's mother Ida Milgrom sought the services of Dina Kaminskaya one of the best lawyers for political cases to defend Anatoly. On applying to the Moscow College of Soviet Advocates to seek their consent, Kaminskaya was more or less expelled from the college. Within six months, she and her husband, another fearless legal campaigner, were expelled from the Soviet Union. Shcharansky's mother and Dina Beilin approached over thirty lawyers to take on his case but without success.[492] Meanwhile, in the summer of 1977 Mark Azbel and Benjamin Fain and two former Prisoners of Zion were allowed to emigrate to Israel, to be followed on 22 March 1978 by two activists close to Shcharansky, Dina and Iosif Beilin. Other stalwart friends of Shcharansky, Vladimir Slepak and Ida Nudel, were arrested and on 21 June 1978 at separate trials she was sentenced to four years exile in Siberia and Slepak to five years.[493] Brezhnev and his associates, notably Andropov, seemed determined to demolish the leadership of the Jewish cultural revival in the Soviet Union, by allowing some to depart to Israel and by imprisoning or exiling others.

Defying his interrogator, Shcharansky survived his ordeal in prison while awaiting trial by making him feel uncomfortable and suspicious that his victim was receiving help from an outside source. Reflecting on this, Shcharansky admitted to his mother that 'I knew I was clever. But I did not know I was so clever'. His morale was further boosted by seeing the Granada television film, 'The Man Who Went Too Far', which the Soviet authorities had to disclose as part of their evidence in his criminal prosecution. He insisted on seeing it three times because one scene showed his wife Avital campaigning on his

---

[491] The Trial of Shcharansky, p.49. Martin Gilbert, Shcharansky pp.177-8 and 225-6.
[492] Martin Gilbert, Shcharansky pp. 200 and 209-10.
[493] Martin Gilbert, Shcharansky pp. 205 and 226-8.

behalf outside the Soviet embassy in London which boosted his morale.[494] He also had the most appalling and grating voice and was inclined to sing loudly to irritate his captors. Although he was offered the services of a court-appointed defence lawyer, S.A. Dubrovskaya, Shcharansky turned this down and was allowed to conduct his own defence. From this procedure, Shcharansky felt some assurance that he was not facing the death penalty for espionage because, if the accused faced such an outcome, he was obliged to be defended by a lawyer.[495]

The prosecution opened their case, after which the lengthy indictment was read to the court and which covered much of the same ground. Shcharansky did not deny his involvement with the documents which were produced in court, the lists of refuseniks and the material put out by Moscow Helsinki Group, even when his participation was marginal. In fact, the manuscript lists of refuseniks were compiled and collated by Dina Beilin, who handed them to Lipavsky to arrange the typing; and that is why the Soviet authorities granted her an exit permit to leave for Israel before the trial, as they wanted all the responsibility for compiling the lists of refuseniks to be placed on Shcharansky's head. He denied that these documents fell under article 64-A of the criminal code, espionage. He pleaded not guilty to such a charge which in any case he deemed to be absurd.[496] Reference was made to a list of 1,300 refuseniks mentioned in an article by the journalist Robert Toth, thereby allegedly exposing the existence of locations where secret work was carried out in the Soviet Union. In fact, most of the individuals refused exit permits were employed at places where no secret work was undertaken. Toth ridiculed the secrecy barrier to emigration. All his information was derived from a briefing session with Dina Beilin, who had conveniently been supplied with an exit visa four months earlier, while

---

[494] Martin Gilbert, Shcharansky pp. 198-9 and 215-16.

[495] The Trial of Shcharansky, pp.42-3.

[496] The Trial of Shcharansky, pp.52 and 54. Martin Gilbert, Shcharansky p.235.

Shcharansky had little to do with the composition of the article. It was alleged that Vitaly Rubin, who had emigrated to Israel, had sent Shcharansky a letter advising him to collect and hand over espionage material. No such letter had ever been dispatched, but during his interrogation Shcharansky briefly caught sight of such a letter of doubtful authenticity addressed to Dr Lipavsky.[497]

Shcharansky in his defence asserted that the Soviet Union having ratified the International Covenant on Civil and Political Rights and other human rights treaties should have brought its own legal code into conformity with these obligations. Because of their failure to do so, a number of anomalies had arisen. There was no emigration law setting out the rules in a coherent fashion and the system was operated in an arbitrary fashion. When the refuseniks had raised this issue with Albert Ivanov, a high-ranking Communist party official in 1976, he replied that there would never be a new emigration law. But this had resulted in numerous hardships for those applying to emigrate which was regarded in any case as an act of treachery; and Shcharansky castigated the system of emigration by invitation only as being wrong. The causes of emigration were religious, cultural, economic and the rising antisemitism induced by Stalin's nationalities policy. Another reason spurring emigration was that there were no Jewish cultural centres in the Soviet Union. In the Jewish autonomous region of Birobidjan, there was not a single school where Yiddish was spoken, and the teaching of Hebrew was forbidden everywhere. The present nationalities policy was a 'reversion to the times of Stalin'. Although he wanted the book by Vladimir Begun, *The Creeping Counter-Revolution* to be submitted as evidence of antisemitism, this was refused by the court. He asserted that the book could be compared to antisemitic tracts published in Tsarist times and under the Nazis, particularly the Protocols of the Elders of Zion. He reiterated that Zionism was the belief of those who wanted to live in Israel

---

[497] Martin Gilbert, Shcharansky p.234.

or considered it to be their native land. In this sense, he was a Zionist. During the war, the Jewish Anti-Fascist Committee had raised huge sums from Jewish communities abroad; why was it wrong now for Soviet Jews to communicate with Jews overseas?[498]

The lists of refuseniks had been compiled before he was involved with the emigration problem and there was nothing secret about them. He had been accused of falsifying the signatures of individuals, who signed collective documents. Shcharansky explained that when this appeared to be the case, the text of the document and the signatures had been copied in one hand by 'the person who made a fair copy of the statement'. The debate on the Jackson Amendment had begun in Congress in 1972 before he had applied to emigrate to Israel and before he was associated with the emigration issue. So too, his contact with foreigners was far from being conspiratorial and one meeting with senators and congressmen had taken place in the foyer of a hotel. As far as trade and the Jackson Amendment were concerned, he had always opted for compromise which would have been 'beneficial to the Soviet Union'.[499]

The prosecutor then questioned Shcharansky about his visit to the village of Ilyinka. In the early nineteenth century, many of the inhabitants of three villages had converted to Judaism; two of these villages had assimilated completely, while Ilyanka held firm, though under official pressure to abandon Judaism. Shcharansky met a number of Ilyinka Jews outside the Moscow Synagogue, who told him that a number of their neighbours had applied to emigrate to Israel. When Matveev heard that the collective farm chairman was holding back 120 invitations to emigrate to Israel, he challenged him about this. To which the chairman replied, 'We don't want you to go to the Zionists. We hate you'. In June 1976, Shcharansky, Slepak

---

[498] The Trial of Shcharansky, pp.54-5. Martin Gilbert, Shcharansky pp.235-6.
[499] The Trial of Shcharansky, pp.55-6. Martin Gilbert, Shcharansky pp.236-7.

and Dr Lipavsky set out for the village of Ilyinka to investigate the emigration situation. Several kilometres from the village they were stopped by police, interrogated for two days and expelled from the area. Nonetheless, Shcharansky and others discovered that there were sixty refusenik families living in the village and ensured that the Moscow Helsinki Group took up their cause, which was also publicised by Robert Toth in the *Los Angeles Times*. The Prosecutor asked Shcharansky whether he had ever visited the village of Ilyinka and he explained that he had not reached it because he had been detained by the police. Despite the evidence produced by the prosecution of four persons from the local collective farm, who did not wish to leave the Soviet Union, Shcharansky told the court he knew that there were seventy persons from Ilyinka who still wished to emigrate.[500]

With regard to document 8, the prosecutor chided Shcharansky that it was unethical to mention the names of sick people in public. Shcharansky responded by stating that this was not the case and by reading some of the medical notes which stated that Leonid Plyushch 'suffers from mania of reformism, needs further treatment' and Sivak shows 'No traces left of emigration mania. Suitable for discharge'. As regards the Moscow Helsinki Group's documents concerning the prisons and camps, Shcharansky declared that the information had been obtained from the prisoners or their relatives. In addition, Shcharansky had now acquired first-hand experience of the conditions in punishment cells. The prosecutor now challenged Shcharansky on the document concerning the lessons from the trials of Malkin and Roitburd. This brought up the contentious issue of whether or not refuseniks should be called up to serve in the army if they were dismissed from their education course or employment. Shcharansky retorted that Malkin's emigration application had resulted in his being expelled from the Institute, where he worked, and being called up in the army, which seemed on the face

---

[500] Martin Gilbert, Shcharansky pp.126 and 237. The Trial of Shcharansky, p.56.

of it to be unfair. When he raised this point with Albert
Ivanov, a member of the Central Committee, he said that
this policy would continue to be enforced, but the court
refused a request by Shcharansky to call Ivanov as a
witness. [501]

A lengthy dispute began on Shcharansky's marital
status, as the court claimed that there were documents
before it which showed he was a bachelor, though he had
married Natalya Shtiglits (Avital Shcharansky) according
to Jewish rites. Rabbi Fishman of the Moscow Synagogue
had asked the Supreme rabbinic authorities in Israel to
annul the marriage because Avital's mother was not Jewish
and they had not married in a synagogue. Shcharansky
objected that these points had already been fully dealt with
and that his marriage certificate (Ketubah) had been signed
by a leading religious authority, Girsh Manevich, but the
court refused to call him as a witness. In any case, his
marital status was a private matter, Shcharansky observed,
not the concern of the court.[502]

After losing his job at the Institute of Oil and Gas,
Shcharansky worked three years as an English teacher and
was attacked by the prosecutor for not paying any taxes.
Shcharansky said that he had tried to pay taxes but that his
payments had been rejected. The prosecutor further
criticised Shcharansky for deceiving the Soviet authorities,
by assisting people to emigrate who did not have relatives
outside. Shcharansky replied that the Soviet system of
emigration insisted on people having 'close relatives' in
Israel, thus stripping them of rights recognized by the
Universal Declaration of Human Rights.[503]

On the 11 July 1978, and the following morning, the
court went into a closed session to hear the espionage
charge. Dr Lipavsky and Leonid Tsypin were called to
prove the charge, giving evidence corresponding to the
details which had already appeared in the newspaper

---

[501] The Trial of Shcharansky, pp.56-7. Martin Gilbert, Shcharansky
pp.236-7.
[502] The Trial of Shcharansky, p.57. Martin Gilbert, Shcharansky p.238
[503] Martin Gilbert, Shcharansky p.239.

articles. Their testimonies were reinforced by those of Ryabsky, an acquaintance of Vitaly Rubin, the academic expert on Chinese philosophy, and Raslin, an ex-refusenik; and Pyotr Adamsky, who had posed as a refusenik for several years, later testified that he had taken a list of Vilnius refuseniks to Moscow, though he had been told that it would be sent abroad to show the fictitious nature of 'refusals on security grounds'. Vitaly Rubin's wife Ina alerted other refuseniks to Ryabsky's dubious status, because although a Communist party member, he had spoken about inviting Richard Pipes, an American academic, to his home, an invitation which was almost immediately withdrawn under suspicious circumstances. Ryabsky claimed that Pipes was an American agent and suggested to Shcharansky in the Rubins' home that the refuseniks should unite with the Soviet dissidents under the umbrella of the Helsinki Final Act on July 4 1975, but the Final Act was enacted a month later and therefore no such conversation could have taken place earlier. When this was put to him, Ryabsky switched the time of the meeting to July 1976. Zapylyaeva testified that she had typed the lists of refuseniks at the request of Dr Lipavsky, but she agreed when Shcharansky questioned her that he had never asked her for any assistance. Two witnesses were called to confirm that they owned the apartments where Shcharansky had telephone conversations with Michael Sherbourne. One admitted that she was in the kitchen for the duration of these calls, presumably hearing little, the other claimed that she heard Shcharansky dictating names over the telephone. Dealing with the material evidence, the court examined the previously mentioned letter of Vitaly Rubin and the questionnaire provided by his wife and Shcharansky's notebooks which contained the full names of fifteen refuseniks. An expert was called to prove that the refusenik lists contained state secrets and that the questionnaire, if completed, would have held highly secret data. It was further alleged that Shcharansky had criminal ties to foreigners, who were connected with intelligence services.[504]

On 12 July, once the closed session had ended, a number of witnesses gave evidence in open court and at Shcharansky's insistence Dr Lipavsky, Ryabsky and Tsypin were recalled. A neighbour of Lidia Voronina, Irina Susikhina, testified that Robert Toth, the journalist, had visited Voronina's apartment several times and on one occasion she saw Shcharansky hand him a text of 30 to 40 pages. But when Shcharansky asked her whether or not she saw what was written on the pages, she answered no. Dr L. Sukhacheva, a doctor at Vladimir prison, where Shcharansky and Orlov had been detained, gave evidence to prove that conditions there were satisfactory. She cited the example of a prisoner called Fedorenko, but document 17 showed that he had lost a considerable amount of weight and had symptoms of paralysis. She declared that the food there 'was, of course, not caviar, neither the black nor the red variety', but 'it was sufficient and of good quality'. A medical orderly, who was employed in one of the Perm region labour camps, claimed that the temperature in the punishment cells there was 18-24 degrees centigrade, a reasonable temperature. Vyacheslav Platonov could not understand his role at the present trial, as he was not acquainted with Shcharansky but knew Ginzburg. He noted that the medical conditions and food in his camp were 'OK, bearable'. In fact, he had been mistakenly brought by the police to the wrong trial.[505]

Abramov, the deputy manager of a canning factory and a mountain Jew, was called, as he had made speeches denouncing Zionism. In answer to a question posed by the Judge, he replied that before the war there were Jewish schools, but they had all closed since no one wanted to study in them. Colonel Yefim Davidovich's daughter, Sonya Gaskova, who had returned to the Soviet Union after

---

[504] The Trial of Shcharansky, pp.58-9. Martin Gilbert, Shcharansky p.241. Natan Sharansky, Fear No Evil pp.202-4.
[505] The Trial of Shcharansky, p.59. Martin Gilbert, Shcharansky p. 241-2, 243 and 245.

making an unsuccessful attempt to settle in Israel, was called as a state witness because at the pre-trial investigation she had highlighted the poor quality of life there. Colonel Davidovich was one of several Minsk Jewish officers, including Lev Ovischer and Naum Alshensky, who applied to emigrate to Israel, but Davidovich died of a heart attack before he was allowed to leave.[506] Gaskova was in a distressed state refusing to answer some questions which Shcharansky put to her, while the Judge overruled other questions, but she refused to incriminate him.[507]

Ryabsky claimed that Professor Richard Pipes had advised Shcharansky to found the Helsinki Watch Group and again repeated that the discrepancy in dates about when the meeting between Richard Pipes and Shcharansky had taken place could be easily answered – it was 4 July 1976. Shcharansky pointed out to him that the meeting could not have taken place in Rubin's home then because in 1976 Vitaly Rubin was living in Israel and Richard Pipes was in the United States.[508] Tsypin declared that Shcharansky was a frequent letter writer, that he collected signatures in favour of the Jackson Amendment, and instructed senators to take a hard line on the amendment. He accused Shcharansky of writing the Malkin and Roitburd letter about being conscripted into the army in an attempt to embarrass the French and Italian party delegates at a Congress of the Soviet Communist party. His conspiratorial meetings took place at a cafe on Kutuzov Prospect, he claimed. But when Shcharansky questioned him about his direct knowledge of what was happening at the Kutuzov cafe, Tsypin admitted that he did not have any direct knowledge but had heard about the meetings from other people – useless hearsay evidence.

According to Tsypin, Shcharansky and his associates wanted to found an organization called 'Sherut Aliya' to encourage emigration. Dr Lipavsky repeated Tsypin's

---

[506] Colin Shindler communication to the author 23 December 2019.

[507] The Trial of Shcharansky, p.60.

[508] Natan Sharansky, Fear No Evil pp.206-7.

evidence about the Malkin and the Roitburd letter. There was a lengthy digression on Dr Lipavsky's part about the film 'A Calculated Risk', of which he declared Shcharansky was the director, commentator and star. He claimed to have taken Shcharansky and Slepak to the Rossiya collective farm to deliver invitations from the American embassy to hasten the emigration of individuals from Ilinka. Shcharansky was on friendly terms with Levitsky and Presel, secretaries at the embassy, who were CIA agents. During the cross-examination session, these three witnesses were evasive, muddled dates and figures and sometimes did not answer questions. At the pre-trial investigation, Lipavsky stated that he was present at a meeting with Senator Brooke, when he brought a draft letter from Senator Jackson to refuseniks, but when questioned now admitted that this was not the case.[509]

On the morning of 13 July 1978, the court proceeded to examine the documents placed before it. First produced were Vitaly Rubin's letter with instructions to Shcharansky and the questionnaire for refuseniks with a note on the back ascribed by a handwriting expert to Ina Rubin. Then there was Dr Lipavsky's statement concerning his enrolment in the CIA and testimony from the Soviet Ministry of Foreign Affairs as to why Robert Toth had been detained after his meeting with Petukhov. Shchransky responded that the first time he saw the questionnaire was at the pre-trial investigation and, despite a plea, he was not allowed to question Petukhov, whose evidence was heard in a closed session. The court next reviewed the lists of refuseniks which were used as evidence to charge Shcharansky under articles 64-A and 70 of the criminal code. A carbon paper allegedly found in Shcharansky's apartment which seemed to bear the same imprints as the lists found in the courtyard of the property, where Robert Toth lived, was produced, but Shcharansky replied that the first time he had glimpsed at this document was during the court proceedings. Shcharansky rejected the notion that his letter of 13 January

---

[509] The Trial of Shcharansky, pp.60-3.

1976 was written at the instigation of Senator Jackson. The prosecutor then put in as evidence the Soviet documentary, 'Purveyors of Souls', which attacked the refusenik movement, and as Shcharansky suggested attracted antisemitic fan mail; and the British television documentary, 'A Calculated Risk', in which Shcharansky's role was exaggerated and his comments misunderstood or distorted. To these items were added correspondence from the Davidoviches from Israel and a number of foreign currency transfers to Shcharansky between 1973 and 1974 totalling 500 foreign currency roubles.[510]

The summing up at the end of the trial began with the prosecutor making a three-hour speech to the court dwelling on Shcharansky's guilt to the applause of an audience packed with government supporters, who interjected the comment from time to time of 'Quite Right!' He condemned the accused not only for his hostile attitude but for his ongoing contact with journalists and diplomats opposed to the Soviet Union. The prosecution found 'premeditation and the presence of intent to undermine the military power of the USSR absolutely clear in Shcharansky's actions'. He asked for a sentence of 15 years' imprisonment in strict-regime camps, the first three years of which to be served in prison.[511]

Shcharansky began by saying that 'I am fully aware that it is an utterly hopeless task to defend myself in this semi-open court with its specially selected audience. All the more so when you consider that I was accused in the official press – the newspaper *Izvestia* – one and a half years before the trial, ten days before my arrest and even a week before a case against me was opened. My social activities were transformed into class ones, and my open activities as a supplier of information were turned into treason and espionage. I have no doubt that the court will support the Procurator's [prosecutor's] demand'.[512]

---

[510] The Trial of Shcharansky, pp.63-4.
[511] The Trial of Shcharansky, pp.64-5.
[512] The Trial of Shcharansky, p.65.

From these generalities, Shcharansky proceeded to observe that all human life did 'not consist solely... of various economic systems in the modern world' and focussed on the national rebirth of the Jewish people. Zionism was born in the aftermath of the Dreyfus affair. Events witnessed by Soviet Jews, such as the foundation of the state of Israel and the alleged 'Doctor's Plot', had made some of them wish to emigrate to Israel. During the 1950s growing national awareness among Jews had landed enthusiasts in prison or labour camps, but during the 1960s the emigration movement had developed. All of his own activities were connected to this emigration movement.[513]

Dealing with the espionage charge and the Senator Brooke episode, Shcharansky showed that Dr Lipavsky's evidence was worthless, as his chronology was completely muddled. In addition, Senator Brooke was a Republican and would not have assisted Senator Jackson's campaign, as he was a Democrat. Shcharansky admitted that he had met the historian Richard Pipes and discussed his book on Peter Struve, but Rybasky had invented what had transpired between them; and again his chronology was flawed and should be discounted. Dr Lipavsky had stated that he and Professor Rubin had tried to persuade Miles, an American diplomat, to stop grain supplies to the Soviet Union, when it was his own view that it would be wrong to discontinue such supplies. 'Shcharansky said that material `clues' – the carbon paper handed in by Lipavsky, the fragment of a list found by the caretaker Zakharov, and the questionnaire with a note from Rubin's wife – contained nothing written in his own hand, and that the first time he saw them was during the investigation'. Nor had he ever given Zapylayeva material to type either directly or indirectly through Dr Lipavsky. Touching on Robert Toth's article 'Soviet Union Indirectly Reveals Centres of Secret Work', Shcharansky said it was based on information personally supplied by refuseniks for transmission for open use in the West. Moreover, Robert Toth's evidence at the

[513] The Trial of Shcharansky, p.65.

251

pre-trial investigation showed many discrepancies between the Russian and the English translation, rendering it useless, but this has not prevented its use in the indictment. Dealing with the charge under article 70, Shcharansky considered it immoral to be facing a criminal charge for defending others. There was nothing amiss with the Helsinki Group documents, and so far as the Pentecostal believers were concerned, he had found them to be honest and open.[514]

In his closing remarks, Shcharansky stated that the chief investigators warned him that because of the position he had adopted he could face the death penalty or fifteen years in prison. But that if he cooperated with them in destroying the Jewish emigration movement, he would be given a short sentence, released quickly and would have the chance of meeting his wife. Five years ago he had applied to emigrate to Israel and was no nearer his dream but he did not regret what had happened.[515]

'I am glad that I have lived honestly, at peace with my conscience, and have not acted against it, even when threatened with death. I am glad that I have helped people. I am glad that I have come to know and have worked with such honest and brave people as Sakharov, Orlov and Ginzburg – people who are carrying on the traditions of the Russian intelligentsia. I am glad that I am a witness to the rebirth of the Jews of the USSR. I hope that the absurd charges against me and the whole Jewish emigration movement will not hinder the liberation of my people. My family and friends know that I wanted to exchange my work as an emigration activist for life in Israel with my wife.'

'My people have been scattered for more than 2,000 years, but wherever Jews have wandered they have always repeated the words: `Next year in Jerusalem!' Now that I am further than ever from my people and from Avital, and

[514] The Trial of Shcharansky pp.66-7.
[515] The Trial of Shcharansky, p.67.

many hard years in prison stretch ahead of me, I say to my people and to my Avital: `Next year in Jerusalem!".[516]

Shcharansky was sentenced to 13 years imprisonment, the first three years to be served in prison, the rest in strict-regime camps. The courtroom crammed with supporters of the authorities erupted into applause at the pronouncement of the verdict and shouted, 'He ought to be hanged'. Throughout the hearing, only Anatoly's brother Leonid was permitted to attend the hearing but not the closed sessions, though his mother went to the court every day her entrance was barred. Numerous diplomats and journalists, who requested permission to attend the trial, were similarly excluded. Shcharansky's friends were corralled into a side street, guarded by police and vigilantes at both ends. In August 1978 Shcharansky was taken to Vladimir prison to begin his sentence.[517]

The Trials of Vladimir and Masha Slepak and Ida Nudel

Among the other refuseniks detained and subsequently tried after Shcharansky's arrest were his mentor Vladimir Slepak and friend Ida Nudel. Lauded as a 'modern Moses', Vladimir Slepak was perhaps the central figure in the campaign for the liberation of Soviet Jewry. He was born into an old Bolshevik family. His father was a true believer, discounting the Nazi-Soviet Pact (1939) and the Doctor's Plot (1953), and naming his son after Lenin and his daughter after Rosa Luxemburg. His mother Fenya was descended from an ancient rabbinic dynasty.

Slepak graduated from Moscow's Aviation Institute as an engineer in 1950 and was employed in an Electro-Lamp factory, which produced military equipment, before moving to another classified research centre. Here he met Masha, who was trained as a doctor but also came from an assimilated Jewish family. Encountering virulent antisemitism in Stalin's final years, their spirits were emboldened by Israel's victory in the 1967 Six Day War, giving them the courage to start leading a Jewish life.

---

[516] The Trial of Shcharansky, p.67.
[517] The Trial of Shcharansky, pp.68-9.

Despite breaking diplomatic relations with the Jewish state after the war, the Soviet Union started permitting a few families to leave for Israel in 1968. Soon the Slepaks began mixing with like-minded young people determined to emigrate and they were given the task of photocopying the first Zionist periodical, *Iton,* which was distributed throughout the USSR. They applied to leave for Israel with their two sons, Leonid and Sanya, in April 1970. They were finally given permission to do so on 14 October 1987. In between the couple were subjected to harassment, frequent raids on their apartment, and Vladimir without employment was arrested ten times. To secure the necessary exit permits, they divorced in 1976, but were still refused. They were told by Andrei Verein, the head of the Moscow visa office, that they were lucky to escape with their lives, and who exclaimed 'Twenty years ago we would have shot you'. Unwavering in their determination, their home became a vibrant hub, where refuseniks and foreign visitors met, and Vladimir spoke on the telephone to activists overseas about the latest phases of the struggle.[518]

On the morning of 1 June 1978, the block of flats where Vladimir Slepak and his wife Masha lived was blockaded. At 4pm, they hung placards from their eighth-floor apartment facing Gorky Street, saying 'Let us go to our son in Israel'. Their eldest son had been allowed to leave, but not their youngest son. A short while later the placards were removed by boat hooks wielded from the flat below. The Slepaks responded by making some fresh placards. Then they were attacked with poles by plain clothes police officers from an adjacent flat, while scalding water was poured on Vladimir's head from the flat above. Eventually, some plain clothes policemen broke down the front door and burst onto the balcony. They allowed the Slepaks time to change their wet clothes and arrested them. A similar police operation took place in the block of flats where Ida Nudel, another prominent refusenik, lived.[519]

---

[518] JC 29 May 2015 p.43 and 15 September 2017 p.22.
[519] A Chronicle of Current Events Nr.50 (1979), p.93.

254

Coordinating her moves with the Slepaks, Ida Nudel went out went out on the balcony of her apartment on 1 June 1978 at six in the evening with a banner displaying the words 'KGB! Give me a Visa!'. Some secret policemen stationed on an adjoining balcony knocked down the placard and hurled stones at her. To stop them, she doused them with water from a bucket which she had ready. Undeterred, Ida went inside and wrote a fresh slogan for the banner on her balcony and also inserted a placard in her kitchen window. Prepared for such an eventuality, the secret police, who had been blockading her flat all day, reached out with a rod with hooks from an adjoining apartment and tore large pieces from her placard on the balcony. A rope with a spanner was lowered from the flat above and swung until it broke her kitchen window. Becoming ever more determined in this confrontation, Ida filled her kitchen window with a piece of cardboard and drew a Star of David on it and placed a new placard on the balcony. At 7.30 pm the policemen went away and later that night Ida removed the placards.[520]

In the evening of June 2 a group of refuseniks, including among others Ida Nudel, Iosif Begun and his wife Alla Drugova, and Leonid Shcharansky, gathered in Pushkin Square to go to the police station to ascertain what had happened to the Slepaks. Here in the square they were surrounded by plain clothes policemen and herded onto a bus. They were taken to a police office, where all the detainees were released, except Ida Nudel. She was then driven to a police station and was informed that she would be charged with 'malicious hooliganism' under article 206, part 2 of the Russian criminal code. She was escorted home to enable a search to be made of her flat, where some placards, paint brushes, books and private papers were removed. Despite this mauling at the hands of the police, Nudel was undeterred and on 4 June and again on 9 June 1978 she went out demonstrating with the Katz family, who wanted to go to the United States for treatment of their

---

[520] A Chronicle of Current Events Nr.50, pp.92-3.

eight months year old daughter, who was gravely ill. They held placards, demanding 'Let us go to Israel!' and 'Let our children go!' On the second occasion, plain clothes police officers confiscated the placards, at the same time yelling 'You've had it too good eating Soviet bread!' 'Traitors!' 'Zionists!' 'Stinking Yids!' 'Hitler didn't kill enough of you!' 'Stalin didn't slaughter enough of you!' Ida Nudel was warned that her action had caused a crowd of 150 persons to gather on the pavement which could have resulted in an accident.[521]

On 21 June 1978, Ida Nudel appeared in court charged with the offence of hooliganism for incidents on 1 June at her apartment and for another one four days later, when she demonstrated on Trubnaya Square in Moscow. In an earlier statement to the authorities, Nudel stated that she had applied to emigrate because of the extreme antisemitism she encountered after 1948. 'Throughout my conscious life, and most of all after I left the Institute, I have been confronted at work, in the street, in newspapers and books, with open hatred, contempt, slander and refined forms of degradation of my national dignity'. She explained subsequently that she had been trying to emigrate for seven years and had not been engaged in any secret work projects. In her final speech to the court, Nudel declared that out of desperation, because her desire to leave went unfulfilled, she decided to protest publicly. 'During these seven years I have learned to walk with my head held high – as a person and as a Jew. These seven years of my life have been filled with struggle, for myself as well as for others. And each time I managed to save the life of another victim [of imprisonment for their beliefs], my heart was filled with an extraordinary feeling, one that has no equal. Perhaps it is akin to what a woman feels after giving birth to a new life. Even if the rest of my life is grey and monotonous, none of you, my judges, can think up a retribution which will gain you revenge for my victorious triumph of these seven years'.[522]

---

[521] A Chronicle of Current Events Nr.50, pp.93-5.
[522] A Chronicle of Current Events Nr. 50, pp.95-100.

On the same day, 21 June, Vladimir Slepak appeared in a People's Court in Moscow charged with a similar offence to Ida Nudel – hooliganism. Masha Slepak was in hospital at the time and had earlier tried to make several interventions to the authorities on her husband's behalf. No other relative or friend was allowed into the court. The prosecutor declared that when a police officer from an adjacent flat tried to take down a placard with a provocative inscription, Slepak grabbed the pole he was wielding, following this up by making threatening gestures and shouting. By his actions, Slepak interrupted the flow of traffic and caused a crowd to gather at both ends of the street, resulting in a disturbance. Vladimir Slepak pleaded not guilty, admitting that he displayed the placards to obtain specific action from various state administrative bodies. His was not an act of hooliganism, but merely an attempt to publicise his cause. For this occurrence, he was sentenced to 5 years internal exile and his appeal was rejected.[523]

On 26 July 1978, Masha appeared in court in a delayed hearing because she had been ill with pancreatitis and heart pains. She denied that she or her husband had indulged in any acts of hooliganism. Proud and defiant to the end, she read a prepared statement to the court: 'In 1970 my family – my husband Vladimir Slepak and two of our children – in accordance with the established legal procedure, handed in an application to go to our relatives in Israel. We received a refusal. Since then we have applied to all the official Soviet departments for permission to emigrate to Israel, where my mother, my son and my sister live'.

'Early in the morning of 1 June this year, some persons unknown to me who had driven up to the entrance of our building at 12 pm the night before in a car with government number plates, fastened our door so that it was impossible for us to leave the building. Driven to despair, my husband Vladimir Slepak and I made a placard saying

---

[523] A Chronicle of Current Events Nr.50, pp.100-2.

`Let us go to our son in Israel' and went out onto the balcony of our flat. I have no doubt that the fate of our family has been decided in advance, and that those of you in the courtroom have only to formalize this decision in a sentence, thus adding new torments to our family's eight years of suffering. For the reasons just given I refuse to take part in this trial. I request that this statement be filed'. Because she had not committed any previous offences, she was given a three-year suspended sentence.[524] But she chose to join her husband in internal exile on a collective farm in Siberia, where he worked as a mechanic.

The Trial of Iosif Begun

Another leading refusenik tried at this time was Iosif Begun, who was one of four Soviet Jews personally 'singled out for attack' in the 1977 television film 'Traders of Souls'. In a letter of protest, Begun offered a robust critique of the film, stating that 'the film persistently suggests to viewers that the Jewish emigrants are not harmless people, but rather that they are betraying their true homeland and are leaving for a State which has only one goal: aggression (on the screen one sees smoke and ashes, bombing and devastation); and the main consequence of this aggression is the murder of children (on the screen one sees disfigured bodies of murdered children)'. The film proposed that the imprisoned Jews were not 'prisoners of conscience', but `hooligans and speculators receiving a just punishment' for having received money from Zionist organizations, pursuing underground `anti-Soviet activity', and meeting American Congressmen, Israeli athletes `and other Zionist agents'. The long film 'leaves the viewer with a deep impression. Its anti-Zionist and anti-Israeli thrust cannot

---

[524] A Chronicle of Current Events Nr.50, pp.102-4.

hide its anti-Jewish essence. An uninformed viewer gets the feeling of dislike and suspicion of all Jews. Those people who try to emigrate, or who get a refusal and try to defend their right to leave, are therefore put in a very difficult and dangerous situation'.[525]

On 17 May 1978, Begun was charged under article 198 of the Russian criminal code for infringing residency regulations, though he was not brought to trial until 28 June because he went on a 42-day hunger strike. In 1971 after applying to emigrate to Israel, he lost his job at the Moscow Engineering Institute, where he was doing post-doctoral research. For five years or more he gave lessons in Hebrew and Jewish culture without the interference of the authorities. But in 1977 he was charged under article 209 part 1 of the Russian criminal code with leading a parasitic way of life for a prolonged period, as teaching Hebrew was not a recognized profession, receiving a sentence of two years internal exile. As he had already been held in custody for a long period, his sentence came to an end on 15 February 1978 and he returned to Moscow. On 10 March 1978, his wife Alla Drugova applied to her local Moscow police station for her husband and father of her two children, Iosif Begun, to be registered as living at her flat. When her request was rebuffed, Iosif appealed to General Pashkovsky, who promised to look into the matter and meanwhile promised that no administrative sanctions would be levied against him. Various other appeals were circulated and on 29 May 1978 the Christian Committee for the Defence of Believers' rights issued a statement defending him.[526]

Meanwhile, Begun was arrested near the building where Dr Orlov was being tried and charged under article 198 of the Russian criminal code with infringing residency regulations. He was brought to trial at a Moscow court still in a semi-conscious state after his hunger strike and, despite requests for a doctor to be called and the trial to be postponed, the judge refused to accede to these requests

---

[525] Martin Gilbert, The Jews of Hope (New York,1985), pp.123-5.
[526] A Chronicle of Current Events Nr.50, pp.103-7.

and ordered that the trial should go ahead. Although extremely weak and shaky, Begun was made to stand by the judge, and when he collapsed, the judge ordered that he be handcuffed and he was lifted up by his handcuffs. For the offence of returning to Moscow to live with his wife, he was sentenced to three years internal exile. In 1981 Iosif divorced his second wife Alla Drugova and she and her son, whom he had adopted, were allowed to emigrate to Israel in 1981.[527]

The Times columnist Bernard Levin praised Begun for his moral rectitude and for the adoption of an intransigent attitude of ethical superiority, with which he out-flanked his Soviet critics. His two trials, suggested Levin, revealed that 'there were some twenty flagrant breaches of Soviet law or the constitution on the part of the authorities... Throughout all this, Iosif Begun has displayed a fortitude in adversity and a courage in resisting oppression that mark him as a truly exceptional being; to read through... a complete collection of the appeals, protests, statements he has sent to various individuals, journals and organizations in his own country and abroad is to catch a glimpse of the best that humanity can do and be. Again and again, it is not his own case he is pleading, but that of some fellow-sufferer or his persecuted people as a whole'.[528]

Sakharov argued that the main purpose of the dissident movement, of which the refuseniks were a vital component, was to change the political attitudes of the Soviet elite. 'Against all the odds', Christopher Andrew and Vasili Mitrokhin concluded, 'dissidents largely succeeded in fulfilling this mission. A small and persecuted minority, powerless save for the strength and courage of its convictions, only feebly supported by the West, defeated a determined campaign to silence them by the world's largest and most powerful security and intelligence service'.[529]

---

[527] A Chronicle of Current Events pp.107-8. Martin Gilbert, The Jews of Hope p.126.
[528] Martin Gilbert, The Jews of Hope p.126.
[529] Christopher Andrew and Vasili Mitrokhin, The Mitrokhin Archive pp.434-5.

Academician Sakharov and his wife Elena Bonner, Dr Orlov, and Anatoly Shcharansky as leaders of the dissident movement, did not falter unlike their predecessors; and when necessary, out-manoeuvred their KGB interrogators in the interminable closed sessions with their debating and polemical skills and in court showed that the cases against them were flimsy constructions, fatally flawed. Around them were a cadre of members of the intelligentsia, poets and scientists and refuseniks, who were brave enough to challenge the secret police and insist on their rights under international and national law codes. People such as Lyudmila Alexeyeva, Alexander Ginzburg, Zhores Medvedev and his brother Roy, Tatyana Velikanova and so on, the list is almost endless.[530] What stands out, though, is the way Anatoly Shcharansky championed the cause of human rights and his insistence at his trial in 1978 that Soviet law on the rights of its citizens to emigrate was subservient to the International Covenants on Civil and Political Rights and other human rights treaties which the Soviet Union had signed. After President Carter's espousal of human rights in 1977 and Shcharansky's own defiant use of them at his trial a year later, human rights featured more and more strongly in the discourse of Soviet Jewry campaigning groups and in the actions and speeches of the new Prime Minister, Margaret Thatcher.

---

[530] Ludmilla Alexeyeva and Paul Goldberg, The Thaw Generation (Boston,1990).Obituaries of Aleksandr Ginzburg The Times 23 July 2002, Zhores Medvedev 18 December 2018, and Tatyana Velikanova 30 October 2002.

Chapter 6 - The Dual Leadership Of Margaret Rigal and Rita Eker

Restructuring the British Soviet Jewry Campaign

As we have seen, Nehemiah Levanon in January 1978 advised British Soviet Jewry organizations to leave the political struggle to their American brethren, while they should concentrate their resources in campaigning for individual refuseniks and revitalizing Jewish culture in the Soviet Union. These pleas were listened to by the National Council in all respects and everyone else, as far as the problem of the drop-outs was concerned. Contention had arisen between the Israelis and the leaders of American Jewry, because as a wider and more secularly-orientated section of Soviet Jews demanded exit visas, as antisemitism mounted, their preferred destination became the United States. Eventually, the Americans and the Israelis came to an agreement on this subject. Meanwhile, Doreen Gainsford emigrated to Israel and a new leadership emerged in the Women's Campaign, their office was re-organized, and they utilised the language of human rights to attempt to exert political influence over the new Conservative Prime Minister, Margaret Thatcher, and through her over President Reagan. In Margaret Thatcher they found a kindred spirit who was sympathetic to their demands for increased emigration from a new low level in the early 1980s; and in the American Union of Councils, they had a radical ally with similar aims. Both groups baulked at the constraints placed on them by the official Jewish leadership, the National Council in Britain and the National Conference on Soviet Jewry in the United States. Moreover, the Women's Campaign gradually placed much less emphasis on disruptive protests and more on their political contacts with the government and officials.

After Soviet intervention in Afghanistan in 1979, relations with the West became frosty and Soviet Jewish emigration plummeted from 21,471 in 1980 to 914 in 1986.[531] The early 1980s were the bleakest years for dissidents and refuseniks in the Soviet Union, who were imprisoned or driven into exile by the KGB and the Jewish campaigners and their allies in the outside world sustained them through these grim years and gave them hope by visits and by expanding their cultural and educational efforts.

Rita Eker and Margaret Rigal
New Leaders of the Women's Campaign

---

[531] Pauline Peretz, Let My People Go. The Transnational Politics of Soviet Jewish Emigration during the Cold War p.344.

Michael Sherbourne
Translator Extraordinary with Shcharansky

When Doreen Gainsford stepped down as leader of the Women's Campaign for Soviet Jewry in 1978, she was replaced by the joint leadership of Margaret Rigal, Linda Isaacs and Rita Eker until Isaacs devoted most of her time to Exodus (a Reform Synagogue Soviet Jewry movement) and the National Council, leaving the control of the 35's to Rigal and Eker, who worked extremely closely together.[532] Mrs Eker also served as vice-chairman of the National Council for Soviet Jewry, the new umbrella organization, thereby introducing a degree of overall coordination into the campaigning. Margaret Rigal belonged to an old Anglo-Jewish family and was attached to the Liberal Synagogue, while Rita Eker was born in England but raised in South Africa and was a keen Zionist. Rigal has been described as charming and very English in manner by her colleague, the debonair Rita Eker.[533] The latter had an easy manner and was a brilliant letter writer, crafting her missives so that

---

[532] NA, FCO 28/3531 Doreen Gainsford to Lord Goronwy Roberts 8 February 1978.
[533] Rita Eker telephone conversation 11 February 2021.

they had the maximum effect on their recipients. Under their joint leadership, a very efficient office organization was set up with Rita Eker running the office administration and Margaret Rigal liaising with M.P.s; both wrote or signed a spate of letters to the Prime Minister Margaret Thatcher in the 1980s, improving on the relationship between her and the 35's which had first been built by Doreen Gainsford. At first, the office accommodation donated to them by well-wishers was spartan and uncomfortable. One office was in a leaking basement, another was in a disused laundry with a gaping hole in the floor from which machinery had been ripped. An office in Finchley Road had shattered windows and rickety floorboards and was so cramped that staff had to work in a lavatory already housing filing cabinets. It was only in 1988 that they moved to superior office accommodation at 779-781 Finchley Road London NW11, eventually fitted with carpets and central heating, and took additional accommodation in these premises in 1992.[534]

When Sylvia Wallis, a founder member, moved to Israel, her position as an organizer of demonstrations was taken over by Rochelle Duke, who developed a close relationship with police officers in the Special Branch and in exchange for information about their next demonstration would receive a tip-off as to the movements of Soviet dignitaries or sporting stars. By July 1977, there were thirty-six women known as front liners, who were prepared to speak at meetings about Soviet Jewry and one hundred and fifty women willing to attend demonstrations at short notice.[535] Doreen Gainsford was the first press liaison officer for the 35's and was succeeded by Joyce Simson, who according to Eker was tough and very persistent. Contact was maintained with provincial branches over the telephone and by means of fortnightly newsletters in the form of circulars which were stuffed into envelopes by volunteers. These circulars contained the latest news about

---

[534] Daphne Gerlis, pp.55-6 and 220. Mark Hurst, p.91.
[535] Daphne Gerlis, pp.54 and 64-5.

refuseniks, thereby permitting 'regular coordinated efforts [to] take place' between London and the provinces.[536] Information about refuseniks in the Soviet Union gleaned from telephone conversations was made available by Michael Sherbourne in the form of transcripts to the 35s and Sylvia Becker would also pass them on to contacts in the Union of Councils for Soviet Jewry in the United States, who if necessary would relay them on to the State Department. Cooperation was thus ensured between the Women's Campaign and the American Union of Councils which had a similar activist orientation. In London, this information was given to the Israeli embassy by the Women's Campaign and to Nan Griefer, the editor of the newsletter *Jews in the USSR*. Griefer in turn also passed on news gleaned from the refuseniks and Israelis.[537]

Since 1980, the task of briefing visitors to the Soviet Union had been taken over by Evelyn Nohr from Rita Eker, who informed them about the potential hazards facing them from the bugging of telephones to their chances of arrest and on their return the travellers were encouraged to compile a report on every refusenik they visited, so that detailed biographies of the dissidents and their families were created. Items the refuseniks urgently needed were noted as were details of their current state of health. Nohr has been a human rights activist all her adult life. As a girl in France, she witnessed the segregation of Jews before they were sent to the gas chambers and in South Africa she became an anti-apartheid activist and volunteered for Amnesty in London. Barbara Lyons and Sue Usiskin prepared detailed biographies of the Prisoners of Zion and the refuseniks which were kept up to date; and each 35's branch was made responsible for several refusenik families and members were encouraged to write letters to them, so that friendships grew between British and Soviet

---

[536] Rita Eker interview and Southampton MS254/A980/1/3/2 'The First Ten Years' draft history.

[537] Daphne Gerlis, pp.85-6.'The first Ten Years' draft history.

families.[538] By 1980 Rita Eker and Margaret Rigal were complaining in the columns of the *Jewish Chronicle* about the shortage of letter writers and appealed to readers to join their ranks.[539]

In a statement incorporated in a report of activities by the National Council for Soviet Jewry for 1981-2 the Women's Campaign admitted that their protests were losing their effectiveness, forcing them to move in new directions. 'We have demonstrated on behalf of Anatoly Shcharansky, other Soviet Jewish Prisoners of Conscience, the Refuseniks, persecuted teachers of Hebrew, as well as against the sale of goods made in labour camps to the unsuspecting British public. More demonstrations have been held in the provinces and outside central London, where the media are more interested, and greater publicity can therefore be obtained. Unfortunately, with the upsurge of violent public protests of all kinds, the media are seldom willing to cover peaceful demonstrations... We have increased our links with the Government, M.P.s, M.E.P.s, the Trade Unions, the Church, and outstanding individuals. Through letters and articles in the press, and interviews and programmes on radio and television, we have continued to try and influence public opinion both here and abroad'.

In response to David Owen's past criticisms of Jewish groups, the 35's declared that 'we have supported other Human Rights organisations working for the victims of persecution in the Soviet Union, including those working for the `Siberian Seven' and against the abuses of psychiatry'.[540] In a meeting with Arieh Handler in 1985, Philip Hurr from the Foreign Office impressed upon him that the Women's Campaign activities were reaching a point where they were 'beginning to become counterproductive... the kind of relentless writing campaign instigated by the[m]... seemed to be of limited

---

[538] Daphne Gerlis, pp.57 and 89-90. 'The First Ten Years' draft history.
[539] JC 22 February 1980 p.20 and 26 September 1980 p.35.
[540] NA, FCO28/6973 National Council for Soviet Jewry Report of activities 1981-2.

value... it had to be borne in mind that replying to the very many letters we received did occasionally mean distracting officials from the real business of trying to do something about human rights in the Soviet Union'. Handler concurred with this, exclaiming 'that Mrs Rigal's activities did not have the approval of the National Council as a whole...'[541] Nevertheless, as we shall see, one of the fresh directions in which the women protesters moved was an increased emphasis on direct pressure on the Prime Minister after Margaret Thatcher formed her new administration early in 1979.

What were the differences between the National Council for Soviet Jewry and the Women's campaign, as many leading women such as Margaret Rigal and Rita Eker were active in both organizations? The National Council had forty-two communal bodies affiliated to it and was regarded as the authoritative voice of the community by the government on Soviet Jewry issues, who were prepared to receive its delegations from time to time; and it had good contacts with academics, sending scientists to Dr Brailovsky's scientific seminars in Moscow. This was achieved through one of its affiliated associations, Scientists for the Release of Soviet Refuseniks. Among the organizations attached to it were the Board of Deputies, the 35's, the Association of Jewish Ex-Servicemen (AJEX), students, various groups of professionals, and the United and the Reform Synagogues. Over time it developed superior links to the All-Parliamentary Committee for the Release of Soviet Jewry than the 35's, especially from the time of June Jacob's chairmanship. But the Women's Campaign was leaner, better organized and had superior contacts with the refuseniks in different communities in the USSR, whom they were able to assist with initiatives in medical care and cultural contact.

According to Andrew Balcombe, the National Council and the Women's Campaign were complimentary organizations and seen as 'more effective for that', as the

---

[541] NA, FCO 28/6973 P.J. Hurr to Mr Macgregor 5 March 1985.

35's and the students were better at calling out their supporters for demonstrations and at harassing Soviet institutions and events. In contrast, the Council was often hesitant at calling for demonstrations because it was worried that not enough members of the community would support them and that the whole occasion would have a negative impact. But the Council could reach into every corner of Anglo-Jewry in Britain and it was truly national in scale, whereas 'outside London the 35's were not so strong, except for certain cities' such as Manchester, Liverpool, Leeds, Glasgow, [and] Birmingham'. Moreover, the campaigners irritated Soviet embassy staff by letting loose mice 'at the Bolshoi performance in London and [by displaying] the huge model of a Russian bear in chains in a shop in the Bayswater Road at the top of the exit from the Embassy Row. The Ambassador saw it every time he left the embassy. I had a line of contact with the embassy. Through these events we were able to make a specific request to the Soviets to reduce such `provocations'. One of the achievements of the Soviet Jewry campaign worldwide was that no Jewish prisoner of conscience in the emigration fight died in a Soviet prison. And they eventually got out'.[542]

The National Council had a budget which ranged from £28,704 in 1987-8 to around £32,000 in 1989, whereas it appears that the Women's Campaign had an annual income in the same period of around £5,000 to cover office expenses, while it also had a charitable arm which raised additional thousands to pay for medication, electrical goods, clothing and other items sent to families in the Soviet Union.[543] But by July 1989 the National Council had accumulated debts of £50,000 which it extinguished by

---

[542] Andrew Balcombe communication to the author 3 September 2020.
[543] LMA, ACC3087/001 Council minutes of National Council 31 March 1988 and minutes of the executive LMA, ACC3087/008 3 May 1989; Rita Eker telephone conversation 11 February 2021.

trying to make payments through a charitable trust.[544] Their financial distress was worsened by the Jewish Agency slashing their annual subsidy from $20,000 to $10,000 in 1989 and the JIA (Joint Israel Appeal) had to come to their rescue.[545] During the 1980s, the 35's concentrated on corresponding with the Prime Minister, sending travellers to the USSR to obtain up-to-date news from refuseniks, sending medical and financial help to those in need, and trying to revive Jewish cultural activities in the Soviet Union. Both the National Council and the Women's Campaign faced growing financial demands and encountered great difficulty in raising the necessary funds to cover their excessive expenditure.

Speaking on behalf of student activists, Howard Rosen stated that the Student and Academic Campaign for Soviet Jewry had attracted 'considerable student support throughout the country and had succeeded in changing NUS's attitude towards Soviet Jewry'. He explained that 'he and his colleagues had come to the conclusion that demonstrations outside the Russian embassy and letters to President Brezhnev were absolutely of no use. He felt that their energies would be better directed into putting pressure on the Foreign and Commonwealth Office'.[546] Whereas many of the Jewish student leaders had socialist or left-wing ideas and were part of the general European student unrest, the 35's were middle-class Jewish ladies, not specifically motivated by feminist ideology but the whole ethos and atmosphere of the 1970s and 1980s was strongly in favour of women's liberation and political participation and it was with these more general ideas that the Women's Campaign was very much in tune.

Despite his unstinting efforts for Soviet Jewry, Greville Janner MP of the All-Party Parliamentary Committee for the Release of Soviet Jewry was egotistical

---

[544] LMA, ACC3087/009 National Council minutes of the executive 24 July 1989.

[545] LMA, ACC3087/008 National Council executive minutes 3 May 1989.

[546] NA, FCO 28/4292 R.P. Campbell 9 October 1980 to Mr Band.

and upset people connected with other sections of the campaign, rendering his group sometimes less effective than it might otherwise have been.[547] He complained to Ijo Rager now based in New York: 'I have heard from various sources that he {Ben Rabinovich's successor in the Israeli embassy in London] has been undermining my efforts behind my back. He was even stupid enough to tell Sacha... that it would be better to keep me out of things because when I am in them, the spotlight has to be on me...Nothing, for example, to involve me in any of the Parliamentary operations (which is, frankly, absolutely ridiculous) and I really cannot allow my efforts to be undermined within our movement in this country'. Although he had been active in the protest movement to free Yevgeny Levich, who was conscripted despite ill health, Greville had been deliberately cut out of the campaign by the Lishka emissary in London. Denying he was self-centred, Greville claimed that he always said that 'it is infinitely better for the others [non-Jewish supporters] to be out in front, rather than us'.[548]

Rising Antisemitism and Secular Soviet Jews become Dropouts on the Way to Israel

In a sensational article in the *New Statesman* in December 1978, Reuben Aiszenstein, a would-be trainee doctor whose studies were disrupted and who later became a Holocaust historian, asserted that antisemitism was the lynchpin of the Soviet political system just as it had been for Russia in Tsarist times. The Six Day War in 1967 and the Soviet invasion of Czechoslovakia a year later gave the anti-Semites in the political establishment the opportunity to replace the ideology of Marxist-Leninism with antisemitism. 'Under the guise of `anti-Zionism' Soviet propaganda has since created a picture of permanent

---

[547] Communication from two respondents, who wish to remain anonymous.
[548] Southampton, MS254/A980/1/2/30 Greville Janner to Ijo Rager 3 November 1975.

struggle between the Soviet Union and its allies on the one hand and the `imperialist' world ruled by the Zionists on the other... When the Soviet Army invaded Czechoslovakia in 1968, Soviet soldiers were told by their political officers that they had saved the Czechs and Slovaks from `two million Zionist counter-revolutionaries'. (The total number of Jews in Czechoslovakia at the time was about 13,000). Today, Soviet officers and men are taught that `Zionists' are responsible for the armaments race and wars because they control 158 of the 163 largest armaments and aircraft corporations in the world: `The largest armaments concern in Western Europe, Vickers Limited, is controlled by international Zionism through the Rothschilds... and Marks and Spencer', declared <u>Red</u> <u>Star</u> , ' the mouthpiece of the Soviet Ministry of Defence'. Shevstov in a novel, *Love and Hate,* brought out in April 1978 in an edition of 200,000, had as its villain Nahum Hotzer, a Moscow Jewish journalist and playwright, who was also a dope-peddler and murderer. His hero, an Aryan Russian scientist, was murdered by Jewish colleagues, who were leaking Russia's nuclear secrets to the Americans. The slain hero was on the brink of revealing that Einstein's role was exaggerated, echoing similar Nazi claims. The book was reprinted in several large editions and made compulsory reading for members of the armed services. More alarming was the current article in the '*Komsomolskaya Pravda* by V. Polezhayev aimed at the twenty million young Komsomols, who were warned against rejecting the ideology and moral values of their parents and grandparents. They were being manipulated by the international Masonic organisations which, in turn, were controlled by international monopolies, but also by International Zionism, this shock element of imperialism and reaction'. Myths of a chilling international Zionist conspiracy linked to the Masons to dominate the Soviet Union reminiscent of the Protocols of Zion were widely peddled by a Moscow-based ideological lecturer, Valery Nikolayevich Yemelyanov. According to Aiszenstein the Russian New Right which was challenging Brezhnev's moderate authoritarian regime for power consisted of five or six groups united by antisemitism and hatred of the West.[549]

P.S. Roland, after analysing Aiszenstein's article for the Foreign Office, disagreed with its conclusions. In the first place, Aiszenstein played down the continuing need of the Soviet Union for Jews in the establishment, particularly the place of scientists among the prize winners, even if their numbers were falling.[550] He also disagreed with Professor Leonard Schapiro, who wrote a critical review of Alexander Yanov's book on *The Russian New Right*, which was heavily cited by Aiszenstein to buttress his contentions. Schapiro disparaged the importance of many of its leaders and stressed that Yanov failed to differentiate influential ideas from those that were simply crazy. The only nationalist supporter to rise to the top of the Communist party was Poliansky, who was recently ousted from the Central Committee. Schapiro continued that 'the evidence for the view that it [nationalism/ antisemitism] is today more than a convenient device by the Soviet leaders to bolster their own hold on power seems to me pretty thin... But this seems to me a long cry from the replacement of communism, which offers a plausible reason for territorial expansion, by Russian nationalism, which does not, and which above all lacks the power to attract foreign fellow-travellers'.[551] Roland agreed with Schapiro that antisemitism could be used 'as, say, a means of discrediting dissent' but 'that for the foreseeable future, at any rate, antisemitism is likely to be carefully controlled – if readily apparent'.[552]

Nonetheless, this academic analysis under-estimated the strength of Soviet media encouragement of antisemitism which caused it to burn like a wildfire within

---

[549] Reuben Aiszenstein, 'The End of Marxism-Leninism' New Statesman 15 December 1978.
[550] NA, FCO 28/3531 P.S. Roland to Mr Lyne 18 December 1978.
[551] Times Literary Supplement 10 November 1978 Leonard Schapiro review of Alexander Yanov, 'The Russian New Right: Right-wing ideologies in the Contemporary USSR'.
[552] NA, FCO 28/3531 P.S. Roland to Mr Lyne 18 December 1978.

the USSR with fuel added by the denials of two Jewish apologists, Begun and Solodar, while at the United Nations the Soviet-sponsored anti-Zionist resolution, equating it with racism, gave this antisemitic campaign international dimensions. Aspects of this international campaign were also reported in the Soviet press. Grigory Vasserman in his travels throughout the Soviet Union saw antisemitism 'as a manifestation of the nationalism of the surrounding peoples, a nationalism 'which prevents the Jews from mingling with the indigenous population, whose main point was to eradicate the soul of the Jew'.[553] Moreover, at the same time as these outbreaks of antisemitism were festering, the KGB and government organs continued their efforts to annihilate Jewish culture within the Soviet Union, by banning any communal organizations, social institutions, and Hebrew classes for children and the teaching of the Hebrew language; and by targeting inspirational teachers, such as Paritsky and Iosif Begun. The most accurate count of the number of functioning synagogues for over two million Jews taken in August 1977 was 69, not a hundred or two claimed by Soviet apologists. Soviet Jewry seemed to be in terminal decline.[554]

In 1977, there was a big crackdown on dissent by the Soviet authorities in an attempt to curb the movement. After punitive sentences were meted out on the main personalities in the Moscow-based Helsinki Monitoring group, namely Yuri Orlov, Ginzburg and Anatoly Shcharansky, the dissident movement 'entered a period of quiescence'. Almost all the dissidents had their home telephone lines disconnected, while contact with the West by mail had according to a State Department report been 'progressively curtailed'. American journalists had been harassed by the Soviet authorities and domestic press reports linked these correspondents to Western intelligence agencies, thereby intimidating Russian citizens who wished to keep in contact with them. All the principals of the Moscow Monitoring group were incarcerated, such as

---

[553] Martin Gilbert, The Jews of Hope (New York, 1985), p.167.
[554] NA, FCO 28/3532 Insight: Soviet Jews vol.4:1 (January 1978).

Shcharansky, for a lengthy term of imprisonment or despatched into internal exile, as happened later in the case of Sakharov. Other potential leaders were encouraged to emigrate.[555] But Shcharansky, who was Jewish, was singled out, by being charged with treason which could merit a death sentence.

Until the mid-1970s, most of the emigrants from the Soviet Union were imbued with religious and Zionist ideals and chose Israel as their destination. But with the passing of time, as Robert Brym pointed out, even the most secular Jews felt threatened by antisemitism and realized that they were superfluous 'in the structure of Soviet nationality relations'. Many chose in the next decade to emigrate in order to enjoy better lives economically and socially for themselves and their children and to gain political and cultural freedom.[556] The United States rather than Israel became the destination of choice for large numbers of these assimilated Jews and the problem of dropouts (noshrim) split the international Soviet Jewry movement. By March 1976, fifty per cent of the emigrants leaving on exit visas for Israel dropped out at the transit camp in Vienna and asked to be sent to the United States or a Western European country. Whereas the Israelis wished to close the offices of the Joint Distribution Committee and the Hebrew Immigrant Aid Society (HIAS) at the transit camp to block the flow of emigrants to the United States, the Americans insisted that distressed Jews had the right to choose whichever country they wished to go to. In the end, the Israeli plan to end all aid to dropouts by 1 February 1977 was shelved because of the opposition it attracted.[557]

Although the problem of dropouts was discussed at the National Council, the dispute was basically one

---

[555] NA, FCO 28/3453 L.R. Kay 'Dissidence: the Current State of Play' memorandum 6 October 1978. State Department memorandum on 'Dissent in the Soviet Union' 24 January 1978.
[556] Robert J. Brym, The Jews of Moscow, Kiev and Minsk. Identity, Antisemitism and Emigration (New York,1994), pp.14-15.
[557] Gal Beckerman, When They Come for Us, We'll All Be Gone pp.356-63.

between the Israelis and Americans and the British Soviet Jewry activists were marginal players in the dispute.[558] The hostile attitude adopted by officials from the Jewish Agency and HIAS to emigrants who did not choose Israel as their destination in Vienna, persisted over the years. In 1985, Rita Eker and her husband met the family of Viktor Kipnis, who had been in refusal for five years and were shocked at the malodorous and shabby hotel accommodation offered to them in Vienna and the frosty reception of the officials from the Jewish Agency to a couple of academics, who stated that they were going to join family in Canada. In contrast, the Jewish Agency placed a comfortably furnished and centrally heated three-bedroom apartment to Israel-bound emigrants. In Peter Moss's report he noted that 'we were particularly interested to learn of the family's recent involvement in Jewish education, especially Kyrill who had regularly attended one of `Moscow's `underground' Jewish study groups'. Apart from the dire situation in Vienna, the family had a difficult transition period of four or five months in Rome, while awaiting their visas and would have to subsist on three hundred dollars, all that they were allowed to take out from the Soviet Union.[559]

Margaret Thatcher Becomes Leader of the Opposition and Embraces the Cause of Human Rights

By good fortune, Margaret Thatcher, the new Leader of the Opposition, was the member for the Finchley constituency which had a large and politically sensitive Jewish population. From the first, Doreen Gainsford, who ran the Women's Campaign, understood that they were speaking the same language about the implementation of the Helsinki Accords and decided to cultivate her, plying her

---

[558] LMA, ACC 3087/001 National Council for Soviet Jewry minutes 15 February 1981.
[559] Southampton, MS254 A980/1/3/2 Report of a Trip to Vienna by Rita Eker and Peter Moss 25/26 November 1985 to meet Viktor Kripnis and his family.

with a non-stop stream of information about the Soviet Jewish dissidents. Spokesmen for the National Council and the wider international movement familiarised her with the language of human rights and encouraged her international interventions on these issues. When Doreen Gainsford departed for Israel at the end of 1978, Margaret Rigal and Rita Eker bombarded Thatcher with the latest news about the refuseniks, particularly Shcharansky, Ida Nudel, and Alexander Paritsky, and on the wider concerns about Helsinki and the implementation of its stipulations about human rights, something that became more pronounced in her own approach after 1977 and 1978 following President Carter's intervention. Thatcher advanced from talking about religious freedom and the right of Jews to emigrate and humanitarian gestures to making general comments about human rights. Gradually, she became identified with this cause on the international stage, particularly among Jewish dissidents in the USSR.

Relying on the advice of Robert Conquest, an outside expert on the Soviet Union, Margaret Thatcher believed that the USSR was bent on world domination. In her first major speech on international affairs given on 26 July 1975 as Leader of the Opposition, she castigated the Labour government for pulling Britain out of the Simonstown naval base, despite the fact that the Soviet Union had 'more nuclear submarines than the rest of the world's navies put together'. The strength of NATO was 'already at its lowest safe limit', and if they lowered the size of their conventional forces any further, they would be faced by the unenviable choice of surrender or using nuclear weapons. The Soviets were 'arrayed against every principle for which we stand'. She noted sorrowfully that 'When the Soviet leaders jail a writer, or a priest, or a doctor or a worker, for the crime of speaking freely, it is not only for humanitarian reasons that we should be concerned. For these acts reveal a regime that is afraid of truth and liberty; it dare not allow its people to enjoy the freedom we take for granted, and a nation that denies those freedoms to its own people will have few scruples in denying them to others'. Since her 'Iron Lady' speech in 1976, she had become sceptical about detente, as she doubted the good faith of the Soviet Union. But like Conquest, she was convinced that so long as Western armaments were kept at the right level, there was little that the Soviets could do to threaten Western interests deeply.[560] At the beginning of 1977 Nicholas Bethell, a Conservative MEP and human rights protagonist, introduced Mrs Thatcher to Vladimir Bukovsky the freed Soviet dissident. Bukovsky advised her, 'much to her delight, that detente was a dangerous myth and that `democratic socialism' was as much a contradiction as boiling ice'. [561]

It was Doreen Gainsford who first exploited the linkage between the plight of the Soviet dissidents and Margaret Thatcher's interest in the wider question of human rights, with the latter's insistence that until satisfactory answers to this question were forthcoming no trust could develop between the West and the Soviet Union as to their future intentions. Margaret Thatcher became Conservative M.P. for Finchley, a constituency with a large Jewish population in 1959; and from the first, her constituents badgered her about her attitude to the challenging situation facing Israel in the Middle East and from the 1970s pressed her on what assistance she could offer to Soviet Jewish dissidents. While her parents had given temporary refuge to a teenage Austrian Jewish girl in April 1939 months before the advent of the Second World War, Mrs Thatcher also shared some of the anti-Jewish prejudices of her time and class, but as she came to know her constituents better she gradually discarded these jaundiced opinions; and set out to persuade Jewish voters in her constituency that they would be welcome if they joined the local branch of the Conservative party. Slowly she came to admire Jews for their values, their scholarship,

---

[560] Charles Moore, Margaret Thatcher vol.1, pp.310-11,332-3 and 553.

[561] Nicholas Bethell, Spies and Other Secrets pp.80-1.

their entrepreneurial skill and their sense of community.[562] The first correspondence which passed between Thatcher and Gainsford on Soviet Jewry was a letter dated 6 November 1974, when the Conservative MP promised to try and 'pop' into a meeting addressed by Sylvia Zalmanson, who was visiting Britain.[563] Four months later she informed Mrs Gainsford that she had written to the Foreign Office about the 36 Soviet Jewish prisoners of conscience.[564]

When she became Conservative Leader of the Opposition on 11 February 1975, Margaret Thatcher was courted by a more diverse body of Jews from communal organizations. After an approach from Lord Fisher, the president of the Board, Thatcher thanked him for bringing 'the four specific cases' of refuseniks to her 'attention'.[565] Sheila King Lassman wrote to her that she was 'one of the many women in your constituency concerned about the plight of Jewish women in the USSR, telling her that 'You will have heard from Anthony Steen of Wavertree that a group of Liverpool 35's would like to meet you at Blackpool next week [at the party conference in October 1975] to discuss this situation. They particularly want to highlight the case of Ida Nudel, the sole survivor of a large family, who were all killed in the Nazi camps'. At the party conference, Mrs. Sylvia Sheff, a leading figure in the Manchester branch of the 35's, met Mrs Thatcher, who asked 'to be kept informed of any violations of the Helsinki

---

[562] Charles Moore, Margaret Thatcher. Not for Turning vol.1 (London,2013), pp.20-1,59,136-7. Margaret Thatcher, The Path to Power, pp.98-9.
[563] Southampton, MS 254/ A980/1/1/31 Margaret Thatcher to Doreen Gainsford 6 November 1974.

[564] Southampton, MS 254/A980/1/1/31 Thatcher to Gainsford 11 February 1975.
[565] LMA, ACC/3121/C1/10 Soviet Jewry Action Committee minutes. Thatcher to Lord Fisher 26 March 1975.

agreement on human rights as committed by the Soviet authorities against Jews'.[566]

Doreen Gainsford continued to cultivate Mrs Thatcher's friendship and advised her that she had learned from a former Soviet government official that letters sent to the Soviet embassy in London started a chain response of queries back and forth to Moscow, and she constantly plied her with information. Gainsford wrote to Thatcher of a visit to this country by a delegation from the Supreme Soviet beginning on 12 May 1975, sending her the latest information about Soviet Jewry and begging her to express her humanitarian views.[567] In February 1976, Gainsford told the Opposition Leader that 35 groups throughout the world had set up a Helsinki Agreement Watchdog Committee and requested a meeting. She was 'totally in agreement with everything Mrs. Thatcher has said of late, and I think that a discussion could be of benefit to both of us'.[568] In August 1976, she supplied Thatcher with the latest information about Ida Nudel.[569] On 12 November 1976 she enclosed a letter sent to all M.P.s about Boris Chernobilsky and Iosif As, two of 52 Jews who had been arrested in Moscow for protesting against the refusal of emigration permits, 'despite the Helsinki Agreement'. Due to pressure from British Parliamentarians and protests from Moscow Jews, they had been released before their trial, which was unprecedented.[570] She urged her to write to the Soviet ambassador about the four latest cases of Jews facing show trials which violated the Helsinki Accords. 'For my own

---

[566] Southampton, MS254/A980/1/31 Sheila King Lassman to Thatcher 1 October 1975. LMA, ACC/3121/CI/10 Soviet Jewry Action Committee minutes 15 October 1975. JC 10 October 1975, p.40.

[567] Southampton, MS 254/A980/1/1/31 Gainsford to Thatcher 12 May 1975, and same to same 17 January 1977.
[568] Southampton, MS 254/A980/1/1/31Gainsford to Edward Leigh 20 February 1976.
[569] Southampton, MS 254/A980/1/1/31 Gainsford to Mrs Thatcher, and Caroline Stephens to Gainsford.
[570] Southampton, MS 254/A980/1/1/31 Gainsford to Mrs Thatcher 12 and 30 November 1976; and 17 January 1977.

part', Mrs Thatcher replied, 'I am waiting to see the outcome of the Belgrade Conference next June which... is meeting to monitor the effects of the Helsinki Agreement. Once this meeting has taken place, I may be in a position to take another initiative'. In the meantime she stated that she wanted to see the information gathered by the Women's Helsinki Watchdog Committee and an appointment was duly arranged for 8 February 1977.[571] On 18 March 1977, Thatcher thanked Gainsford for her recent informative letter, saying 'Please go on sending me all the information that you have on the whole subject. I am busy collecting material for another speech on Helsinki and will naturally be drawing it [to] the attention of the relevant authorities at the time of the Belgrade Conference in the summer'. Telling Thatcher about her intention to emigrate to Israel, Gainsford continued 'You and I have had the discussion in my very early days and agreed the [19]30s and [19]40s must never be allowed to happen again'.[572]

The New Leadership of the Women's Campaign Woos Margaret Thatcher

After Doreen Gainsford left for Israel in 1978, various ladies associated with the Women's Campaign leadership wrote to Margaret Thatcher on the situation of Soviet Jewry before Rita Eker and Margaret Rigal took over the direction of the organization. On 23 February 1978, Thatcher still at this point Opposition Leader of the Conservative party, wrote to Carole Mosheim that 'she was glad to have had the opportunity of meeting you last Friday and of discussing the case of Anatoly Shcharansky...I will certainly continue to do what I can to help him and others who are imprisoned without trial'. In reply, Carole Mosheim mentioned that

---

[571] Southampton, MS254/980/1/1/31 Thatcher to Gainsford 17 and 21 January 1977.

[572] Southampton, MS254/A980/1/1/31 Gainsford to Thatcher 9 February and 18 March 1978.

Dina Beilin, an activist working for Shcharansky, had been given a fortnight to leave the Soviet Union with her family. They were concerned that her departure would coincide with Shchransky's trial to divert press and media attention from it. She continued that the 35's had acquired a film called 'Prisonland' which was made by ex-prisoners now living in Israel, which described 'life as a Prisoner of Conscience'. She suggested arrangements for Mrs Thatcher viewing it and later her secretary returned the cassette of

'Prisonland' which she had borrowed from Mrs Mosheim.[573] In April, Linda Isaacs congratulated Mrs Thatcher on 'the stand taken' by her and 'the other Delegates on Human Rights at the New European Alliance Conference at Schloss Klesheim in Salzburg. We hope that such a stand will not only help Anatoly Sharansky but others like him who have been imprisoned without trial for more than a year, held incommunicado and thus been deprived even of the small comfort of a visiting relative'.[574] On 4 July 1978, Mrs Mosheim again wrote to Margaret Thatcher explaining that Professor Ilya Glezer was visiting this country and asking her if she could squeeze him into her tight schedule with an appointment. She continued somewhat unwisely to mention that 'some of the girls working in this office who are resident in your constituency would be willing to help you or your agent during the forthcoming General Election', thus tying the Women's Campaign to the fortunes of the Conservative party,

---

[573] Southampton, MS254/A980/1/1/31 Margaret Thatcher to Carole Mosheim 23 February 1978 and Alison Ward constituency secretary to Carole Mosheim 17 April 1978. Rita Eker Papers, Carole Mosheim to Margaret Thatcher 7 March 1978.
[574] Southampton, MS254/A980/1/1/31 Linda Isaacs to Margaret Thatcher 24 April 1978 and reply Richard Ryder to Linda Isaacs 2 May 1978.

instead of observing a careful neutrality.[575] As early as 17 October 1978, Matthew Parris on behalf of Margaret Thatcher acknowledged a circular sent by Margaret Rigal 'on behalf of the Campaign to Remove the 1980 Olympics from Moscow'.[576]

On 10 November 1978, Rita Eker and Margaret Rigal addressed the first of a long series of joint letters to Thatcher. 'Have been particularly worried over the last few months', they observed, 'by the rise of official antisemitism within the USSR. The newspapers – both daily and weekly –have featured articles which have developed from anti-Zionism into anti-Judaism and their readers have been encouraged to believe that Jews are manipulating the world communities for their own sinister purposes. Joined to the Jews and synagogues as the object of Soviet scorn are the Masonic Lodges'. A new object of derision had recently been added to the list, that of the 'Bilderberg Club' at which Thatcher had spoken. They wondered if such comments were against the spirit of the Helsinki Agreement? But Richard Ryder of Thatcher's Private Office replied that there was nothing unusual in such attacks.[577] A month later they wrote to Thatcher to congratulate her on going to New York to receive the 'Woman of Conscience 1978 Award', though they were advised that Lady Young would in fact be travelling to New York to accept the award on Thatcher's behalf, and a copy of the Conservative leader's speech was enclosed. The speech was a paean of praise for 'Those who fight for human rights from within countries where they are denied, have courage of a very special kind. For the freedom fighter 'there is only a seeming eternity of

---

[575] Southampton, MS254/A980/1/1/31 Carole Mosheim to Margaret Thatcher 4 July 1978.

[576] Southampton, MS254/A980/1/1/31 Matthew Parris to Margaret Rigal 17 October 1978.

[577] Southampton, MS254/A980/1/1/31 Rita Eker and Margaret Rigal to Margaret Thatcher 10 November 1978, and Richard Ryder to Margaret Rigal 16 November 1978.

imprisonment, forced labour, physical and mental torture, reprisals against his loved ones – and perhaps worst of all the gnawing fear of being forgotten'. In their letter of acknowledgement, Rigal and Eker mentioned Nikolai Sharygin, who had spent ten years in Soviet prison and labour camps, testifying that 'Olympic souvenirs are being manufactured in labour camps and that he actually saw these articles'.[578]

Margaret Thatcher Becomes Prime Minister

On 28 March 1979, the Labour government of James Callaghan lost a vote of confidence in the House of Commons and a general election was held on 3 May 1979. The Conservative party was confident of victory and at the end of April 1979 an official from their Central Office wrote to Margaret Rigal stating that 'Mrs Thatcher was delighted with your kind message. She looks forward to working with you in the future'.[579]

A year later, Professor Leonard Schapiro and Peter Reddaway, two of the country's foremost experts on the Soviet Union, wrote to Margaret Thatcher, recently installed as Prime Minister, stating that 'we are now convinced that the current Soviet campaign to suppress human rights is the worst ever (i.e. since dissent became organized 15 years ago)... even in the present state of East-West tension it would substantially help the cause of human rights in the Soviet union if you and other members of the government were to speak out strongly and persistently to denounce the Kremlin on this issue'. When in 1977 the Soviet authorities started a purge to suppress

---

[578] Southampton, MS254/A980/1/1/31 Rita Eker and Margaret Rigal to Margaret Thatcher 14 December 1978, Richard Ryder to the same 19 December 1978, and Margaret Rigal and Rita Eker to Thatcher 21 December 1978.

[579] Southampton, MS254/A980/1/1/31 Robin Cooke to Margaret Rigal 22 April 1979.

the Helsinki Monitoring groups, the scale of Western protests led by President Carter forced them into a retreat. Now there is a new purge – 'to cleanse the country of dissent before the Olympics – yet Western voices are muted. Thousands of dissenters throughout the USSR have been subjected to systematic KGB intimidation for the last year – dismissals from work, threats of arrest, beatings-up by official thugs – and over 200 who have refused to be intimidated have been subject to long-term arrest or psychiatric internment... Between now and the Olympics we expect the figure of 200 to rise sharply – unless a strong Western protest campaign develops very quickly. Can you help to give a lead?'[580] But Lord Carrington, the Foreign Secretary, was convinced that the major Western objective should be increased pressure to persuade the Soviet Union to leave Afghanistan which they had invaded in December 1979 and that the human rights issue should be held over until the opening of the Madrid review conference on the Helsinki Accords in November 1980. Thatcher was exasperated with the draft reply to Professor Schapiro, allowing it but scrawling 'A typical F.O. reply. Even your efforts [Michael] can't conceal its origin'.[581]

It had been arranged that the Olympic Games would take place in Moscow in the summer of 1980, but the Soviet invasion of Afghanistan on Christmas day 1979 led President Jimmy Carter to declare that the United States would boycott the games. Thatcher as Prime Minister wanted to follow Carter's lead but was reluctantly persuaded to allow the decision whether to attend or not to be made by the various British national sports committees, who decided otherwise.[582]

As early as the summer of 1978, the 35's launched a campaign against the staging of the Olympic Games in Moscow which was well covered in the national press.

[580] NA, PREM 19/1973 Leonard Schapiro and Peter Reddaway to Margaret Thatcher 14 May 1980.
[581] NA, PREM 19/1973 G.H. Walden to Michael Alexander 3 June 1980 and draft replies to Schapiro and Reddaway.
[582] Charles Moore, Margaret Thatcher vol.1, pp.562-3.

Tactics were debated in the National Council. After a discussion with Margaret Rigal, Mrs Eker wrote to Arieh Handler that 'If a group is really going to Moscow to see the Games under the aegis of the National Council [for Soviet Jewry] we suggest once more that they be asked to wear badges expressing their support for Soviet Jewry... such a badge must not have any connection with Israel but might have the Olympic symbol with some Jewish addition... [so that it would] be recognizable by Soviet Jews. At this point I feel compelled to reiterate our concern. Wulf Zalmason told us that when he was arrested in 1970 he met in the labour camps prisoners who were arrested after the 1957 international Youth Festival because they had too much contact with Western visitors ... it was suggested to us by Yoshua [Pratt, the representative of the Lishka in London] in highly emotive terms that Jews who have not applied and who have little or no contact with refuseniks might be emboldened by the Games to approach visiting Jews. I should hate any of them to end up in a labour camp'. Moreover, at the December 1979 meeting 'June [Jacobs, an influential figure in the National Council] emphasised that she was still convinced that there should be a Jewish presence at the Olympic Games in Moscow and that the utmost pressure should be brought to bear before the Olympics for the remaining Prisoners of conscience and refuseniks'. June agreed to warn Eric Graus of the Herut, a right-wing Zionist activist group, that a demonstration in Red Square during the Olympics would be a foolhardy venture.[583]

People were perplexed when Isi Leibler, the international stalwart Soviet Jewry campaigner, visited the Soviet Union in the summer of 1978 to arrange for his travel company to become the official Australian agency for the Olympic Games in Russia in 1980. What they did not comprehend was that he was secretly coordinating his moves with the Lishka and leading refuseniks. Their aim

---

[583] LMA, ACC. 3087/11 Rita Eker to Arieh Handler 26 October 1979 and minutes of honorary officers of the National Council for Soviet Jewry 5 December 1979.

was to draw Jewish visitors to Moscow, where they could mix with the local Jewish community.[584]

In January 1980, Margaret Rigal on behalf of the 35's informed Margaret Thatcher that holding the Olympic Games in Moscow would harm 'Soviet Jews, Baptists and other religious minorities,' and that the KGB action against harmless individuals showed that our forebodings were well-grounded. Joyce Simson, a key figure in the 35's, was arrested with her husband and harassed before their departure from Leningrad airport; they had met Eline Oleynik, a young refusenik in Kiev, who was given a fifteen-day prison sentence; yet another indication of the hard line being pursued by Soviet security officials to foreign visitors before the Olympics.[585] The Women's Campaign briefed MPs, and when there was a debate in the Commons early in the year, Winston Churchill, Jill Knight, and Ian Gilmour, all well-known Conservative backbenchers, spoke in favour of a boycott.[586] Freedom games, a sports event sponsored by the National Council in Birmingham in May 1980 to protest against the conditions of Soviet Jewry, had their impact marred by the action of the Midlands AAA which would not allow their athletes to compete in them, and the wide coverage given to the raid of the SAS to free hostages in the Iranian embassy which blew the other story off the front pages of the national dailies.[587] In these circumstances, all the Women's campaign could do was to mount daily demonstrations outside the office of Intourist, the official Soviet travel agency; but in any case the whole campaign surrounding the boycotting of the Olympic Games was ill-coordinated, confused, and somewhat self-defeating.[588]

At this juncture, the Women's Campaign redoubled their efforts to assist Anatoly Shcharansky, who was

---

[584] JC 4 December 2020.
[585] Southampton, MS254/A980/1/1/31 Joyce Simson to Margaret Thatcher 20 February 1980.
[586] Daphne Gerlis, p.62.
[587] JC 16 May 1980. p.9.
[588] Mark Hurst, Human Rights pp.97-8.

languishing in prison. Having visited Moscow over a weekend early in May 1979 to assess the situation, Mrs Elaine Kibel congratulated Mrs Thatcher on being the first lady Prime Minister of this country and informed her that all the refuseniks 'were delighted with the results of the Election as they felt that you could and would do something to help them. They look upon you with deep affection and hope'. She had met Shcharansky's brother Leonid, who told her that Anatoly suffered from 'severe headaches' and was being punished for not being able to fulfil the prison work quotas. She did hope that Mrs Thatcher could intervene on his behalf and that her government would ensure that 'the `Helsinki Agreement' on Human Rights is upheld throughout the world'.[589] This emphasis on the human rights aspect of the Women's Campaign gained ever-increasing importance throughout Thatcher's premiership.

While wishing the Prime Minister Mrs Thatcher a successful visit to Japan, Mrs Eker and Mrs Rigal reminded her that when she made a short stop in Moscow she should express concern over the continued detention of Shcharansky, suffering from impaired vision, and that Ida Nudel was enduring 'appalling conditions in Siberia'. Bryan Cartledge advised Mrs Thatcher that he did 'not think, in any case that you could have taken these particular matters up with Mr. Kosygin across the supper table'. She agreed, as she was not going to sacrifice her primary objective of arms control and the reduction of nuclear weapons, by unnecessarily upsetting Soviet leaders.[590] At times she was prepared to be more flexible and overstep the limits of the timidity of the Foreign Office, but there were strict limits to her departure from these diplomatic norms.

---

[589] Southampton, MS254/A980/1/1/31 Elaine Kibel to Margaret Thatcher 11 May 1979.
[590] NA, PREM 19/2547 Rita Eker and Margaret Rigal to Margaret Thatcher 25 June 1979; and Bryan Cartledge to Thatcher and to Eker and Rigal both 2 July 1979.

On 16 August 1979, Margaret Rigal on behalf of the
International Committee for the Release of Anatoly
Shcharansky advised Mrs Thatcher that she had spoken to
Avital Shcharansky, who had asked her to forward a copy
of a brief biography of her husband to the Prime Minister.
Her husband had now spent two and a half years in prison
and she was anxious that he should be released from prison
before his health was 'entirely ruined'. In a reply submitted
on Thatcher's behalf, she reiterated that 'Anatoly's story
impressed me profoundly and I can only admire his
fortitude and selflessness. The recent report of his physical
condition is deeply disturbing'. But then the letter bore all
the hallmarks of cautious Foreign Office thinking on
human rights with a caveat that she could only raise some
cases with the Soviet authorities, particularly of those
individuals who were monitoring the implementation of
the Helsinki Agreement. Even so, she had to wait for the
right opportunity to occur to make representations and it
might be necessary for the government to keep such
representations confidential. Nevertheless, she hoped that
pressure from every quarter would lead to his release.[591]
Margaret Rigal begged Thatcher to concentrate all her
efforts on his behalf, as many refuseniks on a recent visit to
Moscow had told her that he personified their struggle to
be free and that their future was 'inextricably bound [up]
with his'. In the files of the Women's Campaign is a copy of
a letter from the Prime Minister to Michael Alexander, one
of her Foreign policy advisers, dated after this
correspondence, with what appears to be Thatcher's
reworking of the reply in much more personal and
vigorous terms. She started by saying that 'I take a very
close interest in all human rights matters in the Soviet
Union' and ended by assuring Mrs Rigal that 'how we

---

[591] Southampton, MS254/A980/1/1/31 Margaret Rigal to Margaret
Thatcher 16 August 1979 and reply of Richard Ryder to Margaret Rigal
3 September 1979.

might most effectively take action on his behalf is under active review'.[592]

Once the Olympics, which for the first time were staged in the Soviet Union, had been concluded in the summer of 1980, the authorities there stepped up their campaign of intimidation against dissidents. Amnesty earlier complained that since a report issued in 1975, 400 more Soviet citizens had been jailed and a hundred more put in mental hospitals. At the British Association conference in Salford in September, Professor Ziman asserted that we need 'to make clear that we scientists are not indifferent to the ill-treatment of Russian, Czechoslovak, Polish, Romanian and other scientists who dare to take the Helsinki agreement at its face value, or to the cat and mouse treatment of Jewish scientists who have sought for years to emigrate from the Soviet Union'. Science today had become a branch of politics: 'it was, for example, inextricable from the arms race. The motive for silence was not prudence but embarrassment'. Moreover, Sir Brian Pippard, Professor of Physics at Cambridge, sent a circular letter to all Fellows of the Royal Society, the premier scientific organization in Britain, urging them to sign a petition on behalf of the beleaguered scientists. 'Because so many of the Russian victims are Jews, and the strongest demands for action have come from Jews in the West', he declared, 'it has unfortunately been all too easy for the whole movement to be dismissed on occasion as some rather disreputable offshoot of Zionism. For this reason I particularly address my plea to non-Jews, like myself...I wish I could believe that by maintaining cultural contacts we might be able to exert a beneficial influence; but conversations with Russian scientists have made clear that they regard this as a delusion. Some, indeed, not themselves victimized, even recommended the total cutting off of all scientific communication on the part of Western scientists...in their view it offers the only chance of

---

[592] Southampton, MS254/A980/1/1/31 Margaret Rigal to Richard Ryder 5 September 1979 and Margaret Thatcher to Michael Alexander 13 September 1979.

ultimately enforcing a more humane attitude. Ever since the cases of Orlov, Shcharansky and Sakharov the argument for such positive action has been gaining support in the West, though not so much in Britain as in some other countries'. The Petition itself called on the Soviet Union to honour its Helsinki commitments on human rights and emigration.[593]

In fact, W.J.A Wilberforce, a Foreign Office official, informed Dr Michael Yudkin in December 1980 that he was speaking the next day at the Madrid review meeting, when he would be mentioning the case of Dr Victor Brailovsky again. Brailovsky was a lecturer in probability theory until he was sacked from the Moscow Radio Technical Institute when he and his wife Irina applied to emigrate to Israel in 1972. He was a key figure in the refusenik movement, holding scientific seminars in his flat in 1977, when Professor Azbel departed for Israel. In this way, he publicised the research of trapped scientific colleagues living in limbo land and kept them abreast of the latest findings in their field from guest lectures by Western scientists. The fourth International Conference on Collective Phenomena was due to be held in his flat in April 1980, and although his flat was ransacked by the police and he was arrested and warned not to go ahead with it, he held it as usual in his apartment. He had also in 1978 resumed the editorship of *Jews in the USSR,* a popular magazine for reviving Jewish culture in the Soviet Union. Wilberforce added in his letter to Dr Yudkin that 'I can assure you that both I and a number of other Western delegations here have done the best we can, by direct appeals for Dr Brailovsky's release [from prison]... Unhappily, all appeals of this kind have so far met with a blank wall of silence; but we can only hope that they may still have some effect'. [594] Dr Brailovsky

---

[593] NA, PREM19/1973 Sir Brian Pippard circular letter and petition September 1980. The Times 3 September 1980. Daily Telegraph 4 September 1980.

[594] LMA, ACC.3087/441 Dr M.D. Yudkin to W.J.A. Wilberforce 18 December 1980.

had been arrested on the second day of the Madrid meeting in November 1980 to show the Soviet contempt for the Western espousal of individuals subject to arbitrary arrest and denied their human rights.[595]

A week later on 18 November 1980, Joan Dale of the Scientific Committee of the National Council wrote to Bernard Levin, *The Times* columnist, to sound out his views about Lord Todd issuing a statement on behalf of the Royal Society for Dr Brailovsky's release from detention. 'Judging by the reaction I have had from Individual Fellows who signed the enclosed [petition] and whom several of us have approached personally, Lord Todd is going to be a very tough proposition unless he is forced into a position where he must take a stand. When I heard Allan [Howard] would be approaching you to ask whether you could write an article on Brailovsky, I thought this would be a perfect opportunity to mention that 278 Fellows had signed a petition supporting Brailovsky amongst others...' She had attended the International Conference on Collective Phenomena in Moscow with Professor Oliver Penrose of Cambridge and, if he wished, 'he would be happy to give him first-hand information'.[596] On 15 January 1981, Bernard Levin urged Russian-speaking 'readers of *The Times* to telephone the Chief Moscow Investigator, Georgyi Ponomarev, or his deputy, Smirnov, to ask the reasons for ... [Brailovsky's] imprisonment, and the nature of the charges to be made against him. Levin gave the telephone numbers of the two officials'. He concluded by saying that 'The persecution of Dr Brailovsky is a scandal that ought to unite the entire body of western science in a plain statement that unless he is freed and allowed to leave the Soviet Union with his wife and children, scientific exchanges will be suspended'.[597]

---

[595] LMA, ACC.3087/067 National Council for Soviet Jewry press release on 13 November 1980.
[596] LMA, ACC.3087/067 Joan Dale to Bernard Levin 18 November 1980. Martin Gilbert, Jews of Hope pp.139-42.
[597] Martin Gilbert, Jews of Hope p.142.

Brailovsky had been warned to cancel the scientific seminars and international conferences and repeatedly chose not to do so, though this was not the issue on which the Soviet authorities decided to prosecute him. They were more concerned with the continuing Jewish cultural revival in the Soviet Union and the blossoming nationalism, despite his journal, *Jews in the USSR*, having ceased publication in the summer of 1979. It was alleged at his trial on 18 July 1981, that in the years between 1973 and 1980 Brailovsky had 'systematically engaged in the preparation and distribution in written, typewritten and other forms of material containing deliberately false fabrications defaming the Soviet regime and the Soviet social system'. The state sought to deny that 'Jews were ... discriminated against in culture and education; second, that antisemitism was a feature of current Soviet society; third, that the Jewish religion was being denigrated; and fourth, that unfair restrictions were being placed on Jewish emigration'. This was the first time these issues had been so openly aired at a trial, and despite a doughty defence on Dr Brailovsky's part, he was convicted and sentenced to five years in exile in an obscure village in Kazakhstan.[598]

In October 1980, Rita Eker in a letter to Margaret Thatcher's constituency secretary confirmed that she had spoken on the telephone to Shcharansky's wife Avital, who relayed the latest news. In a letter to his mother, Anatoly had advised her that he had collapsed in September and had been transferred to the prison hospital. Visits from his family were, however, forbidden because he had written a letter to President Brezhnev on behalf of all the prisoners complaining about their ill-treatment, while an old film of his trial was re-shown on television in which he was 'branded as a traitor and spy'. Michael Alexander, her private secretary, replied on behalf of the Prime Minister, who sent a perfunctory answer, merely saying that she was

---

[598] Martin Gilbert, Jews of Hope pp.143-47.

following these matters closely.[599] When Rita Eker advised the Prime Minister in November 1980 that Avital would be coming on a visit to Britain, Mrs Thatcher while condemning 'the inhuman attitude of the Soviet authorities towards political prisoners' would not make time available to see her. Avital could see a Minister of State at the Foreign and Commonwealth Office as she had done on her last visit in March.[600]

The Women's Campaign was most concerned that Basket 111 which dealt with emigration and human rights was to be included in the CSCE discussions in Madrid, as the 35's protests broadened to cover other well-known Jewish names among Soviet dissidents. Although there had been rumours for some time that the topic was going to be left off the agenda, what spurred the group into action was an article by Lord Bethell in *The Times* stating that its inclusion was in jeopardy. Margaret Rigal had gone to see Stephen Band at the Foreign and Commonwealth Office, who assured her that this was not the case. When Mrs Eker and Mrs Rigal wrote to the Prime Minister about the review meeting of the Conference on Security and Cooperation in Madrid, her private secretary in Downing Street reiterated that their letters with enclosures would be forwarded onwards. 'You will already be aware how closely the Prime Minister follows these matters'.[601] Prior to the opening of the conference, refuseniks and other activists in Tbilisi, Kharkov, Kiev, Moscow and Leningrad staged a 72-hour hunger strike to draw attention to harassment by the KGB and police and obstruction by officials. Once procedural wrangles had been resolved by 14 November 1980, the

---

[599] Southampton, MS254/A980/1/1/31 Rita Eker to Joy Robilliard, Thatcher's constituency secretary, 15 October 1980; and Michael Alexander to Rita Eker 11 November 1980.

[600] Southampton, MS254/A980/1/1/131 Joy Robilliard to Rita Eker 17 November 1980.

[601] Southampton, MS254/A980/1/1/31 Margaret Rigal to M.L. Tait 23 July 1980; and Michael Alexander to Rita Eker 11 November 1980.

Madrid CSCE meeting fell into a regular work pattern.[602] During the first week of the conference, it was addressed by ministers, who referred to the Soviet invasion of Afghanistan and violations of human rights in the USSR and Eastern Europe. Griffin Bell, the American delegate making one of his last appearances for the outgoing Carter administration, praised 'the remarkable group' of Soviet dissidents including Dr Yuri Orlov and Shcharansky. 'He added amidst applause: "When Andrei Sakharov was banished, some of our best hopes for a spirit of security and cooperation in Europe were banished with him'''. The Russians regarded criticism of their human rights record as an interference in their internal affairs but in the second week these matters, including human rights, were addressed in greater detail and the Eastern European countries distanced themselves from the Soviet approach to human rights. At the start of the third week, the conference split into three working groups, each one of which dealt with the individual baskets of the Final Act.[603] The British delegation was well briefed, having received representations from the Board of Deputies, the Women, the Student and Academic Campaign for Soviet Jewry, and Ivan Lawrence M.P. and Peter Archer M.P. from the All-Party Parliamentary Committee, in which there were a good number of non-Jewish M.P.s.[604] On 18 December 1981, two lists of urgent cases were handed to Vice-Minister Ilyvichev, to which were added the topical cases of Boris Chernobilsky, Vladimir Kislik, and Alexander Paritsky (prisoners) and Isaak Shkolnik and Moisei Tonkonogy (refuseniks). John Wilberforce then raised the cases of Shkolnik, Brailovsky, Paritsky, Sakharov and Rudolf Battek

---

[602] NA, FCO 28/4292 Jews in the U.S.S.R. vol.1X:30 November 1980.

[603] NA, FCO 28/4292 Madrid CSCE: State of Play memorandum circa December 1980. Guardian 14 November 1980.

[604] NA, FCO 28/4292 R.P. Campbell to Mr Cummins and Mr Reeve 9 October 1980. D.J. Johnson to M.L. Tait 7 November 1980. J.M. Skinner to Mr Reeve 4 December 1980.

of Czechoslovakia; and H. J. Spence added the names of Paritsky, Kislik and Fridman.[605]

Again, in April 1981, Mrs Eker advised Thatcher that Avital was to be her guest for a week or two and appealed to the Prime Minister to see her. Anatoly had spent three years in various Soviet prisons and a further year in the Perm labour camp. Since December he had been held in solitary confinement and starved, his weight falling to six and a half stone. 'His eyesight... [was] failing and he ...[was] suffering from continual severe headaches which prevent him from concentrating on any subject for more than a few minutes'. He had been sentenced to six months in the punishment cell and could face further charges and be returned to Chistopol prison which had the harshest regime in the country.' Avital Sharansky was convinced that you alone among the leading world politicians, because you are also a woman and a wife, can understand her position. What she wanted was to feel more certain that 'the Western powers are aware of her husband's present situation and doing everything possible to alleviate his sufferings'.[606]

---

[605] NA, FCO 28/4675 H.J. Spence to N.E. Sheinwald 20 December 1981.

[606] Southampton, MS254/A980/1/1/31 Rita Eker to Margaret Thatcher 16 April 1981.

'HOW LONG, O LORD?'

How long, O Lord? Will you forget me for ever?
How long will You hide Your face from me?
How long must I wrestle with my thoughts
and every day have sorrow in my heart?
How long will my enemy triumph over me?
Look on me and answer, O Lord my God...
I trust in Your unfailing love...

(Psalm 13:1/3,5)

*How Much Longer has Avital Shchransky to wait
for Her Husband's Release?*

But it was not until Nicholas Bethell, a Conservative MEP, took up Avital's cause, and implored the Prime Minister to see her, that time was found for a brief interview. Bethell explained that it was a good time for such a gesture while the Madrid review of the Helsinki process was still ongoing and the Jewish communities in North-West London were concerned about the European peace initiative in the Middle East and British arms sales to the Arabian peninsula. In addition, she had already recently been received by the French Foreign Minister.[607] Added pressure came from 'a demonstration during the Moscow Philharmonic Orchestra's performance at the Royal Festival

---

[607] NA, PREM 19/1973 Nicholas Bethell to Caroline Stephens 27 April 1981.

Hall on the evening of 22 April and a demonstration outside the Foreign and Commonwealth Office on the morning of 23 April' by Jewish groups. Avital with Mrs Rigal saw Mr Blaker, a Minister of State on 27 April 1981, when she warned him that without the Prime Minister's intervention, she feared that her husband would after a new trial be returned to prison, where conditions were so harsh that he would die.[608]

Two days later, Mrs Avital Shcharansky accompanied by Lord Bethell had a twenty-minute meeting with Mrs Thatcher. 'Mrs Shcharansky asked for the Prime Minister's public support for her case. The Prime Minister said that she doubted whether it would be helpful to Mrs Shcharansky if she were actively to pursue her husband's case in public. Government representatives regularly argued the case of the dissidents in private... As regards the public aspect, what mattered was that the Prime Minister and other political leaders, should be seen to taking an interest in the case and to be `keeping an eye on things'. This was the most effective means of restraining the Soviet authorities from extreme actions'. Later her guests were entertained to tea and somewhat unusually the Prime Minister bid them farewell on the steps of 10 Downing Street and was photographed with Avital, sending out a clear message of support for Anatoly Shcharansky to his Soviet jailers, thereby throwing a protective mantle over him. At an emergency meeting of the National Council for Soviet Jewry, Avital pleaded with British Jews and the public at large to protest and urge the Russians 'in the name of humanity' to release her husband from prison.[609] Apart from this, there were two powerful interventions to the Prime Minister on behalf of Shcharansky from Lord Flowers, the rector of Imperial College, who had written to the President of the USSR Academy of Sciences about a

---

[608] NA, PREM 19/1973 B.J.P. Fall to Mr Blaker 24 April 1981, and F.N. Richards to Michael Alexander28 April 1981.

[609] JC I May 1981 pp.1 and 9. National Archives, PREM 19/1973 Michael Alexander to Francis Richards 29 April 1981.

fellow scientist and more generally from the film director Bryan Forbes about Soviet repression of dissidents. On some internal government correspondence was a scrawl from Alexander, an official, noting that 'The FCO seems to be keeping up the pressure adequately'.[610]

At the same time, the Prime Minister was coming under pressure from the Yuri Orlov Committee which was set up to assist Shcharansky's mentor and the leading human rights campaigner in the Soviet Union, the imprisoned physicist Yuri Orlov. Thatcher responded that she sympathised with the views of the Orlov Committee, who wished to intensify efforts for Orlov among scientists and would ask the British members of the CERN Council to raise this matter there.[611] CERN was the European scientific body which collaborated with the Soviet Union in scientific research.

Aside from this, Margaret Rigal later asked Mrs Thatcher to include Ida Nudel's name in the agenda of the United Kingdom delegation to the UN Conference of the Decade for Women. She was 'a prime example of a woman's fight for the rights of women and men against tyranny', and a key figure in the dissident movement. Thatcher replied that she had asked the delegation to utilize 'any suitable occasion to publicise the case and to bring it to the attention of the Conference'.[612] Despite the Prime Minister's help, this was at quite a low level of diplomatic intervention.

Like Shcharansky, Nudel was deeply involved with the Moscow Helsinki Watch Group led by Yuri Orlov and

[610] NA, PREM 19/1973 Brian Flowers to Academician A.P. Alexandrov 18 May 1981.Thatcher to Lord Flowers 29 May 1981 and Thatcher to Michael Alexander 19 January 1981, and Michael Alexander to Forbes 26 January 1981.

[611] National Archives, PREM 19/1973 John Eades to Thatcher 26 January 1981, and Thatcher to Eades 12 February 1981.

[612] Southampton, MS254/A980/1/1/31 Margaret Rigal to Thatcher 12 May 1980 and Thatcher to Rigal 9 July 1980. NA, PREM 19/2547 Paul Lever to Mike Pattison 2 July 1979 and Mike Pattison to Margaret Thatcher of the same date.

Alexander Ginzburg. Nudel declared that 'Shcharansky was absolutely right when he stressed the connection between the Jewish movement and the dissident movement. If you don't think like the authorities, you are a dissident. If you're not loyal to the system, you're a dissident...[the dissident leaders were imprisoned in 1978, the same year that Nudel, Shcharansky and Slepak, all of whom supported the human rights movement, were also sentenced]'. She wrote letters and sent packages to refuseniks, who were imprisoned on false charges. 'When Ida found that a prisoner was ill, she would send telegrams to doctors, get the information to refusenik circles in Moscow or Leningrad, and thence to the West. She has received hundreds of letters from prisoners and one of her dreams is to publish a book of these letters. They tell it all. They give you an idea of their inner lives, how their Jewishness has evolved and how it changes, and how the[ir] support is going on'.[613]

Towards the end of 1981, Rita Eker wrote to the Prime Minister, informing her that they had recently formed a Women's Committee for Polina Paritsky to assist this tragic family. Her husband Alexander had just been given a totally undeserved sentence of three years in a labour camp. Also enclosed were biographical details of the family, an essay by their daughter, Dorina, and the curriculum vitae of their son Isaak now living in Israel. On 3 February 1982, Mrs Eker confirmed that as yet she did not have the prison address of Alexander and that Mrs Paritsky was terrified that her remaining children were to be taken from her and placed in an orphanage. She hoped that 'when Madrid reconvenes on February 9th, the British Government will make strong representations on behalf of Alexander Paritsky'.[614] Replying to Mrs Eker's earlier letter, the Prime Minister declared that as she would know from her Foreign Office contacts, Alexander 'Paritsky's case was raised by

---

[613] Louis Rapoport, 'Refuseniks. The Captive Israelis', Jerusalem Post International Edition 5 July 1986.
[614] Southampton, MS254/A980/1/1/31 Rita Eker to Margaret Thatcher 19 November 1981 and Rita Eker to Joy Robilliard 3 February 1982.

the leader of our delegation to the CSCE Review in Madrid at the time of his trial. Lord Trefgarne, Parliamentary Under-Secretary at the Foreign and Commonwealth Office, raised the general question of Soviet violation of human rights, including the plight of Soviet Jews, with the Soviet Ambassador last November'. Paritsky had now arrived at a labour camp in the Soviet Far East.[615] This was all at a quite a low level of diplomatic representation for Paritsky, as neither the Foreign Secretary nor the Prime Minister was intervening on his behalf. Nor had the British government position hardened at the end of the year, so that in October 1982 the government were not contemplating moving beyond raising his case at the CSCE meeting 'or in direct bilateral contacts with the Soviet authorities'.[616]

At a dinner to celebrate the 220th anniversary of the Board of Deputies in December 1981, Margaret Thatcher as guest of honour devoted lengthy passages in her address to the difficulties facing Soviet Jewry. 'More Jewish people have been harassed and brought to trial this year than in the past ten years together. There has been renewed suppression of Jewish cultural activity, including the banning of Hebrew study groups and raids on the homes of Hebrew teachers in Moscow. It is hardly surprising that the number of Jews who wish to leave is rising. But the rate of emigration, which reached 50,000 in 1979, is falling. It may be under 10,000 in 1981'. Besides making life worse for Jews, the Soviet authorities denied them the right to emigrate. 'These actions are contrary to the humanitarian provisions of the Helsinki Final Act... HMG's concern has been made clear in Parliament, in Madrid and in the Human Rights Commission of the United Nations. We have conveyed to the Soviet Union at a high level our concern about abuses of human rights. We shall continue to take every suitable opportunity to reiterate that concern'. She

---

[615] Southampton, MS254/A980/1/1/31 Margaret Thatcher to Rita Eker 17 March 1982.

[616] Southampton, MS254/A980/1/1/31 A.J.Coles to Margaret Rigal and Rita Eker 5 October 1982.

mentioned five of the leading refuseniks. 'Anatoly Shcharansky and Vladimir Slepak both leading members of the Helsinki Monitoring Group in Moscow, who are suffering cruelly in prison and in internal exile. Viktor Brailovsky, who courageously organised scientific seminars in Moscow and was arrested a year ago... Ida Nudel, known as the guardian angel of Soviet Jewish prisoners and their families, who was exiled to Siberia three years ago. Boris Kalandarev, a young student held for the past two years in a labour camp'. Then there was the worsening situation of Jews in the Ukraine. 'I think, for example, of Alexander Paritsky. Like Brailovsky, he tried to teach those deprived of work and education because of their beliefs... A system which denies its people the right to think for themselves and to worship as they wish is fundamentally unjust'. In the future she believed 'there would be changes for Soviet Jews'.[617] Nevertheless, the Prime Minister was exaggerating the high level of diplomatic intervention she had made on behalf of Soviet political prisoners whether in the case of Paritsky or Shcharansky, as she did not want to put too much pressure on the Soviet authorities; her first priority remained the reduction of nuclear weapons and troop concentrations in Europe and her activity on behalf of human rights activists and refuseniks was constrained within safe Foreign Office guidelines.

By the beginning of 1982, Margaret Thatcher was beginning to rethink her strategy as to what approach she should adopt to the Soviet Union as regards their Jewish population, but it was hardly in a much more confrontational direction. 'As you know', Thatcher remarked to Rita Eker, 'I take a close interest in all human rights matters in the Soviet Union...The treatment of refuseniks such as Ida Nudel casts grave doubt on the commitment of the Soviet authorities to their humanitarian

---

[617] Southampton, MS254/A980/1/1/31 Margaret Thatcher speech at the 220th anniversary dinner of the Board of Deputies at the Guildhall on 15 December 1981.

obligations under the UN Covenant on Civil and Political Rights and the Helsinki Final Act. Ida Nudel's case is of particular concern to me. I have recently exchanged letters with Ida's sister in Israel, Mrs Elena Fridman. I also drew attention to her plight in my speech to the Board of Deputies last December.' These indirect moves would have hardly been of much diplomatic concern to the Soviet Union. 'We are disturbed by the recent reports of Ida's health [she had heart problems] and of the conditions in which she is being held as punishment for her strong desire to emigrate to Israel...We have recently conveyed to the Soviet authorities at a senior level our concern about a number of particularly deserving cases, including that of Ida Nudel. I do not think further such representations at the present time are likely to be useful'.[618] Possibly this means stepping up the level of diplomatic intervention to Foreign Minister level, as it was usual to have twice yearly exchanges, in which such matters were raised, but from what ensued this was unlikely the case as yet.

Margaret Thatcher was flying to the United States in June 1982 to have a meeting with President Reagan. Margaret Rigal advised her that 'Recent visitors have been asked by many leading Refuseniks to beg the American administration to link the Grain Talks with the Emigration of Soviet Jews. During May only 205 Jews were allowed to leave the Soviet Union; less than seven a day. With half a million waiting for permission to emigrate this means total despair. Split families now have little hope of reunifying and our post is full of appeals from parents deprived of their children and children frantic with worry over their aged parents. Now is the right moment for him to insist that the freedom of movement guaranteed by the Helsinki Agreement is honoured by the USSR'. She ended by apologizing for approaching the Prime Minister at this difficult time.[619]

---

[618] Southampton, MS254/A980/1/1/31 Margaret Thatcher to Rita Eker 26 March 1982.

During the summer of 1982, Avital Shcharansky approached Greville Janner, who passed her plea for help on to Neil Thorne, a Conservative MP, who had better contacts with Downing Street. Mrs Thatcher told him that she had been informed that 'The British delegation to the CSCE meeting in Madrid have raised Mr Shcharansky's case several times both in plenary sessions and privately with the Soviet delegation. Foreign and Commonwealth Office Ministers have also brought the case up on a number of occasions. Lord Carrington referred to it in his Churchill Memorial lecture in October 1981 and the Prime Minister herself mentioned Mr Shcharansky in a speech to the Board of Deputies in December 1981'. [620] This was hardly a rebuke made directly at the Foreign Minister level and was part of the moderate line pursued by the government. Avital Shcharansky and Anatoly's mother were growing increasingly desperate about his isolated state, fearing that he was no longer alive. So Rita Eker in July 1982 approached the Prime Minister. After seeking information from the British embassy in Moscow, the government cast doubt on these rumours. Francis Pym, the new Foreign Minister, in these circumstances did not think it 'appropriate to make a special demarche to the Russians at this stage' but would raise Shcharansky's situation with the Soviet ambassador when he met him in September or ventilate it when the Madrid review meeting reconvened in November.[621]

Shortly before Yom Kippur, the Day of Atonement 1982, messages from former refuseniks and Prisoners of Zion now based in Israel were sent to Mrs Eker, who relayed them on to the Prime Minister. For many months

---

[619] Southampton, MS254/A980/1/1/31 Margaret Rigal to Margaret Thatcher 3 June 1982.

[620] NA, PREM 19/2547 Neil Thorne to Derek Howe 24 June 1982; Derek Howe to John Coles 28 June 1982; and 5 July F.N. Richards to John Coles with draft reply to Neil Thorne.
[621] NA, PREM 19/2547 A.J. Coles to F.N. Richards 21 July 1982 and same to the same 29 July 1982.

Anatoly Shcharansky had languished 'in an internal punishment cell which is so horrible that even by Soviet law a prisoner cannot be kept there for more than fifteen days'. To prompt the authorities to free him from his isolation, Anatoly was starting a hunger strike on Yom Kippur to draw worldwide attention to his plight. These appeals were signed by the biggest names in Soviet Jewry, including among others Professor Benjamin Fain, Dina Beilin, Ilana Fridman, Silva Zalmanson, Mark Dymshits, and Josef Mendelevich.[622]

In a letter sent to Andrew Balcombe, the President of the National Council, for the third Brussels Conference on Soviet Jewry, Margaret Thatcher reiterated her support and said that she was 'disturbed by the recent drastic cut-back in emigration and intensified campaign of persecution... The obstacles placed in the way of those seeking freedom of movement and freedom of religious belief stand in stark contradiction to the provisions of the UN Covenant on Civil and Political Rights and the Helsinki Final Act which the Soviet Union solemnly undertook to observe'. Although our efforts to subject 'Soviet human rights performance to rigorous public scrutiny... both bilaterally and through the CSCE process may not bring immediate results, we continue to hope that in time the Soviet authorities will be persuaded to change their policies of repression'.[623]

Margaret Thatcher Wins a Second Term

Apart from the Soviet Jewry campaign, Mrs Eker and Mrs Rigal were partisan supporters of the Tory leader, and perhaps aligned the Women's Campaign too closely to the Prime Minister which would have been dangerous had she lost a snap election which she called after the Falkland

---

[622] NA, PREM 19/2547 separate appeals from former refuseniks and Prisoners of Zion 28 September 1982.

[623] NA, PREM 19/2547 Ian Kydd to A.D. Balcombe I September 1982 with Thatcher message to Brussels 111 Conference.

Islands War. Enthusing with Thatcher, they sent her congratulations on the happy result of the military victory. 'We are convinced that the fight for freedom is indivisible and that the unshakeable resolve shown by this country will benefit all who are struggling for the rights recognised by the United Nations Human Rights charter'.[624] As usual at the end of the year, they sent the Prime Minister a special calendar prepared by the 35's portraying refuseniks, who were currently in the news. Of the 48 refuseniks featured in the calendar in 1981, only one had been allowed to leave. They added that 'In the last fortnight `Final Refusals' have been given to long-term Refuseniks in Moscow and Leningrad – a life sentence for those involved'.[625] Despite savage cuts to social services and unemployment standing at three million, the Conservatives were returned on 9 June 1983 with a majority of 144 in the general election, and Mrs Eker and Mrs Rigal sent Margaret Thatcher flowers as a token of their appreciation for her 'magnificent victory' and her 'concern for Soviet Jewry'.[626]

The General Secretary Leonid Brezhnev, who had been ailing for some years and had been becoming increasingly rigid, died on 10 November 1982, opening the succession to Yuri Andropov, the former KGB chief, to whom Thatcher put out diplomatic feelers. At the beginning of 1983 Mrs Milgrom, Shchransky's mother, visited the Chistopol prison, where he had been on hunger strike for four months, to see the prison governor. Avital appealed to the Prime Minister, saying that he was now being 'forced-fed every three days', so that his very survival

---

[624] Southampton, MS254/A980/1/1/31 Margaret Rigal and Rita Eker to Thatcher 16 June 1982 and Thatcher's private secretary to Rigal and Eker 18 June 1982.

[625] Southampton, MS254/A980/1/1/31 Rita Eker and Margaret Rigal to Margaret Thatcher 21 December 1982.

[626] Southampton, MS254/A980/1/1/30 Tessa Gaisman to Rita Eker and Margaret Rigal 14 June 1983; and Eker and Rigal to Margaret Thatcher 18 June 1983. Margaret Thatcher, The Downing Street Years (London,1995), p.304.

was in danger. In her reply, the Prime Minister in an open letter to Avital commended his defiant action, stating that his stance had caught the attention of people of many faiths and nationalities, 'symbolising as it does the right of every citizen to the basic freedoms of movement and non-violent dissent'; and was influencing British public opinion. 'A decision by the new Soviet leadership to release your husband and allow him to join you in Israel would be not only a humanitarian gesture, but also a step towards better East-West relations. I earnestly hope that they will take this step'.[627] Francis Pym, the Foreign Secretary, 'raised Shcharansky's case with the Soviet Ambassador and the Soviet Foreign Minister in September 1982'. He now added in 1983 that 'A number of our partners and allies have also made high-level representations in recent months'. In Pym's view, the best course would be for the group of Ten member states of the European community to make joint representations to Andropov, but because it was impossible to reach a consensus within the group the plan was dropped. Margaret Thatcher to her credit had insisted that nothing less than Shcharansky's release from prison would be a sufficient gesture by the Kremlin. Pym saw the Soviet ambassador in London again in February, who warned that 'outside pressure could only be counter-productive'. Pym insisted that the British public was concerned about Shcharansky's health and Popov promised to report this. [628] Arieh Handler, the chairman of the National Council, thanked Thatcher and Pym, and particularly the former, for the government's intervention and for the lead she gave in the fight for basic human rights which 'has had an enormous effect on the whole campaign not only in this

---

[627] Southampton, MS254/A980/1/1/30 Margaret Thatcher to Avital Shcharansky 14 January 1983.

[628] NA, PREM 19/2547 Roger Bone to John Coles 19 January 1983; draft despatch to European partners by Roger Bone 21 January 1983; A.J. Coles to Roger Bone 24 January 1983; Francis Pym to Moscow embassy 7 February 1983; and Roger Bones to A.J. Coles 8 February 1983.

country but throughout the western world'.[629] An alternative almost madcap plan suggested by Lord Sieff, the Zionist leader, to exchange Shcharansky for the British spy Geoffrey Prime was vetoed by the Prime Minister.[630]

In March 1983, in response to an invitation from the Women's campaign to send a message of encouragement for a tree planting ceremony in honour of Anatoly Shcharansky, Mrs Thatcher despatched a message of support and affirmed that the government would continue to make the strongest representations to the Soviet authorities on his behalf.[631] In June, Avital Shcharansky added her name to the congratulatory letter with flowers from the 35's on Thatcher's general election triumph.[632]

Having learned in the same month of June 1983 that because of the swelling of his hands and feet Anatoly was finding it difficult to write, Avital sought the advice of a cardiologist Professor Allan Ross of the George Washington University Medical Center. His diagnosis was Anatoly suffered from a condition known as 'angina pectoris' because of his chest pains complicated by an irregular heartbeat. 'Appropriate management would include hospitalization followed by a battery of examinations'.[633] On 5 July 1983, his mother Mrs Milgrom and his brother Leonid were allowed to speak to Anatoly through a glass screen at Chistopol with a message from the KGB that if he asked for his release from prison on medical

---

[629] NA, PREM 19/2547 Arieh Handler to Francis Pym and the same to Margaret Thatcher 8 February 1983.
[630] NA, PREM 19/2547 Lord Sieff interview with Robert Armstrong 4 February 1983 and F.E.R Armstrong 7 February 1983.

[631] NA, PREM 19/2547 Avital Shcharansky to Margaret Thatcher 10 January 1983. Southampton, MS254/A980/1/1/30 Rita Eker to Margaret Thatcher and Joy Robilliard to Rita Eker both 11 March 1983.
[632] Southampton, MS254/A980/1/1/30 Rita Eker and Margaret Rigal to Margaret Thatcher 18 June 1983.
[633] NA, PREM 19/2547 Report of Professor Allan Ross of the George Washington University Medical Center on Anatoly Shcharansky 9 June 1983.

grounds it would be granted. He told them that the worst part of his 110-day hunger strike which ended in January 1983 was the forced feeding by his jailers. 'They tied him up, beat him when he was nearly unconscious and then forcefully pried open his mouth causing wounds and lacerations in his throat that of course did not heal in his condition and caused him considerable pain'. Afterwards 'he would try to turn the radio on full volume in order to revive himself from his state of near unconsciousness'. For the last few months before their visit, he had been kept in 'hot-house' conditions being given lenient prison treatment, such as better food and sewing one sack per day, instead of eight, without being punished. In February he had started another hunger strike to aid another prisoner. After his prolonged hunger strike his medical condition worsened, leaving him with a heart condition, he became pale and jaundiced and his hair fell out. Between 14 January and their time of meeting, he told his mother, that his weight had increased from 77 lbs to 121 lbs so as to make him 'presentable'.[634]

Leonid advised his brother that Andropov in a letter of 21 January 1983 written to Georges Marchais, the head of the French Communist party, hinted at the possibility of Anatoly's early release. He advised his mother and brother that he would not appeal to the Supreme Soviet to release him, as 'every day that I am in prison is a continuation of the illegal situation that began with my trial'. He had never deviated from the prison regime, but it was the prison authorities who had been violating their own regulations. 'So on what basis should I appeal? Any appeal would be inappropriate...I strongly urge you to find a way to convey to those people who are active politically and in public life, to all my good friends, to those working and fighting in [sic on] my behalf... those who insist on my innocence give them my warm thanks. Write them that I can make no appeal to the Soviet authorities but... the absence of an

---

[634] NA, PREM 19/2547 report of Ida Milgrom's meeting with her son Anatoly Shcharansky telephoned to Avital Shcharansky on 8 July 1983.

appeal will not have a negative effect on any decision regarding my release. Any positive decision will not depend on letters'. Anatoly ended the conversation, by saying that lodging an appeal was 'something I will not do'; it was an implicit admission of guilt. This was a clear hint that he wanted continued pressure from political leaders in the West backed by public demonstrations. From the point of view of the new leader Andropov, working towards a solution to this impasse was a priority, as it was resulting in much unwelcome, negative publicity for the Soviet regime; and it is apparent that the new policy was implemented as far back as January.[635]

Avital was again back in London from the United States to press the case for her husband's release and was staying with Lord Bethell, who arranged another meeting between her and the Prime Minister. On 15 July 1983, Avital handed Mrs Thatcher a copy of the medical report and the transcript of Mrs Milgrom's interview with her son. 'She argued that the concluding stages of the [Madrid] Conference offered an opportunity to secure her husband's release. It was inconceivable that the Madrid Agreement should be signed if it did not provide for the release of people like her husband. The Americans had earlier assured her at the highest level that they will not sign the Agreement unless there was complete understanding with the Soviet Union that Shcharansky would be released. She was worried to read in the press reports that the West was going to sign and that the Russians had proposed to release some dissidents but not her husband'. The Prime Minister admitted that the West was going to sign, as the Madrid Agreement provided for expert meetings on human contacts and for a European disarmament conference. But all she could offer were vague assurances that she would use 'every possible opportunity to bring pressure to bear on the Soviet Union' for the release of Anatoly.[636] It was a weak

---

[635] NA, PREM 19/2547 report of Ida Milgrom's meeting with her son Anatoly Shcharansky telephoned to Avital Shcharansky on 8 July 1983. Martin Gilbert, Shcharansky pp.388-90.
[636] NA, PREM 19/2547 A.J. Coles to Roger Bone 15 July 1983.

and unwelcome response, leaving everything to the Americans and not offering support at the highest levels of the British government. Meanwhile, Avital had given an assurance not to tell the press anything about the interview other than that the Prime Minister wanted to be updated on the latest position.[637]

In private bilateral exchanges at the Madrid review meeting, Max Kampelman, the head of the American delegation, was able to speak to his KGB contact Kondrachev in the spring of 1983 and avoid sending messages through the Foreign Minister Gromyko. He informed Kondrachev that the Soviets were not abiding by their human rights commitments given at Helsinki. As a start, they could release a few controversial dissidents. Kondrachev assured him that Shcharansky would be released unconditionally if he requested to be released. Kampelman asserted that Shcharansky would not ask for a pardon or sign anything which indicated his guilt but he could ask to be released on health grounds. Kondrachev checked with higher authority that this meant that he would be freed not only from prison but the Soviet Union. We have seen that when this proposition was put to Anatoly by his mother on 5 July, he rejected it because he saw it as an admission of guilt. Max Kampelman put Shcharansky's answer to Kondrachev in Madrid, who said 'Everything is now off'; but this was unacceptable to Kampelman, who retorted that letter or no letter the deal stood.[638]

During a reception at the French embassy in Moscow on 14 July 1983, Adamyshin, the head of the First European department at the Foreign Ministry, drew the British ambassador aside to tell him that the Americans were insisting on 'Soviet performance' in the human rights field, particularly over Shcharansky, and that the Russians would not yield to 'blackmail'. The ambassador said that the British government also attached major importance to

---

[637] NA, PREM 19/2547 David Wolfson to A.J. Coles 14 July 1983.
[638] George P. Shultz, Turmoil and Triumph. My Years as Secretary of State (New York,1993), pp.273-4.

human rights and 'was deeply concerned over the treatment of Shcharansky'. Adamyshin replied that 'the Soviet government had not at any time given any assurance to the Americans that Shcharansky would be released before or after the conclusion of the Madrid meeting'; and that no Soviet representative had given any such assurance, including Kondrachev. The ambassador told Adamyshin that his understanding 'was that the US government had been given to understand that the Soviet government would take action over Shcharansky'.[639] Later Kovalev, the deputy Foreign Minister and the nominal head of the Soviet delegation at Madrid, recited the usual litany that the USSR would brook no interference in its internal affairs. However, if the Soviets came to a decision which was in line with American wishes, this was coincidental. But when George Shultz, the Secretary of State, met Gromyko on 8 September 1983 and maintained that the Russians had made a commitment through Max Kampelman, the leader of the American delegation at Madrid, to release Shcharansky, Gromyko continued to deny this.[640]

On 14 July 1983, despite her son's admonitions, Mrs Milgrom sent an appeal to the Supreme Soviet asking for Shcharansky's release from prison on medical grounds. On 26 August she received a reply from one of the Deputies, stating that his request for a pardon had been rejected. No matter that Mrs Milgrom replied that 'she had not asked for a pardon, but for his release on medical grounds', nothing more transpired.[641]

The Third World Conference on Soviet Jewry was held in Jerusalem from 15 to 17 March 1983, when Dr Rhodes Boyson, an Education Minister, was visiting the country, and he read out a statement from the British Prime Minister, as the previous Brussels conference had been

---

[639] NA, PREM 19/2547 Sutherland Moscow to FCO telegram 15 July 1983.
[640] NA, PREM 19/2547 Sutherland to FCO telegram 15 July 1983.George Shultz, Turmoil and Triumph, pp.273-4 and 369-70.
[641] Martin Gilbert, Shcharansky p.391.

postponed on security grounds. This was at the suggestion of Greville Janner. Later, Arye L. Dulzin, its chairman, wrote a letter thanking Mrs Thatcher for her contribution. 'It was important that your voice be heard from Jerusalem, so that Soviet Jews will know that the free world is with them, and so that the new leader in the Kremlin will understand your care and concern about human rights for Soviet Jews, primarily their right to leave unharassed, so that they can join their families in their historic Homeland – Israel'; and a letter of thanks also came from Handler on behalf of the National Council.[642] Once again there was linking of the cause of Soviet Jewry with the more general campaign for human rights which as we have seen was used more and more extensively in correspondence; and an indication of the growing coordination between the different Soviet Jewry groups.

Repression and the Cultural Revival of Soviet Jewry

Once Andropov became leader, he failed to implement an economic or political reform programme because he could not break free of his Stalinist training, his KGB background and his experience of the Hungarian uprising. Economic reform was his long-term aim, after which political reform could follow. Andropov felt that he had to intensify his repression of refuseniks to boost his own credentials among his colleagues, as this was the regime consensus; and he was implacable in his resolve to halt emigration and to wipe out the revival of Jewish culture within the Soviet Union. Yet despite his authoritarianism, he stood out intellectually among the rather humdrum Soviet leaders, 'Andropov was absolutely brilliant'. [643]

---

[642] NA, PREM 19/2547 A.J. Coles to S.T. Crowne 10 March 1983; Arye L. Dulzin to Margaret Thatcher 23 March 1983; Dr Rhodes Boyson MP to Margaret Thatcher 23 March 1983.
[643] William Taubman, Gorbachev. His Life and Times (London,2017), pp. 141,143-4 and 191-2. 'Was Andropov of a Jewish family?'

During the fifteen months of his term as Soviet leader between 1983 and 1984, Andropov conveyed a clear message to Israel through a loyal regime journalist that 'Whether you like it or not, the saga of mass Jewish emigration from the Soviet Union has reached its end'. The dispatch added that 'it was "openly said" in Moscow that "the last train has left the station"'. From a peak of 50,000 emigrants in 1979, the numbers sunk to 88 in Andropov's last full month in office. He was determined to crush the leaders of the refusenik movement, by sponsoring trials and harsh sentencing and during his fifteen months in office none of the Prisoners of Zion were allowed to leave. He held the cultural revival of Soviet Jewry, the Hebrew classes, the religious seminars, and 'the ferment of Jewish national aspirations', in equal disdain. Shortly before assuming the supreme office, he declared that he was opposed to the 'festering sore' of false cultural demands by those whom he described as 'bad elements'. Between November 1980 and June 1982, a monitoring group recorded well over thirty incidents involving the suppression of Jewish cultural activity in the USSR, many involving the harassment of groups rather than one individual.[644] Hence the Hebrew teacher Iosef Begun was held incommunicado in prison for eleven months and then in October 1983 given a sentence of 13 years deprivation of liberty. Hence Dr Yuri Tarnopolsky was sentenced to three years in a labour camp for organizing a Jewish university in Kharkov for children of refuseniks unable to obtain higher education. Hence Moshe Abramov, a religious Jew in Samarkand, was allotted a similar sentence for encouraging religious practice among young Jews.[645]

---

https:/www.quora com; and 'USSR leader reportedly hid Jewish roots to advance in party.' JTA 18 June 1999.

[644] LMA, ACC 3087/18 National Council Cultural Committee 'memorandum on the continuing suppression of Jewish culture in the Soviet Union' circa June 1982.
[645] Jerusalem Post international edition 19-25 July 1984. Martin Gilbert, 'The man who closed the Soviet gates'.

Andropov disrupted the scientific seminars by jailing and exiling its main organizer Dr Victor Brailovsky. In early July 1984, the KGB interrogated Ephraim Katzir, the former President of Israel, who was detained in Leningrad when he tried to visit a Soviet Jew for whom he was carrying gifts; and four Israeli scientists were expelled for meeting Soviet Jewish activists and long-term refuseniks.[646]

The more the cultural revival of Soviet Jews was repressed the more they were inspired to defy their oppressors, a response which evoked massive assistance from Western Jewry. Prestin and Professor Benjamin Fain set up a new, more popular samizdat journal in 1975 called *Tarbut* (Hebrew for culture) with explanations of the Jewish festivals, the principal dates of the religious calendar and recipes.[647] Before she left for Israel in 1978, Zelda Harris, a prominent member of the Women's Campaign, was instrumental in helping to set up the Cultural Committee of the National Council for Soviet Jewry in February and campaigned vociferously for persecuted educators. The Committee was designed to support 'Jewish cultural and educational facilities in the Soviet Union' and was initially promised funds of up to £5,000 in its first year of operation. It was intended that members of the Committee would 'liaise with `tourist briefers' to improve coordination with the material going in'.[648] In July 1978, just before her departure, Zelda Harris wrote to Peter Levy that 'Cynthia [Jacobs] and the other girls have been terrific, apart from sending books with tourists and collating the requests from the USSR, many books have been sent by post'. Annette Spiers obtained 'fairly large quantities of books from publishers' and encouraged Soviet Jewry groups to send them to their own refusenik families. 'In the case of B'nai B'rith we received a donation and mailed their adopted families books which we considered suitable'. Cynthia

---

[646] Jerusalem Post international edition 8-14 July 1984.

[647] Gal Beckerman, p.337.

[648] LMA, ACC 3087/017 National Council Cultural Committee June Jacobs to Zelda Harris 6 February 1978.

Jacobs was 'very motivated and extremely well organised' but was worried about cuts to the income of her office due to the shortage of funds. 'It is vital that the office continues to function, especially now when all attention is focussed on the trials and how to "get at the Russians", the ongoing struggle for Jewish identity is something which does not hit the headlines'. Zelda was disappointed that a meeting of rabbis set up by Dov Marmur, a Reform rabbi, and the Chief Rabbi on this subject at her suggestion could have taken place without any report being forwarded to her. Nevertheless, she was glad to have been present 'at the kick-off' of an important strand of the campaign.[649]

When Zelda left for Israel, the joint leadership of the Cultural Committee was assumed by Jean Balcombe and Cynthia Jacobs. Four years later, the situation had hardly changed for the better. Information was compiled on all the ulpanim, Hebrew language classes, and Jewish cultural seminars taking place all over the Soviet Union. With the assistance of educationalists and rabbis and former refuseniks who now lived in Israel, suitable educational material was sent to the USSR. Cultural material on the festivals and Haggadot, narrating the exodus from Egypt on Passover evening, and children's booklets on Israel were produced on airmail paper. Books were sent by Wizo, Emunah, B'nai B'rith, students, various youth groups and so on to individuals, not all of whom were refuseniks, in the Soviet Union, but all of whom wanted to receive Jewish literature. The subjects covered included the Hebrew language, Jewish history, philosophy and culture. Although the despatch of the books was carefully monitored and claims were made with the Post Office if they were not received, owing to the difficulty of communicating with individuals in the USSR, only a rough estimate of their receipt could be made. On this basis, it was estimated in 1982 that 33%-50% of the items sent were delivered to their recipients. Contacts were made with the

---

[649] LMA, ACC 3087/017 National Council Cultural Committee Zelda Harris to Peter Levy 28 July 1978.

Foreign Office during the Madrid Conference to review the Helsinki Final Act in order to brief members of the British delegation on the cultural harassment of Soviet Jewry. A resolution was passed at a meeting of European MEPs in Paris urging the survival of Jewish culture in the Soviet Union which the chairman promised to pass on to the Director-General of UNESCO and at a conference of that body in London in July 1982 every delegate was informed about the confiscation of a UNESCO publication on the 'Social Life and Values of the Jewish People' by the Soviet authorities. Regular discussions were held with the Department of Industry about the Soviet interference with the post. The interdenominational Committee for Soviet Jewry, Conscience, and the National Council set up an academic support group for the Hebrew language in the Soviet Union, who protested against the persecution of educationalists; and their efforts were bolstered by VISA, the writers committee for Soviet Jewry. In conjunction with the Chief Rabbi's Office, the Cultural Committee initiated the formation of Soviet Jewry groups in United Synagogue congregations.[650]

In January 1983, Cynthia Jacobs sent George Rigal a batch of books which he wanted for posting to an individual in Riga. George was the husband of Margaret Rigal and, as in the case of the Ekers, the spouses contributed hugely to their wives' campaigning efforts. Among the books which Cynthia supplied were the Shapiro dictionary, the *Luach Hapoalim Hashalaim*, the *Tarbut* book and tape for Hebrew self-taught and the *Sifron le Student alef*. 'From past experience', she indicated that the first three books should arrive, the *Sifron le Student* was occasionally allowed and the *Tarbut* book and tape were 'new and untried'.[651] All the books were geared to the learning and teaching of Hebrew. Cynthia Jacobs was also

---

[650] LMA, ACC 3087/17 National Council Cultural Committee report circa July 1982.
[651] LMA, ACC 3087/111 Cynthia Jacobs to George Rigal 10 January 1983.

in regular contact with another member of the 35's, Ruth Eker, because she was constantly arranging for travellers to visit different cities in the Soviet Union. She informed Mrs Eker 'I have a parcel of books prepared for Marik Feldman of Lvov – is there a contact in either of the two big towns that we can leave them with? Also, I have books for David Soloveitchik in Kharkov. Perhaps they can be left with Yakir in Moscow via Paritsky – unless you have a better or more direct connection'.[652]

Throughout 1983, the Women's Campaign had concentrated on bringing Alexander Paritsky's case as well to the attention of the British government with the latest family news because he was one of the leaders of the Jewish cultural revival in the Soviet Union. When Rita Eker informed the Prime Minister about the illness that had affected their daughter, her private secretary answered that he hoped it would be treated soon, and that Alexander's case had been raised with the Soviet ambassador in October 1982 and by the British delegation at the CSCE Review meeting in Madrid on four separate occasions. Alexander was due to be released from the punishment block on 13 April and pressure would be maintained for his release from the labour camp.[653] In the middle of the summer, Rita Eker renewed her supplications on behalf of the family, as Mrs Paritsky was out of work and was receiving hospital treatment, but the greatest anxiety was caused by Alexander's physical condition. On 4 November 1983, Mrs Eker sent the Prime Minister a circular which had been sent to all adopters of the family about the deterioration in Alexander's health.[654] The only response of the Thatcher

---

[652] LMA, ACC 3087/111 Cynthia Jacobs to Rita Eker 19 December 1985.
[653] Southampton, MS254/A980/1/1/30 William Rickett to Rita Eker 15 March 1983.

[654] Southampton, MS254/A980/1/1/30 Rita Eker to William Rickett 7 July 1983, and Timothy Flesher to Rita Eker 19 July 1983. Eker to

administration was to say that they would raise his case again when a suitable opportunity arose.

Again, in March 1984 Mrs Eker informed Mrs Thatcher of the latest concerning news about Paritsky, who was released from hospital after being treated for high blood pressure. He was classified as an invalid by the prison doctor and recommended to do light work, instead of which he had been placed in solitary confinement since 24 January for allegedly breaking prison regulations. Three other prisoners were promised early release for testifying against him. Mrs Thatcher's private secretary advised Mrs Eker that the letter and the circular would be placed before her when she returned from a European Council meeting in Brussels, without eliciting a promise of further action.[655] In September, Mrs Eker wrote to the Prime Minister that she was delighted to inform her that Alexander Paritsky had been released from prison and had returned to his wife and family in Kharkov and urged her to send him a message; but Mrs Thatcher did not 'regard it as appropriate, or necessarily in Mr. Paritsky's best interests, to send him a message' – a less than robust response to a cry for help and more typical of the cautious Foreign Office approach.[656]

The Madrid review meeting of the Helsinki Accords was held against an unpropitious background of the Soviet invasion of Afghanistan, the declaration of martial law in Poland and the shooting down of a Korean airliner on 1 September 1983. Despite this, the British and Americans successfully pushed for a concluding document with incremental gains for human rights. Applications for permission to marry persons of other nationalities or for family reunification were to be decided within six months.

Rickett 4 November 1983, and David Barclay to Eker 8 November 1983.

[655] NA, PREM 19/2547 Rita Eker to William Rickett 15 March 1984 with circular to adopters of the Paritsky family. Southampton, MS254/A980/1/1/30 David Barclay to Rita Eker 19 March 1984.
[656] NA, PREM 19/2547 Rita Eker to Margaret Thatcher 10 September 1984; and David Barclay to Rita Eker 13 September 1984.

Nor were applicants to be discriminated against. Expenses incurred in connection with such applications were to be related to a sum no more than the average monthly wage. Visitors from all the participating states were to have unrestricted access to their diplomatic missions. The Madrid document affirmed religious freedom, a boon for Jews and Baptists in the Soviet Union and Catholics in Czechoslovakia.[657] Workers' rights to join and organize trade unions were recognized. In his concluding remarks on 9 September 1983, George Shultz listed his 'heroes' who gave their masters no rest, Polish workers, Czech intellectuals, East German clergy and Soviet dissidents of every description. He called for freer emigration from the USSR, especially by Jews.[658]

Andropov died on 9 February 1984 after only fifteen months in office to be succeeded by Konstantin Chernenko, who remained in command for just over one year. He was an elderly hardliner who was sick and barely able to function.[659] At the same time, Avital Shcharansky asked Margaret Thatcher to mention her husband's very dismal situation and the increasing persecution faced by Soviet Christians and Jews when she visited Moscow to assess the new leader. 'As you know ', Peter Ricketts a Foreign Office official informed a colleague, 'the Prime Minister did not in fact raise the question of human rights during her meeting with Mr Chernenko'. Her unwillingness to raise the topic was hidden behind a public relations smokescreen that her exchanges with the new Soviet leadership 'must of necessity remain confidential'. Thus, David Barclay responded to Mrs Eker and Mrs Rigal that he was 'not in a position to give you an account of the Prime Minister's exchanges with the new leadership as these must of

[657] NA, FCO 28/6424. Jorg Kastel, 'The CSCE Meeting in Madrid 1980-3'; and FCO 28/5963 A.J Williams despatch on the Madrid meeting from 8 February to 25 March 1983. D.K. Sprague to Mr Smith 31 March 1983.
[658] NA, FCO 28/6424 UKDEL Madrid to FCO 9 September 1983.
[659] William Taubman, Gorbachev pp.192-3.

necessity remain confidential. But as you know, Mrs Thatcher has repeatedly made clear her attitude to the question of human rights abuses in the Soviet Union and specifically to the case of Anatoly Shcharansky', thereby ignoring Avital's plea.[660] A request by the Women's Campaign for Mrs Thatcher to write a forward to a booklet by Martin Gilbert on Shcharansky and to be the sole patron of a concert held in his honour was fielded with an equally subtle and misleading excuse. 'To do so would identify her in a very clear way with a particular name, when there are so many victims of Soviet repression about whom she receives representations'.[661]

At the end of October 1983, the Prime Minister at the request of Arieh Handler, the chairman of the National Council, received a delegation from the Praesidium of the International Council for Soviet Jewry which was meeting in London.[662] 'Since then we have seen many reports of continuing harassment and denial of basic rights, above all the right to emigrate, by the Soviet authorities', Mrs Thatcher reiterated in a public statement two years later to the same organization which she again made at Handler's request. 'In working for better relations between Britain and the Soviet Union and for an improvement in East/West relations generally, we have not and will not soft pedal on human rights and respect for the CSCE commitments'. Handler later informed the Prime Minister that when the Praesidium met in Washington in September 1985, a 'small delegation was received by President Reagan who expressed his great pleasure when reading your

[660] NA, PREM, 19/2547 Rita Eker and Margaret Rigal to Margaret Thatcher 13 February 1984; and David Barclay to Eker 27 February 1984.

[661] NA, PREM 19/2547 Rita Eker to Margaret Thatcher 19 December 1983; R.B. Bone to J.A. Coles 6 January 1984; and A.J. Coles to Rita Eker 9 January 1984.

[662] LMA, ACC 3087/1 November 1983 Arieh Handler to Margaret Thatcher 1 November 1983.

message'.[663] Again, Handler as chairman of the National Council had much better access to the Prime Minister and at the Speaker's reception for the Board of Deputies had a quick chat with her, enabling him to mention that Ida Nudel was suffering from cancer.[664] Whereas the National Council was taken politically seriously by the Prime Minister and she met representatives from time to time, she invariably rebuffed attempts by the Women's Campaign to speak to her directly. Theirs was an epistolary romance with the Prime Minister always hinting that she would concede more on human rights than she was actually willing to give. Even when the chairman of the National Council pleaded with Margaret Thatcher to receive a deputation of women leaders on 27 April 1983, the date of Ida Nudel's birthday, the attempt was rejected as were invitations to concerts sponsored by the umbrella organization.[665]

In June 1983, Thatcher formed a new government and moved Geoffrey Howe from the Exchequer to the Foreign Office. Early in 1984, Howe met Gromyko at a CSCE meeting in Stockholm for an exchange of views. Howe saw this as an opportunity to put human rights as an item on the agenda, listing 'some of the most important names. Andrei Sakharov, his wife Elena Bonner and Anatoly Shcharansky. Gromyko was immediately dismissive... "You have lowered the tone of this conversation. I have no intention of discussing such matters with you"'. Next time Howe touched on the subject in Moscow in July 1984, Gromyko 'ignored it completely'. Undeterred, Howe returned 'to the charge' in New York at a luncheon in September, where the General Assembly was meeting. 'Quite deliberately, I raised some human-rights names with

---

[663] LMA, ACC 3087/286 Arieh Handler to Thatcher 28 August 1985, and Margaret Thatcher's statement September 1985; and Handler to Thatcher 13 September 1985.

[664] LMA, ACC 3087/286 Arieh Handler to Thatcher 15 May 1985.
[665] LMA, ACC 3087/286 Arieh Handler to Margaret Thatcher; and16 October 1984 same to the same.

him as we left the table to take our coffee when no one else was in earshot. His reply was just as prompt and even more brutal: "Sakharov", he said, taking up one of my names apparently at random, "Sakharov". That is the Russian for sugar. No thank you. I don't take sugar with my coffee'. He was grinning dismissively'.[666]

Now Margaret Jacobi took up the issue of the non-delivery of mail to the Soviet Union, eliciting a reply from the Prime Minister herself. Governments had the right to intercept incoming mail which was prohibited under their internal regulations and confiscate it, so that the exporting country could only establish the fate of a particular item and notify the sender accordingly. While complaints by the British postal authorities had been ignored, representations by the Department of Trade and Industry had been equally fruitless.[667]

Earlier in 1984, Yosef Mendelevich and Avital Shcharansky went on a tiring two-week European tour to awaken public opinion about Soviet Jewry and the Prisoners of Zion, particularly Anatoly Shcharansky to coincide with the Stockholm CSCE talks which opened in January. In a letter of thanks to Rita Eker, they praised the Women's Campaign, saying that they 'received, as always, positive reports and encouraging support for all our plans. When we arrived in London, our press conference was all arranged by our friends in [the] `35[s]'. This really could have been enough, but [the]`35[s]' stood behind us for the entire duration of our journey. This foresight and generosity filled us with wonder and joy. Whenever we had any difficulty in making a connection, printing material, making a news release or simply in financially making ends meet, we had a friendly, warm, helpful base to phone home to, ready to share our struggle. When we ran into the problem of arranging a meeting with the British Foreign Minister in London, `35[s]' succeeded not only in quickly

---

[666] Geoffrey Howe, Conflict of Loyalty (London,1995), pp.351-2.

[667] Southampton, MS254/A980/1/1/30 Margaret Thatcher to Margaret Jacobi 24 April 1984.

setting an appointment but also in housing us comfortably within walking distance of the meeting place, as the Minister would only receive us on Shabbat'.[668]

With the Soviet government tightening their repressive regime, 48 former Prisoners of Zion, including Yosef Mendelevich, Mark Dimshits, Sylva Zalmanson and Raisa Palatnik, sent an appeal to the US Congress and the governments of Canada and Western Europe on 14 August 1984, which Evelyn Nohr forwarded to Mrs Thatcher. They expressed indignation that Anatoly Shcharansky had to undertake a hundred-day hunger strike to protest against his illegal isolation from the outside world and in May Iosif Begun started a hunger strike against his worsening prison conditions and ended up in the prison hospital. They appealed to the outside powers to save the lives of these two sick prisoners and to help nullify a new Soviet law reminiscent of Stalin's era which allowed prison authorities to add up to three years imprisonment after a prisoner had served his term. Evelyn Nohr forwarded her the appeal because of the interest that Mrs Thatcher took in the case of Shcharansky.[669] Thatcher expressed general concern over the state of Russian Jewry, adding that Sir Geoffrey Howe, the Foreign and Commonwealth Secretary, had raised the case of Shcharansky when he had met the Soviet Foreign Minister, Gromyko in July 1984 as a continuing example of the plight of Soviet Jews.[670]

In December 1984, an appeal from Mark Nepomniashchy on behalf of his daughter's fiancé Jacob Levin, who was charged with anti-Soviet activities for trying to lead a Jewish life, was passed on to the Prime Minister. Nepomniashchy, too, had his home searched and had been interrogated more than once and ordered to stop

---

[668] Rita Eker Papers, Yosef Mendelevich and Avital Sharansky to Rita Eker and Margaret Rigal circa January 1984.

[669] Southampton, MS254/A980/1/1/30 Evelyn Nohr to Margaret Thatcher 21 August 1984 enclosing the appeal of 14 August 1984.
[670] Southampton, MS254/A980/1/1/30 Joy Robilliard to Evelyn Nohr 1 October 1984.

teaching Hebrew and to cease observing the Sabbath and Jewish festivals. Col. Krasnov of the Jewish department of the Odessa KGB threatened to put him in prison. Likewise, Levin was told that he would be placed in a cell with homosexuals, while his intended wife would be put into a cell with criminals, who would rape her. Nepomniashchy appealed for help to free Jacob Levin from prison and to allow him and his daughter to go to Israel.[671]

Martin Gilbert Joins the Campaign for Soviet Jewry

Meanwhile, Avital Shcharansky tried a new tactic in her campaign to secure her husband's release by appealing to public opinion worldwide. She persuaded Martin Gilbert, the eminent Oxford historian and chronicler of Churchill's life, to write a biography of Anatoly in the hope that he would be freed from detention and be reunited with her in Israel. He was also a pioneering historian of many aspects of the Holocaust. Martin Gilbert had visited the refuseniks in the Soviet Union at the beginning of 1983 at the urging of a Mr Shenhar from the Israeli embassy in London and was soon a powerful and enthusiastic advocate of their cause.[672] Between July 1983 and January 1986, Gilbert toiled at producing this memoir of Shcharansky, as his release continued to fade into a distant future. In line with his historical treatment of Jews, he presented Shcharansky as a 'Hero of Our Time' and his re-telling of the lives of the boys who survived the concentration camps, he depicted as a 'Triumph over Adversity'. To compile his biography, Gilbert interviewed refuseniks in Israel, who had been in the circle around Shcharansky in Moscow and outside activists, who knew him. Michael Sherbourne gave Gilbert the benefit of his long-term association with Shcharansky and the latter's colleagues in Moscow; and Rita Eker also

---

[671] NA, PREM 19/2547 appeal from Mark Nepomniashchy 4 December 1984.
[672] JC 15 July 1983 p.4. Communication of Michael Beizer to the author 9 August 2020.

made material available. He wrote to Enid Wurtman, whom he had met at the Third World Conference on Soviet Jewry in Jerusalem in March 1983, that 'Without you and Dina [Beilin] there would have been (1) no book (2) A very inferior book'. He recalled the time when he had addressed a meeting of former refuseniks in her flat in Jerusalem in the summer of 1983 and had been 'so nervous'.[673] In September 1983, Avital arranged a rally in Jerusalem at which she read out a defiant letter from her husband stating his refusal to confess as a spy in exchange for his freedom; and it was pertinent that Martin Gilbert and Dov Shilansky from the Israeli Prime Minister's office were chosen as the other speakers.[674]

During his visit to the Soviet Union in March 1983, Martin Gilbert visited refuseniks in Moscow and Leningrad and struck up an enduring friendship with many individuals. Interweaving their stories with historical background and information, he wrote a passionate and lively account of his travels entitled *The Jews of Hope* (1984) which was well received worldwide, thereby throwing a protective mantle over them. Since Elie Wiesel published *The Jews of Silence* in 1963, much had changed with a quarter of a million Jews allowed to leave the Soviet Union and a partial revival of Jewish culture. In the preface, Gilbert added the thought that 'Cut off from the world, the Jews of hope refuse to bow down to superior force, or to accept the threat of never being allowed to leave the Soviet Union'. When Martin Gilbert said goodbye to Yuly Kosharovsky and spoke of their meeting again in his house in England, he replied 'You are invited to my house in Israel'. The Jews of silence had morphed into the Jews of hope. The book was also a useful vehicle for publicising Anatoly Shcharansky's continued detention in the bid to secure his release.[675]

---

[673] Enid Wurtman Archives, Martin Gilbert to Enid Wurtman 19 March 1986.
[674] JC 23 September 1983, p.2.
[675] Martin Gilbert, The Jews of Hope: The Plight of Soviet Jewry Today (New York, 1985).

In an updated epilogue to the Penguin edition
published some two years later in 1985, Gilbert complained
that the number of Jews receiving exit visas had dwindled
from 51,000 in 1979 to 896 in 1984. 'Of the forty refusenik
families mentioned in... [the earlier account], the only three
granted an exit visa in the past two years were Boleslav
Dubin from Minsk; Eduard Erlich, of the Leningrad Society
for the Study Jewish Culture; and Evgenia Utevskaya, the
girl who had so courageously challenged the police
evidence in a Leningrad courtroom in August 1981'. In the
summer of 1984, she wrote to the British Prime Minister,
Mrs Thatcher, appealing for support to be allowed to
emigrate. In September Mrs Thatcher answered, expressing
'very real concern' about the difficulties facing Soviet Jews.
A month later Evgenia and her family received exit visas.[676]

Margaret Thatcher Cultivates Mikhail Gorbachev

From her days as the Opposition leader, Margaret Thatcher
arranged seminars at which experts presented papers and
spoke on various topics, including the Soviet Union, and
when she became Prime Minister she continued this policy.
There were two views on the evolution of the USSR, one
was that the Western and Soviet system had so many
features in common that democracy and the politics of
compromise would eventually be adopted by the Russians;
the other was that totalitarian states were different from
democratic ones and would never produce a democratic
leader. While sympathising with this last viewpoint,
Thatcher believed that authoritarian systems could never
completely crush the individual, as proved by the
emergence of dissidents such as Sakharov, Bukovsky,
Ratushinkaya and the refuseniks. At one of these seminars
Professor Archie Brown presented a paper in which he
asserted that 'a movement for democratizing change
[words underlined by Mrs. Thatcher on her copy of
Brown's paper] can come from within a ruling Communist

---

[676] Martin Gilbert, The Jews of Hope 1985 Epilogue pp.223-4.

party as well as through societal pressure'. After her continuing disappointment in the case of Andropov and Chernenko, she placed her hopes in the rising aspirant for leadership, Mikhail Gorbachev, whom intelligence sources had identified as a possible reformist, and invited him to visit Britain on 15 December 1984. 'As head of political intelligence at the London station [of the KGB], Oleg Gordievsky was responsible for briefing Moscow on what Gorbachev should expect in his meetings. He was also briefing MI6 on Soviet preparations'. To facilitate the success of the visit, Gordievsky even passed on the agenda for the visit to Gorbachev which was given to him by MI6.[677]

Because of the continuing rivalries in Anglo- Jewry, no representative body was able to meet with Gorbachev during his visit and put the case for the increased emigration of Soviet Jews to him. As Sir Sydney Hamburger noted to Handler: 'You... explained all the problems that had arisen and the difficulties of effecting a coordinated approach by the Board, the National Council and the Chief Rabbi, or even an agreed representation by me of these on behalf of the whole community'.[678] This lack of coordination continued after Arieh Handler became chairman of the National Council, despite his emollient style of leadership.

During Gorbachev's time in Britain, he smiled and laughed and answered Mrs. Thatcher's questions in a non-polemical manner and 'was a sharp debater'. The Prime Minister asked him why in particular constraints had been placed on Jews wishing to emigrate to Israel. He claimed that eighty per cent who had applied to leave were allowed to do so. Thatcher responded that this was not her information. Then he claimed that the others had been working in jobs connected with national security, a remark

---

[677] Margaret Thatcher, The Downing Street Years pp.452-3. Charles Moore, Margaret Thatcher vol.2 pp.110-11. The Times 15 September 2018.
[678] LMA, ACC.3087/214 Sir Sidney Hamburger to Arieh Handler 12 March 1985.

which Thatcher thought it best to ignore. The Prime Minister, however, found many of his other answers straight-forward and concluded 'I like Mr. Gorbachev. We can do business together'. On the other hand, his views on human rights issues seemed to have lagged far behind his other responses. To Neil Kinnock, the Labour leader, who asked him about Shcharansky, he 'responded with a volley of obscenities and threats against "turds" and spies like Shcharansky. Prison was "where he would stay"... and Britain would "get it right in the teeth" in a "merciless" denunciation of its own human rights violations if that was the game it wanted to play'. When pressed by St. John-Stevas MP on the Soviet failure to honour its human rights commitments, he threatened to retaliate by '"exposure" of British sins in this field'. Nevertheless, Geoffrey Howe found that when questioned on this issue, Gorbachev unlike Gromyko gave a detailed response 'with some original turns of phrase'. Meanwhile, Gorbachev cut short his visit to London to rush back to Moscow, as he had heard that Dmitry Ustinov, the Defence Minister, had died and he wanted to participate in the scramble for power because Chernenko's health was deteriorating.[679]

[679] Margaret Thatcher, The Downing Street Years pp. 459-63.William Taubman, Gorbachev pp.196-201. Charles Moore, Margaret Thatcher vol.2 pp.231-43. NA, PREM 19/1394 Mikhail Gorbachev a personal assessment by K.A. Bishop 3 January 1985; and draft assessment by Geoffrey Howe to George Shultz circa January 1985.

Chapter 7 – Mikhail Gorbachev And Glasnost

Mikhail Gorbachev Becomes General Secretary and Allows Shcharansky to Emigrate

When Gorbachev became the Soviet leader in 1985, he was relatively unknown to Western statesmen and they hurried to meet with him to ascertain his intentions. He assembled a new team and struck a hard bargain with the West to exchange Shcharansky for spies and clear that stumbling block to good relations with the United States and Europe out of the way. He began to promote glasnost, a spirit of openness in Soviet society, but what did this mean and how far would he go in allowing other notable detainees to be free to go abroad or return to their homes and for Jews to be permitted to leave in much greater numbers? He was a poor administrator and by his indecisiveness inadvertently drove Soviet society to chaos and economic ruin, while glasnost and his policy of perestroika (restructuring) unleashed powerful forces of nationalism which he found difficult to control.[680] He used the leaders of the Soviet Jewry movement as hostages to be surrendered for some concession from the West; and at the end of 1987 it was still hard to understand in which overall direction he would go. Under his rule the numbers allowed to emigrate climbed from a new low of 914 in 1986 to a modest 8,155 at the end of 1987.[681]

On 11 March 1985, Mikhail Gorbachev at the age of 54 was elected as General Secretary and as the youngest member of the Politburo was presented with an opportunity of reshaping the country's ailing economy and moving its relationship with the United States in new directions. After his predecessor's funeral, Gorbachev met Vice-President Bush and the Secretary of State George Shultz. Bush brought up the issue of human rights, telling the Soviet leader that it was an issue 'extremely important

---

[680] Vladislav Zubok, The Fall of the Soviet Union (New Haven, 2021).
[681] Pauline Peretz, Let My People Go p.344.

to the president and the American people'. The denial of Jewish emigration, the persecution in the Soviet Union of Hebrew teachers, the treatment of dissidents, of Shcharansky, Sakharov, Begun and Orlov, 'all presented central issues that we wanted to approach and discuss, consistent with the spirit and letter of the Helsinki Accords'. To this Gorbachev responded in an 'agitated way', by charging that America violated human rights within its own territory and beyond its borders, but nevertheless offered to appoint rapporteurs on human rights on both sides to discuss the issue. Bush was happy to take up this suggestion and accorded a personal invitation from President Reagan for him to visit the United States to forge a more constructive relationship. Leaving aside the question of human rights, Gorbachev agreed that they had had a useful exchange of views.[682] Until Gorbachev assembled his own team, replacing Gromyko as Foreign Minister with Eduard Shevardnadze in 1985 and selecting Anatoly Chernyaev as his principal foreign policy adviser a year later and also having input from Georgy Arbatov, Anatoly Dobrynin, and Aleksandr Yakovlev, there could be no movement on important foreign policy issues, such as President Reagan's Strategic Defence Initiative, but human rights were an area in which the Soviet leader's views were still somewhat retarded.[683]

What were the influences that shaped Gorbachev's outlook? His grandfather Andrei Gorbachev was a hardworking peasant proprietor, who by dint of extra effort advanced his family into the middle ranks of the peasantry. For being unable to fulfil impossible quota demands, he was sentenced to forced labour in a camp near Irkutsk in Siberia, where his task was to cut and haul timber. On his release for commendable hard work, he was put in charge of a pig farm on his collective farm. His other grandfather Pantelei Gopkalo joined the Communist party in 1928 and in the following year being a gifted organizer was chosen

---

[682] George Shultz, Turmoil and Triumph (New York,1993), pp.528-33.
[683] William Taubman, Gorbachev His Life and Times (London,2017), pp.221 and 253-4.

to set up the first collective farm in Privolnoe in the Ukraine. Promoted several times, Pantelei eventually joined the district procurement office which supervised the delivery of grain and other crops. During the great famine in the Ukraine because of Stalin's forced collectivisation programme, Pantelei was arrested on false charges of organizing a Trotskyite cell in 1937 and after his charge was reduced was sentenced to fourteen months in prison. On his release, he told his family how after his arrest, he had been blinded by a bright light, how the interrogator broke his arms and beat him. His brutal treatment and torture seared itself into the family's collective memory.[684] Gorbachev studied law at Moscow University before moving after graduation to an agricultural college and was remembered as an outspoken student. His close friend at Moscow University Zdenek Mlynar became a key colleague of Alexander Dubcek in Prague. During the time of the alleged Doctors' Plot against Stalin in 1952, Volodya Liberman, a Jew and a decorated ex-serviceman, was thrown off a bus by antisemites and arrived three hours late for his class. Liberman at a meeting in the law school was questioned by another student for his loyalty, only to be defended by Gorbachev, who denounced his accuser as 'a spineless beast'. But although not personally antagonistic towards Jews on an individual basis, he could later indulge in antisemitic rhetoric against those Jews who wanted to abandon the Soviet Union.[685]

With the accession of a new Secretary General in Moscow, Margaret Thatcher seized the opportunity to travel there for exploratory talks. Rita Eker on behalf of the Women's Campaign sent her good wishes for the journey and renewed her dialogue with the Prime Minister by discussing the problems of Soviet Jewry in terms of human rights. 'We hope', she continued, 'that the good relationship you established with Gorbachev during his visit to the United Kingdom will prove fruitful both for the contacts

---

[684] William Taubman, Gorbachev p.11-19.
[685] William Taubman, Gorbachev pp.41-58.

between our two countries and for the Human Rights issue which is so close to our hearts. Now, as always, the victims of Soviet religious persecution are relying on you to act as their champion'.[686]

On 10 July 1985, Mrs Eker arranged a meeting with the Prime Minister for Avital Shcharansky, accompanying her on the visit. In a briefing paper, the Prime Minister was advised that 'Mrs Shcharansky is making a round of Western capitals lobbying on behalf of her husband in the hopes that a "final heave" by Western leaders at the Helsinki Tenth Anniversary [meeting] will secure his release. Our impression from the Russians when we raised Anatoly Shcharansky's name in the margins of the Ottawa Human Rights' Meeting was that, if anything, they are more determined than ever not to be seen to be backing down in response to Western pressure on high profile cases'. Charles Powell, who was becoming one of the closest foreign policy advisers of Mrs Thatcher, sent her a minute offering her advice as to what she should say at the meeting: 'Difficult as it is to do so, the task of the Prime Minister is to steer Mrs. Shcharansky towards a lower profile approach. Her present tactics appear to be making the Russian more obdurate & defiant'.[687]

The Prime Minister had already interrupted her busy schedule to see the Parliamentary Wives for Soviet Jewry in June 1985 because of the importance she attached to their cause; and here just over a week later she was meeting with Avital Shcharansky and Rita Eker on a Soviet Jewry issue. Avital entreated 'the Prime Minister to join with other Western leaders in exerting maximum pressure on the Soviet Government in the run-up to the Helsinki 10th Anniversary Meeting and the United States/ Soviet Summit to obtain the release of her husband'. Mrs Eker maintained that maximum pressure had to be kept up on

---

[686] NA, PREM 19/2547 Rita Eker to Margaret Thatcher 12 March 1985; and Mark Addison to Eker even date.
[687] NA, PREM 19/2547C.R. Budd to C.D. Powell 9 July 1985, and minute by Powell.

the Soviet authorities. 'The evidence was that conditions for would be émigrés [emigrants] had become stricter under Gorbachev'. Mrs Thatcher did her best to disabuse Avital, saying that she saw no 'grounds for hope for his early release'. She urged her 'to consider the possibility that too much publicity for her husband's case might actually damage him because the Soviet authorities would find it difficult to back down'. Mrs Shcharansky responded that her husband had become a symbol for the hopes of all of those trapped in the Soviet Union and that 'sufficient pressure would embarrass the Soviets and cause them to relent'.[688] What the Prime Minister meant by further action was that Geoffrey Howe, the Foreign Secretary, would meet Shevardnadze on the Soviet side at the Anniversary Meeting in Helsinki, when he would raise individual cases, including Shcharansky's, but if that failed the government would try a 'lower profile approach'.[689] Unlike Avital, the Prime Minister refused to see her husband as the symbol for the hopes and aspirations of the refusenik community. Hence in succeeding months, the British government left negotiations for his release to the Americans.

For the time being Gorbachev's pronouncements after his elevation to high office on foreign affairs were stale and flat, and the flagrant abuse of human rights as far as detainees were concerned continued. Relaying the latest information about Anatoly Shcharansky from his mother, the leaders of the 35's conveyed to Mrs Thatcher that 'having spent six months in the prison of his labour camp from March until September...[he] was then sentenced to a further six months in prison until March [1986]. During the time he had been in prison he had had no visits and his last letter was written in October so there had been no word from him for three months. Anatoly was punished last March because he went on a hunger strike in protest against the withholding of his mail. His mother fears that he may have resumed his hunger strike as there has been no word

---

[688] NA, PREM 19/2547 C.D. Powell to C. Budd 10 July 1985.

[689] NA, PREM 19/2547 briefing paper 10 July 1985.

from him'. When Mrs Milgrom conferred with officials, 'she was assured that the "December letter" was on its way and that Anatoly had been seen by two doctors and that his health was satisfactory... Avital was told that her husband's weight has now been reduced to 40 kilos (6 stone 4lbs)'. The Women's Campaign leaders asked Mrs Thatcher to tell the Soviet authorities that if they were being serious about detente, they should free Shcharansky. Replying to Mrs Rigal and Mrs Eker on the Prime Minister's behalf, Mark Addison assured them that ministers were continuing to impress upon the Soviet authorities that British public opinion was disturbed and that the treatment of these brave people was unacceptable.[690] Meanwhile news came through that Alexander Paritsky had suffered a severe heart attack in prison.[691]

George Shultz, the Secretary of State, believed that human rights were a crucial issue dividing his country from the Soviets and that unless they recognized its importance to the Americans, the relationship between them would not change for the better. Overcoming the objections of his expert advisers, Shultz on a trip to Moscow in November 1985 met Gorbachev and decided to ask if he could take Shcharansky and Ida Nudel with him on his return flight, knowing that it would probably incur a negative response. He would at least compel the Kremlin to register the significance of the issue for the United States. To Shultz's delight, Gorbachev responded that if the United States gave up some of its illusions about Soviet policy in Africa and Asia, maybe the Soviet Union could move on to other matters, such as human rights.[692] Reports started to appear in the West German press at the beginning of 1986 that Shcharansky and Andrei Sakharov were to be exchanged

[690] Southampton, MS254/A980/1/1/30Margaret Rigal and Rita Eker to Thatcher 7 January 1986; and Mark Addison to Margaret Rigal and Rita Eker 23 January 1986.
[691] Southampton, MS254/A980/1/1/30 Rita Eker to Thatcher 3 February 1986.
[692] George Shultz, Turmoil and Triumph pp.586,588-9, and 594-5.

for East bloc agents but then it appeared that Shcharansky alone was to be swapped for these spies. When Shultz feared that Shcharansky would be urged to sign a letter making an admission of guilt to secure his release, on checking with Avital she assured him that Anatoly would sign nothing. At American insistence in the negotiations, when a deal had been agreed, Shcharansky crossed the Glienicke bridge to West Germany on 11 February 1986 first, following which the East and West exchanged their spies. Speaking recently about his walk to freedom, Shcharansky recalled that the trousers he had been given by the Soviet authorities were too large and that his main concern when crossing the bridge was securing them to prevent them from falling down.[693] From this time onwards Anatoly Shcharansky adopted the Hebrew name of Natan and henceforth called himself Natan Sharansky.

Immediately news came through about Sharansky's freedom Margaret Thatcher seized the opportunity to highlight her own role in his release from captivity. The contents of the message were delivered to Avital by the British embassy in Tel-Aviv with the warning that the full text would be issued after delivery to her. 'My dear Mrs Shcharansky, I cannot tell you what wonderful news it has been to me personally, and to everyone in this country, that your husband is now free. For all who are concerned about Human Rights in the Soviet Union', note the constant refrain in this message about human rights, 'he had become a symbol of the brave individual willing to stand up against the repressive machinery of the Soviet state. His struggle to maintain his religious and personal integrity in near-impossible conditions was an inspiration to us all. And of course your own untiring efforts have played a most important part in achieving today's happy result'.[694] In a

---

[693] George Shultz, Turmoil and Triumph pp.706-7. Martin Gilbert, Shcharansky Hero of Our Time (Harmondsworth,1987), pp.414-5. Natan Sharansky at Bafta on 5 November 2019.
[694] PREM 19/2547 Geoffrey Howe to British embassy Tel-Aviv 11 February 1986.

careful re-writing of history Natan Sharansky had now in the eyes of British officialdom become a fighting symbol of the refusenik community or perhaps the wider Soviet dissident ranks. The publication of Martin Gilbert's biography of Sharansky subtitled 'A Hero of Our Time' three months after his release in February 1986 further boosted Sharansky's prestige internationally and the refusenik cause. Originally Gilbert was asked to write the biography as part of the campaign to secure his release from prison and the Soviet Union, though this happily proved to be unnecessary.[695]

Shimon Peres, the Israeli Prime Minister, heralded Sharansky's release as a great moment in the history of the Jewish people. More than this, it was also a pivotal moment in the relationship between the West and the Soviets, but at the time its significance was difficult to interpret – it might have been a meaningless gesture to placate Western public opinion or it might have been the first glimmer of trust in the tense relationship between the two superpowers. Charles Powell, the Prime Minister's close adviser, informed Mrs Eker that 'the problem of Jewish emigration is an issue that the Prime Minister and her colleagues have raised on numerous occasions in contacts with the Soviet leadership. It is our hope that the much-welcomed release of Anatoly Shcharansky this week will be followed by a positive change of attitude on the part of the Soviet authorities to emigration, and, indeed, to the general question of respect for human rights'.[696]

Martin Gilbert Boosts the British Soviet Jewry Campaign

Since his trip to Moscow and Leningrad early in 1983, Martin Gilbert threw his considerable international prestige and influence behind the campaign for Soviet Jewry. He

---

[695] JC 15 July 1983 p.4. Communication of Michael Beizer to the author.
[696] Southampton, MS254/A980/1/1/30 Charles Powell to Mrs Eker 17 February 1986.

called for a flexible approach in the international protest movement. As he wrote to Arieh Handler of the National Council, 'I am sorry that my contribution at Washington ran into stormy waters. I am not political, and certainly have no wish to tread on toes. But you know that my only concern is to help our people get out'.[697] In March 1983, he met Michael Beizer, a refusenik in Leningrad, who was conducting tours of the city to show visitors and local people the sites connected with the city's past Jewish inhabitants; and encouraged him to smuggle out his researches with the help of foreign tourists which were diligently translated by Michael Sherbourne into English. The material was then assembled by Gilbert and embellished with maps and plans of the city. During a second visit to Leningrad in August 1985 by Gilbert and a further visit from Michael Sherbourne in 1987, they conferred with Michael Beizer and various outstanding points were sorted out and the book was published in the United States as *The Jews of St Petersburg: Excursions Through a Noble Past* (1989), helping him to become a professional historian when he moved to Israel.[698] Every refusenik Martin Gilbert met on his trips to the Soviet Union became 'a devoted pen friend... [for whom he campaigned tirelessly]. Despite the thousands and one things he was working on, Martin kept in touch with letters and postcards, often sent registered with return receipts to confirm that they had not been intercepted by the KGB'. Michael Beizer 'personally received more than one hundred letters, some activists twice as many'.[699] For the refuseniks in Leningrad the early years of Gorbachev's rule were clouded with the arrest and sentence to three years imprisonment each for Roald Zelichenok and Vladimir

---

[697] LMA, ACC3087/139 Martin Gilbert to Arieh Handler 19 September 1985.
[698] Michael Beizer, The Jews of St. Petersburg: Excursions Through a Noble Past (Philadelphia, 1989), introduction by Martin Gilbert; and Michael Beizer to the author 9 August 2020.
[699] Michael Beizer tribute to Martin Gilbert International Churchill Society 2015.

Lifshits and the KGB began collecting evidence against Beizer because his book on 'The Jews of St. Petersburg' was published in a samizdat.[700]

As we have seen, the publication of *The Jews of Hope: The Plight of Soviet Jewry Today* by Martin Gilbert in 1984 and in an updated version in 1985 publicised the claims to freedom for many refuseniks, whom he met on his trip in 1983; and invested them with some measure of international protection. Nor was this all the help he extended to them; he wrote about the current problems of individual refuseniks over many years in the *Jerusalem Post, Jewish Chronicle, Forward* and the *Daily Telegraph, Guardian* and *Independent*, assisting them to obtain exit permits. Writing in the *Jewish Chronicle* at the end of December 1987, Martin Gilbert mentioned that he had addressed the United Nations in Geneva in February as a representative of the British government, when he issued an appeal on behalf of Ida Nudel, Vladimir Slepak, Victor Brailovsky and other long-term refuseniks.[701] Later Martin Gilbert quietly assisted some of his friends from the Soviet Union in finding homes and employment in Israel.[702]

Help also came from Donna Wosk, a Jewish academic from California, who pleaded with Mrs Thatcher to intercede with Mr Gorbachev to allow her husband Michael Beizer to join her in the United States. The Gorbachev image of 'glasnost was nothing more than a public relations gimmick... a mask for continued repression of human rights and human dignity. Hebrew teachers continued to be imprisoned in the Gulag. Jews and Dissidents are still fed into psycho prisons and injected with psychotropic drugs which amount to nothing less than `psychic murder...' She also despatched a separate appeal to Gorbachev.[703]

---

[700] Michael Beizer to the author 11 August 2020.
[701] JC 25 December 1987 p.3.
[702] Telephone conversation with Rita Eker 11 February 2021.
[703] Southampton, MS254/A980/1/3/32 Donna L. Wosk to Thatcher 30 January 1987; and same to Gorbachev 1 February 1987.

Scientists for the Release of Soviet Refuseniks

In addition to the ceaseless efforts of the Women's Campaign and Martin Gilbert on behalf of Soviet Jewry, there was the resourceful intervention of a constituent body of the National Council, the Scientists for the Release of Soviet Refuseniks (SRSR). It was one of the best-run organizations associated with the National Council and hugely influential and its Co-Chairmen were Professor E.P. Wohlfarth of the mathematics department of Imperial College and Professor Michael Yudkin of Oxford. Its very efficient co-ordinator was Joan Dale, a public-spirited individual in whose house Colin Shindler spoke for the first time to a meeting of ladies which led to the foundation of the Women's Campaign. Joan Dale worked in close harmony with Rita Eker and they corresponded and sometimes had lunch together, while Mrs Eker liaised between the SRSR and the Medical Committee.[704] Nine members of the Royal Society, the most prestigious scientific institution in the country, Jewish and non-Jewish, served as patrons of the SRSR, at least three of whom were Nobel laureates. Professor E.P. Wohlfarth of the SRSR was invited in the summer of 1987 to sit on the executive of the National Council, while Dr Jonathan Sutton became a full-time campaign officer of the SRSR and for a period utilised the National Council's offices.[705] In turn the SRSR was affiliated to the International Federation of Scientists for Soviet Refuseniks, in which scientists from twelve nations were represented but the most dynamic associations were from the United States, Britain and France. Particularly noteworthy was the Committee of Concerned Scientists based in New York. The main activities of the International Federation and leading campaigners were intervening with governments on behalf of beleaguered colleagues in the Soviet Union and trying to attract more consistent support

---

[704] Southampton, MS254/A980/1/3/106 Joan Dale to Rita Eker 19 August 1987.
[705] Southampton, MS254/A980/1/3/106 Newsletters of the SRSR 22 September 1986 and 9 July 1987.

from colleagues in the West to attend the refusenik scientific seminars in the USSR to keep them abreast of the latest trends in research in their specific fields and to disseminate the findings of these trapped scientists. News about the situation of specific refusenik scientists was given to colleagues at national and international conferences for computer science, biochemistry, physics and so on and they were asked to sign petitions and write letters to the Soviet authorities.

The situation for Soviet refusenik scientists was still perilous in the years 1984 into the spring of 1987. Take the case of Professor David Goldfarb (1919-1990). In June 1984 Dr Michael Yudkin travelled to the USSR to participate in a meeting of the Federation of European Biochemical Societies in Moscow and at the same time visited a number of refuseniks. On his way to visit Professor Goldfarb he was stopped and questioned by militiamen. He brought to the attention of the West the plight of Goldfarb, who had been promised an exit visa, but was summoned to attend the KGB offices. Here Professor Goldfarb was warned that he was 'attempting to take [secret] bacterial strains out of the country' and was involved with 'disseminating anti-Soviet literature'. In fact, the strains were not secret and had been obtained from a Western source. From Moscow Dr Yudkin journeyed to Leningrad, where he again visited refuseniks. On 3 July, he was with Dr Evgeny Lein when they were stopped by militiamen and Lein was taken away in one direction, Dr Yudkin in another to a police station. He was forced to empty his pockets and his bag, resulting in a notebook being confiscated. A request to telephone the British consul was refused. He was informed that he was suspected of anti-Soviet agitation and espionage and advised to keep his activities confined to science.[706] In response biologists in the United States and Britain urged colleagues not to supply bacterial strains for research to their Soviet counterparts until the charges against Professor Goldfarb were dropped. This resulted in a new charge

---

[706] Southampton, MS254/A980/1/3/106 Newsletter of the SRSR 18 July 1984.

against the Professor of supporting the moratorium campaign.[707]

However, Professor Goldfarb's son Alex had been allowed to leave the USSR some years earlier and having settled in the United States was anxious that his parents should join him there, especially as Professor Goldfarb was crippled with diabetes and heart disease. Professor Goldfarb was asked by the KGB to incriminate the American journalist Nicholas Daniloff by signing papers but refused to do so, thereby sacrificing a chance to leave the Soviet Union. One of his toes was amputated because of diabetes and he required further surgery. Alex asked Mr Armand Hammer, the chairman of the Occidental Petroleum Company, who had close business ties with the Soviet Union and was used as a go-between by American Presidents, to assist him. Meanwhile, Professor Goldfarb had risen to the top of the American priority list of Soviet citizens denied exit visas to reunite with relatives in the United States. On a visit to the Soviet Union in October 1986, Dr Hammer intervened with Mr Dobrynin, the Washington ambassador, who said he could do nothing. But the request reached Mr Gorbachev, who, to escape from the international opprobrium which this case was causing and the scientists' pressure over releasing bacterial strains for research, granted permission. On 16 October, Professor Goldfarb because of ill health was strapped into a reclining chair and whisked away to the United States with his wife on Mr Hammer's private jet. After Professor Goldfarb's death in 1990, his daughter Olga was given exit visas for herself and her two daughters in May which was in accordance with her father's last wishes.[708]

Dr Evgeny Lein, was a senior scientist at the Research Institute of the Cellulose Industry. He was sentenced to two years corrective labour on a spurious charge of assaulting a policeman, three years after applying to emigrate. To

---

[707] Southampton, MS254/A980/1/3/106. Nature (January 1985).
[708] New York Times 26 February 1990. Southampton, MS254/A980/1/3/106 Newsletter of the SRSR 22 September 1986. Australian Jewish Times 1 May 1987.

escape a new charge of parasitism, he was compelled to work as a stoker at a site, where he was exposed to a high level of noise which made him deaf in his right ear. Dismissed from his employment after requesting a transfer, he was given a thrashing by plainclothes policemen, who concentrated their blows on his left ear. Dr Lein and his wife Irina were only allowed to leave for Israel in 1989, after a long international campaign on their behalf. Another refusenik, Joseph Berenshtein, an engineer, was given a sentence of four years in a labour camp in Zhitomer in the Ukraine, after applying to emigrate. In his cell he was slashed by other prisoners with broken glass across his face and eyes, severely damaging his eyesight. When his wife and grown-up daughter visited him in prison, they could not recognize him, so changed had a 45-year-old-man become.[709] Many scientists and mathematicians remained trapped in the Soviet Union, despite intensified international campaigning, but a few fortunate individuals were granted permission to leave in Gorbachev's early years in power. The Khachaturyans obtained exit visas, while the Goldshtein brothers were expected to follow them on 20 April 1987.[710]

Professor Philip Siegelman of the Scientists for Sakharov, Orlov and Shcharansky, an organization supporting Soviet dissidents, wrote to Professor Wohlfarth of the SRSR on 24 April 1986 complaining that 'We have just been through a disheartening effort to get the [American] National Academy of Sciences to take a serious position on human rights in its negotiations with the Soviet Academy for the re-establishment of bilateral exchange programs. The new exchange agreement has just been published revealing that human rights considerations are virtually invisible. This is massively disappointing to us (and to Dr Elena Bonner with whom we have been conferring) though

---

[709] Southampton, MS254/A980/1/3/106Newsletter of the SRSR 12 February 1985.
[710] Southampton, MS254/A980/1/3/160 Newsletter of the SRSR 14 April 1986.

not surprising. What is also very distressing is the unwillingness of NSAS members to speak out in protest'.[711]

The Nuclear Explosion at Chernobyl

A couple of days later, on 26 April 1986 at 1.23 am, a nuclear reactor at an atomic power station at Chernobyl near the town of Pripyat in the Ukraine exploded, thrusting a massive amount of radioactive material into the night sky, more than ten times the amount generated by the bomb dropped at Hiroshima. More than 336,000 inhabitants were too slowly evacuated from the surrounding area after exposure to radioactive material by the Soviet authorities, some later dying from the early onset of cancer. In the Soviet Union news of the event was suppressed until Swedish scientists detected excessive levels of radiation which did not come from their own reactors. On I May, despite the high levels of radiation, a May Day parade went ahead, as Gorbachev insisted on holding it, brushing aside pleas not to do so; and Western broadcasts alerting people to the dangers of radiation were jammed.[712] On 14 May Gorbachev addressed the nation on television, admitting the disaster. The clean-up operations almost bankrupted the country, forcing Gorbachev to accelerate economic reforms which he had proposed delaying until the 1990s, but he never could make up his mind about introducing a completely free market economy or abolishing collective farms; but the disaster persuaded him to sign a nuclear non-proliferation treaty with President Reagan in 1987 in order to save defence costs. Grachev claimed that Gorbachev 'crossed a psychological barrier' after Chernobyl freeing him to take 'more decisive action', though his later dithering with economic reform makes this seem doubtful. Like his mentor Andropov, he proceeded cautiously,

---

[711] Southampton, MS254/A980/1/3/160 Professor Philip Siegalman to Professor E.P. Wohlfarth 24 April 1986.
[712] Serhii Plokhy, Chernobyl. History of a Tragedy (London,2019), pp.84-6,121,177-8, and 186-8.

wasting time appeasing the hardliners, by introducing the anti-alcohol drive and campaigning against unearned income and individual labour activity. While he allowed Sakharov's wife to travel to the United States for medical treatment, he appeased members of the politburo, by caustically remarking that Elena Bonner's influence on her husband showed 'what Zionism is'.[713]

The Women's Campaign and Soviet Dissidents Educate Margaret Thatcher on Human Rights

Throughout 1986 there seemed to be little progress on humanitarian gestures, apart from the release of Sharansky and Dr Yuri Orlov's forced expulsion and deprivation of Soviet citizenship in October. At the end of the year, Sakharov was released from internal exile and allowed to return to Moscow. Prominent dissidents and others not so well known, however, languished in goal or in a state of limbo. In April 1986, Mrs Eker wrote to the Prime Minister enclosing a letter from Mrs Orlovsky, pleading with her to intervene on behalf of her sister Maria and her husband Vladimir Slepak, a well-known refusenik.[714] In May, Mrs Thatcher planned to visit Israel and Mrs Eker and Mrs Rigal wrote wishing her a 'successful visit...and...an opportunity to relax for a while and enjoy the sunshine'. They also commended her for the support given to Jews, who wished to leave the Soviet Union. In her reply, the Prime Minister mentioned that she hoped 'to meet a member of Ida Nudel's family to mark my support for the continuing campaign to secure her release'.[715] During her visit to Israel from 24-27 May, Mrs Thatcher met Natan Sharansky and heard 'at first hand some of his experiences, as well as ... witness[ing] the

---

[713] William Taubman, Gorbachev pp.240-51.
[714] Southampton, MS254/A980/1/1/30 Rita Eker to Thatcher 4 April 1986 and Henrietta Orlovsky to Thatcher April 1986.
[715] Southampton, MS254/A980/1/1/30 Rita Eker and Margaret Rigal to Thatcher 20 May 1986 and Thatcher to Rita Eker 22 May 1986.

joy of his freedom'. Although she refused an invitation to attend a dinner in his honour in London, she sent a public message of support to a meeting at the Albert Hall on 21 September 1986, hailing him as 'the symbol of the brave individual standing up to the repressive machinery of the state'; and promising that her government would not forget the plight of those still not allowed to leave.[716] The Prime Minister was saddened by Mrs Eker's letter in October, reporting that once again the Paritsky family had not been allowed to leave the Soviet Union.[717] Such was Mrs Thatcher's reputation, that an increasing number of Russian Jews living in Israel whose close family were still trapped in the Soviet Union begged her to intervene with the Soviet authorities on behalf of their relatives. A visitor to the Soviet Union brought back a letter from the Tufeld family in December specifically addressed to the Prime Minister, urging her 'as a good mother, kind & responsive' person to help them be reunited with their only son Igor in Israel.[718]

Apart from this ceaseless correspondence, the two leaders of the 35's exploited every conceivable opportunity to contact the Prime Minister, when they wrote to her on the wider issues of the campaign because they knew she was always ready to listen to them. They exclaimed how distressed they were by reports in the British press that 'only the American delegates refused to sign the final draft at Berne which would have excluded Israel from those countries where reunification of families was to be expedited'. The Soviet Union thought that 'when it comes to the crunch, Jews are regarded as less important than the

---

[716] Southampton, MS254/A980/1/1/30 Rita Eker and Margaret Rigal to Thatcher 5 June 1986 and same to the same 11 June 1986; and Thatcher to Rita Eker and Margaret Rigal 8 September 1986.
[717] Southampton, MS254/A980/1/1/30 Charles Powell to Rita Eker 12 November 1986.
[718] Southampton, MS254/A980/1/1/30 Rita Eker to Thatcher 8 December 1986 and Izolde and Vladimir Tufeld to Thatcher December 1986.

rest of the human race not only within the USSR but worldwide'. Since they were confident that this was not her view and the document had not been signed, it was not too late to undo any harm. 'Please for the sake of four to five hundred thousand Soviet Jews waiting for exit visas, do not arrange for any agreement with the USSR which excludes the Jews and Israel'.[719]

In November 1986, Sir Geoffrey Howe, the Foreign Secretary, met Eduard Shevardnadze, the Soviet Foreign Minister, for a bilateral meeting on human rights and various other matters, such as the Middle East and fishing rights around the Falkland Islands, while leaving aside the subject of arms control. Sir Geoffrey said that of the personal cases that he had handed him in New York, the case of Laptev had been settled. On the wider issue of human rights cases, he was glad to see the resolution of the cases of Sharansky and Orlov. 'He did not propose to go through the list which was well-known, ranging from people like Sakharov to Ratushinskaya [a poet]. We were glad to see that she had been released from prison but were concerned that she was unable to get an exit visa to come to England for medical treatment... Shevardnadze understood that there was no time to go through the full list of cases. But he wanted to make the point that all countries should bring their laws, institutions, and rules on human contacts and rights in line with the relevant CSCE and UN documents. He recognised that the Soviet Union had much to do, and it was already doing a lot. They were also prepared to bring their laws into line with the Berne Agreements, which had been reached but not adopted. They would look at specific requests, taking considerations of humanity into account'.[720] This showed considerable movement and flexibility on the Soviet Union's part, a sign perhaps of progress.

---

[719] Southampton, MS254/A980/1/1/30 Rita Eker and Margaret Rigal to Thatcher 30 May 1986.
[720] National Archives, PREM 19/3174 Telegram 169 from Vienna to London November 1986.

Accompanied by Lord Bethell, Dr Yuri Orlov (1924-2020), a physicist and founder of the Helsinki Monitoring group with such refuseniks as Sharansky and Vladimir Slepak, saw the Prime Minister on 28 November 1986 in order to brief her before her meeting with Gorbachev. A session with photographers was arranged before the meeting, a strong hint to the Soviets that she had broad sympathy for his views. Orlov had already sent her important documents outlining his ideas for Russia's future and recounting his prison experiences and those of internal exile from 1977 until 1986. His worst moments were being accused of theft by other prisoners, who had been broken and suborned by the prison authorities, and spending time in the isolation cell for legitimate complaints. In the cell, where the temperatures were below freezing, the bunks were wooden planks held together by metal strips which were bitterly cold. 'Every night I used to rub the planks with my hands to warm them up. Then I would lie down, fall asleep, wake up again ten minutes later because of the cold, start rubbing the planks again with my hands, and so on hour after hour getting just a few minutes sleep at a time'. He was deprived of citizenship against his will, expelled from the Soviet Union, and granted refuge in the United States.[721]

In his thoughts on Russia's future, Orlov claimed that 'the world's main guarantee of peace...is not disarmament but the building up of trust and confidence between peoples. For instance, Britain and France both have nuclear weapons, but you're not going to use them against each other. Your links are too close for that. The same sort of links must be built up between the Soviet Union and the West, and this can only be done by making the Soviet Union a far more open society, allowing a free press, non-violent dissent, different political ideas and foreign travel. Disarmament is not the main thing. Nuclear weapons can never be entirely done away with... they can always be rebuilt if a country feels threatened by conventional forces.

---

[721] National Archives, PREM 19/3174 Yuri Orlov's Experiences 1977-86.

So the only way to prevent it is by confidence-building measures, as envisaged in the [Helsinki] Agreement. Millions must be allowed to travel – and freely, without being guarded all the time as they are now. And this is why the human rights movement is so important'. While these reforms cannot be implemented overnight, they will take a shorter time than Gorbachev envisages. 'The great barrier, I think, is not Gorbachev himself or the top leadership, but the middle ranks of the Soviet bureaucracy who have so firmly dug in to the system as it exists today. The KGB, for instance, is a very strong negative force. They want to preserve their power and role in society. Implementation of my ideas would reduce this power. I still have some hopes in Gorbachev. It's too early to say, though. We'll have to see. He has improved things over criticism of the authorities. Regional Party secretaries, for instance, can now be criticised in the press. So can ministers, but not the Central Committee or the Politburo. One can criticise the police, but not the army and certainly not the KGB'.[722]

In a scintillating analysis on the position of the Jews and other dissidents in Gorbachev's Soviet Union, Orlov contended that 'the situation over Jewish emigration has got worse. Even fewer are being allowed to leave than before Gorbachev got to power. I think though that this is a card that Gorbachev and the leadership will play if and when it comes to the point that they need better relations with the West and a more liberal policy at home. All these concessions over human rights, myself included, are cards in Mr Gorbachev's hands. And he plays them when it suits him. For the moment Jewish emigration is not necessary for him, so they stay in the Soviet Union as hostages, for the moment, ready to be used in the future'. He explained to President Reagan that 'he should defend and try to free the Soviet Union's political prisoners, who are as it were the pioneers of this openness that we want'. Anyway there were not a huge number of political prisoners. 'The number

[722] National Archives, PREM 19/3174 Yuri Orlov's Ideas for Russia's Future November 1986.

of actual political dissidents in prison, those sentenced under Articles 64 (treason) and 70 (anti-Soviet agitation), I would put at something between 200 and 300, not counting collaborators with Nazi Germany or those genuinely guilty of spying for the West...The number of those convicted on other less serious political charges, under Article 190 which carries a maximum of three years imprisonment, is harder to calculate. There are people who refuse to serve in the army, the Pentecostals for instance, or Jews who wish to emigrate, or others who simply object to serving as a matter of conscience. The figure of 10,000... is too high, but it may be in the range of 2,000 to 3,000'. Without the implementation of reforms guaranteeing openness, peace cannot be maintained.[723]

When Thatcher met Orlov, she told him that she had read his briefing papers and agreed that 'we should not treat relations with the Soviet Union as being only a matter of arms control. The genius of the Helsinki Accords was that they gave the West a locus for asking about human rights in the Soviet Union. Without that, the Soviet Union could always have argued that these were purely internal issues'. Because of the shortness of time, Orlov stated that he wanted to deal with one specific issue, that 'was Shevardnadze's proposal for holding a human rights conference in Moscow'. The Prime Minister was grateful for his advice on staging such a conference in Moscow and the necessity, if it was held there, to have strict stipulations as to who would be able to attend. She was extremely sceptical about 'any promises made by the Soviet Union about the conditions for such a conference would be honoured...Once we got locked into discussions with the Soviet Union, the West would be driven by a compulsion to compromise which the Soviet Union would exploit. She would therefore try hard not to have it in Moscow'.[724]

---

[723] National Archives, PREM 19/3174 Yuri Orlov's Ideas for Russia's Future November 1986.
[724] National Archives, PREM 19/3174 Charles Powell to Colin Budd on PM's meeting with Dr Orlov 28 November 1986.

Orlov was of the opinion that while at the Vienna Review conference which opened on 4 November 1986 everyone was speaking about human rights, the majority were unwilling to name the Soviet Union for its flagrant abuse of these rights. 'Most of the western delegations have failed to mention the names of individuals who should be released immediately from prison, labour camps, exile or psychiatric detention, or of the refuseniks who have waited many exhausting years to leave the country', he remonstrated.[725] George Shultz's speech at the opening session was sharp in tone and named more specific cases than the Foreign Secretary on behalf of the European states. Despite opposition from colleagues, he mentioned Sakharov.[726] 'It is essential to demand, openly and persistently, a universal political amnesty in the USSR, Orlov continued... This would lead to the release of at least 800 political prisoners, first and foremost the 40 or so who monitored the observation of human rights agreements. At the very top of the list should be Dr Andrei Sakharov, Anatoly Kosryagin [a psychiatrist imprisoned for exposing abuses]... writer Anatoly Marchenko, the Jewish leader Iosif Begun and Professor Naum Meiman and his wife, who has cancer. It is crucial to lay down in the text of the next concluding document the unassailable rights of citizens to monitor human rights'.[727] The outcome of the continued pressure by the United States and the European states in Vienna was that Dr Sakharov was released from internal exile in December 1986 by Gorbachev, who spoke personally on the telephone to him, to show by this concession to the Western powers that he was prepared to negotiate with them. In addition, the poet Irina Ratushinskaia and Igor Gerashchenko were allowed to leave for London.[728]

Undeterred by this concession, Dr Orlov pressed Thatcher on 29 December to 'raise the question of a

[725] The Times 26 November 1986.
[726] National Archives, PREM 19/3174 Charles Powell 'Essential Facts' November 1986.
[727] The Times 26 November 1986.
[728] George Shultz, Turmoil and Triumph p.749.

universal political amnesty in the USSR, both openly, in public statements, and privately, in closed discussions' at her forthcoming high-level meetings in Moscow. This would result in the freeing of at least 800 political prisoners. Since the two had last met Anatoly Marchenko, a political prisoner, had died after prolonged hunger strikes and Academician Sakharov had pleaded for the release of prisoners of conscience. He further requested that she should not sign a concluding document in Vienna, unless the USSR agreed to a political amnesty, claiming added support for his viewpoint from Sharansky and others in the Helsinki Monitoring group.[729] Following advice from the Foreign Secretary, Thatcher replied that she was 'not convinced that we should necessarily refuse to sign the final document if the USSR do not agree to a complete political amnesty. My fear is that this could stop us from following up the Vienna meeting, and thus actually deprive us of the advantage the Helsinki Accords offer in providing a forum for continuing public scrutiny of the Soviet human rights record'.[730]

At the end of 1986, Rita Eker and Margaret Rigal sent the Prime Minister the 35's calendar, wishing her and her family 'a happy and peaceful new year'; and remarking that 'Despite the token gesture by the Soviets in releasing a few of the leading activists, the situation of the Prisoners of Conscience is as terrible as ever'. In the typewritten section of the reply, Mrs Thatcher acknowledged that the calendar would 'serve as a constant reminder during the year of the tragedy and injustice still suffered by so many Jews in the Soviet Union'. In a few lines penned in her own hand, she thanked them 'for the lovely flowers which will give us so much pleasure although we remember those who would love to see them'. If nothing else, this correspondence illustrates the rapport which existed between the two ladies

---

[729] National Archives, PREM 19/3174 Yuri Orlov to Thatcher 29 December 1986.
[730] National Archives, PREM 19/3174 Lynn Parker to Charles Powell 13 January 1987; and Thatcher to Yuri Orlov 15 January 1987.

and the Conservative leader. At the same time, there was always the risk that if they were too close to the government, they might damage their cause with the Opposition when it came to power.[731]

Surveying the situation over the past year in the Soviet Union, the National Conference on Soviet Jewry, an American body, published an analysis. Jewish emigration from the Soviet Union in 1986 was 914, a twenty per cent drop from 1,140 entitled to leave in 1985, the year of Gorbachev's accession.' Despite Soviet gestures in a few high visibility cases, such as those of Natan Sharansky and David Goldfarb, (or non-Jewish dissidents, such as Yuri Orlov and Andrei Sakharov), nearly 380,000 Jews await being processed for emigration, among them 11,000 refuseniks, and Prisoners of Conscience... who have been harassed, attacked, arrested and imprisoned because they may wish to emigrate, or teach Hebrew. The persistent harassment and intimidation of Jewish self-study efforts to sustain culture and religion continues. Despite a discernible shift in tactics since General Secretary Gorbachev assumed leadership of the Communist Party of the Soviet Union, the results of the shift, such as the new emigration decree, proved to be merely tactical and cosmetic'. The new emigration code which became effective on 1 January 1987 narrowly defined family as including only parents, children and siblings, thereby making it impossible for hundreds of thousands to apply for exit visas.[732] This somewhat gloomy survey echoed in greater detail the assessment of the Women's Campaign leaders to Mrs Thatcher.

Nor on the cultural front were the auguries any better for Jews in the Soviet Union. The Chief Rabbi Immanuel Jakobovits had been in touch with the Soviet ambassador to

---

[731] Southampton, MS254/A980/1/1/30 Rita Eker and Margaret Rigal to Thatcher 30 December 1986; Mark Addison to Mrs Eker 2 January 1987; and Margaret Eker to Mrs Eker 2 January 1987.
[732] Southampton, MS254/A980/1/3/32 National Conference on Soviet Jewry, 'The Illusion of Glasnost' circa 1987.

Britain, Leonid Zamyatin, a wily operator, skilled at deflecting awkward questions from Western journalists, about a proposed trip to Moscow by a delegation from the Conference of European Rabbis in order to discuss matters affecting Soviet Jewry.[733] Jakobovits had been to the USSR once before at the end of 1975, when he had been hoodwinked by the KGB by participating in a Potemkin tour and only meeting middle-ranking officials, so that his impressions were superficial and his assessment somewhat over-optimistic. Activists, such as Professor Alexander Voronel, head of the Soviet Immigrants Aliya Committee, claimed that the Chief Rabbi had been deceived by clever Soviet propaganda. What irked him was a comment attributed to Jakobovits that there was no antisemitism in the Soviet Union, which seemed to betray his naivety. Aliya activists were incensed by the assurance given to him by the deputy head of Ovir (the visa bureau) and repeated by Jakobovits that '98.6 per cent of all emigration applications had been granted and that the 1.4 per cent would not be a permanent group, thus indicating that the present 'refuseniks' too would sooner or later be allowed to leave'. Activists claimed that only a third of visa applications were granted per month and that 'well over 100,000 visa applications pending have been refused'. Part of the vehemence behind the attack was the frequently quoted remark of the Chief Rabbi that 'efforts for aliya must be equalled by efforts to secure religious and civil rights of Jews, who remain in the USSR'.[734]

Since the visit of Jakobovits in 1975, the situation on the ground among Soviet Jewry had in certain respects changed for the better. There had been a small religious revival. According to Yirmiyahu Branover, Professor of Magnetohydrodynamics at Ben Gurion University, speaking in April 1984 there were about 2,000 people who had returned to Judaism and perhaps as many as 10,000 people connected to the movement. Older people, who had

[733] The Times 7 August 2019 obituary of Leonid Zamyatin.
[734] JTA news bulletin 8 January 1976.

a yeshiva education, had encouraged the spiritual revival. 'The returnees believe in the importance of sharing whatever they learn whether it is the Hebrew alphabet, halachah [rabbinic law], or a bit of Chumash [the Five Books of Moses] and [the] Rashi [commentary]. People who visit Russia and see the ba'alei t'shuva [religious penitents] walking in the streets of Moscow with their payot [sidelocks], black suits, and black hats, risking arrest by the KGB, can't believe their eyes'. Branover had migrated to Israel in 1972 and was chairman of an organization of Orthodox immigrants from the Soviet Union known as Shamir which had published a hundred book in Russian on Jewish subjects, including translations of the Pentateuch, the Ethics of the Fathers, and Yehuda Halevi's Kuzari , a classic medieval philosophical text.[735]

But the whole movement had also been immensely boosted by Western visitors. Ernie Hirsch made a trip to Moscow from London in 1979 and was appalled by the living conditions but stimulated by the thirst for spiritual knowledge among the Jews in the Soviet Union. In 1981 he founded an organization known as RRJ, Russian Religious Jews. 'Working around the clock, Ernie and his family would pack suitcases, brief and debrief their emissaries, raise the necessary funds and keep meticulous records – all from their Hendon home. Information about the Community's needs was provided by Rav Eliyahu Essas... Every fortnight, a team of two agents was sent to Russia – often one would give shiurim [religious lessons] and the other would attend to logistics. Ernie handpicked men and women who could teach Torah and attend to communal needs, making sure to send a variety of role models, including dayanim [judges of rabbinic courts], rabbonim and professionals. A staggering 246 individuals made the journey – with many travelling twice'. Rav Essas communicated regularly with Mr Hirsch, informing him as to which supplies and teachers were needed. Two festival prayer books were brought in by visitors and the visas

---

which had a record of this would be complied with by switching other books in their place. For the festival of Tabernacles lulovim [palm branches]would be smuggled in bunches of flowers, while etrogim [citrons] were passed off as fruit for making tea.[736] In addition, the National Council for Soviet Jewry established an office for the Support of Jewish Culture in the Soviet Union to produce specific study programmes on Judaism, Israel and Jewish life in the Diaspora and self-teaching kits and guides for teachers; they aimed to introduce more specific information to tourists to avoid the mistakes of the past; and they issued a guide for posting books to the Soviet Union.[737]

A Delegation from the Conference of European Rabbis hoped to receive an invitation from the Council for Religious affairs, after an agenda had been agreed, and a chance to meet Mr Gorbachev. Among the items placed on the agenda were opportunities for Jewish education of children with parental approval, the availability of religious textbooks and instruction in elementary Hebrew, and cultural programmes on the Jewish tradition and its history for adults; opportunities for Western rabbis to serve Jewish communities in the Soviet Union for one or two years, where such officials were not available; easy access to kosher food in shops and restaurants for Soviet citizens and foreign tourists; and the provision of Jewish old-age homes and cemeteries. Freedom was sought for Soviet Jews to emigrate to Israel without hindrance, and 'in the case of security considerations after a maximum of five years... Most anxiously we seek the release of Jewish prisoners and internal exiles on humanitarian grounds, particularly when the sentence arose from a charge involving the pursuit of Jewish culture and Hebrew studies'. As expected, Zamayatin in his reply parried their request, by confirming

---

[736] Aviva Landau, 'To Russia with Love and Mesiras Nefesh', Hamoar (September 2017).
[737] Alyth Gardens Soviet Jewry Archive, National Council for Soviet Jewry, Working Group for the Support of Jewish Culture and Education in the Soviet Union leaflets.

that the Council for Religious Affairs would be ready to receive a delegation on a religious visit, while other questions could not be discussed, as they had nothing to do with the religious aims of the visit; and that the Chief Rabbi of Moscow would send an official invitation when they applied. He also demanded an answer to a wholly irrelevant letter, in which he claimed there was widespread antisemitism in Britain which the Chief Rabbi dutifully answered in a separate communication.[738]

In rebuttal of the Soviet ambassador, the Chief Rabbi thanked him for the confirmation that the delegation of European rabbis would be received by the Council for Religious Affairs and emphasised that while they would be happy to meet Chief Rabbi A. Shayevich in Moscow as well as other Jewish leaders and groups, it had never been suggested in the correspondence that he would act as their host. The twelve specific items on the agenda were 'all of Jewish religious concern to us as rabbis'; and noted that if there was to be 'any meaningful discussions between rabbis and the Soviet leadership', they 'must feature' on the agenda; and asked for the name and address of the person on the Council for Religious Affairs to whom he was supposed to write about the proposed visit. He assumed that this person was familiar with their correspondence and the items on the agenda. This was a 'genuine attempt' to promote 'religious freedom', 'by removing the plight of millions of our co-religionists as a major obstacle to better understanding and goodwill'.[739]

As the Prime Minister was visiting the Soviet Union in March 1987, the Chief Rabbi sent her copies of his correspondence with the Soviet ambassador about religious freedom, remarking that the response had been 'distinctly unsatisfactory'; and requested a short meeting with her to discuss this. Charles Powell stated that the Prime Minister

---

[738] NA, PREM 19/2547 Rabbi Immanuel Jakobovits to Leonid Zamyatin 24 November 1986; and same to the same 2 December 1986.
[739] NA, PREM 19/2547 Rabbi Immanuel Jakobovits to Leonid Zamyatin 15 December 1986.

would be delighted to see him on 9 March but suggested that he should either speak for all the Soviet Jewry groups, who would also wish to be heard because of the forthcoming visit, or that one or two of their representatives should accompany him.[740] However, the Board of Deputies and the National Council for Soviet Jewry appear to have insisted on a separate appointment and the Chief Rabbi conferred with the Prime Minister at a re-scheduled appointment, when she promised to pass on his request for an official invitation for a delegation of European rabbis to visit the USSR.[741] She seems to have digested the Chief Rabbi's concerns, for at a meeting with Edgar Bronfman of the World Jewish Congress she told him that 'it is impossible for Jewish culture to flourish in Russia'.[742]

In the new year, it was announced that the Prime Minister's forthcoming visit to the Soviet Union would take place between 28 March and 2 April 1987. At once the leaders of the 35's voiced their concerns to the Prime Minister. Refuseniks in Moscow had asked them to transmit a message to her that they remained 'adamant that neither the USA[n]or Great Britain should make trading arrangements or lift existing sanctions in order to persuade the Soviet Authorities to grant them the rights that have already been promised under the United Nations Human Rights Charter. They expressed strong fears that some well-intentioned people might suggest altering the Jackson-Vanik Amendment or in other ways weakening the West's position. The Refuseniks hope that you will visit them whilst you are in Moscow and they are most anxious that you should see a representative group not only the most prominent academics'. The two ladies informed Mrs Thatcher that the Soviet authorities were harassing Natasha Khassina, who since Ida Nudel's arrest in 1978 had taken

[740] NA, PREM 19/2547 Rabbi Immanuel Jakobovits to Margaret Thatcher20 January 1987; and Charles Powell to Jakobovits 22 January 1987.
[741] JC 13 March 1987, p.48 and 10 April 1987, p.1.
[742] JC 16 January 1987, p.10.

over the task of looking after the welfare of prisoners of conscience; and appealed to the Prime Minister to visit or telephone her to ensure her safety. Charles Powell replied that the question of trust was central both to security concerns and human rights. This made 'it essential to maintain the pressure for progress in parallel on both human rights and security matters, as well as other areas (e.g. Afghanistan) where Soviet behaviour is unacceptable'.[743]

Dr Iosif Begun was employed as a radio engineer with a research institute but was dismissed from his position on applying to emigrate and started working in menial jobs and as a Hebrew teacher. When he demanded that the teaching of Hebrew be officially recognized and stopped working, he was arrested in March 1977, charged with parasitism and sentenced to two years exile in Siberia. When he returned to Moscow, he was charged with breaking residency restrictions for ex-prisoners, prosecuted and sentenced to three more years in exile. Freed, he returned to Moscow in 1981 and resumed his teaching activities. But at the end of 1982 Yuri Andropov, the ex-KGB chief, became the Soviet leader and was determined to crack down on the refusenik movement which was causing a brain drain of educated Jews, many of whom were technocrats, whom he believed the ailing Soviet economy could not afford to lose. This time Begun was charged with anti-Soviet agitation or propaganda, a charge which could carry a seven-year gaol sentence, followed by five years in internal exile. All this treatment of Begun was meant to terrorize the remaining refusenik community. At the beginning of 1987, Gorbachev declared an amnesty for about 140 political prisoners, who included Hebrew teachers and Jewish activists, such as Begun, as part of his broader initiative for a rapprochement with the West; and in February they were released from confinement. The

---

[743] Southampton, MS254/A980/1/1/30 Rita Eker and Margaret Rigal to Thatcher 22 January 1987; and Charles Powell to Rita Eker and Margaret Rigal 10 February 1987.

amnesty may also have been in small measure a response to the demands of Orlov and his associates. As there was some haggling when Begun was offered his release for signing a statement, he was one of the last of the political prisoners to be freed from the Chistopol punishment gaol. Fearing that his father was not going to be released, his son, Boris Begun, and about twenty other persons demonstrated at the Arbat shopping centre in Moscow for several days until they were beaten up by KGB thugs in front of the world's press, who received similar treatment.[744] Within a short time, while on a visit to Washington, Georgy Arbatov, an adviser to Gorbachev, announced on 15 February 1987 Begun's release. A day later Mrs Eker wrote to the Prime Minister that despite claims that the refusenik leader Iosif Begun was to be released from prison, his wife had not been told anything and had merely been referred back to the KGB and Mr Gromyko, consequently she was very distressed. 'She... begged me to appeal to you personally on her behalf as she is sure you will understand what she is feeling'.[745] Fortunately the report was correct, Begun was freed from prison and returned to Moscow, though he and his wife had to wait another year until they were permitted to emigrate to Israel in January 1988.

On 6 March 1987, Colin Shindler, who possessed some expertise on Soviet Jewry, and three other Finchley constituents of Margaret Thatcher met her to discuss their concerns before her trip to Moscow later in the month. Shindler's companions spoke about their adopted Russian families, the Feigins and the Yosefeviches, and showed the Prime Minister a short two-minute film on the Feigins. The question of the non-delivery of mail was discussed in detail. 'Although a number of individual cases were mentioned, she stated that she would raise the general problem with suitable general illustrations. She would leave a list of specific cases with the Soviets... Sir Geoffrey Howe would

---

[744] Gal Beckerman, pp.430-2 and 507-10.
[745] Southampton, MS254/A980/1/1/30 Rita Eker to Thatcher 16 February 1987; and M.J. Hartley to Mrs Eker 17 February 1987.

also discuss the problem with Shevardnadze...She repeated the point that Jewish emigration and human rights were definitely on the agenda `as always'. She regarded the talks as taking place at a unique time in the development of the USSR and was looking forward to the meeting... She commented that Gorbachev had to fight a huge, entrenched bureaucracy --`not a small one like ours' – and there were many vested interests. The issue of Jewish emigration was a sensitive one in terms of Soviet infighting and she implied that it could be used as a political football...[and] it was not at all clear whether Gorbachev would overcome his opponents... Friends in America who continually visited the USSR warned her not to regard Gorbachev's Russia in the same light as Dubcek's Czechoslovakia'.[746]

Colin Shindler felt that 'despite hints that 10-12,000 hard core refuseniks would be allowed to leave, [there was] no movement as yet...Soviet hints that the cases of these 10-12,000 refuseniks would be "reviewed" could still mean that there would be a negative answer and no emigration'. Long-term refuseniks, such as Slepak, Nudel, Kosharovsky, Prestin, Ovsischer, Lerner and Abramovich were in 'despair', as 'there was no end in sight'. He was still uncertain whether Gorbachev was 'genuine', only his future action over a six to nine-month period would show. He was also concerned that the Prime Minister was confused between the number of applications from Soviet Jews to relatives in Israel for invitations to emigrate and the number of these applicants who actually received the emigration visa, the vizov, from the Soviet authorities – a much smaller number than the original number of 400,000. Shindler told the Prime Minister that 'it was possible that having allowed out the 10-12,000 hard core refuseniks the Soviets would refuse to accept new applications. The first degree relations law seemed to indicate a drift to finally stop emigration'.[747]

---

[746] Southampton, MS254/A980/1/1/30 Colin Shindler, memorandum on 'Meeting with Mrs Thatcher on Soviet Jews' 6 March 1987.
[747] Southampton, MS254/A980/1/1/30 Colin Shindler memorandum.

The Moscow refusenik community were very concerned about this last point, sending a message to Mrs Thatcher through a visitor that 'The new complementary set of rules governing those requiring to leave the USSR state (Article 24) that applications will only be considered for re-unification at the invitation of husband/wife, father/mother, son/daughter, brother/sister. Thus any family without such a relative will for all practical purposes be prevented from emigrating for generations to come'.[748] As regards state secrets, Thatcher observed that some Jews were in sensitive positions barring them from emigrating quickly, but she was aware that it was used as a catch-all excuse to stem emigration, something that also exercised the minds of the Moscow refusenik community. Shindler commented that 'She was concerned for the plight of the refuseniks in the context of the general struggle for human rights and made no attempt to sort out its various components'. He concluded that Soviet Jewry was 'on the agenda in a general fashion but low down on the list of [Thatcher's] priorities'.[749] Perhaps too sweeping a conclusion on his part when arms control and human rights were so intimately linked in Thatcher's mind and that of her close advisers. Moreover, 'She believed that the current strategy of publicity and protest was the right one and she would help at all times'.

Organized jointly by the National Council for Soviet Jewry, the Student and Academic Campaign for Soviet Jewry, the Union of Jewish Students and the Women's Campaign, there was a mass protest outside the Soviet embassy on 8 March 1987. Hundreds of young people from youth movements and universities marched down Kensington High Street, shouting in unison, 'What do we want? Freedom! When do we want it? Now! One, two, three, four, six, eight, let our people emigrate'. The rally was headed by Lord Bethell, Sir Keith Joseph MP, the Duke of

---

[748] Southampton, MS254/A980/1/1/30 Neville S. Conrad to Sir David Wolfson 17 February 1987.
[749] Southampton, MS254/A980/1/1/30 Shindler memorandum.

Devonshire, Greville Janner MP and Hugh Dykes MP. When they exited nearby underground stations, the demonstrators were each issued with a piece of string, holding the string they formed a human chain symbolically linking the Soviet and Israeli embassies.[750]

This rally was followed up by a delegation from the Board of Deputies and the National Council for Soviet Jewry on 19 March 1987 to the Prime Minister comprising Dr Lionel Kopelowitz, June Jacobs and Neil Bradman and Joe Lobenstein of the Agudas Israel, a right-wing Orthodox organization. A scientist, publisher and property developer, Neil Bradman had only in the last eighteen months emerged in the leadership ranks of the National Council, of which he was now its chairman, and was the principal spokesman. He indicated that he wanted the vast bulk of the 400,000 Soviet Jews who had applied for an invitation from Israel to emigrate, to be given permission to leave. The West should not ask for too little. He touched on the statement made by Samuel Zivs of the Soviet Anti-Zionist Committee that 10,000 Jews had asked for their requests to be considered – a figure disputed by the Soviet ambassador, who dismissed that number as a pure invention. June Jacobs then spoke about the individual cases, such as Ida Nudel, declaring that if Mrs Thatcher was going to visit a dissident, she should also meet with a Jewish refusenik. Mr Lobenstein insisted on the Jews' right to practise their religion. According to her advisers, the Prime Minister asserted, religious practice was incompatible with Marxist-Leninist principles and that freedom for Jews to practise their religion would not be possible. She was genuinely surprised to learn that there were only six prisoners of Zion waiting to be freed. She agreed that it was important to concentrate on numbers, not individual cases.[751]

On 24 March 1987 Dr Orlov had another meeting with the Prime Minister, in which he gave her further advice on how

[750] JC 13 March 1987, p.6.
[751] LMA, ACC 3087/286 Neil Bradman report of a delegation to Margaret Thatcher 19 March 1987.

to handle the human rights issue in her talks in Moscow. 'The Prime Minister said that she would need to pitch what she had to say about human rights in her speeches and television interviews so as to encourage people like Mr. Orlov but not to irritate the Soviet authorities to the point of being counter-productive. Mr. Orlov agreed that this was a delicate balance. He suggested that the Prime Minister should express satisfaction with what had been achieved. She might refer to the need for open frontiers. But so far as possible she should avoid appearing to criticise the state of affairs in the Soviet Union, emphasising the advantages enjoyed by the West. People would get the point. She might also explain that arms control and human rights were just two aspects of the wider problem of security. The Soviet people had been indoctrinated to think that disarmament and peace were one and the same thing. This was a fallacy. Arms control would only be achieved when trust and confidence were established between countries, and that would only happen when the Soviet Union accorded its people basic human rights'. He was of the opinion that Gorbachev had kept some religious activists in prison as well as a number of persons connected with the Ukrainian Helsinki Monitoring Group. 'His own assessment was that Gorbachev was working very closely with the KGB in managing the release of certain well-known dissidents to obtain maximum impact on public opinion in the West while doing nothing about those whose names were not widely known. It was a very artful exercise'. Nevertheless, there were indications that the Soviet Union was beginning to respond to pressure from the West. 'He had heard of contacts between the US and Soviet delegations at the CSCE Conference in Vienna in which the Soviet side had asked directly what the US would regard as acceptable concessions on human rights'. [752]

Before her trip to Moscow on 28 March 1987, the 35's leaders wrote to Thatcher, advising her that long-term

---

[752] National Archives, PREM19/3174 Charles Powell to Lynn Parker on the PM's meeting with Dr Orlov 24 March 1987.

refuseniks, even those with first degree relatives abroad, had recently had their applications turned down; and followed this up with a letter enclosing 'some heart rending appeals which have just reached this office'. They went on to say that 'As you know Soviet Jews themselves are convinced that you, and only you, among Western leaders really have their concerns at heart. If you return and there is no improvement they will indeed feel that their last hope has gone'. In a highly personal gesture, they sent her a gift of a scarf for her visit; and the Prime Minister's foreign policy adviser Charles Powell in a scribble added to the reply declared that he had given Mrs Thatcher the gift which they had enclosed with their previous letter. 'She was delighted & will take it with her'. He also flattered them, saying 'You know how very much she admires your organisation and the work you do and I am sure she will have the interests of those whom you represent very much in mind when she is in Moscow'.[753]

Apart from this, Margaret Thatcher sent one refusenik, Mrs Nina Nadgornyi, an unusually candid letter commiserating with her on the fate of her talented son, who was not permitted to emigrate 'in breach of the commitments ... freely entered into under the Helsinki Final Act' and outlining what she was doing and what she hoped to say to Mr Gorbachev.' When Tim Renton was in Moscow in January he was told that measures were in hand to facilitate the number of departures from the Soviet Union. I very much hope this is true. I shall certainly press for this in my conversations with Mr. Gorbachev in Moscow. I send you and your family my warmest wishes and my hopes that you all will soon be allowed to emigrate to Israel'.[754]As this message filtered through refusenik circles, it enhanced Mrs Thatcher's image as the beneficent fairy godmother,

---

[753] Southampton, MS254/A980/1/1/30 Rita Eker and Margaret Rigalto Thatcher 25 February and27 March 1987; and Powell to Mrs Eker27 March 1987.
[754] Southampton, MS254/A980/1/3/106 Margaret Thatcher to Mrs Nina Nadgornyi 10 March 1987.

who at a mere flick of her wand could work modern miracles.

Another indication of the improved atmosphere in the relationship between the superpowers was a meeting in Vienna between representatives from the International Federation of Scientists for Soviet Refuseniks and delegates from ten of the nations attending a CSCE session. Sir Antony Williams, the British Ambassador to the Madrid and Berne CSCE meetings, chaired the discussions which lasted for five hours. The scientists were impressed on how well-briefed the diplomats were on the cases of individual refuseniks, while the diplomats were surprised at the seniority of the scientists who attended the talks. The diplomats conveyed a reluctance to be swayed by the fresh image of liberalism presented by the Soviets and were critical of the new regulations governing departure of its citizens from the Soviet Union, as they did not have meaningful replies from their Soviet counterparts to their detailed questions. The scientists were happy to receive explanations as to the inner working of the CSCE sessions which they felt would be useful for their own lobbying activities. A meeting was also arranged between a few representatives of the scientists and two of the Soviet delegates, in which the general refusenik situation was discussed and then there was a focus on specific cases. The scientists drew the attention of their Soviet colleagues to the plight of Iosif Begun, Alexander Ioffe, Solomon Alber, Ya'acov Alpert, Irina and Victor Brailovsky, Abram Englin, Victor Fulmacht and Benjamin Charny, who was ill with cancer.[755]

During her talks in Moscow at the end of March and the beginning of April 1987, Mrs Thatcher argued for the retention of nuclear weapons and was opposed to Gorbachev's plan for the denuclearisation of Europe, as this would leave the Soviet Union with a superiority in conventional forces and chemical weapons. She then went to lunch on Monday with Sakharov and other former

---

[755] Newsletter of SRSR 19 February 1987.

dissidents, impressing on them the need to continue to support Gorbachev when he encountered difficulties because of the opposition he was facing. In the afternoon, the talks covered human rights and the question of Soviet Jewry. The following morning, Thatcher had breakfast with refuseniks at the British embassy. Among the invitees was Iosif Begun, who was selected because the Prime Minister wanted to put him in the spotlight and under her protective mantle. Nonetheless, she wrote in her memoirs that 'Theirs was a disturbing tale of heroism under mainly petty but continual persecution' – a somewhat naive remark on Thatcher's part. 'Every obstacle, short of total prohibition, was put in the way of their worship and expression of cultural identity. They were discriminated against at work – if they found work. They told me that giving private tuition was the easiest way to earn a living: for these were educated people whose talents the Soviet state should have been able to draw upon. One of their leaders, Iosif Begun, brought me a Star of David, which he had carved out of horn while he was in prison and which I have always kept'.[756]

Amplifying this account, was a letter from Charles Powell to a Mrs Beryl Greenberg stating that 'During her talks with Mr. Gorbachev last week the Prime Minister expressed the hope that Soviet Jews who wished to emigrate would be allowed to do so. Mr. Gorbachev said that the Soviet Government considered all humanitarian cases very carefully and would continue to deal with them attentively, with positive results where possible. The latest figures for Jewish emigration confirm an accelerating increase since the start of the year'.[757] A week later a similar reply was sent to Rita Eker and Margaret Rigal with the additional observations that 'The Foreign Secretary also raised this question with the Soviet Foreign Minister and

---

[756] Margaret Thatcher, The Downing Street Years (London,1993), pp.482-4.
[757] Southampton, MS254/A980/1/1/30 Charles Powell to Beryl Greenberg 10 April 1987.

handed him a list of Soviet citizens refused exit visas about whom the Government have received representations in recent months. Mr. Shevardnadze undertook to look into the cases listed and I can confirm that some of those you mentioned were among them'. There were also 'recent reports that the Soviet authorities may be preparing to allow large numbers of refuseniks to leave'.[758]

More significant perhaps was the congratulatory letter sent by Neil Bradman on behalf of the National Council to the Prime Minister and the meeting he arranged for Natan Sharansky with her on 6 May 1987. 'I wish to record our deepest appreciation for the manner in which you expressed support for the rights of Soviet Jews both prior to and during your most successful visit to the USSR... I know from my personal conversations with ex-refuseniks now in Israel and their compatriots still in Russia, how much they all welcomed your public statements and unprecedented action as a Head of Government in meeting with Dr and Mrs. Begun and Mrs Rosa Ioffe'.[759] He followed this letter up by securing a wide-ranging discussion at Downing Street between Sharansky, who was on a visit to Britain, and the Prime Minister. Among the topics Sharansky wanted to focus on, were the relaxation of restrictions on emigration and religious worship which the West should be seeking; the new emigration law and its treatment in the Vienna CSCE talks; and the government's approach to economic and cultural sanctions and the degree of cooperation in science and technology.[760] All this was in line with the fresh thinking as regards foreign policy recently adopted by the United States.

Shultz, the American Secretary of State, placed the real turning point in his negotiations with the Soviet Union

---

[758] Southampton, MS254/A980/1/1/30P. A.Bearpark to Rita Eker and Margaret Rigal 15 April 1987.
[759] LMA, ACC.3087/286 Neil Bradman to Margaret Thatcher 10 April 1987; and the same to the same 14 April 1987.
[760] LMA, ACC. 3087/286 Neil Bradman to Charles Powell private secretary to Margaret Thatcher 1 May 1987.

over human rights in his talks starting on 13 April 1987, when he visited Moscow and marked the occasion by participating in a Seder, a Passover festive meal, with a group of refuseniks. Among them were the Slepaks, to whom Shultz showed photographs of the grandchildren they had never seen, for the others he brought mementos. Shevardnadze had always insisted that the Soviets would make adjustments which suited them, not measures which were forced on them. Having run through all the commitments of Helsinki on human rights and inducements such as trade, Shultz decided to change his tack and adopt a fresh approach. He asked for a half-hour of private time with Shevardnadze and Ambassador Dobrynin, on whose advice Gorbachev relied. Speaking very slowly from a prepared statement, so that a Soviet Foreign Ministry official could take a verbatim note, Shultz argued that the economic progress that the Soviets sought could not be achieved 'unless the Soviet system is changed sharply, in ways that stimulate the creativity and drive of individuals. In the information age, success will come to societies that are open and decentralized and provide lots of room for individual initiative... Your interests and ours will not be served if the future is marked by growing economic asymmetry between East and West. But that will happen if the Soviet Union does not become a full participant in the information revolution'. Such a failure will lead to heightened tension and insecurity which neither of us want.' You believe that human rights consist of jobs, housing, health care, and economic benefits. The only way your society is going to be able to fulfil those rights is to permit your people a greater degree of what we regard as human rights: freedom of speech, movement, expression, and personal choice... And practically speaking, when human rights are allowed to flourish, and economic `right' consequently flourish also, then the problem you face with regard to pressure for emigration will diminish'. We do not regard changes over human rights as a concession, but as something which would further improve

369

our relationship.[761] Shevardnadze later told Shultz privately in September 1989 that he went over the notes of this meeting `carefully with Gorbachev and others in the leadership', and that what I had said `had a profound impact'.[762]

As his arm control talks with Gorbachev on the same visit were going well, the Soviet leader said that Shultz could raise any other issue, so he chose human rights. Gorbachev railed at him that, by attending the Seder with Soviet citizens, he was stirring discontent. 'You deal only with a certain group of Jews, people who do not like it here and have complaints and show no interest in the millions of other Soviet Jews who are out of your field of vision'. Shultz responded by putting a positive interpretation on Gorbachev's remarks and exclaiming that 'I welcome your comments as indicating that if Jews want to practise their religion, to learn Hebrew, to teach it to their children, that is all right with you'. Why don't you see how many wish to emigrate, perhaps not many will take this opportunity. He had a big aircraft available and he did not doubt that the reporters would be willing to give up their seats to the refuseniks. In reply, Gorbachev attacked the United States record in dealing with its minorities in contrast with the Soviet Union which had a good 'record on relations between nationalities, self-determination, and autonomous areas for even the smallest group'. So long as Gorbachev could place his criticism on the record, Shultz felt that he was comfortable discussing human rights. It was progress of a kind.[763]

Among the Leningrad refusenik community, things seemed to be changing for the better in early 1987 because of the interventions of Martin Gilbert and Donna Wosk. Despite their three-year prison sentences, Zelichenok was released in February and Lifshits returned home in March.

---

761 George Shultz, Turmoil and Triumph pp.886-9.
[762] George Shultz, 'Epilogue' in The Jewish Movement in the Soviet Union. Yaakov Ro'l (Baltimore,2012), pp.424-5.
[763] George Shultz, Turmoil and Triumph pp.894-5.

A demonstration on behalf of Michael Beizer by seven refuseniks on 23 March 1987 resulted in permission for him to emigrate to Israel. On 10 May 1987, Michael Beizer completed his customs declaration at Pulkovo airport before embarking on the flight to Israel, when a fellow refusenik, Yuri Shpeizman, asked to look at it as an aid to completing his own form. Shpeizman had been ill for a number of years with a heart problem and indications of cancer. He was ordered by a customs officer to open his tefillin [phylactery] boxes, replying 'You can open them yourselves, but they will no longer be kosher and I will be unable to use them again'. That confrontation resulted in a heart attack, and poignantly Yuri died on route to Israel in Vienna. Yuri and his wife, a Hebrew teacher, had been waiting for exit visas for ten years and had not seen their grandchildren.[764]

Despite these optimistic news stories, nothing appeared to be happening in the short run. In response to the lethargy of the Soviet authorities, Mrs Eker and Mrs Rigal raised the disquieting case of Mrs Rimma Sosna, a refusenik, whose daughter lived in Britain, with the Prime Minister. They advised her that Mrs Sosna had 'demonstrated in the centre of Leningrad with twenty-four other long-term refuseniks [on 23 April 1987] and they intend to continue to press for a positive response from the authorities in line with the previous promises given to you and Sir Geoffrey. She is begging you to enquire why despite all assurances, she has been refused again'. She will be sixty-three in a couple of weeks' time. She had not worked since she and her late husband applied to go to Israel in 1974. 'She is entirely isolated from her family in Wembley Park and she is surely a suitable subject for Mikhail Gorbachev's well-publicised liberal intentions. If Rimma Sosna's refusal on grounds of `state security' is to be

---

[764] Michael Beizer to author 11 August 2020 and his 'First Day of Freedom' Soviet Jews' Exodus website.

prolonged still further, there is no reason at all to believe that other long-term refuseniks will be allowed to leave'.[765] Then came another appeal for Mrs Thatcher to take action on the diplomatic level for Mrs Katya Yusefovich of Moscow, who was 'six months pregnant with serious heart defects and other complications' but wanted to go to Israel with her husband and four children. She intended to demonstrate on 27 April in Pushkin Square, and for a time the couple had been on a hunger strike. The Prime Minister was well acquainted with this case, as some of her constituents had recently come to see her about it. When answering Mrs Joyce Simson, who was a prominent figure in the 35's organization, Charles Powell sought to reassure her that Leonid Yusefovich's name had been included in the list of names of those wishing to emigrate handed to Eduard Shevardnadze, the Soviet Foreign Minister, by Sir Geoffrey Howe.[766]

Not so much appeared to have changed in Gorbachev's Russia when a delegation of M.P.s led by Peter Archer Q.C. from the All-Party Parliamentary Committee for the Release of Soviet Jewry were denied visas for a visit to the Soviet Union in February 1987. They raised the plight of seven long-term refuseniks whom they wished to present with their annual award, with the Prime Minister. Mrs Thatcher assured Peter Archer that the British ambassador in Moscow 'protested strongly to the Russians about 'the refusal of their visas; and that when she met Iosif Begun during her recent visit she had presented him with their annual award. There had also been a frigid response from the Soviet ambassador in London when Peter Archer addressed a complaint to him about the Parliamentary delegation being refused entry visas to his country.[767]

[765] Southampton, MS254/A980/1/1/30 Margaret Rigal to Thatcher 23 April 1987.
[766] Southampton, MS254/A980/1/1/30 Joyce Simson to Margaret Thatcher 24 April 1987; and Charles Powell to Simson 11 May 1987.
[767] Southampton, MS254/A980/1/1/30 Margaret Thatcher to Peter Archer 21 April 1987; and L. Zamyatin to Archer undated.

Seen through Rita Eker's eyes in May 1987, the situation in the Soviet Union was still viewed as gloomy. Glasnost had not spread to the refuseniks and the ex-Prisoners of Zion, who were being held against their will in the USSR. It was an uphill struggle to counter Gorbachev's incredibly effective publicity for the new spirit of openness in Soviet society. The Women's Campaign was in a precarious financial situation and she pleaded with her American well-wishers for funds. 'We are spending three times the amount of our budget and are deeply in debt, due to the 220 American students whom we briefed this season', she admitted to David Frisch. 'The cost of goods, clothing, food and medication [for Russian Jews] far exceeds any amounts we have received, not only from you as one of our most generous benefactors, but also from our many friends throughout the world'. She begged him to increase his donation, 'so that we can fulfil the great need to send in medics, scientists and people who will give hope to those who are without. Thousands of pounds are needed to send in cancer drugs. Thousands of pounds are needed to fund engineers and scientists of the Refusenik community who are prepared to travel throughout the USSR to give support and encouragement to the Jews in remote places'.[768]

Travellers briefed by the Women's Committee, who visited Kishinev, Odessa, Dushanbe and Lvov, were instructed to make only one telephone call to refusenik families to set up appointments for security reasons and were advised only to leave drugs with individuals in charge of medical committees. Second-hand clothes were not given to refusenik families because they might find them difficult to sell and such a gift could hurt their pride.[769] The travellers on returning from a trip to the USSR sometimes reported their suspicions that certain refuseniks were working with the KGB. They also brought back messages

---

[768] Southampton, MS254/A980/1/3/32 Rita Eker to David Frisch 19 May 1987.
[769] Southampton, MS254/A980/1/3/32 Rita Eker to Hinda Cantor 3 November 1987.

373

and requests from refusenik families, particularly for electrical goods of all kinds, but advised that visitors should 'not bring expensive Western items of luxury such as French perfumes or frilly underclothing'. Nor were jeans a useful item anymore. What was wanted were 'cameras, tape recorders... T-shirts with inscriptions (these go over other items in parcel and are used to bribe prison guards to allow rest of package to go through to prisoner), VCRs, jogging shoes and sports clothing with Western insignia'. Visitors were also asked to obtain 'black caviar and India tea from Berioska shops, for use as currency in prison'.[770] Attached to the Union of Councils in the United States, a body with whom the Women's Campaign maintained close links, was the International Physicians Commission for the Protection of Prisoners, which sent consultants in various specialities to the USSR to examine physically sick refuseniks and assess their condition. Detailed medical notes were compiled on each individual with recommendations for treatment or a note that such persons needed treatment in the United States or Israel.[771] On occasions, refuseniks ordered expensive equipment, such as tape-recorders and cameras, as they had been dismissed from their employment and needed them for a livelihood; but later travellers discovered that they had been sold in order to generate income. The same was sometimes the case with expensive drugs ordered for sick relatives. It, therefore, became imperative that all such requests had to be very carefully vetted.[772] Nor had much changed on the cultural front by March 1987. Books sent through the post still only had a 40%-50% chance of safe arrival and conditions were deteriorating still further, whereas if these

[770] Southampton, MS254/A980/1/3/106 Joan Dale to Rita Eker 2 June 1986 and same to same 11 June 1986.
[771] Southampton, MS254/A980/3/33 Linda Opper of the International Physicians Commission circular 18 July 1988; MS254/A980/1/3/32 Dr Soffer to Rita Eker Urgent Medical Notes 23 October 1987. Daphne Gerlis, p. 178.

[772] Daphne Gerlis, p.178.

items were carried by travellers a 99% success rate was guaranteed.[773] The Foreign Office, nevertheless, in July instructed the British ambassador in Moscow with an optimistic assessment of the human rights situation in the Soviet Union, though there were still reservations on the rate of progress. They 'Welcome[d] recent progress in the list of personal cases Secretary of State handed to you in March. One last effort would eliminate the problem. Would have a major impact on image of the Soviet Union in U.K. Welcome[d] also recent releases of dissidents, increase in emigration, but growing public/ parliamentary concern and refusal of Ovir [the emigration visa office] to accept new applications to emigrate. Hope no intention to create a ring fence'.[774] Again, not all influential figures within the Conservative party were enthusiastic supporters of the approach adopted by the Women's Campaign and in part followed by the Prime Minister. Neil Bradman, the chairman of the National Council, noted the contents of a letter which he had received from Norman Tebbit, the Tory party chairman, which had a quite different tone. 'We shall continue to press the Soviet Union to abide by their Helsinki commitments... Experience suggests that rigid linkage between human rights issues and culture or trade with the Soviet Union is not fruitful; and does little to help those who are suffering. Our general principle is to expand contacts, not to cut them, as a means of influencing the Russians towards more civilised behaviour'.[775]

At this point in the summer of 1987, there was a serious outbreak of turf warfare in Manchester between the Manchester Council for Soviet Jewry led by Sir Sidney Hamburger and the Manchester branch of the Women's Campaign which was defused by the adroit tactics of Neil

---

[773] LMA, ACC 3087/18 National Council Cultural Committee 2 March 1987.
[774] National Archives, FCO58/4681, telegram July 1987 Secretary of State to British ambassador in Moscow July 1987.
[775] Southampton, MS254/A980/1/3/32 Norman Tebbit to Neil Bradman 26 May 1987.

Bradman, assisted by the cooperation of Rita Eker and Margaret Rigal. The clash between Hamburger and Sylvia Sheff JP chairman of the Manchester 35's group echoed the earlier strife in London between some of the more lethargic male politicians in the Board of Deputies and the National Council and the Jewish women, who adopted fresh publicity tactics and moved on to the political high ground hitherto reserved for men and regarded as sacrosanct.

Sylvia Sheff was a feisty and strong-minded lady who organised a series of demonstrations in Manchester during the visit of the Georgian State dancers in June 1987 and the Bolshoi Academy Ballet Company and the Kirov Opera Company between 12 and 16 August. After the earlier visit of Sharansky to Manchester, Sylvia was convinced that his strategy of the 'need to maintain the pressure and protest' was correct, because talk of 'glasnost' masked 'the continuing human rights violations'; and she drew special attention to the fate of Yuri Shpeizman who had recently died in Vienna on his way to Israel.[776] Sir Sidney Hamburger, who sat on the boards of many voluntary associations and public bodies, believed that Sylvia Sheff's aggressive campaigning methods upset members of the public and were counter-productive; and instead, he tried more peaceful ways of protesting and was snubbed at the last minute when a promised meeting with the management of the Bolshoi Academy was unexpectedly cancelled. He claimed, however, that he was given time to air his views about Soviet Jewry on the local radio station and that his organization's posters after the performance were well received by the public. He called on members of the Manchester Jewish community not to participate in the 35's demonstrations outside the theatre where the Bolshoi ballet troupe were dancing, when there had been serious problems with mobilizing the community and students and their parents would be away for the summer. He denounced Sheff as being self-centered and for her lack of cooperation with his Manchester Council for Soviet Jewry,

---

[776] LMA, ACC.3087/215 Leningrad letter in memory of Yuri Shpeizman 28 May 1987; Sylvia Sheff to Sir Sidney Hamburger 12 June 1987.

by not attending meetings, but there was also evidence to show that she had been making overtures of willingness to cooperate.[777] Thanks to Neil Bradman's diplomatic intervention, by being present at a meeting of the Manchester branch and then holding an executive meeting of the national body in Manchester, peace terms were threshed out: the affiliates of both organizations undertook to campaign independently of each other and not to criticise each other publicly. Margaret Rigal and Rita Eker agreed with a certain input from Baruch Gur, the Lishka representative, that 'we must put the whole matter behind us and not give anyone an excuse for fresh vilification'. [778]

Undeterred by the risks of identifying too closely with one political party and one political figure, the leaders of the Women's Campaign for Soviet Jewry boldly congratulated Mrs Thatcher on her success at the general election on 11 June 1987. Accordingly, Powell wrote to the two ladies declaring that 'The Prime Minister has asked me to thank you for your kind message of congratulations on the outcome of the General Election. I know she will do everything she can to support your cause'. Trying to boost their friendship with Mrs Thatcher still further, the two ladies next wrote to her on her birthday on 12 October 1987 offering her 'Many happy Returns', 'a pleasant and successful year' and 'good health for you and your family'; and at the same time with a flourish added that 'We know Ida Nudel and all who have received permission to leave the Soviet Union during the last twelve months would wish to add their good wishes to ours'.[779]

---

[777] LMA, ACC.3087/215 Sylvia Sheff to Sir Sidney Hamburger 16 July 1984 and 1 July 1986. Sir Sidney Hamburger to Neil Bradman 9 June 1987; and same to same 12 June 1987. Sheff to Hamburger 1 July 1986. Manchester 35's to Sir Sidney Hamburger 13 August 1987. Sylvia Sheff to Neil Bradman 17 August 1987.

[778] LMA, ACC.3087/215 Neil Bradman to Sir Sydney Hamburger 21 August 1987; and Margaret Rigal to Neil Bradman 2 September 1987.

[779] Southampton, MS254/A980/1/1/30 Charles Powell to Rita Eker and Margaret Rigal 15 June 1987; and Margaret Rigal and Rita Eker to Margaret Thatcher 12 October 1987 and Thatcher to the same 22 October 1987.

*Freedom at last! Shcharansky greeted by Shimon Peres
after arriving in Israel*

Rita Eker with Natan and Avital Shchransky

The Release of More Prominent Jewish Leaders

From the beginning of September and into October 1987, suddenly prominent refuseniks such as Victor Brailovsky, Ida Nudel and Vladimir Slepak, were given exit visas and Naum Meiman waited expectantly beside his phone. In addition, on 30 October it was announced that a three-day summit would be taking place in Washington starting on 7 December between President Reagan and Gorbachev. In fact, Professor Meiman, a leading mathematician and nuclear expert, and an important figure in the Moscow Helsinki Monitoring Group, was not given permission to leave until January 1988. But did this herald a real change in Soviet policy or were these visa concessions placebos to placate the West? [780]

Given an education steeped in Russian culture, Ida Nudel had as a young girl read Pushkin and Lermontov to the Soviet nation on the radio. At the age of seventeen, she started to become interested in Jewish traditions and after becoming aware that the Jews had returned to their ancient homeland felt obliged to follow. In 1970 she applied for permission to emigrate to Israel but was refused because of the knowledge she had acquired while working as an economist for the Moscow Institute of Planning and Production. In the summer of 1972, she led a protest against the arrest of the refusenik Vladimir Markman at the central office of the Soviet Communist party. Meanwhile, in the same year, her sister Elena and her husband were allowed to leave for Israel. Coming into contact with the Prisoners of Zion, she was soon immersed in a campaign to assist them, by obtaining items from tourists, such as warm underwear, vitamins, and chocolates, which could be bartered with guards for favours. Hence she became known as their 'Guardian Angel'. Sometimes Albert Ivanov, an official of the Central Committee of the Communist party, would listen sympathetically to her complaints about the conditions her adopted prisoners were enduring. For

[780] Beckerman, p.519. Associated Press News 26 January 1988.

unfurling a banner from her Moscow apartment in June 1978, she was sentenced to four years in internal exile in Siberia. Defiant as ever in court she described the last seven years as the most wonderful in her life, she could hold her head high as a human being and Jew, with the same joyful spirit as a woman giving birth. While in Siberia, she was put under constant surveillance by the KGB. Hoping to return to Moscow at the end of her sentence, she was given 72 hours to leave and then hounded by the police for six months as she tried to find a place where she could settle. A friend in Tartu Estonia, whom she had helped in prison camp, suggested she find a home there but when she went to a house with rooms to let, the clerk said, 'You're not registered anywhere. How's that possible? Get out of here right now, or I'll call the militia'.[781]

Eventually, a man who had sent her packages while she was in exile found a home for her in the small town of Bendery in Moldavia. After four days, she was summoned before the local police chief, who was furious that she had managed to become registered in his district. A big man, he ranted at her which she stoically endured until his fury subsided. Nudel said: 'You're a man. You have a gun. You have many aides who can kill me. Why are you shouting?' My manner, and my spirit, were my only weapons. 'Why are you afraid of me?' I asked him. He was no fool. He calmed down, ashamed that he had shouted hysterically at a small woman and had been 'bested'. He let Nudel go. She lived alone for two years in a two-room peasant hut with her pet collie dog as a companion. It took two years for her to make her quarters habitable, piping in water and installing electricity. Her day-to-day existence was grim, especially for a woman with a heart condition, carrying water and coal to her home and standing for hours in long queues to shop. Initially, she tried to befriend the few Jews in the town, organizing a Hanukah party for about thirty persons but the police came along and broke it up, warning

---

[781] Louis Rapoport, 'Ida Nudel's Long White Night', Jerusalem Post international edition 5 July 1986. Beckerman, pp. 383-4 and 425-6.

them that they would suffer in their workplace for attending such an event. People who had attended the party then boycotted her. While in exile in Siberia, Nudel had received 12,000 letters from well-wishers in 51 countries, an indication of worldwide support. Consequently, Nudel possessed an inner serenity. 'I'm safe, secure in my heart', she observed. 'But the Jews of Bendery don't have this feeling, this inner security'. They do not feel that anyone in the West is interested in their fate. She resumed her old activity sending packages to refuseniks imprisoned on trumped-up charges.[782]

Meanwhile, her married sister Elena Fridman now in Israel started a worldwide campaign for Ida Nudel's right to emigrate, enlisting the support of political leaders in the United States and Britain as well as the actress Jane Fonda. Through her many telephone conversations with Michael Sherbourne, Ida Nudel had been able to convey the latest news to him about the Prisoners of Zion, with whom she was in touch; and he also strengthened her resolve, when her spirits were low, as she had received a threat to incarcerate her in a psychiatric hospital.[783] All this up-to-date information on Ida and other refuseniks was passed by Michael Sherbourne to members of the Women's Campaign, particularly to Rita Eker, who disseminated it more widely in their campaigning and through alerting MPs. In April 1984 Jane Fonda was allowed to visit Ida. To her surprise, Ida also was able once again to telephone her old friends Andrei Sakharov and Elena Bonner and welcome them in Moscow after they returned from administrative exile.[784]

When Vladimir Slepak informed his father in 1969 that he wished to leave the Soviet Union, the old-style Bolshevik denounced him as a traitor and refused to speak to him. Yet nine years later when he was told his son was sentenced to five years internal exile, he suffered a heart

[782] Louis Rapoport, 'Ida's Long White Night'.
[783] Gerlis, pp.170-1.
[784] Hurst, pp.106-7. Beckerman, pp.500-1

attack and although a life-long atheist, muttered Hebrew prayers before his death. Vladimir, his wife Masha and sons Alexander and Leonid first applied for exit visas in April 1970. Following the 1967 War, Slepak began to feel a strong Jewish identity and started writing letters and appeals to the United Nations in the process emerging as an activist Jewish leader. Vladimir worked as the laboratory head of the Moscow Scientific Institute of Television Research, while his wife Masha was employed as a doctor. Since 1970 their flat had been constantly raided by the police, and books, letters and photographs were confiscated. Having been forced to testify in the Second Leningrad Trial in 1971, he was twice imprisoned in that year on charges which were never revealed to him. In June 1978, Vladimir and Masha Slepak were arrested for displaying a banner from the window of their eighth-floor apartment, proclaiming 'Let Us Go to Our Son in Israel'. For this defiant act, he was sentenced to five years in internal exile in Siberia, in which his wife voluntarily joined him. On his release on 2 December 1982, they journeyed back to Moscow. Before Passover 1987, their son Alexander staged a 17-day hunger strike in front of the Capitol building in Washington to draw attention to his parents' 17-year wait for an exit visa. At the same time, the American Union of Councils for Soviet Jews called on the National Conference for Soviet Jewry, the B'nai B'rith International, the NJCRAC, and Student Struggle for Soviet Jewry 'to join together in an international effort to free Vladimir and Masha Slepak'. The beginning of the hunger strike was marked by a rally on the steps of the Capitol on 27 March joined by senators and Congressmen and leaders of the Soviet Jewry campaigning organizations; and a series of rallies across the United States culminated in one held in Washington on 12 April 1987 which was addressed by Dr Orlov, Natan Sharansky, and Elie Wiesel. Soviet Jewry groups in Britain, France, Israel and Belgium were called upon to stage their own rallies at the same time.[785] The campaign to free the Slepaks continued, when Vladimir and Masha attended the Seder Service at the American embassy in Moscow a few days later in April.

Throughout the 1970s and 1980s, the 35's did their best to assist the Slepaks' campaign for the right to emigrate to Israel but their action was intermittent. When Joyce Simson visited Moscow in 1979, she met Masha Slepak outside the main synagogue, who told her that her husband had been exiled to Siberia and was in poor health. On 9 May 1979, a story appeared in the *Daily Telegraph* that the Women's Campaign was trying to arrange for a doctor to see Vladimir. While in exile, Vladimir's morale was boosted, as he heard in a BBC broadcast that the 35's were demonstrating on his behalf.[786] At the 1979 TUC conference in Liverpool, Women's Campaign members demonstrated in ghostly attire with placards demanding the release of Ida Nudel and Vladimir Slepak. Through this intervention, six trade union leaders appealed to the Soviet authorities for their release; and a petition signed by 600 delegates on behalf of the refuseniks was dispatched to Brezhnev.[787] But there is no clear evidence that the 35's took up the Union of Councils clarion call for international demonstrations on behalf of Vladimir in April 1987, though it is possible that they transmitted news of the campaign to the Prime Minister's office.

The All-Party Committee for the Release of Soviet Jewry, particularly its secretary and moving spirit, Greville Janner M.P., tried to do all it could for the Slepak family; and Greville developed a close relationship with them, frequently speaking on the telephone to them. When the younger son of the family Leonid was thirteen, Greville listened in tears, as he recited the traditional blessing before the Torah reading in Hebrew on the telephone and

[785] National Archives, PREM 19/3174 Memorandum of Pamela Cohen, Union of Councils for Soviet Jews 12 March 1987 and case history of Vladimir Slepak. Los Angeles Times 1 December 1987.
[786] Gerlis, pp.97,98,232-4,239,244,258,259,269.
[787] Hurst, p.95.

arranged for a number of Jewish boys in England to celebrate his barmitzvah for him by proxy.[788] Working in conjunction with the All-Party Committee, the Women's Campaign plied them with relevant material, so that they could raise questions in Parliament about individual refuseniks. For instance, in 1983 Alec Woodall asked the Minister of State, Malcolm Rifkind, if he had discussed the situation of Vladimir Slepak and Alexander Lerner, with Soviet authorities.[789]

Although he was regarded by many as the father of the immigration movement, Vladimir Slepak did not receive the same red carpet treatment as that accorded to Ida Nudel and Sharansky when they arrived in Israel. However, when their plane touched down at Ben Gurion airport on 26 October 1987, Vladimir and Masha were greeted by a hundred former Soviet Jews.[790] The main thrust for their new-found freedom came from supporters in the United States, while the British campaign only played a subsidiary role in their release. With great perceptiveness, Vladimir analysing the current emigration situation, remarked in a speech in Los Angeles that 'the jailing of those who wished to emigrate had ended for Soviet Jews, and the number of exit visas has increased .... But in 1979...more than 50,000 Jews were allowed to leave the Soviet Union. Gorbachev wants to "raise the effectiveness of the Soviet economy"... But he understands, he's smart enough, [to see that] everything is linked one with another. For this he needs credits, new technology...from the West. So he must have a good face. So to fulfil his reforms in economics, he has to change something in the internal society...But he wants to make it as less as possible'. Slepak thought that if Gorbachev undertook real reforms, he could at the same time lose control over the Soviet system. He

---

[788] Gerlis, p.115.
[789] Hurst, p.100.
[790] Jewish Chronicle 30 October 1987, p.5.

warned that the USSR was thus going through a 'very dangerous' transitional period.[791]

At the end of the year, despite all the promises, there had been no mass migration of refuseniks, even if some outstanding members of the Russian Jewish community had been allowed to emigrate because they were exposed by the spotlight of a worldwide publicity campaign and there was active political campaigning on all levels on their behalf. Margaret Thatcher was due to hold brief talks with Mr Gorbachev at the Brize Norton airbase on 7 December 1987, as his aircraft touched down on its way to Washington prior to a summit meeting with President Reagan; and once again the two ladies from the Women's Campaign were prompted to write to the Prime Minister with their thoughts for this meeting. 'Last week, Mr. David Mellor, repeated in the House of Commons, the words he had used in Vienna: "No human rights, no genuine security, no deal". In the last few weeks more long-term refuseniks have been given fresh refusals. The detentions last week in the Soviet Union might have occurred under Brezhnev or Andropov; "Glasnost" appears to have been forgotten... Many families on whose behalf you spoke when you were in Moscow, are still in the Soviet Union. We are anxious that the case of the thousands of those waiting should be highlighted rather than a few individuals, but the prolonged refusals being given to those who have already waited for more than ten years, blatantly illustrates the denial of human rights now taking place. Please fulfil the hopes of thousands of Soviet Jews who are relying upon you and make Mr. Gorbachev understand that you know and will not ignore his failure to grant the basic human rights to so many of his fellow citizens'.[792]

Following up on the Prime Minister's Guildhall speech outlining her foreign policy objectives, Neil Bradman, the chairman of the National Council, wrote an

---

[791] Los Angeles Times 1 December 1987.
[792] Southampton, MS254/A980/1/1/30 Margaret Rigal and Rita Eker to Thatcher 1 December 1987.

enthusiastic and supportive letter to her. 'I fervently hope that in all your discussions with Soviet leaders and officials,' he asserted, ' you will emphasise that for Glasnost and Perestroika to succeed and achieve some at least of the goals set by Mr Gorbachev, requires that the Soviet authorities have the confidence to permit the fulfilment of the objectives we seek. Letting all Jews who wish to emigrate do so would assist in building Western confidence and contribute to economic restructuring'.[793] Of all the chairmen of the National Council, Neil Bradman established the best rapport with the Prime Minister, Margaret Thatcher, and communicated with her on the most regular basis; and in this respect was the most effective.

A month later, Neil Bradman reported to his executive on a briefing he had received about the results of the Brize Norton meeting between the Prime Minister and Mr. Gorbachev. 'The Prime Minister had raised the Soviet Jewry issue together with other Human Rights problems in a general way. Mr. Gorbachev's responses were surprisingly "prickly". These matters, however, formed but a small part of their general discussions. The Foreign Secretary, in his meetings with Mr. Shevardnadze, went into greater depth, presenting lists of outstanding cases. Shevardnadze accepted the lists and said that perhaps these were matters that could best be discussed when Sir Geoffrey visits Moscow in February 1988. It was interesting to note that Shevardnadze sought to diffuse the situation when Mr. Yakovlev interjected heatedly. Although it was confirmed that Isaak Tsitferblit and the Nodgorny family, among others appeared on the list, the Chairman felt we ought to enquire about the entire Foreign Office list'.[794] What the consultation between the British government and the Gorbachev team seemed to show was that it still elicited

---

[793] LMA, ACC 3087/286 speech of Margaret Thatcher at the Lord Mayor's banquet 16 November 1987; and Nel Bradman to Margaret Thatcher 26 November 1987.
[794] LMA, ACC 3987/008 minutes of the Executive of the National Council 23 December 1987.

the usual stone-walling response from Gorbachev and Yakovlev but that Shevardnadze the Foreign Minister appeared to be adopting a fresh and more receptive attitude.

Natan Sharansky Organizes the Biggest Ever American Rally for Soviet Jewry

On 6 December 1987, there was the biggest rally of the American Jewish community ever, when more than 250,000 people gathered on Washington's National Mall, a day before Gorbachev's arrival at Andrews Airforce base. If the American Jewish establishment had enforced its will, there would have been no such meeting. From across the United States Jews arrived in Washington on chartered buses, 1,000 such buses coming from the New York area. One man alone had been campaigning for a major rally since he had arrived in Israel early in 1986 and that man was Natan Sharansky, who had changed his name since he had emigrated. He kept on reiterating that 400,000 Soviet Jews wished to leave the USSR, whereas the American Jewish establishment put these figures as 10,000 to 20,000. By the time news of the date of the summit was disclosed, there were only five weeks left for Sharansky to embark on a whirlwind tour of thirty American cities to generate enthusiasm for the rally. David Harris, the executive director of the American Jewish Committee, was given leave to work closely with Jewish federations and other philanthropic institutions to organize the rally with contingents coming from all parts of the country.[795]

Yet there were still mixed messages coming from Gorbachev. Coinciding with the Washington rally was a pre-summit demonstration of seventy-five refuseniks in Smolensky Square outside the Foreign Ministry offices in Moscow, which was brutally dispersed by hundreds of plainclothes KGB officers and officially inspired individuals calling themselves peace demonstrators. Peter

---

[795] Forward 17 November 2017.

Arnett, an American television commentator, who was trying to film the scene, was knocked to the ground and detained for four hours, while other Western journalists were roughed up. The journalists recognized the peace demonstrators as KGB men, who had broken up a peaceful rally in February in favour of Dr Iosif Begun. A number of Moscow refusenik demonstrators were detained for a short while and then released. An equally harsh response happened in Leningrad, where a planned demonstration was prevented from taking place with thirty refuseniks being dispersed by force and four of them being sentenced to ten days' imprisonment. Notwithstanding these happenings, on the eve of the summit the authorities allowed 73 veteran refuseniks to leave, including Pavel Abramovich, Professor Alexander Ioffe and Viktor Fayermark.[796]

At the Washington rally, which opened with the blowing of a shofar and Pearl Bailey singing 'Let My People Go,' American Jewish leaders demanded free emigration for Soviet Jews without calling on the Reagan administration to make any concessions in return to Gorbachev. Thousands of placards held aloft echoing the message of the song, proclaimed 'Let My People Go', the original slogan of the student movement. Morris Abram, the chairman of the National Conference and of the Conference of Presidents of Major American Jewish Organizations, spoke tactfully, stressing that glasnost did not seem to apply to Jews. He continued that 'We want to believe that the release of highly visible refuseniks is not a publicity stunt, but we observe that in 1979... Brezhnev released six times as many Jews as Gorbachev in 1987'.[797] 'Angered by the dispersal of a demonstration by Soviet Jews in Moscow, former refuseniks who spoke... demanded that the Reagan Administration institute direct linkage between Jewish emigration and US-Soviet trade and cultural ties'. Vladimir Slepak asked where was glasnost

---

[796] Jewish Chronicle 11 December 1987, p.3.
[797] JTA news bulletin 7 December 1987, Beckerman, pp.525-6.

when Jewish demonstrators in Moscow were beaten? 'We must not allow the Soviet Union to get credits or most favoured nation status until all our brothers and sisters are free'. Yosef Mendelevich, another former Prisoner of Zion, thundered that he was outraged that a meeting had been set up between Gorbachev and sixty American business leaders. He urged the administration to adopt a policy of 'no trade, no aid', until sixty thousand are permitted to emigrate each year. Sharansky also denounced the meeting with business leaders, declaring 'They forget how dangerous it is to trade without concern for moral issues'. He told the mass protest that it did not matter whether Reagan was stronger than his opponent or whether Gorbachev would be willing to permit emigration. 'It is we, it is our struggle which makes governments in the free world strong. It is our struggle which can make the Soviet government willing to reopen the gates of the Soviet Union'.[798] Many of the recently released refuseniks also lit the candles on a gigantic menorah to celebrate the forthcoming festival of Hanukah, the annual Jewish celebration of religious and cultural freedom. Perhaps the most important remarks were delivered by Vice-President George Bush, who promised that 'Human rights will be high on the agenda for the summit. I will personally raise it with Mr Gorbachev. I will not be satisfied until the promise of Helsinki is a reality... Let's not see five or six or 10 or 20 refuseniks released at a time, but thousands, tens of thousands – all those who want to go'.[799]

According to reports, President Reagan began an opening session with Gorbachev by discussing human rights, particularly those Jews not permitted to leave. He mentioned the mass rally in support of Soviet Jewry and the impressive number of participants but avoided speaking about the issue publicly. To this Gorbachev later responded

---

[798] Jewish Chronicle 11 December 1987, p.3. JTA news bulletin 7 December 1987.
[799] JTA news bulletin 7 December 1987.

that he 'was not on trial and you are not to judge me' and compared the USSR's emigration policy with the United States restrictions on the entry of immigrants. At a meeting with senators, the Soviet leader said 'Take a look at your own record on human rights, while you criticise ours'. He promised to examine every case, conceding that 'We will limit the question of security and intelligence and information', where there is refusal of exit permits on grounds of being in possession of state secrets. However, the Soviet Foreign Ministry spokesman Gennadi Gerasimov conceded that the Washington rally had made its point about the need for Jewish migration; and in a conversation with Shultz after the summit, Morris Abram elicited the information that they were no longer talking about individual cases and that 'Gorbachev understood, perhaps, for the first time, the enormous pressure that had been generated in Washington for the case of Soviet Jewry'.[800] The high point of the summit was the signing of the INF (Intermediate Forces Nuclear) Treaty which scrapped all land-based intermediate range (300 to 3,000 miles) missiles capable of carrying nuclear weapons over the next three years, and in doing so tried to put the relationship between Washington and Moscow on a new footing. In their talks with Gorbachev, the senators reiterated that an improved Soviet human rights performance would boost the chances of Senate ratification of the arms control treaty, a point which must also have weighed on him.[801]

Charles Powell summed up the British government's position at the end of the year to the leaders of the 35's, by remarking that 'As you know the Prime Minister takes a particular interest in this question... Although the numbers of Jews allowed to leave the Soviet Union have increased

---

[800] Southampton, MS254/A980/1/3/33 Soviet Jewry Update of the National Conference on Soviet Jewry February 1988. Jewish Chronicle 11 December, pp.1 and 3 1987. Henry L. Feingold, Silent No More: Saving the Jews of Russia, the American Jewish Effort,1967-1989 (Syracuse, NY, 2006), p.274.
[801] Jewish Chronicle 11 December 1987, p.3.

encouragingly this year the Prime Minister is aware that for every fortunate individual or family who is allowed to leave many more must continue their long and distressing vigil for exit permission. I can assure you that they will not be forgotten: the Government will continue to press the Soviet authorities to honour all its human rights commitments and in particular to grant all Jews who so wish the right to leave their country'. Much the same remarks were contained in a personal letter sent by Margaret Thatcher to a Mr and Mrs Knobil, who raised the issue of the emigration problems encountered by the Lein, Gashunin, and Archipova families. They were informed that Sir Geoffrey Howe, the Foreign Secretary, had handed his Soviet counterpart 'a list of refusenik cases which included that of Eugeny Lein'.[802] Nonetheless, a month after the Washington summit the Soviet authorities tightened their emigration procedures in Leningrad and Moscow; and despite assurances to the contrary, the teaching of Hebrew was still not recognized as a legitimate profession, its teachers being arrested on charges of parasitism. In 1919, the Soviet government decreed that Yiddish was the Jewish language and disparaged Hebrew, which was later vilified as the language of an enemy Zionist state, Israel. Aleksey Magarik, a Moscow teacher of Hebrew, had been arrested in March 1986 and sentenced to three years in a labour camp. Similar sentences continued to be meted out to other Hebrew teachers, Vladimir Lifshits, Yuliy Edelshteyn and Leonid Volkovsky, though all were subsequently released.[803] Yet from these contradictory policies, it was still difficult to ascertain in which overall direction Gorbachev would go.

---

[802] Southampton, MS254/A980/1/1/30 Charles Powell to Mrs Rigal 17 December 1987 and Margaret Thatcher to Mr and Mrs Knobil 31 December 1987.
[803] Soviet Jewry update February 1988.

Chapter 8 - Mass Emigration

In 1988, Mikhail Gorbachev was still moving slowly and cautiously, still uncertain in which direction he wanted to take the Soviet Union. Towards capitalism and a free market or did he want many of the controls of a planned economy to remain? In the latter case, he would have to keep many of the Jewish scientists and engineers in the Soviet Union. He moved rapidly to ensure that there were exit visas for many prominent Jewish dissidents to leave, thus clearing a backlog of well-known names and undermining the international campaign for Soviet Jewry. For the numbers of Jews permitted to leave the USSR rose slowly from 18,919 in 1988 to 71,196 in the following year, quite out of proportion to the number wishing to emigrate. When in 1990, the number suddenly shot up to 181,802, was this part of some grand design or gesture on the Secretary General's part or was it forced on him by the economic chaos and seething nationalism in the different republics, unleashed by perestroika, re-structuring, and glasnost, openness, and the hidden cost of the nuclear explosion in Chernobyl? Although Gorbachev mouthed the right words as regards human rights, did he really believe in them and were the changes in the Soviet legal code sufficient to bring them into line with the UN Charter and into line with international human rights law and the Helsinki Accords, to which the Soviet Union nominally subscribed?

The Soviets Allow More Well-Known Refuseniks to Leave To Ease Western Pressure

By Passover 1988, all the prominent refuseniks at the Seder attended by Shultz had been allowed to emigrate and so were some well-known names on whose behalf British groups campaigned such as the Paritskys.[804] Rita Eker and Margaret Rigal wrote to Thatcher that 'Now that the Paritskys are at long last safely in Israel, we should like to

---

[804] George Shultz, Turmoil and Triumph p.887.

thank you once more for all the help and assistance you have given this long-suffering family'.[805] Nevertheless, others such as Vladimir and Isolde Tufeld remained trapped in limbo land because of specious security considerations. In his reply, Charles Powell stressed that Mrs Thatcher was 'very distressed to hear of Mrs Tufeld's condition and shocked at the Soviet authorities' refusal to allow her husband to be with her at this crucial time. We have conveyed our concern to the Soviet authorities both through the Soviet Embassy and the Foreign Ministry in Moscow. We have not yet had any response'.[806] For the Tufelds as for many refuseniks, Margaret Thatcher had become almost a mythical figure, an all-powerful good mother, whose intervention could redeem them from the house of bondage and ease their journey to Israel.

Among refusenik scientists who had been allowed to leave during the last few months and had arrived in Israel by 4 February 1988, were many familiar names: 'Iosef Begun, Lev Elbert, Victor Fulmacht, Alex Ioffe, Alexander Lerner, Vladimir Lifshitz, Arcady Mai, Vladimir Slepak, Aba Taratuta, Evgeny Yakir, Leonid Yusefovich and Victor Fairmark, who has arrived in England to join his American wife. Others who have received permission and will be leaving shortly include: Pavel Abramovich, Solomon Alber, Leonid Byaly and his wife Judith Ratner, Vladimir Dashevsky, Abram Kagan... Vladimir Prestin, Alexander Roitburd, Lev Shapiro, Valery Soyfer and Leonid Volvosky and Felix Kochubievsky whose son sadly died in a motor accident in Israel last year'. Although after a campaign by Oxford students, Boris Nadgornyi had been granted permission to emigrate, his father Professor Edward Nadgornyi and his mother Nina, despite promises, had still not been granted exit visas. On arriving at Vienna, Professor Lerner declared that during the last few months

---

Southampton, MS254/A980/1/1/29 Rita Eker to Thatcher 17 May 1988.
Southampton, MS254/A980/1/1/29 Charles Powell to Rita Eker 29 January 1988.

emigration applications for Jews without first degree relatives had been relaxed but now the Ovir offices in Kiev, Leningrad and Moscow had toughened their approach and were strictly enforcing them.[807] Prospects for 1988 were thus not quite so sanguine as appeared.

However, in a concession to the Prime Minister, the Soviet ambassador in London expedited the passage of Mrs Sosna from the Soviet Union because her family lived here. By July 1988, Mrs Rimma Sosna was reunited with her son Boris in London, whom she had not seen since 1974, when he was given permission to leave Leningrad.[808] In addition, Professor Baum wrote to Margaret Thatcher that 'you were kind enough to write a warmly supportive letter to Mrs Nina Nadgornyi, the Moscow Refusenik. More recently, I notified you of the good news that her son, Boris, the subject of that correspondence, had finally received an exit visa from the Soviet Union'. Nevertheless, his parents remained 'beleaguered in Moscow on the spurious excuse of possession of State secrets by his father, Professor Edward Nadgornyi'; and their son Boris would be grateful if you would let him have a message of support for his parents.[809] Mrs Thatcher had also written a helpful letter to Leonid Finkelstein, a former Soviet Jew living in Britain, assuring him that the case of his son joining him in Britain had been taken up by the Foreign Secretary, Sir Geoffrey Howe; and that she 'very much hope[d] that this will lead to progress'.[810]

On Monday 15 February 1988, the British Foreign Secretary met his Soviet counterpart, Shevardnadze, in Moscow and presented him with a list of 35 persons not granted exit permits, pleading publicly for understanding

---

[807] Newsletter of SRSR, 4 February 1988.
[808] National Archives, PREM 19/3174 Charles Powell to Thatcher 21 April 1988. Jewish Chronicle 29 July 1988, p.10.

[809] National Archives, PREM19/3174 Professor H. Baum to Thatcher 9 June 1988.
[810] Jewish Chronicle 8 January 1988, p.6.

and warning that there could not be trust unless there was progress on Afghanistan, arms control and human rights. Baruch Gur, the representative of the Lishka at the Israeli embassy in London, said that half the names on the list were Soviet Jews. In addition, Shevardnadze agreed to set up bilateral talks to discuss human rights issues, though the Kremlin quickly tried to renege on this agreement but were dissuaded after pressure from the Foreign Office.[811] On Tuesday morning, Sir Geoffrey had breakfast with a new generation of refusenik leaders, Yuli Kosharovsky, Mrs Natalia Khasina and Mrs Tatiana Ziman, and three Christian human rights activists. 'One of the memoranda presented to Sir Geoffrey complained about the problem of "poor relatives" – those unable to leave because they are unable to obtain affidavits from remaining relatives or former spouses which state that they pose no financial burden'. Other memoranda dealt with the iniquities of the emigration laws and the procedures which caused immense hardship for Soviet Jews. On Tuesday, he had talks with Gorbachev and there was a magnificent reception arranged for him in the Kremlin. At the press conference, the Foreign Secretary added that two years ago there had been almost 20 cases of those with relatives in Britain who had been unable to join them, but now the list had been whittled down to one.

Kosharovsky asserted that glasnost had provided a cover, allowing antisemites to hold meetings throughout the country making false accusations against Jews, while Jews were barred from holding counter-demonstrations. The allegations in 'The Protocols of the Elders of Zion' were widely disseminated, so that the Jews were accused of wishing to seize control of the wealth and power of the Soviet state. If the doors of the Soviet Union were thrown open, he believed that 500,000 Jews would choose to leave. But the authorities also resorted to propaganda to limit the impact of the refusenik movement, besides jailing them. Samuel Zivs, the deputy chairman of the Soviet Anti-

---

[811] LMA, ACC 3087/008 minutes of the executive of the National Council 17 February 1988, and 22 June 1988.

Zionist Committee, claimed that 'Ninety per cent of the Refuseniks left the Soviet Union last year. There are no more than 1,200 requests for emigration visas waiting to be processed...We do not believe that 400,000 people want to leave. This is pure imagination'.[812] The refusenik leaders feared that the Soviet authorities were winning the propaganda war, by allowing well-known personalities such as Shcharansky, Nudel, and Slepak to leave, while encumbering the mass of Soviet Jews with countless regulations to entrap them.[813]

The National Council and Women Intensify and Widen Their Campaign

Between 1986 and 1988, the National Council for Soviet Jewry and the Women's Campaign stepped up their efforts to make the wider British public aware of the iniquities of the Soviet regime as regards human rights, despite their signing the Helsinki Final Act, by trying to maximise their support from trade unions, the Churches and the media. Turning first to the trade unions, in the mid-1970s Doreen Gainsford appointed Rosalind Gemal as the Trade Union officer of the 35's and Gemal contacted the Electrical, Electronic, Telecommunications and Plumbing Union, NALGO and the AEU about Sender Levinson, a metal worker, who had been dismissed from his employment in 1975 and sentenced to a term of imprisonment for applying to emigrate to Israel. He had been charged with parasitism, though his wife and children were allowed to depart for Israel. As many members and leaders of the unions were adherents of the Communist party, they rebuffed these overtures, while others supported the Palestinian cause and were hostile to Israel. Still others were antisemitic and unsympathetic. Rachele Kalman was shocked by the rabid antisemitism she encountered from rank and file trade

---

[812] Jewish Chronicle 19 February 1988, pp.1 and 2.
[813] Jewish Chronicle 26 February 1988, p.4.

unionists, though not from members of the executive, when she tried to distribute leaflets on human rights at the Brighton TUC conference in 1978. The leaflet outlined the rights denied to Russian Jewish workers, when they tried to emigrate, including freedom of speech, freedom of assembly and religious worship, and called on the TUC conference to support a charter for basic human rights in all countries. Every year the annual conferences of individual trade unions were held in Brighton and Blackpool or Bournemouth, at which local branch members of the Women's Campaign attended to harangue delegates and hand out leaflets. In July 1986, Alan Sapper, the General Secretary of the Association of Cinematograph and Television Technicians, took up the case of Alexei Magarik, a young musician, who had been sentenced to a term of imprisonment and not allowed to practise his profession. Sapper visited Russia in November talking to trade union officials, after which Magarik's prison term was halved. In August 1987, an appeal was made to trade unions to adopt a refusenik family, to which NALGO responded by adopting the Yelistratov family, who had been refused exit permits for sixteen years.[814]

As Trade Union officer of the Women's Campaign over a period of fourteen years, Rosalind Gemal corresponded with every trade union and tried to persuade as many as possible to insert articles on human rights and the plight of manual workers refused exit permits in their journals to heighten awareness of members lacking in knowledge of conditions in the Soviet Union. In the archives of the 35's deposited in Southampton, are countless trade union files and until these are evaluated it is impossible to assess accurately the overall effectiveness of this campaign.[815] What is clear, however, is the failure of these remonstrations to make much more than a limited impact on the General Secretaries of the TUC during the mid-1980s. In 1984 Rita Eker and Margaret Rigal wrote to Len Murray that they understood that a number of trade

---

[814] Daphne Gerlis, pp.121-9.
[815] Daphne Gerlis, p.128.

unions had written to him enclosing relevant biographies of Jewish workers in the Soviet Union, who had been dismissed from their employment because they had applied to emigrate to Israel. The Soviet authorities were in breach of Convention 111 dealing with discrimination in employment, a matter which was going to be discussed at the International Labour Organization conference in June. 'We are aware that the TUC has already passed on some of those [cases] to the ICFTU [International Confederation of Free Trade Unions] and we enclose more than a hundred similar cases which may help the ICFTU in its evidence'. In reply, the secretary of the international department of the TUC stated that their 'representative in the ILO Committee on the Application of Conventions and Recommendations [would raise] the allegations that the Soviet authorities are in breach of Convention 111'.[816] On 26 June 1986, the international secretary informed Mrs Gemal that they took up 'such cases informally and without publicity in the course of contacts with Soviet trade union representatives, and would be reluctant to pursue the suggestion that the TUC should adopt a family on the list, which could undermine our approach'.[817]

In August 1986, Mrs Rosalind Gemal tried to gain support for a resolution at the TUC conference in September which drew attention to the fact that despite a 'unanimous resolution on human rights in the Eastern Bloc' in 1978, it 'seems never to have been implemented'. She wrote with the request to Alan Tuffin of the Union of Communication Workers, as he had always been sympathetic to the plight of Soviet Jews. The Women's Campaign was unhappy with the attitude of the International Department of the TUC which would only make informal approaches and was 'desperate to get the names of those Soviet Jews who are suffering dreadfully in

---

[816] Southampton, MS254/A980/1/3/48 Rita Eker and Margaret Rigal to Lionel Murray 13 April 1984; and Michael Walsh to Mrs Eker and Margaret Rigal 17 April 1984.
[817] Southampton, MS254/A980/1/3/48 Michael Walsh to Rosalind Gemal 26 June 1986.

the Soviet Union to the attention of the TUC'. If he was willing to speak for the motion, she would send him details of a refusenik to use as an example out of the hundreds in their lists.[818]

Christian clergymen of different denominations and church members aided the activities of the Interfaith Committee of the National Council in London and at events at the local level, which included some churches adopting individual refuseniks and sometimes congregants making small donations. Within the Church of England, there was cooperation with the campaign for Soviet Jewry in Birmingham, Oxford and Manchester in the late 1970s but it was difficult to generate much long-term enthusiasm from the mass ranks of Christian clerics.[819] When the Revd. Marcus Braybrooke of the Council of Christians and Jews was approached in November 1985 about having clergy sermonise or make mention of Soviet Jewry on the Sunday before a forthcoming summit between President Reagan and Gorbachev, he could not promise to do much about activating the clergy but would appeal to the ex-Archbishop of Canterbury Lord Coggan to add his voice in the church press which he did.[820]

From 1977, there was an Interdenominational Committee of the National Council, run by the charismatic Reform Rabbi Dow Marmur, which gradually evolved in the 1980s into the Interfaith Committee under the chairmanship of Mr S.S. Levin, a stalwart of the United Synagogue. Both found it increasingly troublesome to obtain the necessary quorum for holding regular committee

---

[818] Southampton, MS254/A980/1/3/48 Rosalind Gemal to Alan Tuffin 15 August 1986.

[819] LMA, ACC.3087/162 Oxford Interdenominational Committee Margaret Curtis to June Jacobs 12 March 1978, Birmingham Interdenominational Committee Renee to Jean Karsberg 18 October 1978, and National Council press release 1978 about 120 Christian clergy in Manchester attending a conference on Soviet Jewry.

[820] LMA, ACC.3087/106 Arieh Handler to Marcus Braybrooke 1 November 1985; Joy Paul to Handler telephone message 4 November 1985; Joy Paul to Marcus Braybrooke 7 November 1985; and press release from the CCJ 8 November 1985.

meetings and tended to confine their activities to sponsoring an annual seminar for Christian clergy on Soviet Jewry sponsored by a prominent bishop.[821] Support from the Catholic Church was minimal, apart from some nuns and Cardinal Basil Hume, who was willing to be outspoken on the issue. As noted in Chapter 4, the Anglican Bishop David Shepherd and his wife assisted the Liverpool branch of the Women's Campaign by demonstrating on the evening of the Day of Atonement, when Jews were unavailable. In 1974, Christian clergymen participated in a prisoners' lunch in Croydon. Donald Soper and the United Reformed Church passed several resolutions in 1979 in favour of Soviet Jewry. Elsie Lucas, a resident of Edinburgh, who was associated with Keston College which investigated the persecution of Christians in the Soviet Union, was a great supporter of the refuseniks, participating on a march in London; these are just a few of multifarious examples. In turn, the 35's campaigned for Pastor Vins, imprisoned as a Baptist, and Dr Koryugin, a supporter of the Campaign Against Psychiatric Abuse and for Veronica Rostropovich, the sister of the cellist.[822]

However, the National Council was never able to establish close relations with either the British Council of Churches or Keston College. The secretary of the former, Canon Paul Oestreicher, made clear that his visit to the Soviet Union was primarily concerned with arms control and disarmament and that their treatment of minorities affected these issues; the word Jew was not mentioned. And when Arieh Handler asked him later to take action, as the

---

[821] LMA, ACC.3087/161 Rabbi Dow Marmur to all members of the Interdenominational working group 3 May 1977. ACC.3087/166 S.S.Levin to Professor Chimen Abramsky 11 January and Abramsky to Levin 27 January 1983; and S.S. Levin to all members of the Interfaith Committee 28 February and 11 May 1983. ACC.3087/165 Interfaith seminar at Westminster Cathedral 17 February 1982.
[822] Daphne Gerlis, pp.129-35. LMA, ACC.3087/192 Elsie Lucas to Arieh Handler 10 May 1983 and Handler to the same 20 May 1983; and Elsie Lucas to Joy Paul 24 March 1984; and Joy Paul to the same 9 April 1984.

position of Jews in the USSR had deteriorated, there was no follow-up correspondence.[823] Attempts by Andrew Balcombe of the National Council in 1980 to set up a joint religious programme with Christians on the BBC Russian Service were rebuffed by the director of Keston College, the Revd. Michael Bourdeaux, as being useless because of the negative attitude of the BBC producers. This was a fair comment, but when three years later Arieh Handler tried to set up a meeting with the director, his suggestion was stymied with the excuse from his secretary that he was too busy travelling after the award of the Templeton prize, but that he could meet the research director instead.[824]

Liaison with the churches by the 35's was initiated by Delysia Jason before her departure for Israel and was taken over in 1975 by Margaret Rigal, who contacted twenty-one bishops, evoking a varied response. In 1987 she reactivated the interfaith committee under the auspices of the National Council. It was launched as the Interfaith Committee of the Rights of Jews, Christians and Muslims in the USSR and the Bishop of Oxford, Revd. Richard Harries, served as its chairman. In May 1988, there was a weekend of prayer, when a piece composed by Rabbi Zalman Kossowsky was recited in synagogues, churches and mosques. On 24 October 1988, United Nations Day, a meeting of all three faiths took place with appraisals of the situation facing each faith in the Soviet Union being given by experts. Christian clergymen in their sermons began mentioning the dire situation facing Jews in the USSR who planned to emigrate. On the debit side, some Christian groups were eager to obtain the names and addresses of refusenik families, because they were at a low point psychologically and were an easy target for missionary activities; and this sometimes

---

[823] LMA, ACC.3087/071 Paul Oestreicher to Arieh Handler 18 October 1984; and Handler to the same 26 February 1985.
[824] LMA, ACC.3087/192 Arieh Handler to Michael Bourdeaux 13 March 1984; and Caroline Andrews secretary of the director to Handler 23 May 1984.

made Jewish groups cautious and wary about seeking their assistance.[825]

Great effort was expended by campaigners in trying to gain the interest of local and national newspapers. When she started as the press officer of the Women's Campaign, Joyce Simson was shown by Kevin Keighley of the *Guardian* how to write a press release, as her early efforts were somewhat amateurish. Blessed with a booming voice, Joyce relied on *chutzpah* to gain entry to correspondents, passing herself off as Mrs Simpson, as the BBC Foreign Editor was almost impossible to reach.[826] In addition to the quality press, the 35's and Barbara Oberman's group found that the popular press were often happy to publish stories illustrated by photographs of glamorous young ladies. The Women's Campaign also had good contacts with the local London newspapers, including the *Hendon Times*, the *Ilford Recorder*, the *Enfield Times* and the *Croydon Advertiser*. The 35's featured in the BBC 'Panorama' programme and the ITV 'World of Action' series, one of which so entranced Shcharansky when he was in a Soviet prison...[827] Apart from the 35's, there was Michael Sherbourne, who was on the telephone almost every evening with his contacts in the Soviet Union relaying the latest information about refuseniks and dissidents to the Women's Campaign and the Union of Councils in the United States, from where the latest news was forwarded to the Foreign Office and the State Department. The Soviet Jewry campaign benefited from the assistance of *The Times* columnist Bernard Levin, who wrote many enthusiastic articles promoting the cause and from the Soviet affairs expert, David Floyd, in the *Telegraph*. With his first piece on the Prusakovs which was published on 4 July 1972, Bernard Levin produced a stream of articles on refuseniks and such non-Jewish dissidents as Sakharov, Solzhenitsyn, and Father Gleb Yakunin in a polished and witty style.[828] Strenuous efforts were made by

---

[825] Daphne Gerlis, pp.131-5.
[826] Daphne Gerlis, pp.97,102-3.
[827] Interview with Barbara Oberman and Daphne Gerlis, pp.102-3.
[828] Daphne Gerlis, pp.106-7.

the Women's Campaign to ensure the utmost accuracy in all their published material, so that they were established as an unimpeachable source for any story attributed to them.

In the USSR, the refusenik and dissident leaders briefed foreign correspondents, when this was possible, and tried to have the names of Prisoners of Zion displayed on banners in photographs, as this gave them some measure of protection if the photographs were reproduced in the Western press.

The Women's Campaign Counters Gorbachev's Propaganda and Highlights Human Rights

John Simpson acutely pinpointed why the persistent protests by the Women's campaign were so important in the 1980s, when the public were bamboozled by Gorbachev's slogans of glasnost and perestroika. 'Once Gorbachev had made his mark, it was very easy to think that everything was now all right with the Soviet Union, when it clearly wasn't. What the 35's did wasn't always popular at the time because people liked Gorbachev and wanted to believe that Moscow had changed. I think that by reminding us that it hadn't changed nearly enough, they did a great deal of good. And in the end the people of Russia themselves showed that they didn't feel things had changed enough'.[829] There was always close cooperation between the independent-minded Martin Gilbert and the Women's Campaign. His articles on the tribulations of Soviet Jewry appeared in the world's press and his critical support bolstered the whole movement, when the more moderate larger communal organizations were often prepared to settle with Gorbachev for fewer concessions.

In March 1988, Margaret Rigal informed the National Council for Soviet Jewry of 'the proposed visits of the Red Army Ensemble, the Moscow State Circus and the Kirov Ballet. The 35's...would be maintaining a presence at all

---

[829] Daphne Gerlis, p.187.

venues visited by the Russians and asked that affiliates be so informed'.[830] The Women's Campaign always had a hard core of supporters who could be relied upon to attend these demonstrations at all times and the 35's persisted with this policy of making visitors from the Soviet Union feel uncomfortable and unwelcome.

At the request of the National Council, Mrs Thatcher on 15 July 1988, received a delegation of four from the International Council of the World Conference on Soviet Jewry, comprising Neil Bradman, its chairman, Dr Lionel Kopelowitz, the President of the Board, Edgar Bronfman, the President of the World Jewish Congress and its Director-General, Israel Singer. 'Mr Bronfman reported... on his meetings with Eduard Shevardnadze, the tone of which was decidedly "upbeat" and centred around opportunities for furthering culture and religion in the Soviet Union. Statements had been made that rabbis and teachers would be allowed in the Soviet Union and that facilities would be available for the training of rabbis and teachers. Mr Bronfman had been informed that a gradual rise in emigration to a level substantially above the current rate, though less than 50,000 per annum would be permitted'. The Prime Minister seemed to echo President Reagan's view that decisions had been made at the top of the Soviet leadership which had not filtered down through the ranks of the bureaucracy. She seemed to indicate that Western governments and the campaign for Soviet Jewry should be prepared to acknowledge the advances in the Soviet attitudes.[831] Mrs Thatcher, who had hitherto been sceptical that Jewish culture could be resuscitated in the Soviet Union, now appeared to accept Bronfman's viewpoint. But the interpretation put on the report of the meeting by the Jewish press was misleading in that they inferred that the Prime Minister declared that Britain would

---

[830] LMA, ACC 3087/008 minutes of the executive of the National Council 23 March 1988.
[831] LMA, ACC 3087/008 minutes of the executive of Soviet Jewry 20 July 1988.

not be satisfied with the emigration figures until all Jews who wished to leave were granted exit permits.[832]

Despite the lack of direct personal access, the correspondence between the Women's Campaign and the Prime Minister grew with an ever-widening group of refuseniks appealing to her. Now it was the turn of five refuseniks from Leningrad led by Dr Roald Zelichenok, who used Mrs Eker as an intermediary to dictate a letter to Mrs Thatcher over the telephone. 'In recent weeks refuseniks and Soviet Jews have been deeply shocked', it began, 'to hear that one after another the countries of the West have agreed to the proposal to hold a human rights conference in Moscow. We have also been encouraged by the fact that you and Sir Geoffrey Howe continue to oppose the idea completely under present circumstances. We, in common with thousands of other Soviet Jews are denied human rights. We are refused the right to leave the country. We are discriminated against for being Jewish. Many of us have been thrown out of work for applying to leave the country or for being involved with normal Jewish life. Our sons and daughters suffer anti-Semitism in school and face quotas on entry to higher education. The Soviet Union has broken promise after promise about human rights. They have introduced regulations and procedures, such as the 1987 "emigration" rules, which contradict their international obligations... We are living proof that the Soviet promises in this area are worthless. We are grateful for your firm support and we know that you will continue to have the strength to speak out for us when you meet Mr. Gorbachev'. Mrs Eker added in her covering letter that her request for visas for herself and Mrs Rigal to spend a weekend in Moscow with a delegation of Parliamentary wives had just been refused.[833]

---

[832] Jewish Chronicle 22 July 1988, p.8.
[833] Southampton, MS254/A980/1/12/29 Dr Raoul Zelichenok and others to Margaret Thatcher 24 October 1988; and Rita Eker to Thatcher 25 October 1988.

In his reply to Dr Evgeny Lein, one of the signatories of the appeal, P.A. Bearpark, stated that 'I am sure you will be heartened by 'the words of the Prime Minister in a recent address to Friends of the Hebrew University, who said the following: 'When it comes to the proposal to hold a human rights conference in Moscow in a few years' time, I assure you that we shall consider attending such a conference only when the Soviet Union has implemented the commitments which it has accepted in (the Helsinki) accords. Reports of the imminent release of political prisoners is encouraging. But we wait to see whether these assurances will become fact...We will not rest until the citizens of the Soviet Union obtain the basic human rights and fundamental freedoms enshrined in the Soviet Constitution and in international commitments undertaken by the Soviet authorities.[834] In a separate letter, Mrs Eker was informed that the Prime Minister was 'very disappointed that our representations in London and Moscow failed to reverse the Soviet authorities decision. It is unfortunate that certain parts of the Soviet bureaucracy still appear untouched by glasnost, and it is to be hoped that this refusal will not affect any other visits to the Soviet Union you might wish to make. It is precisely the sort of problem which you have encountered which underlies our reluctance to agree to the Soviet proposal for a Moscow Human Rights Conference'.[835]

Similar letters to that despatched to Dr Lein were sent to all the other signatories of the appeal, including Dr Zelichenok. In a personal letter to a Mr. R. Selby, the Prime Minster noted that 'the Women's Campaign for Soviet Jewry (35's) called on William Waldegrave in the Foreign Office on 28 September, and he is taking a close personal interest in this case. He will be raising it specifically during his forthcoming visit to Moscow (which is provisionally scheduled for early December) when he also hopes to meet

---

[834] Southampton, MS254/A980/1/1/29 P.A. Bearpark to Evgeny Lein 4 November 1988.
[835] Southampton, MS254/A980/1/1/29 P.A. Bearpark to Mrs Eker 4 November 1988.

the Zelichenoks personally. I can assure you that we are doing everything possible to help the Zelichenoks in their tragic plight and that, more generally, we are working hard to convince the Soviet Union of the need for lasting fundamental changes in their system so that there can be no more cases like this'.[836] Fortunately, on their return from their visit to the Soviet Union the Parliamentary wives reported to Mrs Thatcher 'the happy news that (Alek) Roald Zelichenok and his wife Galina are going to be granted permission to leave the USSR to come to Israel'.[837]

After travellers returned from the Soviet Union, they brought back a letter from a group called 'Jewish Women for Emigration and Survival in Refusal' signed by 39 women and another letter signed by one of them Anna Sofman which Mrs Eker again passed on to the Prime Minister. The group appealed to Mrs Thatcher on the eve of her summit with Mr. Gorbachev and noted that 'Your repeated applications to the Soviet officials, and your firmness and the consistency of your position in [on] human rights have supported us during many long years. Please do not let our hopes die now. Moreover, you have great influence with the Soviet officials, and that is why many of our friends have left the USSR during the last two years. The situation of families in refusal is becoming worse every day. The secrecy restrictions...are patently absurd and illegal. The physical and mental health of our families has deteriorated under these conditions. Surely it is also wrong that a former husband and wife can influence our refusal'. Finally, there came the appeal to 'Mrs Thatcher, not only as a Prime Minister but also as a woman and a mother and one of the most active protectors of our interests: Please help us to emigrate from the USSR. Please convince Mr Gorbachev not to mock at our children and our husbands

---

[836] Southampton, MS254/A980/1/1/29 Margaret Thatcher to Mr. R. Selby 4 November 1988.

[837] National Archives, PREM19/3186 Sarah Meyer to Margaret Thatcher 18 December 1988.

and parents and LET US GO'.[838] Mrs Thatcher's role in the negotiations was gaining mythical dimensions, as she was regarded as a mother and protector with invincible power. Anna Sofman in her own private appeal to the Prime Minister, as she had also signed the letter from the women's group, explained that she was the wife of Lev Sofman, a long-term refusenik, was the mother of a son Boris aged five and was expecting another child. 'In addition I can say that not long ago our family have got [a] new refusal till 1991 (it was said by phone from the Supreme Soviet of the USSR)'. She warned that she would go on hunger strike when her baby was a month old. Once again, there was the appeal to Mrs Thatcher, as she had 'great authority with the Soviet officials. I apply to You as You are a woman and a mother. I plead [with] you to help our family to realize our human right and our long-year dream to leave the USSR'. In his reply, Charles Powell asked for a copy of Anna Sofman's biography which Mrs Eker sent to Mr. Wheeler of the Soviet department of the Foreign Office. As was her usual practice, she also enclosed the Women's Campaign calendar for 1989 which highlighted a number of refusenik cases. She ended by saying that 'the Refuseniks are relying on the Government's stand on Human Rights and know that Mrs Thatcher will not let them down'.[839] Again and again, the Women's Campaign emphasised the human rights aspects of the trapped Soviet Jews situation, as they were keenly aware that this was common ground they shared with the British government and the Americans.

Another theme which started to be underscored increasingly in the correspondence between the Women's Campaign and the Prime Minister was the necessity of the

---

[838] Southampton, MS254/A980/1/1/29 Women's Group of Refuseniks to Thatcher 26 November 1988; and Rita Eker to Thatcher 30 November 1988.
[839] Southampton, MS254/A980/1/1/29 Anna Sofman to Thatcher 26 November 1988; Rita Eker to Thatcher 30 November 1988; and Rita Eker to Charles Powell 29 December 1988.

Soviet Union agreeing to changes in its emigration policy before the British government could consent to the holding of a human rights conference in Moscow in 1991. In particular, they wanted the right of emigration to be accepted as inalienable as guaranteed by the UN Declaration of Human Rights and the International Covenant on Civil and Political Rights which the Soviet Union had signed; and not limited to the reunification of families of first degree relatives as set out in the new emigration regulations which came into force in January 1987.[840] Mrs Eker sent the Prime Minister comments concerning the concluding document of the Vienna CSCE meeting prepared by refuseniks at the Moscow International Seminar on Humanitarian Problems. They were concerned about the draft concluding document because it only made recommendations which were open to a wide variety of 'interpretation of concrete proposals without imposing any obligations on the participants who systematically violate the agreements they sign'. They asked for the following items to be included in the concluding document, the main points of which were:

1. 'The CSCE countries solemnly guarantee their citizens the right of freedom of emigration'.

2. 'The CSCE countries pledge to legally ensure the guarantee to the right of emigration'.

3. 'The CSCE... demand that any restrictions on exiting a country should be of an exclusive character and should be stated strictly and fully by law. This law should establish periods of restrictions and contain legal guarantees against the arbitrariness of the authorities'.

4. 'The CSCE countries demand that the principle of reunification of families should not replace the right of emigration...'

7. 'The CSCE countries find the practice of forceful deprivation of citizenship of people leaving their country as a hindrance of their right to return as it is stated in the

---

840 Henry L. Feingold, Silent No More p.245.

Declaration of Human Rights and the International Covenant on Civil and Political Rights'.

The proposals had been forwarded by the Moscow refuseniks to the Union of Councils of Soviet Jews, an activist American Jewish pressure group, with whom the British women worked closely. As they had already been sent to the British delegation in Vienna, Mrs Eker thought that the Prime Minister might also want to see them. The Union of Councils sent copies of the memorandum to President Reagan, Shultz, Congress and delegates from the 35 nations of the CSCE. As can be seen from an examination of the proposals, their main purpose was to prevent the Soviet Union from evading its obligations by hiding behind vague security concerns and ensuring that emigration existed as a right, not tied to the need for a family reunion.[841] Charles Powell sought to assure Mrs Rigal that if the conference was to be held in Moscow, the Soviet Union would have to maintain its recent improvement in human rights and to accept that they 'must be respected as of right and that it will ensure open conditions for the Conference itself'.[842]

Powell reiterated the substance of the last letter, when answering a Mr. H. Wolfson, adding these rights have been denied to the 'Raiz and Uspensky families, whose circumstances are particularly distressing'.[843] The weekly circular of the Women's Campaign dated 19 December 1988, noted that we are being inundated with reports that the Americans 'are said to have bargained 150 Long-Term Refuseniks against their signature' to the concluding document. Because 'Such an ending in Vienna would assume a Human Rights Conference to be held in Moscow

---

[841] Southampton, MS254/A980/1/1/29 Rita Eker to Thatcher 9 November 1988 with memorandum from the Moscow International Seminar on Humanitarian Problems 2 November 1988.
[842] Southampton, MS254/A980/1/1/29 Charles Powell to Margaret Rigal 9 December 1988.
[843] Southampton, MS254/A980/1/1/29 Charles Powell to Mr. H. Wolfson 12 December 1988.

in 1991', members should write to Margaret Thatcher and
Sir Geoffrey Howe appealing to them not to sign the final
document until Moscow met the requisite conditions.[844]

President Reagan Presses for a Deal Over the 1991
Human Rights Conference in Moscow

Nonetheless, the mood against participating in a future
human rights conference in Moscow was softening in
Western capitals by October 1988. 'But in recent weeks,
both the French and the Americans have weakened in their
opposition to this', Charles Powell warned the Prime
Minister, 'while the Russians have explicitly made
agreement to a conference in Moscow a pre-condition to all
human rights follow-up'. George Shultz, the Secretary of
State, informed Sir Geoffrey Howe, the Foreign Secretary,
that 'The Soviets have already improved their performance
with regard to the areas the U.S. has consistently raised:
prisoners, emigration, jamming, bilateral cases, and
institutionalization [of reform]. If they are willing to make
the further efforts we might require, we'll have payment in
advance for a meeting in Moscow'. Powell advised the
Prime Minister that unfortunately it was uncertain whether
the Americans would insist on their pre-conditions and in
some cases their meaning was obscure. For instance, 'do
political prisoners include prisoners of conscience? The
French seem to agree at any price. We risk a rout... Clearly
we cannot single-handedly block the outcome of the
Review Conference. But I think we could make greater
efforts than are suggested in the FCO [Foreign and
Commonwealth Office] letter to bind other Western
governments to a tough set of pre-conditions for a meeting
in Moscow'. Thatcher agreed with his advice, commenting
'especially with a visit to Poland in view'; and to the

---

[844] Southampton, MS254/A980/1/1/29 circular of the Women's
campaign for Soviet Jewry 19 December 1988; and Mrs Juliet Keen of
the Brighton branch of the 35's to Thatcher 27 December 1988.

suggestion that she should try to enlist President Reagan's support.[845]

A message was sent by Mrs Thatcher to President Reagan on 20 October 1988 by the secure link to stiffen the American terms for such a conference. She explained that she was worried that the Soviets would interpret the West's acquiescence in their proposal to hold a human rights conference in Moscow as a sign that they had done enough and exploit it for propaganda purposes. Hitherto, our support has 'sustained those individuals in the Soviet Union who have shown such courage in campaigning for human rights in their own country. All their hopes and faith will crumble if they think we have been hoodwinked into agreeing to a Moscow human rights conference. There is still a very long way to go before the Soviet Union truly accepts that human rights are God-given and cannot be taken away by the State... What I propose now is that we should aim to agree clear, specific criteria which would have to be met, and be seen to be met, if the West was to consider attending a conference in Moscow. If the two of us can do this, we should be able to persuade our other Allies to rally to that position. Without such clear criteria, the Soviet Union would have every opportunity to backslide on their commitments'. Geoffrey Howe would be in touch with George Shultz to agree these criteria.[846] A positive response came back from the President, stating that 'You and I should remain personally in touch on this important issue. I am convinced, as you are, that our cooperation is essential to a firm alliance stand'.[847]

Details of the American pre-conditions for such a conference were negotiated between Ambassador Yuri

---

[845] National Archives, PREM19/3174 George Shultz to Sir Geoffrey Howe circa October 1988; and Charles Powell to Thatcher 13 October 1988; and Charles Powell to Thatcher 19 October 1988.

[846] National Archives, PREM19/3174 Thatcher to President Reagan 20 October 1988; and Charles Powell to Lyn Parker 20 October 1988.

[847] National Archives, PREM19/3174 President Reagan to Thatcher 28 October 1988.

Dubinin and George Shultz in Washington. Shultz informed Shevardnadze that he welcomed the news delivered by the Soviet ambassador about the 29 prisoners of conscience who had been pardoned or paroled. Other names on the American list included prisoners denied their liberty for political or religious reasons, including those convicted on other charges – a polite way of saying framed on fraudulent criminal charges. These included psychiatric detainees, while the British would have added those sentenced to internal exile. The United States, Shultz said, would expect all the additional cases to be resolved as well. During September and October 1988 he was pleased to observe that 45 persons were granted permission to leave the USSR, but there were other persons deemed by us to be equally deserving who were denied permission to emigrate. There were a number of other cases which the United States expected to be resolved and which had already been raised in bilateral talks, involving divided families, blocked marriages and separated spouses. There was also the need for a clear commitment to end jamming in unequivocal terms. What the United States was seeking were public assurances by the Soviet Union that it intended 'to take certain steps in 1989 – specifically, to allow the rate of emigration to continue to increase' and to end jamming – [all] 'would provide important indications for the future'. The United States was looking to those articles in the criminal code classified as 'anti-Soviet agitation and propaganda' which were used to define political and religious crimes to be substantially abolished or amended. He believed that the Soviet Union had begun to satisfy these requirements, but before agreeing to the Moscow conference the United States would like to see the resolution of the specific cases mentioned and clear evidence that further reforms will be undertaken.[848]

---

[848] National Archives, PREM19/3174 Eduard Shevardnadze to George Shultz 7 November 1988 and George Shultz to Eduard Shevardnadze 8 November 1988. J.S. Wall to Charles Powell 10 November 1988.

The United Kingdom delegation reported that Shultz was convinced that the Vienna CSCE meeting could be concluded by 20 January 1989 before he left office; and that the Russians would try to meet the conditions for a conference in Moscow. The United States had now agreed to an economic conference, so long as it was not held in Prague. To conclude the agreement the Americans were willing to lower the bar on human rights issues which was worrying. Schifter, the American assistant Secretary of State, found only 80 long-term refuseniks, that is, persons denied permission to leave for ten years when they had twice applied to the visa office, which was too low a figure. The British thought that those denied the right to leave for five years was sufficient to be included in this category, while the Canadians under pressure from the Beth Tzedek Soviet Jewry Committee organization believed that there were 1,900 long-term refuseniks, which in the British view was too high a figure. Moreover, it was doubtful whether agreement on the dubious psychiatric cases could be concluded by 20 January next. Within Congress and the State Department, there were many who thought that Schifter was over-eager to reach agreement with the Russians on the Moscow conference, and was, therefore, too accommodating to their viewpoint.[849]

According to a Foreign Office assessment of the current state of Anglo-Jewish opinion, 'The so-called 35's are very much the hard line of the Soviet Jewry lobby in the UK. They seem to have heard that the Americans are wobbling on their conditions for agreeing to a Moscow human rights conference although the letter does not say so... The National Council for Soviet Jewry with whom we are also in regular contact tell us that a decision to agree to a Moscow conference in circumstances where everyone else is prepared to go along with it would be accepted by the majority of the Jewish lobby so long as significant and real

---

[849] National Archives, PREM19/3174 UK delegation CSCE Vienna to the FCO November 1988. Wendy Eisen, Count Us In pp.255 and 318-19 n.29.

improvements such as the release of all the long-standing refuseniks had been achieved'.[850] This was not quite the case because the Student and Academic Campaign for Soviet Jews refused to endorse the Moscow conference so long as Jews were refused visas on spurious grounds and antisemitic groups continued to flourish.[851]

On 7 December 1988, Gorbachev addressed the United Nations on disarmament and human rights questions. Soviet democracy, he proclaimed, would be placed on a more regular basis, referring in particular to freedom of conscience, glasnost and public association. Further, 'In places of confinement there are no persons convicted for their religious beliefs'. According to the analysis of the British ambassador in Moscow, this was less broad a category than Gorbachev's previous definition of 'all those whom the West regards as political prisoners'; and it was not clear whether this definition applied to those detained in psychiatric hospitals.[852] Gorbachev continued that naturally this did not preclude people being charged with espionage or terrorism whatever their political or ideological beliefs. 'The problem of exit from and entry to... [the Soviet Union], including the question of leaving it for family reunification, is being dealt with in a humane spirit... As you know one of the reasons for refusal to leave is a person's knowledge of secrets. Strictly warranted time limitations on the secrecy rule will now be applied' – this was progress the British ambassador observed. 'Every person seeking employment at certain agencies or enterprises will be informed of this rule. In case of disputes, there is a right of appeal under law'. Taking a swipe at the Soviet Jewry campaigners, he asserted that 'This removes

---

[850] National Archives, PREM19/3186 Cecily Woolf to Margaret Thatcher 12 October 1988; and Lyn Parker to Charles Powell 17 October 1989.
[851] National Archives, PREM 19/3186 Justyn Trenner to Margaret Thatcher 26 January 1990.
[852] National Archives, PREM19/3174 Rodric Braithwaite Moscow to the FCO December 1988.

from the agenda the problem of the so-called `refuseniks".
However, he confirmed that the Soviet Union would
participate more fully in the CSCE human rights
monitoring arrangements, leaving appeals concerning the
interpretation and implementation of agreements to the
International Court of Justice; and that the jamming of
international broadcasts would cease.[853]

The Soviets had previously indicated that they
intended to lift the security restrictions on 120 refusenik
cases, of whom 50 of these would-be emigrants had been
informed of this by 6 December 1988.[854] However, it soon
became apparent that the cessation of the jamming of
international broadcasts would not be applied to Israel. By
the end of 1988, 18,965 Jewish emigrants had been allowed
to leave, double the total of the previous year. There had
also been a sudden surge of Jews wishing to leave the Soviet
Union in the closing months of 1988. Speaking to the World
Conference on Soviet Jewry, Nehemiah Levanon of the
Lishka declared that, 'When the Soviet Union is behaving
as if it recognizes the right of the Jews of the USSR to
emigrate to Israel, when the harassment of Jewish activists
trying to teach and study Hebrew and to develop Jewish
cultural activity has stopped, we are obligated to weigh
carefully what we will demand from the present regime
and what we will do in the face of new opportunities...Do
not disarm', was Levanon's warning. 'There is still more to
do'.[855]

Instructions were issued by State Department
officials to the American ambassador in Moscow to convey
to Shevardnadze that the United States was not prepared to
reach prompt agreement on the outstanding human rights
issues and thus bring the Vienna meeting to a close. When
Ambassador Schifter (1923-2020) heard about this, he

---

[853] New York Times 8 December 1988.
[854] National Archives, PREM19/3174 Rodric Braithwaite Moscow to
the FCO December 1988.
[855] Henry L. Feingold, Silent No More p.263. Wendy Eisen, Count Us In
pp.258-9.

approached Shultz and they agreed that he would carry an oral message to Moscow countermanding this, as he was leaving for the Soviet Union on the next day, 11 November 1988. Schifter played a crucial role with his Soviet counterpart Anatoly Adamishin, with whom he was on excellent terms, in brokering a deal. Schifter told Soviet Foreign Ministry officials provided there was progress on a number of human rights issues and an early conclusion of the Vienna CSCE meeting provision would be made for a Moscow conference on human rights.[856] He had entered the United States as a boy of fifteen and both his parents, whom he left behind in Europe, perished in the Holocaust. He was determined not to let this opportunity for an agreement slip by and shouldered the weight and moral obligations of his background. He argued that there had been tremendous progress on emigration and divided family cases, though emigration should be recognized as a right in accordance with the universal declaration of human rights. While quite a number of divided family cases had been resolved, there were some 20 American reunification cases which were still outstanding. It was important that all these cases were resolved, as it was difficult to see why Sergey Petrov, an artist, with no access to secrets for more than ten years was refused permission. The United States hoped to see the same resolution of the six cases on President Reagan's list which were recently presented to Chairman Gorbachev, namely Stolar, Vasily and Galina Barats, Yuly Kosharovsky, Lev Lukyanenko and Leila Gordiyevskaya – most of these names were those of well-known refuseniks. There were also a number of dual nationals, who would be allowed to renounce their Soviet citizenship to facilitate their departure to the United States. We would welcome confirmation that all prisoners of conscience convicted under explicitly political provisions of the Soviet criminal code would be released from any form of punishment and internal exile. We would further welcome the resolution of

---

[856] Anatoly Adamishin and Richard Schifter, Human Rights, Perestroika and the End of the Cold War (Washington, 2009), pp.166-72.

cases, where Soviet citizens have been convicted of ordinary crimes or confined to mental hospitals for political reasons. It was noted that a suitable mechanism had been implemented for the review of questionable psychiatric cases; and that permission would be granted to American psychiatrists to examine all the case records. As far as long-term refuseniks were concerned, the regularization of the secrecy restrictions announced by Chairman Gorbachev at the UN would go a long way to resolving this problem. On 2 December, the United States embassy presented a list of refusenik cases which were of special concern and there was also the list compiled by CSCE Commission of Congress, and the United States looked forward to the prompt resolution of these cases. Additional information about Soviet intentions to abolish key articles of the criminal code and on future legislation regarding religious freedom and human rights was required. As great progress has been made over the past three years, Secretary Shultz believed that the remaining issues could be resolved quickly.[857]

On 21 December 1988, Charles Powell scribbled on a confidential memorandum the note that 'We have reached the point of decision. Even with the advances registered, any decision to accept a Moscow Conference must surely be conditional on Soviet performance, not promises. Agree we send the attached message to President Reagan?' To this, the Prime Minister responded by answering 'Yes'. Under combined external pressure and the need to reform Soviet society, improvements had occurred 'undreamed of only two or three years ago'. 13 of the 22 political and religious prisoners have been released, while the Americans were going to go through other names known in the West case by case. 18 of the 56 refuseniks of major concern to the United Kingdom had emigrated or been given permission to emigrate or had their secrecy ban lifted.

---

[857] National Archives, PREM19/3174 Moscow Human Rights Conference instructions to the United States ambassador 15 December 1988.

Jewish emigration had substantially increased. There were no outstanding bilateral cases on the British list, though the government continued to pursue the Gordievsky and Badanova cases. The United States government had been asking the Soviet authorities to grant permission for Gordievsky's wife and daughter to visit him in Britain, so that the family could discuss their future. Gordievsky was, of course, the former KGB operative, who had defected to Britain. Stephen Wall on behalf of the Foreign Secretary concluded that 'Shultz proposes to recommend to President Reagan that the US government should agree that the Moscow Conference can go ahead. The Americans believe that resolution of this issue remains crucial to the conclusion of the CSCE negotiations, and the start of the Conventional Stability Talks... the Foreign Secretary considers that, if the Americans decide to accept a Moscow Conference, we should be prepared to join them. He does not believe that any UK national interest would now be served in standing out – in near or even total isolation – against agreeing to the Moscow Conference. It would, however, be essential to make clear that our agreement to it was wholly conditional on continued advances on the Soviet human rights front between now and the holding of the conference in 1991'. The Prime Minister should write to the President reiterating that acceptance of the conference in Moscow was conditional on this basis.[858]

There followed a letter to the President, beginning 'Dear Ron' and ending 'every good wish to you and Nancy for Christmas'. The thrust of the message was that 'We must make it clear to Moscow, publicly and privately, that our agreement to attend a Moscow Conference in 1991 is strictly conditional on continued progress meanwhile, which we will monitor closely: and that we shall not reach

---

[858] National Archives, PREM19/3174 J.S. Wall to Charles Powell 21 December 1988.

a final decision on attendance until it is clear that the Russians have actually implemented their undertakings'.[859]

On 1 January 1989, Charles Powell noted that General Powell telephoned to say that President Reagan, Shultz and he had discussed the prospects of reaching agreement in Vienna and agreeing to a Moscow Conference on human rights in 1991. It appeared that the President 'had pretty well made up his mind that he wanted to conclude the Vienna meeting before he left office'. As regards human rights, General Powell insisted that Britain draft some words about conditionality, since the State Department was reluctant to do so.[860] The next day, Powell warned the Foreign Office that the proposed Moscow Conference was still controversial in Britain with a large number of M.P.s putting down a Motion against it and 'there was considerable pressure from human rights and Jewish organisations'.[861] The President's reply to Margaret Thatcher's message was regarded as unsatisfactory because it failed to say explicitly that Western 'participation in a Moscow Conference would be conditional upon the Soviet Union implementing in full its undertakings'.[862] In a fresh memorandum to the Prime Minister, Powell suggested that Britain should conditionally agree to a Conference, provided we can tie the Americans...to the points set out in the attached message from you to the President'. Thatcher agreed to send a message on these lines to Reagan. The American press release about consenting to the Moscow Conference was better than Charles Powell anticipated, especially noteworthy was the key phrase: 'lack of future and institutionalised progress made to date will cause us to

[859] National Archives, PREM19/3174 Margaret Thatcher to President Reagan December 1988.
[860] National Archives, PREM19/3174memorandum by Charles Powell to Thatcher 1 January 1989.
[861] National Archives, PREM19/3174 Charles Powell to the resident clerk FCO 2 January 1989.
[862] National Archives, PREM19/3174 Charles Powell to the resident clerk FCO second message 2 January 1989.

reconsider our decision to attend a Moscow Conference in 1991'.[863]

On 3 January 1989, Powell reported to the Prime Minister that 'there were those in the Administration who were keen to see the United States agree to a Moscow Conference: and others who saw the prospect of a Conference in 1991 as very useful leverage upon the Soviet Union to continue to improve its human rights performance'. The President had joined the ranks of the latter. What was disturbing was General Powell's emphasis on flexibility in the United States' approach to human rights in the Soviet Union, so Britain decided to go on its own way when the text of their press statement was agreed.[864]

Among the points raised in the American statement which was couched in vague terms, were the significant progress made in human rights in the Soviet Union, including 'the release of hundreds of political prisoners and exit permission for many people long refused the right to emigrate', while 'emigration rates...are substantially higher'. The British press release was much more specific: 'The great majority of family reunification cases have been resolved (the long-outstanding United Kingdom list was cleared last year)'.

'Jewish and other emigration figures have increased substantially and many long-term refuseniks have been allowed out'.

'Conditions on which refuseniks are allowed to emigrate have been substantially eased'.

'All prisoners committed under the explicitly political and religious articles of the criminal code are being released and

[863] National Archives, PREM19/3174 Charles Powell to the Prime Minister memorandum 2 January 1989 and same to same 3 January 1989.
[864] National Archives, PREM19/3174 Charles Powell to Lyn Parker 3 January 1989; and same to the same second letter of the same date.

the Soviet authorities have undertaken to review all other outstanding cases'.[865]

The British statement declared explicitly that 'Our attendance at the Conference in Moscow will depend upon progress in the human rights field being maintained' and went much further than the American statement. Specifically, this included 'effective guarantees of free speech, freedom of religion, freedom to emigrate, as well as genuine judicial independence; people are no longer imprisoned (including in psychiatric wards) for their political and religious beliefs; there are no remaining long-term refuseniks who are denied their right to emigrate'. Because she had the solid backing of the British Women's Campaign and other activists, Margaret Thatcher felt freer than the United States to maximise her demands on Gorbachev as regards human rights; and stiffened President Reagan's resolve to overcome State Department willingness to take a softer American line, though Reagan nearing the end of his term as president was determined to reach an agreement with the Soviet Union.[866] Shultz felt that that the human rights criteria which the British were trying to impose on the Soviet Union tied them to a concrete set of proposals, while the United States wanted to adopt a more flexible approach as to whether or not they would participate in the proposed conference.[867] At the end of the day the American press release was so much vaguer than the British and a disappointment to Soviet Jewry campaigners.

Behind what was a successful conclusion to the negotiations, was a campaign by the Union of Councils, a more radical American Soviet Jewry organization, in which Donna Wosk played a prominent role, by compiling regularly updated lists of Prisoners of Zion which were

---

[865] National Archives, PREM19/3174 Colin Powell Washington to Charles Powell January 1989; and Charles Powell to Colin Powell.
[866] National Archives, PREM19/3174 Charles Powell to Lyn Parker FCO with a copy of the press release 3 January 1989.
[867] National Archives, PREM19/3174 Charles Powell to Lyn Parker second letter of 3 January 1989.

passed on to the Women's Campaign and Martin Gilbert.[868] Gilbert continued to use this information to write articles in the international press outlining the predicament of refuseniks, who were still trapped in the Soviet Union. At the beginning of 1988, for instance, he arranged a breakfast at the Hilton Hotel, Park Lane for Natan and Avital Sharansky 'to discuss the ways and means of bringing home, to the Jewish and wider communities, the particular problems faced today by the refusenik movement in the Soviet Union'.[869] These updated lists were also sent by Donna Wosk to Richard Schifter, the Assistant Secretary of State, but she left it to his discretion which names to include in the final list agreed at these negotiations.

On 20 January 1989, George H.W. Bush was inaugurated as President and on 6 March his new Secretary of State James Baker announced some new foreign policy guidelines based on fundamental human freedoms. While looking forward to nuclear arms reductions, he announced that the United States was exploring ways of accelerating the removal of its chemical weapons in Germany; and that removing the imbalance in conventional forces between East and West must be the primary focus of arms control. There should be freedom to organize in the workplace; freedom to express political differences; freedom to exchange ideas and information as well as freedom of movement; and freedom from military intimidation or attack. Although some progress towards these freedoms had been achieved through the CSCE process, more was needed by way of changed Soviet military deployments and respect for human rights.[870]

---

[868] Southampton, MS254/A980/1/3/33 Donna Wosk to Rita Eker 4 August 1988; Donna Wosk to Paul Summerfield 6 September 1988; Donna Wosk to Rita Eker 14 December 1988; and Donna Wosk to Richard Schifter 14 December 1988.
[869] Enid Wurtman Papers, Martin Gilbert to Wurtman 13 January 1988.
[870] National Archives, PREM19/3174 UK delegation Vienna to FCO speech by James Baker 6 March 1989.

Under the auspices of Professor Joel E. Lebowitz of Rutgers University, the Committee of Concerned Scientists sent a letter to Mr Gorbachev signed by 1,600 scientists from all over the world, 'pressing him to clear the decks of Soviet scientists who have been refused permission to emigrate for years. They attached to their message the names of 243 scientists refused for 5-10 years and 213 refused for 10 years or longer. Included were 21 who have been refused for 15 years or more'.[871]

In March 1989, travellers returned to London with fresh appeals addressed to the Prime Minister from two Moscow-based refusenik groups with overlapping membership which Rita Eker forwarded to Margret Thatcher. One was the Legal Seminar on the Emigration Problems, the other was the Public Committee for Monitoring Visa Office Work. They wished to draw Mrs Thatcher's attention to the current situation that despite Gorbachev's pronouncements to the United Nations in December 1988 and the conclusion of the Vienna negotiations in January 1989, 'over one hundred Jewish families (more than 300 men, women and children) are continually refused exit visas for reasons of "state secrecy". For all of these Families over ten years has passed since their first request to emigrate. It has been even longer since they handled "sensitive" information. Whether or not this material should still be considered secret was already controversial in the 1970s. At today's rates of technical and scientific progress, this claim has become increasingly ludicrous. In addition, a large group of would-be emigrants (the so-called "poor" relatives) are not even allowed to apply for exit visas because their relatives refuse to sign an affidavit guaranteeing the absence of financial claims. Often the signature of this document becomes the object of extortionate demands'. While there was no legal machinery for appealing against the illegal acts resulting in refusals, the Soviet government continued to flout the provisions of the international agreements which it had signed. 'In short,

---

[871] Southampton, MS254/A980/1/3/34Committee of Concerned Scientists of New York 8 February 1989.

the impression is created that the Soviet Authorities are intentionally preserving the institution of long term refusal in order both to discourage Jewish emigration and influence international public opinion by sporadically freeing selected individuals to create a benevolent atmosphere for summits, official visits, etc. In the last two months, this "fresh trade" together with the whole issue of refuseniks has disappeared from the political scene. The Soviet Authorities and press have announced that the problem no longer exists. But we are still here'. To overcome this arbitrariness and lawlessness, we have tried everything, including appeals, demonstrations and hunger strikes. 'Everywhere we meet only silence, indifference and the ever-tightening screw of repression'. The signatories begged the Prime Minister to raise the question of the flagrant violation of human rights, when she met Mr Gorbachev.[872]

Paul Gray, Thatcher's private secretary, advised Rita Eker that as regards the Moscow Conference the government had 'been very careful to make clear, both privately and publicly, that our attendance at this Conference nearly three years hence will depend on our being satisfied that Soviet assurances have been implemented. We believe that the Russians now have a significant extra incentive to live up to our human rights standards and that we can make effective use of this'. Enclosed was a Foreign Office statement which summarized Britain's continuing requirements for the conference to be held in Moscow. Significant progress had been made on a number of human rights issues by the Soviet Union, it noted. Thus 'the great majority of family reunification cases have been resolved (the long-standing United Kingdom list was cleared last year; Jewish and other emigration figures have increased substantially and many long-term refuseniks have been allowed out; conditions in which refuseniks are allowed to emigrate have been

---

[872] Southampton, MS254/A980/1/1/29 Leonid Stonov and others to Thatcher 1 March 1989.

substantially eased; all prisoners committed under the explicitly political and religious articles of the criminal code are being released...; the jamming of Western broadcasts to the Soviet Union has ceased'. By 1991, Britain expects to see a new criminal code implemented, the abolition or amendment of the political and religious articles, and people no longer imprisoned in psychiatric wards for their religious and political beliefs. There would be no long-term refuseniks denied their right to emigrate. All of this would have to be supported by 'effective guarantees of free speech, freedom of religion, freedom to emigrate, as well as of genuine judicial independence'.[873]

The earlier appeals from the two organizations of refuseniks were followed in April 1989 by a group describing itself as the representatives of the poor relatives. 'Our group consists of the refuseniks not allowed to leave on the ground[s] of the lack [of] the affidavits from their close relatives (mother, father, former wife or former husband if there is any common child)'. More precisely the government demands that we present them with documents proving that our close relatives do not have any claims on us. We have no legal means of compelling the production of such a document, so that we can only ask for it. In most cases, the reasons why no document is forthcoming has nothing to do with a material claim. 'Sometimes it is the fear for the career ...revenge, the lack of objective information about Israel, the absence of free emigration in the USSR'. On numerous occasions we have tried to ask the courts to define the 'presence or absence of...material claims' but they have refused to do so, while the emigration office will not accept notarised documents. 'Most of us are unemployed, the great number consist of single women who turned out to be in an awful position without money and without opportunity to bring up their children in a proper way. There are invalids who cannot

---

[873] Southampton, MS254/A980/1/1/29 Paul Gray to Rita Eker 30 March 1989 with the Foreign Office statement on the Moscow Conference.

receive demanded medical support'. Despite promises in the last two years, a new law dealing with the problem of poor relatives has not been produced. In order to strengthen Mrs Thatcher's position, when she met Gorbachev, who was on a three-day visit to Britain beginning on 5 April 1989, the group intended to hold a demonstration in front of the British embassy in Moscow on 3 April.[874]

Gorbachev Visits London and Frees the Samoilovich Family

The talks between Thatcher and Gorbachev mostly concerned arms control, the modernization of short-range nuclear weapons.[875] But the Prime Minister also pursued her revised human rights agenda and 'made it known to the Russians that she would insist on freedom of emigration and the freeing of long-term refuseniks'. Sir Geoffrey Howe, the Foreign Secretary, asked Eduard Shevardnadze, his counterpart, whether the Soviet Union would enshrine human rights legislation into law. Mrs Thatcher added later that Gorbachev had promised that such legislation would be implemented. As conciliatory gestures before Gorbachev's visit, it was announced that Georgy Samoilovich, a long-term refusenik, would be allowed to come to Britain for medical treatment and 14 refusenik families, many of whom had been held back on grounds of knowledge of state secrets, had been granted exit permits.[876]

As part of the CSCE review meetings, the London Information Forum was held in the capital between 18 April and 12 May 1989. Among its aims were 'to press Russians and East Europeans to comply fully with their

[874] Southampton, MS 254/A980/1/1/29 Y. Seminovsky and others to Thatcher circa April 1989.

[875] Margaret Thatcher, The Downing Street Years p.786.

[876] Jewish Chronicle 7 April 1989, p.1 and 14 April 1989, p.3.

commitments under the Helsinki Accords in the field of information, by highlighting existing shortcomings'; 'to encourage direct personal contacts between media experts from the West and East'; to encourage the Soviet Union and Eastern Europeans to 'relax controls and unwarranted censorship' and strive for 'greater openness to information carried by information technology'.[877] The Prime Minister opened the conference with a major address on freedom of information. She stated that in 1941 President Roosevelt delivered an address in which 'He looked forward then to a world founded upon four essential human freedoms. First among the four he put freedom of speech and expression, everywhere in the world. Nearly fifty years later we have still not fully achieved that freedom in all European countries'. It is clear from the changes in the Soviet Union and Eastern Europe that the central command system for economies 'has quite plainly failed... It is clear too from the priority which General Secretary Gorbachev is giving to political change and greater openness, in which we wish him every success. Now, with the microchip, we are fast moving into a new age of information technology... Countries which try to insulate their people from these developments, which try to limit access to information, to control the use of photocopies, to restrict contacts with foreigners, do not just fail to live up to their commitments under the Helsinki Accords, they condemn their people to lower standards of living and to a second-rate existence'.[878] Some of the argument in Thatcher's speech sounded like an updated version of Shultz's exchanges with Shevarnadze in April 1987.

On the other hand, there had been a marked improvement in the free flow of information and the cultural opportunities open to Soviet Jews by the summer of 1989, as noted by the Cultural Committee of the National Council. 'Now, not only can tourists take in many new

---

[877] National Archives, PREM19/3174 J.S. Wall to Charles Powell 8 March 1989.
[878] www.margaretthatcher.org/document/107642.

books, but most Jewish books sent by post are arriving. We must therefore take the opportunity of sending in much larger quantities of books than ever before. However, it is essential that most of the books should be printed in Russian or Russian/Hebrew and cooperation with Soviet Jews in Israel would help to ensure that the translations are good and that any teaching books are suitable to the Russian mentality'.[879] By September 1989, Cynthia Jacobs was suggesting that 'the focus should be on support for the chedarim [Hebrew classes] and children's education in the Soviet Union...This would involve the sending in of books and educational materials – videos and tapes, the sending in of teachers , and perhaps helping to fund the translation and production into Russian of suitable material...'[880]

While pressure was mounting from refusenik groups in the USSR over the backlog in dealing with long-term refusenik cases, there was still a steady flow of appeals concerning individual families. Mrs Lurie requested a meeting with the Prime Minister before Mr Gorbachev's visit about her parents but was told that she was too busy and was requested to make an appointment with William Waldergrave, the Foreign Office Minister. She was advised that the Prime Minister remained 'very concerned about her parents' case, that the Government is continuing to do all it can for your parents and that she will be raising the continuing refusenik problem with Mr Gorbachev when he comes to London'.[881] Mrs Eker passed on two letters shortly before the Gorbachev visit, one from Mrs. Prilutzkay, the other from her twin daughters. 'These letters are addressed to you personally', Mrs Eker continued, 'because, as you well know, every Soviet Jew believes that you are the key

---

[879] LMA, ACC 3087/18 National Council Cultural Committee 31 July 1989.
[880] LMA, ACC 3087/1821 September 1989.
[881] Southampton, MS254/A980/1/1/29 Paul Gray to Anna Lurie 30 March 1989.

to their freedom and that their faith in you is absolute'.[882] Both girls were very roughly manhandled when they demonstrated for exit visas which they and their mother could not acquire, as their father would not sign the necessary document. They were in a highly distressed state and were receiving medical treatment. Their father, after moving out when they were five, had not bothered to keep in touch with them since and had a new family. In Israel they had family who would welcome them, a grandmother and other relatives. Meanwhile their mother was continuing with her demonstrations, for which she was due to appear in court.[883] Charles Powell assured Mrs Rigal that the government was 'aware of the circumstances of this family – they have recently been included among those refusenik cases on which we press the Soviet authorities'.[884]

Prior to Mikhail Gorbachev's visit to London in April 1989, June Jacobs suggested at a meeting of the executive of the National Council that the lobbying campaign would have to be presented in a more 'sophisticated and professional manner' than in the symbolic actions undertaken in the early and mid-1970s, as there were no more Prisoners of Zion. She proposed that there should be a one-day mass lobby of Parliament arranged by the Board of Deputies.[885] It was agreed that members of the public, who were requested to write to M.P.s, should be given clear-cut guidance of the lines along which they were to write; and that the message of the campaign must include the idea of 'no new refuseniks'.[886] Neil Bradman added that the Council would repeat its earlier briefing of M.P.s, trade

---

[882] Southampton, MS254/A980/1/1/29 Rita Eker to Thatcher 3 April 1989.

[883] Southampton, MS254/A980/1/1/29 Margaret Rigal to Margaret Thatcher 24 April 1989; and appeal of Masha and Vicky Prilutzkay circa April 1989.

[884] Southampton, MS254/A980/1/1/29 Charles Powell to Margaret Rigal 5 May 1989.

[885] LMA, ACC3087/008 minutes of the executive of the National Council 19 October 1988.

[886] LMA, ACC3087/008 minutes of the executive of the National Council 16 November 1988.

unionists, businessmen and journalists.[887] At the centre of the campaign would be the slogan, 'WHY ARE WE WAITING', which would refer not only to the long-delayed changes in the emigration laws and the laws affecting religious and cultural activity, but also the lack of implementation of the undertakings in the human rights document signed recently in Vienna. It was hoped to deluge M.P.s with 40,000 letters, while the All-Party group of M.P.s would sponsor an early day motion on the day of Gorbachev's visit.[888] Within the past year a new organization had been set up called Refusenik – Public Action for Soviet Jewry; both the founders Lionel Salama and Michael Isaacs had been trained in advertising and wanted to use a well-targeted sponsored campaign in the press to counter Gorbachev's sophisticated public relations methods. Their spokesman on the National Council declared that they had decided to place advertisements in the press before Gorbachev's visit and would cooperate with the Council. All the affiliated groups on the Council agreed that 'there would be no collective event or rally' out of a fear that if they did not attract enough support to the event, it would damage the campaign.[889]

The National Council sought interviews with William Waldegrave, the Minister of State at the Foreign Office, Neil Kinnock, the Opposition leader, and Norman Willis, the general secretary of the TUC to express their concerns about the 'impediments' to emigration and the lack of religious and cultural freedom in the Soviet Union.[890] Mrs Thatcher made known to the Russians that she would insist on freedom of emigration and the freeing of long-term

---

[887] LMA, ACC 3087/008 minutes of the executive of the National Council 18 January 1989.

[888] LMA, ACC 3087/008minutes of the executive 8 February 1989.
[889] Jewish Chronicle 15 July 1988, p.14 and LMA, ACC 3087/008 minutes of the executive of the National Council 22 February 1988.

[890] Jewish Chronicle 31 March 1989 p.3.

refuseniks according to Neil Bradman.[891] From the moment Gorbachev arrived, the Student and Academic Committee mounted a vigil outside the Soviet embassy; and a celebrity roster, including Felicity Kendall, Andrew Sachs, Joanna Lumley, Bernard Levin, and Susan Hampshire, read out names of thousands of refuseniks when Mr Gorbachev called on the Prime Minister in Downing Street. Lawrence Littlestone, the executive director of the National Council, asserted that the Prime Minister had confirmed that Gorbachev had promised legislation that 'would enshrine the right to leave', though concessions offered over the case of George Samoilovich and a few other refuseniks were not enough. Because of the pressure from the British Soviet Jewry campaign, the Soviet embassy responded by issuing a statement on human rights, in which the refusenik situation was given a prominent place.[892]

Disputes within the National Council over the tactics to be employed during the Gorbachev visit and its aftermath opened fissures in its ranks. Although its chairman, Neil Bradman, said little publicly, he was furious that the Student and Academic Campaign for Soviet Jewry would not be bound in respect of meetings with ministers; and remarked on 1 March 1989 that in his capacity as a donor he would no longer fund the council.[893] In addition, a new organization called '1991 Watch' was set up by the 35's, SACSJ and Refusenik to put out information prior to the human rights conference in Moscow. Its first leaflet was denounced by Bradman as being 'politically counter-productive', because it listed conditions to be fulfilled by the Soviet authorities for the conference to go ahead which were less onerous than those demanded by the Prime Minister.[894] There was also a feeling of optimism, a notion

---

[891] Jewish Chronicle 7 April 1989, p.1.
[892] Jewish Chronicle 14 April 1989, p.3.
[893] LMA, ACC 3087/008 minutes of the executive of the National Council 1 March 1989.

that they were in the final stretch of a victorious campaign, that they could ease the pressure on the Soviets. Bradman 'believed that there were still a number of people in our movement who were frightened to acknowledge that we were in sight of winning what we had been campaigning for. That is the right of Soviet Jews to leave as of right'. [895] He was a scientist and wealthy businessman, who was a generous donor and his withdrawal of funding immediately plunged the National Council into a financial crisis. Its executive director claimed that it had debts of £30,000 owing to the Inland Revenue, in addition to which they were £8,000 overdrawn in the bank and had outstanding bills amounting to £8,000.[896] In these dire circumstances, the Jewish Agency refused a request by the National Council for a lump sum donation of £28,000 to cover two years' annual grants. Instead, they reduced their annual payment from $20,000 to $10,000. A fresh injection of funds from a handful of donors tidied them over the immediate crisis, but all the office staff had to be given notices, apart from the executive director.[897] The National Council also received a loan of £10,000 which its new chairman, John Fenner, a City lawyer, announced would keep their office open until the new year.[898]

Having received a letter from Robert Hicks MP with his constituent's query about the current position of human rights in the Soviet Union, the Prime Minister gave him a sober but hardly glowing assessment of the situation. 'While there have been substantial improvements in the Soviet attitude to human rights under Mr. Gorbachev, we

---

[894] LMA, ACC 3087/008 minutes of the executive of the National Council 9 April 1989.
[895] LMA, ACC 3087/008 minutes of the executive of the National Council 29 March 1989.
[896] LMA, ACC 3087/008 minutes of the executive of the National Council I March 1989.
[897] LMA, ACC 3087/008 minutes of the executive of the National Council 3 May 1989.
[898] LMA, ACC 3087/010 minutes of the executive committee of the National Council 13 November 1989.

recognize that there remains a long way to go. Recent changes reflect a more liberal interpretation of existing rules rather than the fundamental reform we are seeking: we therefore regularly press the Soviet Union on the wider need for institutionalised reform, as well as on individual cases. We raise these concerns through our Embassy in Moscow, through the Soviet Embassy in London and at the regular UK/USSR bilateral talks on human rights'.[899]

One refusenik over whom the Prime Minister took immense trouble was George Samoilovich, a senior scientific lecturer in applied mathematics. Ultimately he was allowed to leave the Soviet Union with his family and emigrate to the United States, but this was only after an international campaign involving governments and the American Union of Councils for Soviet Jews, and the British Women's Campaign and the International Physicians Commission. Along the way to this success story, there were numerous tussles with the Soviet Union's many-tentacled bureaucracy which was as obstructive and evasive in the age of Gorbachev as in the days of his predecessors. Samoilovich (born in 1922) served in the air force as an eighteen-year-old and was demobilized in 1972 with the rank of lieutenant-colonel-engineer. From 1958 he served as a senior official in the scientific research organisation of the Ministry of Defence until his retirement from the military. But in all those years he worked in the fields of applied mathematics and mechanics and the main results of his work were published in open academic journals and books. He explained that he had 'never taken any part in the activity connected with any... technical units or kinds of military techniques and never used any technical data of them'. From the end of 1972, he had no connection to classified information, as he 'worked in a civil institute of computerizing economics control (Ministry of instrument-making industry) as a chief of laboratory' before being dismissed when he applied to emigrate in

---

[899] Southampton, MS254/A980/1/1/1/29 Margaret Thatcher to Robert Hicks 20 April 1989.

1979. Although his wife and son had no connection with secret work, they were not allowed to emigrate either because of him. In any case, the work with which he was involved was now 18-20 years old. 'Is it possible that so long ago in the Soviet Union there were such works in the military field which hold their actuality on a level of state secret till now? And that is in a time of speedy scientific and technological progress?'[900]

When he and his family became refuseniks in 1979, he allowed his cramped apartment to be used as a centre where Western doctors could examine Jews ill with cancer. He became friendly with these doctors, particularly an American one called Professor Richard Rosenbluth. In July 1988, George Samoilovich fell ill and, when a tumour appeared on his neck, his wife Vera, who was a doctor, insisted that he had it investigated and it was diagnosed as lymphoma but treatment was delayed. Having heard this, Dr Rosenbluth, the director of an oncological department of the Hackensak Medical Center in New Jersey came to Moscow with an offer to treat him free of charge in his clinic. From doctor friends, Samoilovich knew that the methods of treating lymphoma cancer of the throat in the Soviet Union were antiquated unlike those in the United States. Together with Samoilovich's wife and son, Dr Rosenbluth visited the All-Union Oncological Centre in Moscow to obtain a document confirming George's diagnosis in order to show it to the officials in Ovir, the office for visas and registration. After they obtained the necessary certificate which involved a protracted argument, they hurried to the OVIR office on 2 August to show it to an official. He suggested that the best way to obtain permission was not to apply on grounds of treatment, but for a temporary visit. However, he claimed that such an invitation could only come from the United States, so they all hurried to the American embassy. To the

[900] Southampton, MS254/A980/1/1/29 George Samoilovich to Margaret Thatcher 14 January 1989 and biographical record of the same date. Daphne Gerlis, pp.203-5.

Ovir official's surprise, Dr Rosenbluth obtained an invitation for the visit from the American consular authorities. On 8 September, George's wife was orally informed that he could not be granted a visa on grounds that he possessed knowledge of state secrets.[901]

Help arrived from overseas. Linda Opper, director of the International Physicians Commission together with Marilyn Tallman, director of the Chicago Council for Soviet Jews, visited the Soviet Ministry of Public Health, and after speaking to the deputy minister, procured a document stating that George could go abroad for treatment over a period of two months accompanied by another person to assist him. But after waiting one month, he again received a refusal from Ovir on grounds that he had knowledge of state secrets. These refusals sparked an international campaign led by the American Union of Councils for Soviet Jews and the British Women's campaign for Soviet Jewry which worked in close cooperation with added input from the International Physicians Commission and the student organization Visov. Demonstrations were held in front of embassies and consulates in Britain and the United States in the course of which Dr Rosenbluth and several other doctors were arrested while demonstrating in New York. The Union of Councils worked with the State Department and George had several meetings in Moscow with Richard Schifter, an assistant Secretary of State, who was intimately involved with the human rights negotiations with the Soviet Union. He promised his assistance. The British Campaign involved Jewish organizations in France and members approached Lord Plumb, who induced the European Parliament to pass a resolution on 19 September 1988 to aid Samoilovich's campaign. He also put his case to Mr Gromyko. The British government 'expressed concern at official level on Mr Samoilovich's behalf in recent weeks',

---

[901] Southampton, MS254/A980/1/1/29 Rita Eker to Margaret Thatcher 19 January 1989 with a letter of George Samoilovich to Margaret Thatcher 14 January 1989 and biographical note of the same date. Daphne Gerlis, 205-7.

claimed Lyn Parker. 'The Foreign Secretary raised the case with Mr Shevardnadze in New York on 26 September. He was told that the matter would be looked at again'. On 12 October 1988, Mrs Cecily Woolf of the Brighton 35's branch had a fifteen-minute interview with Mrs Thatcher in which she raised concerns about the Samoilovich and Shoiket family cases. It was agreed by the Prime Minister that Mrs Woolf could inform the press that these particular refusenik cases had been discussed. Staff from the American, British and Dutch embassies in Moscow were in constant contact with George as were a constant flow of visitors.[902]

Through the efforts of the Women's Campaign and the British Medical Campaign for Soviet Jewry, George was sent an invitation on 18 January 1989 from Professor Daniel Catovsky that he would personally treat George at the Royal Marsden Hospital. Rita Eker and Joyce Simson telephoned him, advising him to address a personal appeal to the Prime Minister, Margaret Thatcher. He agreed to do this, despatching his appeal through two visitors from Leeds, who agreed to take it back to England. A day later, this appeal was sent by Rita Eker to the Prime Minister. On 21 February 1989, George again received a refusal of his application to be allowed to travel abroad for treatment. Contact with the British embassy in Moscow now became intense and there were almost daily telephone calls from Rita Eker, Joyce Simson and Liz Phillips of the 35s. As Gorbachev was visiting Britain on 5 April 1989, Thatcher intimated that she expected Samoilovich to be allowed to visit Britain for treatment prior to his visit. On 2 April, George heard through a telephone call from Pamela Cohen of the Union of Councils that Ambassador Schifter had advised her that he had heard through diplomatic channels that travel restrictions on George would be lifted. The next day Rita Eker telephoned him to confirm that the news was true. Following this, the deputy chief of OVIR telephoned

---

[902] Daphne Gerlis, pp.207-9. National Archives, PREM19/3186 Lyn Parker to Charles Powell 6 October 1988; and Nigel Wicks to Lyn Parker 12 October 1988.

to say that he could collect a foreign passport and travel to London for treatment. More time elapsed while George prepared a document saying that he did not object to his family joining him abroad, which he left at the OVIR office. In exchange for the passport, George had to surrender his interior one. He then went to the British embassy, where he deposited his foreign passport for the necessary permissions.[903] The Foreign Secretary was utterly astonished that the Women's Campaign had 'got wind' of the situation before he had from American sources, as he wanted to ensure that the British received 'a share of the credit' prior to the story breaking.[904]

George, after successful treatment in the Royal Marsden Hospital as an out-patient in the winter of 1989, was delighted when his son Victor telephoned him in the summer stating that he and his mother had finally been given permission to leave Moscow. Rita Eker on behalf of George and his family wrote to Margaret Thatcher to thank her for all her 'efforts' which had resulted in 'this happy outcome'.[905] When George Samoilovich thanked William Waldegrave, the Minister of State at the Foreign and Commonwealth Office, he responded with a warm handwritten note. 'I was immensely touched to receive your letter... I was only one amongst very many -- led by the Prime Minister Thatcher – who pressed the justice of your case. I am delighted we were successful and wish you and your family great joy in the future. Meanwhile we shall not rest until there is a just emigration law in place in the Soviet Union, and full observance of that law'.[906] The Prime Minster also responded to George with a handwritten

---

[903] Daphne Gerlis, pp.207-17. Southampton, MS254/A980/1/1/29 Margaret Thatcher to John Wheeler MP 15 May 1989.
[904] National Archives, PREM19/3186 Geoffrey Howe to Rodric Braithwaite April 1989; and Braithwaite to Howe April 1989.
[905] Southampton, MS254/A980/1/1/29 Rita Eker to Margaret Thatcher 2 August 1989; and Caroline Slocock to the same 7 August 1989.
[906] Southampton, MS254/A980/1/1/29 William Waldegrave to George Samoilovich 2 October 1989.

response, praising him and others like him who had won by their 'own faith and courage. I am so glad we were able to help'.[907]

But it was not until October 1989 that Mrs Eker was able to pass on to the Prime Minster the news that 'George, Vera and Victor Samoilovich are now happily reunited in Vienna. They will be flying to England on Friday, 20 October. George's dream is that he and Vera should thank you personally for all that you have done for them. He is convinced that without your personal support, his story would never have achieved a happy ending'. They were holding a celebration for George in their office on 26 October, to which the Prime Minister was invited and they hoped she could put in an appearance, even if it was for five minutes. Following her usual response to such invitations, the Prime Minister claimed that she was too busy for a personal meeting.[908] Nonetheless, she attended a British Technion dinner on 2 November 1989, when on a self-congratulatory note she exclaimed that 'We are seeing long-standing [refusenik] cases resolved, and none has given me more pleasure than that of George Samoilovich'.[909]

However, the Prime Minister was on occasion willing to attend a dinner of a representative body of Anglo-Jewry, such as the Board of Deputies or an innocuous institution, such as Friends of the Hebrew University. It was all a delicately balanced manoeuvre not to appear too closely allied to campaigning groups or individual refuseniks which would upset the Soviets and introduce a jarring note in their relationship. George retired to New Jersey with his

---

[907] Southampton, MS254/A980/1/1/29 Margaret Thatcher to George Samoilovich 3 October 1989.

[908] Southampton, MS 254/A980/1/1/29 Rita Eker and Margaret Rigal to Margaret Thatcher 17 October 1989; and Amanda Ponsonby to Rita Eker 23 October 1989.

[909] Southampton, MS254/A980/1/1/29 Margaret Thatcher address to the British Technion Society 2 November 1989.

wife Vera and son but his daughter-in-law was not given permission to join them until 1993.[910]

Every opportunity was exploited by Rita Eker to press the government to take action. A bunch of flowers was sent to Mrs Thatcher in the hope that when she attended a performance of the Bolshoi ballet, she would speak to the diplomatic corps about the many unresolved refusenik cases. Unfortunately, the Prime Minster did not have time to attend the performance.[911]

Despite these concessions over individual cases by Gorbachev, many refuseniks still remained trapped in the Soviet Union. 'It is now six months since the Final Document was ratified in Vienna and promises made at that time by the Soviet Government have been broken', declared Rita Eker and Margaret Rigal in a letter to Margaret Thatcher in the summer of 1989. 'Hundreds of Soviet Jews are still waiting to leave without any change in their situation and the legislation that was due to be published is still only a matter of speculation... Would it be possible for you to inform the Soviet authorities that their lack of performance in the last six months bodes ill for any hope that they will fulfil their undertakings in the next year. Unless and until they turn their promises into action, participation in the Moscow Human Rights Conference remains in doubt'. In his reply on behalf of the Prime Minister, Paul Gray stated that the problem of long-term refuseniks is still far from resolution, despite the Soviet commitments, under the CSCE arrangements, to resolve all outstanding human rights cases within 6 months of the Vienna Conference'. The government was making the Soviets aware of their concern, most recently by Mr Waldegrave summoning the Soviet ambassador to the Foreign Office to discuss a range of cases. As if the 35s had no intimate knowledge of this, he claimed that the

---

[910] Daphne Gerlis, p.217.
[911] Southampton, MS254/A980/1/1/29 Rita Eker and Margaret Rigal to Thatcher 4 July 1989; and Amanda Ponsonby to the same 5 July 1989.

government's most recent success was the permission given to the Samoilovich family to leave. He ended on a reassuring note, by saying that 'until Soviet promises are turned into deeds our attendance at the Moscow Conference will be in question'; and that government efforts would not cease until the refusenik problem was finally resolved by the introduction and implementation of legislation.[912]

At the beginning of September, the leaders of the 35's raised the case of Dora Kazachkov, whose seventy-seventh birthday it was and whose son had spent the last thirteen years in prison and Soviet labour camps. During that time she had only been allowed to see her son on three occasions. After an internal trial, he was now languishing under a harsher regime in the Chistopol prison. Her message to Mrs Thatcher was that 'as a mother, she must understand that all I want is my son to be with me till I die'. Rita Eker and Mrs Rigal pleaded with the Prime Minister that when she met Mr Gorbachev on a stopover in Moscow she should ask him to permit Mikhail Kazachkov to join his mother in Leningrad. They also presented Mrs Thatcher with 'a list of 1,800 names of Soviet Refuseniks, Waitniks and activists'. Armed with this list, they hoped that she would remind Mr Gorbachev that neither had the problem of the refuseniks been resolved nor had the promised legislation to ease emigration been introduced.[913] Charles Powell in his response admitted that during her brief visit the Prime Minister 'had a very wide range of issues to cover, and there was not time to raise all matters of concern affecting Soviet Jews, or to pursue individual cases. The Prime Minister did, however, raise the refusenik problem, and the need for early legislative reform'. He mentioned that when the Foreign Secretary met Shevardnadze in New York on 29 September, he had raised a number of individual cases as

---

[912] Southampton, MS254/A980/1/1/29 Rita Eker and Margaret Rigal to Thatcher 25 July 1989 and Paul Gray to the same 11 August 1989.
[913] Southampton, MS254/A980/1/1/29 Rita Eker and Margaret Rigal 2 September 1989.

441

well as that of Mikhail Kazachkov. Gorbachev declared that those who wanted to leave the Soviet Union could do so and legislation would be introduced shortly. In a letter to Elliot Lister, Powell provided important additional information that 'We are sending a delegation to the USSR in October both to raise individuals' cases, including Mikhail Kazachkov and Dimitri Berman, and to discuss the draft legislation on human rights which is coming before the Supreme Soviet. The team will also be going outside Moscow to have a look at the human rights situation on the ground. The conclusions reached by the team will, of course, be one factor in our eventual decision on whether or not to attend the Moscow Conference in 1991' – a remarkable insight into overall government policy. In a more general policy statement attached to the letter, the Foreign Office claimed to have resolved satisfactorily '70% of refusenik cases and over 80% of cases involving prisoners of conscience.'[914]

In December 1989, Margaret Rigal wrote to the Prime Minister complaining that delegates at the All Soviet Congress of Jewish Cultural Associations 'were insulted and jostled by members of Pamyat' – an antisemitic Russian organization. A similar ambivalent attitude to former Soviet Jews was shown when Natan Sharansky was refused a visa to attend the funeral of Andrei Sakharov. In a rebuttal of the Women's Campaign complaints, Powell stated that embassy staff had attended the Congress; and that although Pamyat members distributed leaflets and jostled delegates, embassy staff saw no serious effort at disruption, while the police were at hand to prevent the counter-demonstration getting out of hand. The British embassy believed that the Congress was a success with delegates airing their views on a wide range of issues.[915]

---

[914] Southampton, MS254/A980/1/1/29 Charles Powell to Rita Eker and Margaret Rigal 6 October 1989; and Powell to Elliot Lister 21 September 1989 with attached policy statement.
[915] Southampton, MS254/A980/1/1/29 Margaret Rigal to Thatcher 19 December 1989; Charles Powell to the same 11 January 1990.

1990: a Turning Point and the Beginning of
Mass Migration

At the end of 1989, it was still uncertain in which direction Gorbachev would move. Soviet Jewish emigration had climbed to 71,196 in 1989 exceeding the cap of 50,000 indicated by Edgar Bronfman, but it soared to 181,802 in 1990 and remained at a high level for the next three years, reaching 178,566 in 1991, 108,292 in 1992 and 102,134 in 1993.[916] Why did the conditions for emigration change so much by 1990? In many respects, despite a belief in the rule of law in a limited fashion, Gorbachev was an old-fashioned Communist functionary, skilled at dissembling and covering up problems from the public. In the summer of 1987, the trial was concluded of the operators who shut down the nuclear reactor at Chernobyl, but the scientists, who were to blame for the flawed design of the reactor were exonerated by Gorbachev and never faced prosecution. He was now free to implement his economic and political reforms and in a spirit of openness, glasnost, encouraged local cultural elites to rebel against the party under the banner of perestroika, restructuring, and unleashing nationalist forces within the Soviet Union which he could not contain. Gorbachev was forced at the same time to expend millions of roubles to rehabilitate areas blighted by the nuclear disaster and to pay for the medical care of tens of thousands suffering from the after-effects of radiation.[917] The disaster at Chernobyl and its consequences in exacerbating growing Ukrainian nationalism, contributed mightily to the break-up of the Soviet Union, as Russia with nearly 150 million inhabitants and the Ukraine with 50 million were the most populous republics in the Soviet Union.[918]

---

[916] Pauline Peretz, Let My People Go p.344.
[917] Serhii Plokhy, Chernobyl: History of a Tragedy (London,2019), pp.281,299,310,321.
[918] Serhii Plokhy, The Last Empire. The Final days of the Soviet Union (London,2020), pp.xxxi,54-65.

The economy was overwhelmed, forcing Gorbachev to seek financial sustenance from the West, but he continued to dither and did not switch the economy over rapidly enough to a market one, as his advisers pleaded with him to do under their '500 day' plan.[919] By the spring of 1989, there was certainly more freedom, but the economy was disintegrating and 'many items were unobtainable in the shops: razor blades, soap, toothpaste, butter and salami sausage'.[920] An additional factor in Gorbachev's calculations, was that by the late 1980s most Soviet experts were coming round to the view that it might be expedient to release tens of thousands of highly trained Jewish technocrats, as the central planning apparatus was unravelling and the demand for labour was falling.[921] On the other hand, with the KGB's apparatus still intact and antisemitic parties allowed to air their venomous views, Gorbachev believed that the Jews were sufficiently cowed not to depart en masse.

The new more democratic reforms also set free nationalist sentiment and unrest throughout the Soviet republics which Gorbachev suppressed by force. In Tbilisi, the capital of Georgia, Soviet troops fired on a crowd of protesters on 29 April 1989, killing twenty-one protesters and wounding many others. On 19 January 1990, Soviet troops entered Baku in Azerbaijan to suppress a movement for independence. In Vilnius in Lithuania on 13 January 1991, thirteen civilians died in clashes with troops, but the epicentre of the unrest was the Ukraine, where the Chernobyl disaster had occurred and where the memory of the famine of 1931-4, for which Stalin was blamed, and in which 3.9 million Ukrainians perished, persisted. [922]

---

[919] William Taubman, Gorbachev. His Life and Times pp.521-30.
[920] Nicholas Bethell, Spies and Other Secrets (London,1994), p.353.
[921] Robert J. Brym, The Jews of Moscow, Kiev and Minsk pp.72-3.
[922] Amy Knight review of Vladimir Bukovsky, Judgment in Moscow: Soviet Crimes and Western Complicity 16 January 2020 New York Review of Books; and Serhii Plokhy, Chernobyl: History of a Tragedy pp.320-21. Anne Applebaum, Red Famine. Stalin's War on Ukraine (London, 2018), p.xxiv.

Against a background of economic chaos and rising nationalism and antisemitism in the republics of the Soviet Union, secular Jews felt unsafe and uncertain of the future for their children and themselves. To the surprise of the Soviet authorities, thousands of these secular completely-assimilated and detached Jews queued for visas to Israel in January 1990 outside the Netherlands consular section in Moscow which was handling such matters, as diplomatic relations had not yet been restored with the Soviet Union.[923] This was a portent of what was to happen in the rest of 1990 when the surge of Jewish immigrants reached unheralded numbers. Massive fear of what would happen in the future caused a panic among Soviet Jews and an unexpected avalanche of applications for visas.

Having made a short visit to Moscow, Rita Eker relayed to the Prime Minister the refuseniks' widespread concern about the rising antisemitism in the Soviet Union which could only lead to physical violence. Jews could no longer cherish any hope of living safely there. To this onslaught, Powell replied that a legislative reform process was underway. There were now over a hundred synagogues functioning in the Soviet Union, while hundreds of Jewish cultural groups were burgeoning. 'However, only half of the Jewish cultural groups in the USSR have official recognition; there are still a number of long-term refuseniks who continue to be denied permission to leave the USSR; there are still some prisoners including Soviet Jews who continue to be imprisoned on the flimsiest of pretexts... William Waldegrave discussed these issues with a group of Jewish representatives in Moscow earlier in the month... we shall underline to the Soviet authorities the need for fundamental and permanent reform...' [924]

Pamyat was a political party on the extreme fringes of Russian conservatism which emerged in 1985 and was openly antisemitic. According to Walter Laqueur, it enjoyed the support of no more than ten per cent of the

---

[923] Henry L. Feingold, Silent No More pp.282-3.
[924] Southampton, MS254/A980/1/1/29 Rita Eker to Thatcher 17 January 1990; and Charles Powell to the same 5 February 1990.

population. It revived the myth of the 'Protocols of the Elders of Zion' that the sinister forces of the 'monster of world masonry, Zionism and imperialism' were trying to obliterate Russian culture and in the updated version Americanize it. Some of the old ideas of the Protocols were resurrected in the claim that the Moscow metro had been mined so as to explode one day and destroy all the government institutions. At its meetings, members appeared in black shirts, calling for 'de-Zionization', the banning of 'mixed marriages', the 'deporting of Jews and other minorities' and 'cleansing Russian intellectual life of Marxist and liberal influences'. While many of Pamyat supporters came from the backward elements of society unhappy at change and modernism, it also enjoyed the patronage of Ilya Glazunov, a leading artist, and Valentin Rasputin, a popular writer about Siberian village life and sections of the bureaucracy. Hence although incitement to racial hatred was a crime under Russian law, there was a reluctance on the part of officials to prosecute members of Pamyat; rather they were treated as misguided patriots.[925] There was also the publication of a vicious tract, Rusofobiya (1989), by Igor Shafarevich, a distinguished mathematician, who blamed Jews for the violence perpetrated under Lenin and Stalin and for their supposed degradation of Russian culture and history. He became co-chairman of the National Salvation Front, the main anti-Yeltsin faction.[926]

During the course of her visit to the Soviet Union, Mrs Eker was handed a letter from the Prager family, who felt trapped in the USSR, which she forwarded to the Prime Minister. Charles Powell on Margaret Thatcher's behalf agreed that cases such as that of the Pragers were unsatisfactory. But nevertheless reiterated that the government utilised 'every suitable opportunity to raise

---

[925] Walter Laqueur, The Long Road to Freedom. Russia and Glasnost (London,1989), pp.135-45.
[926] Robert Horvath, The Legacy of Soviet Dissent: Dissidents, Democratisation and Radical Nationalism in Russia (London, 2005), pp.150-1,237.

individual cases with the Soviet Government (most recently the Foreign Secretary met Mr. Shevardnadze on 19 December [1989] and during UK/USSR bilateral talks on human rights in Moscow on 9 January). We shall now include the Prager family among these cases'.[927] On the other hand, other refuseniks of long standing were being allowed to emigrate because of the representations being made by the British government and their transatlantic allies. On 17 April 1990, the Prime Minister was happy to inform Leslie Donn that 'Olga and Ephraim Dinkin, whose cases we have raised with the Soviet authorities on numerous occasions, have now been given permission to emigrate'. On 11 May, Rita Eker wrote to the Prime Minister enclosing a letter from the Moscow refusenik leader Leslie Stonov in which he related the news that 'the other day ... our family was granted a permission to leave the country. He expressed to her, 'to Mr. Douglas Hurd, Secretary of State for Foreign Affairs, to the other members of the government, to the Parliament and to all the British people my profound gratitude for your steadfast efforts to release Soviet refuseniks and political prisoners. I know you have made a great contribution to our release. After the long 11 years of waiting, I cannot find the words to express my feelings of obligation and gratitude'.[928]

At the same time, despite some improvements in the situation in the Soviet Union, many of the old problems remained, or were exacerbated by the new freedoms introduced by the Gorbachev reforms. 'We welcome the increased freedom of expression and association in the USSR, but this does have a darker side', the Prime Minister acknowledged. 'Groups such as Pamyat have been free to express their inflammatory and racist views. The recent

---

[927] Southampton, MS254/A980/1/1/29 Rita Eker to Thatcher 19 January 1990; and Charles Powell to Rita Eker 31 January 1990.
[928] Southampton, MS254/A980/1/1/29 Margaret Thatcher to Leslie Donn 17 April 1900; and Rita Eker to Margaret Thatcher 11 May 1990 enclosing Leonid Stonov to Thatcher 6 May 1990. Charles Powell to Rita Eker 25 May 1990.

calls for pogroms are particularly abhorrent. We have made clear our concerns about these developments'. Further, the Ministry of the Interior has 'announced that it was investigating an incident at the Central House of Writers at which Pamyat allegedly broke up a meeting of reformists'.[929] In a follow-up letter to Sylvia Sheff, a leader of the Women's Campaign in Manchester, Charles Powell, asserted that 'More widely, we shall continue to bring home to the Soviet authorities that, as part of their efforts to create a law-based state, they should ensure that all are free to enjoy their religious and cultural freedoms without fear of persecution or harassment. Most recently, our concerns were underlined by the Foreign Secretary to Mr. Shevardnadze during his visit to the USSR, 9-12 April'.[930]

At the end of May, Mrs Eker and her colleague reflecting on her experience during a recent visit sent the Prime Minister 'several items on recent anti-Semitic outrages, but these can only give a very slight idea of the atmosphere of terror spreading throughout the whole of the USSR'. What the leaders of the 35's were most concerned about was their recent 'list of Soviet Jewish Refuseniks, Waitniks and Activists, totalling 2,200 families. As this shows, there are still many refuseniks who have already waited for more than 10 years, and others being refused for the first time on the same absurd pretexts. Too many others, the `Poor Relatives' are still unable to register their applications to leave as their former spouses or elderly parents will not sign the Notarised Financial Waivers that may be dangerous for themselves in the future'.[931]

Margaret Thatcher in her reply admitted that 'the human rights performance' of Gorbachev had 'some way to go before the problems facing Soviet Jewry are resolved once

---

[929] Southampton, MS254/A980/1/1/29 Margaret Thatcher to Leslie Donn 17 April 1990.
[930] Southampton, MS254/A980/1/1/29 Charles Powell to Sylvia Sheff 30 April 1990.
[931] Southampton, MS254/A980/1/1/29 Margaret Rigal and Rita Eker to Margaret Thatcher 29 May 1990.

and for all... there are now unprecedented numbers of Soviet Jews leaving the Soviet Union, but as you point out there remain a minority of refuseniks who, for inexplicable reasons, continue to be denied permission to leave. We shall continue to raise individual cases with the Soviet authorities, and to underline to them the need to ensure that the new Soviet law governing emigration provides a permanent solution to this outstanding problem'. She was also hoping to meet some activists to hear about their various concerns during her visit to the Soviet Union in the second week of June 1990.[932]

Meanwhile, with a limited income and staff, the National Council for Soviet Jewry started to run down its activities doing less in the area of monitoring and more in encouraging cultural activities in the Soviet Union. In February 1990, its chairman, John Fenner, was happy to announce that he had secured a commitment from the JIA (Joint Israel Appeal) for a grant of £25,000 per annum for a period of two years. The Board of Deputies agreed to house the Council's truncated office staff consisting of its executive director and find accommodation for its Contemporary Jewish Library.[933] Dr Gur's office at the Israeli embassy, where he was acting as Nativ's liaison officer with the British campaign, was closed shortly afterwards and it was announced that he would not be replaced.[934] Despite these setbacks, the executive of the Council continued to believe that the political campaigning should go on for at least another eighteen months.[935] Because of the fast-changing situation in the Soviet Union, the National Council continued to shift its focus to the

---

[932] Southampton, MS254/A980/1/1/29 Margaret Thatcher to Margaret Rigal 7 June 1990.
[933] LMA, ACC 3087/010 minutes of the executive of the National Council 22 February 1990.
[934] LMA, ACC 3087/010 minutes of the executive of the National Council 23 April 1990.
[935] LMA, ACC 3087/010 minutes of the executive of the National Council 5 February 1990.

promotion of cultural awareness among Jews in the Soviet Union in line with the new policy adopted by the National Conference for Soviet Jewry in the United States.[936] Its chairman had a meeting with the Chief Rabbi, who wanted the Council to establish a supervisory arm to promote the twinning of communities, both religious and secular, in the United Kingdom with those in the Soviet Union. A prime concern was the training of teachers, who were to be sent there.[937] Cynthia Jacobs 'noted that congregations within the United Synagogue were twinning their members and the Synagogue directly with towns around the Soviet Union and suggested that this activity be taken up on a larger scale'.[938] Mrs Rigal mentioned that she and her husband and the 35's were despatching Jewish literature to people all over Russia and continued to receive requests for children's books and Hebrew material.[939] The National Council sponsored three Soviet Jewish historians for the Spiro Institute training course in Jewish history, while the Institute of Jewish Education invited 15 teachers from a Riga school to tour Jewish schools and sample training courses in London.[940] A coalition of religious bodies and individuals in Israel were 'concerned with the `spiritual absorption' of Soviet Olim [immigrants] and with [religious] activities in the Soviet Union'. An organization called Keter was training emissaries to go to the Soviet Union, unfortunately without any liaison with the Conference of European rabbis or Anglo-Jewry. By September 1990 John Fenner, the chairman of the National Council, reluctantly concluded that the Council could not

---

[936] LMA, ACC 3087/010 minutes of the executive of the National Council 13 November 1989.
[937] LMA, ACC 3087/010 minutes of the executive of the National Council 8 January 1990.
[938] LMA, ACC 3087/010 minutes of the executive of the National Council 23 April 1990.
[939] LMA, ACC 3087/010 minutes of the executive of the National Council 23 April 1990.
[940] LMA, ACC 3087/010 minutes of the executive of the National Council 23 July 1990.

raise sufficient funds to sponsor the Chief Rabbi's ambitious twinning programme.[941]

Although Soviet Jews were now free to some extent to travel to Israel and elsewhere, the Soviet Union played on the fears of the Arab states, with whom they were friendly, and incited them to raise objections to the emigration of Soviet Jews to Israel. An Egyptian diplomat 'expressed disgust with Soviet tactics which were trying to place all the blame on the United States, accusing the latter of conniving in Israeli attempts to send the immigrants to the occupied territories and of closing the gates to emigration to America. They were also accusing the Americans of financing the operation. The Soviets had even told the Arabs that they were prepared to go to the Security Council to protest against the American behaviour'.[942] At the same time, the Prime Minister was sharply critical of the Israeli government, objecting to the fact that too many of the immigrants were being settled in the West Bank, the Golan heights and the suburbs of East Jerusalem, though their status in international law was unsettled.[943]

The Prime Minister visited Russia, the Ukraine and Armenia between 8 and 10 June 1990 at the invitation of Mr Gorbachev. Jonathan Arkush of the National Council spoke 'to the Foreign Office to express concern over the draft law on emigration... [as] it appeared that the Prime Minister will not be dealing with the substance of the law, though it will surface in discussions among officials'.[944] Rita Eker in a more tactful note told Margaret Thatcher that 'We were thrilled to hear that you laid a wreath at Babi Yar on behalf

---

[941] LMA, ACC 3087/010 minutes of the executive of the National Council 10 September 1990.

[942] National Archives, PREM 19/3186 Ambassador in Cairo to FCO February 1990.

[943] National Archives, PREM 19/3186 Geoffrey Howe to ambassador in Tel Aviv April 1990.

[944] LMA, ACC 3087/010 minutes of the executive of the National Council 5 June 1990.

of the [30,000] Jewish women and children murdered and buried there. It was an imaginative and much-appreciated gesture and we are all most grateful. Thank you for receiving the Soviet Jewish Refuseniks and for bringing up their cases with the Soviet Authorities. No doubt you have heard at first hand the fears felt by many Soviet Jews over the increasing anti-Semitic violence within the USSR and you will understand how anxious we are that those who wish to leave should be allowed to emigrate while they are still unharmed'.[945] Two days later, the ladies sent another letter asking if Dr Leonid Stonov could have a brief meeting with the Prime Minister to personally thank her for the help without which he would have been unable to leave the Soviet Union. Replying on her behalf, Charles Powell sent the usual letter claiming that her schedule was too full to find a space to see him.[946]

On the occasion of the Jewish New Year on 19 September 1990, the leaders of the Women's Campaign applauded the Prime Minister 'for the stand you have taken over the Gulf crisis. We are grateful to you for the leadership you have given in the field of human rights and we applaud your refusal to allow the violation of a country's peace and security'.[947] This was followed up a month later by a request for the Prime Minister to receive a delegation of members of both Houses of Parliament together with the leaders of the Women's Campaign from London and the provinces on 10 December 1990 – Human Rights Day. 'As you know', they continued, 'despite the enormous improvement in the USSR in the field of Human Rights, there are hundreds of long-term refuseniks still being given fresh refusals and a growing number of new

---

[945] Southampton, MS254/A980/1/1/29 Rita Eker and Margaret Rigal to Thatcher 12 June 1990.
[946] Southampton, MS254/A980/1/1/29 Rita Eker to Charles Powell 14 June 1990; and Charles Powell to the same 14 June 1990.
[947] Southampton, MS254/A980/1/1/29 Rita Eker and Margaret Rigal to Thatcher 19 September 1990; correspondence secretary to the same 20 September 1990.

applicants who are also being refused on the same old pretexts. With the worldwide welcome of ...Gorbachev's new measures, these refuseniks are terrified that they will be forgotten and their hope and trust is entirely dependent on your continuing championship of their cause. They rely on you completely'.[948] The request was accompanied by a bouquet of flowers after what had turned out to be a difficult and contentious Conservative party conference for Margaret Thatcher and no doubt was meant to show unflagging support from the Women's Campaign and to boost the Prime Minister's resolve.

On behalf of the Prime Minister, Charles Powell reiterated that 'despite the heartening trend under Mr Gorbachev's leadership towards a greater respect for human rights, there is still a long way to go. We shall not forget the remaining refuseniks and shall continue to press the Soviet authorities on both long-term and new cases until there is a satisfactory outcome to all. Our concerns were made clear during the Prime Minister's visit to the Soviet Union in June and by the Foreign Secretary in Moscow in September, when he met Jewish leaders'. They had also discussed the new emigration law with the Soviet authorities. Unfortunately, the Prime Minister had too crowded a schedule to receive a deputation from the Women's Campaign, as usual distancing herself from the campaign so as not to upset Gorbachev, but offered her Minister of State, William Waldegrave, who would be available to meet the delegation.[949]

On 22 November 1990, Margaret Thatcher announced that she would not contest the second ballot for the leadership of the Conservative party, after inadequate support in the first ballot, and made her final speech as Prime Minister. On the same day the leaders of the

[948] Southampton, MS254/A980/1/1/29 Rita Eker and Margaret Rigal to Thatcher 15 October 1990; and Amanda Ponsonby to Rita Eker 15 October 1990.
[949] Southampton, MS254/A980/1/1/29 Charles Powell to Rita Eker and Margaret Rigal.

Women's Campaign wrote to her, saying that they could not 'describe our sense of loss and dismay at the news of your resignation. We have tried over the years to express our gratitude to you for the help you have given us in our campaign, but we know that we have failed to convey the depth of our feelings. We can only say now that the numbers arriving in Israel are a tribute to you. Without your support they would still be in the Soviet Union. Thank you for all you have done and please be sure that we shall be, as always, asking for more assistance in the future'. Six days after the letter, Margaret Thatcher formally resigned as Prime Minister and in that sense it was slightly premature.[950] In response to some fact-finding sheets sent by the 35's, Charles Powell asserted that the majority of cases mentioned by them were already on the Foreign Office list of refuseniks and prisoner cases which were raised regularly with the Soviet authorities but thanked them for their assistance which enabled the government to keep their lists up-to-date. The passing of a new law of freedom of conscience and religion was an encouraging sign. Rita Eker and Margaret Rigal ended the year by sending Margaret Thatcher one of their special calendars highlighting a number of refuseniks, and wishing her 'a happy, prosperous and peaceful 1991'.[951]

On 29 November 1990, the leaders of the Women's Campaign despatched a warm letter of congratulation to John Major on his succeeding Margaret Thatcher as Prime Minister. Charles Powell conceded that 'Although unprecedented numbers of Soviet Jews are now being allowed to leave the USSR, there are still both long-term and more recent cases where exit visas have been denied'. The government promised to press Soviet authorities about these cases, while at the same time urging them to adopt

[950] Southampton, MS254/A980/1/1/29 Rita Eker and Margaret Rigal to Thatcher 22 November 1990.
[951] Southampton, MS254/A980/1/1/29 Charles Powell to Rita Eker and Margaret Rigal 24 November 1990; and Rita Eker and Margaret Rigal to Margaret Thatcher 20 December 1990.

the new emigration law to end 'the refusenik problem. Once and for all' – a continuation of Margaret Thatcher's policy.[952]

Nevertheless, during the spring and summer of 1991, the leaders of the Women's Campaign made one last attempt to rekindle Margaret Thatcher's enthusiasm for the cause. Before a trip she was making to Moscow in May 1991, they wrote to her reminding her that 'there are still thousands of Soviet Jewish families unable to leave and each week brings more refusals. We are sending you one typical case -- the Molodchikovs of Kiev, chosen because [t]his refusal extends to 1998. We are also enclosing biographies of Solomon Smolyar, whose dying wish is to reunite with his sons in Haifa; the tragic Sorkin family of Penza and the Bodner brothers of Tashkent facing a prolonged and totally unjustified `Trial' in Alma Ata'. They also approached her requesting a meeting to seek her advice about a new scheme they were contemplating to aid Soviet Jews.[953]

Margaret Thatcher sent the leaders of the Women's Campaign a letter from Douglas Hogg, the new Minister of State, who in the absence of the Foreign Secretary overseas, summarised the current human rights situation in the Soviet Union. 'The specific human rights cases mentioned by' them 'are all ones we have raised regularly with the Soviet authorities, including the run-up to the Prime Minister's visit to the Soviet Union in March. Douglas Hurd discussed the emigration problem with the Soviet Foreign Minister Bessmertnykh during his subsequent visit, and the current position was looked at in detail during a recent round of official talks on human rights issues. The cases of refusenik Solomon Smolyar and prisoners Felix and Roman Bodner were specifically highlighted by FCO officials'. The government was also 'encouraged by the fact that the

---

[952] Southampton, MS254/A980/1/1/29 Charles Powell to Rita Eker 17 December 1990.
[953] Southampton, MS254/A980/1/1/29 Rita Eker and Margaret Rigal to Margaret Thatcher 2 and 9 May 1991.

Supreme Soviet have now adopted a new law on emigration, which will allow Soviet citizens to receive on request passports for foreign travel except in certain specific cases. We still have some worries over the provisions for denial of permission to travel, on grounds of "state secrets": these provisions are wide-ranging and might be open to abuse. It is also unfortunate that the law will not come into effect until 1 January 1993... We shall continue to encourage the Soviet authorities... to re-double their efforts to create a law-based society in which all are able to enjoy fundamental freedoms without fear of harassment or persecution'.[954]

On 12 July 1991, the leaders of the Women's Campaign renewed their appeals for help to Margaret Thatcher, telling her that 'in the last eighteen months two hundred thousand Soviet Jews have reached Israel, indeed a modern miracle, but even now new applicants are being refused and long term refuseniks are having their refusals confirmed yet again'. As she was regarded as the prime mover of this twentieth-century exodus, they appealed to her to persuade President Gorbachev to release the remaining refuseniks from 'the quicksands of Soviet bureaucracy'. Caught as they were in civil disorder and rising Russian nationalism, the refuseniks were trapped in a difficult situation. Nor did a further appeal in November to the former Prime Minister to grant them an interview to discuss their plan to help the newly arrived immigrants in Israel elicit a more positive response.[955] In March 1992, Mrs Eker and Mrs Rigal on some happy family occasion for the Thatchers, sent the former Prime Minister their best wishes.[956] This was to be their last contact.

---

[954] Southampton, MS254/A980/1/1/1/29 Douglas Hogg to Margaret Thatcher 5 June 1991; and Margaret Thatcher to Rita Eker 12 June 1991.
[955] Southampton, MS254/A980/1/1/29 Rita Eker and Margaret Rigal to Thatcher 12 July 1991; and the same to the same 1 November 1991; and Lois Stuart-Black to Rita Eker 4 November 1991.

Summing up the results of a CSCE human rights meeting held in Copenhagen in June 1990, Lawrence Littlestone informed the executive of the National Council of the advances that had been made with 'regard to the condemnation of antisemitism and guarantees of religious and cultural freedoms'.[957] Among the Foreign Office delegation were Neil Bradman, a vice-president of the National Council, Jonathan Arkush, a member of its executive, and Mrs Sylvia Sheff of the 35's. 'A proposal to outlaw hate propaganda on grounds of race or religion is being co-sponsored by the Soviet Union and Canada... Jewish organisations present at Copenhagen are pressing for antisemitism to be explicitly mentioned in the final wording'.[958] In previous legal agreements 'antisemitism had always been covered by such general terms as "racism", "racial and ethnic hatred", or "persecution on religious grounds"'. In the Copenhagen agreement, the participants committed themselves to 'take effective measures, against incitement to violence...based on national, racial, ethnic or religious discrimination, hostility or hatred...', and to "protect persons and groups", as well as their property, "who may be subject to threats or acts of discrimination, hostility or violence" on these grounds'. They undertook to pay special attention to problems of racial prejudice or hatred in education.[959] Littlestone 'reported on the changed atmosphere between this and previous meetings and pointed in particular to the ease of access to members of the Soviet delegation'. There was a 'high degree of cooperation among Soviet Jewry lobby groups in presenting the case in a coherent fashion. He believed that this method was not only effective, but also appreciated by delegations... the Council's expertise was

---

[956] Southampton, MS254/A980/1/1/29 Rita Eker and Margaret Rigal to Margaret Thatcher 18 March 1992; and Lois Stuart-Black to Rita Eker and Margaret Rigal 24 March 1992 and 15 June 1992.
[957] LMA, ACC 3087/010 minutes of the executive of the National Council 23 July 1990.
[958] Jewish Chronicle 15 June 1990, p.2.
[959] Jewish Chronicle 6 July 1990, p.44.

called upon... by the British delegation not only to offer advice but also to clarify information received from other sources and Soviet responses to their own enquiries'.[960]

At a CSCE meeting held in Paris later in the year, 34 nations represented in the organisation adopted a resolution, stating that 'the religious identity of national minorities will be protected'. These 'minorities had "the right to express, preserve and develop" their religious identity "without any discrimination". The resolution also expressed the determination of the signatories "to struggle against all forms of racial or ethnic hatred, antisemitism, xenophobia or bias"'. While it was regarded as a great step forward that the Soviets signed a document condemning antisemitism, refuseniks remained sceptical until they saw how this approach was applied in specific circumstances. At the conference, Vadim Zagladin, a close aide of Gorbachev, announced that representatives of the World Jewish Congress would participate in the planning for the next human rights conference in Moscow.[961] With hindsight, it appears that the Soviets were carefully choreographing the requisite moves to court Western public opinion, so that there would be no snags in the staging of the next human rights conference in Moscow. It was also noteworthy that Gorbachev refrained from making a speech for internal consumption condemning antisemitism.[962]

In September 1991, Moscow hosted a meeting of the CSCE for the first time. John Fenner, chairman of the National Council, attended as a non-governmental officer of the British delegation. Sir John Robson, leader of the British delegation, claimed that advances had been made by the Soviet authorities in the commitment to the independence of the judiciary, the press and media. The

---

[960] LMA, ACC 3087/010 minutes of the executive of the National Council 23 July 1990.
[961] Jewish Chronicle 23 November 1990, p.33
[962] LMA, ACC 3087/010 minutes of the executive of the National Council 25 October 1990. Jewish Chronicle 23 November 1990, p.33.

British statement demanded changes in their emigration law, the clear demarcation of a distinction between 'state secrets' and real national security. 'It also called for an appeals procedure, cheaper passports, and a reversion of the rule by which would-be emigrants have to prove that there are no outstanding claims from dependant relatives'.[963] Privately Fenner admitted that 'The Moscow conference did not succeed in the area of national minority rights, the final document displayed "very weasely language". However, it did reflect the decay of central and Eastern Europe which had yet to establish a new structure'. Fenner felt that Teimouraz Ramishvili, the head of the Human Rights division of the USSR Foreign Ministry, was sympathetic, but there was a power struggle going on between the centre and the republics.[964] When the Ukraine voted on 1 December 1991 to become independent, the old USSR was at an end. A new union known as the Commonwealth of Independent States was created, of which the Russian Federation, the Ukraine and Belorussia were members.

When a briefing session was held at the Foreign Office on 6 March 1992 prior to the preparatory meeting for Helsinki, Lawrence Littlestone was invited on behalf of the National Council. A summary of the conclusions reached at the Prague meeting of the CSCE council was circulated, from which it was clear that following the complete turnover of staff within the CSCE unit at the FCO the question of human rights had been downgraded from a Foreign Office perspective. 'Joyce Simson, of the 35's Women's Campaign, broached a[n enquiry about the] problem of pan-European antisemitism and asked how the CSCE proposed to deal with it. The response from Mr Tate was that racism and xenophobia is a matter of grave concern in Europe, however, to specify one form, and perhaps not necessarily the most important form, could be

---

[963] Jewish Chronicle 27 September 1991, p.5.
[964] LMA, ACC 3087/010 minutes of the executive of the National Council 4 December 1991.

invidious and would not necessarily benefit Jews' – an unsatisfactory response which appears even worse with hindsight. While the Moscow meeting and the Paris charter contained 'clear references to antisemitism as a form of racism, and as an area of educational concern, the Prague summary quite deliberately ignores it'.[965]

The dissolution of the Soviet Union and the large-scale exodus of Jews from it created a whole new series of problems. When Mrs Eker visited Russia early in 1992 she was struck by 'the absolutely dire circumstances now pertaining in Moscow. The need for additional food supplies cannot be overestimated and medicines are in short supply and in many areas are non-existent. She noticed many people begging in the streets and is fearful of the rise in anti-Semitism'.[966] This shortage of food was not limited to one region, as the National Council was already supporting the work of the Central British Fund which was despatching food parcels to Moscow, Lvov and other centres.[967] During the mass exodus of Jews from the former Soviet Union to Israel, Christian missionaries were active. There were problems on board the ships operating from Odessa to Haifa which had partially been organized by the Ebenezer Trust, a missionary body, and the Jewish representatives on the ships. 'Mr Littlestone noted that the buses from the Ukraine are still travelling, that missionaries are still increasing their activities inside the former Soviet Union and in Israel itself where Hebrew-Christian congregations are already established'.[968]

Jonathan Arkush declared in October 1991 that according to the best estimates 'at least 3,000-5,000 families

[965] LMA, ACC 3087/010 memorandum of Lawrence Littlestone on Foreign Office briefing session 6 March 1992 in minutes of the executive of the National Council.
[966] LMA, ACC 3087/010 17 February 1992.
[967] LMA, ACC 3087/010 minutes of the executive of the National Council 4 June 1991.
[968] LMA, ACC 3087/010 minutes of the executive of the National Council 21 January 1992 and 17 February 1992.

throughout the Soviet Union were being denied exit'. The Vaad, the umbrella organisation of Soviet-Jewish cultural associations, he believed, took an ambivalent attitude towards them, holding the view that they should no longer be given political priority when their destination was uncertain. Margaret Rigal responded that the majority of the long-term refuseniks still saw Israel as their ultimate destination.[969]

She well summed up the exit visa restrictions which still persisted at the end of 1992. In January 1992, President Yeltsin of the Russian Federation issued a decree that 'the laws concerning secrecy and security should be those of the former USSR. Russian emigration authorities are therefore refusing exit-visas to anyone who had secrecy rating unless and until that particular secret has been declassified... The absurdity of the refusals is well-known... Some of those refused hold an international passport and have in the past been given a passport for international travel. Nevertheless, they are refused permission to emigrate. Others have been refused because they work on aeroplanes which have since been sold to America. Some worked on research projects on satellites which are now being used worldwide. When they appeal to their various past employers they are merely informed that the secrecy rating has not been changed'.[970]

Reflecting on their past work together, Rita Eker told Greville Janner that they had been 'very privileged to have witnessed a modern miracle and we are sure that you share our delight that so many Jews from the former Soviet Union are now safely in Israel...We look back on our cooperation with you and your [All-Party Parliamentary] Committee over the years with enormous pride'.[971] As she explained some years earlier, the refuseniks 'will be greatly heartened to know that our Parliamentarians are concerned over their

---

[969] LMA, ACC 3087/OIO minutes of the executive of the National Council 29 October 1991.
[970] Southampton, MS254/A980/1/1/38 Margaret Rigal to Lady Cocks 24 November 1992.
[971] Southampton, MS254/A980/1/1/45 Rita Eker to Greville Janner 8 May 1997.

fate and that they will continue to ensure the question of human rights will always feature uppermost in any negotiation with the Soviet Union'.[972] Members of the All-Parliamentary Committee raised questions about individual refuseniks in the House after prompting from the National Council or the 35's and in the 1990s these were automatically referred to the Foreign Office for action.[973] Greville and his wife with Dame Peggy Fenner MP visited the Soviet Union in 1989, for which he thanked Rita for her 'immaculate and invaluable' briefing and again in 1991, with a larger group of five 'continually active and devoted' MPs.[974] Occasionally, there were momentary hiccups between the two organizations as an occasion when Greville rebuked Rita Eker for sending out Nicholas Bethell's Conservative party pamphlet under the auspices of the 35's, for which she apologized profusely.[975] Relations were sometimes more fraught between Greville and other sections of the Soviet Jewry campaign and sometimes with the representatives from the Lishka at the Israeli embassy; yet to his credit Greville recognized that it was better from a public relations viewpoint, if his non-Jewish colleagues in the Parliamentary Committee took the lead.

However close was the relationship between the Women's Campaign and the MPs on the All-Parliamentary Committee, it is probable that the ties of the National Council with the Parliamentary Committee were even closer and its input more considerable. When June Jacobs was chairman of the National Council, she implemented a scheme with Tim Sainsbury MP in the late 1970s , whereby

[972] Southampton, MS254 A980 1/1/45 Rita Eker to Greville Janner 8 August 1988.

[973] Southampton, MS254 A980 1/1/45 Rita Eker to Bryony Rudkin Greville's assistant 23 July 1991.

[974] Southampton, MS254 A980 1/1/45 Emma Grossman to Margaret Rigal 16 October 1989; and Greville Janner to Rita Eker 18 October 1991.

[975] Southampton, MS254 A980 1/1/45 Greville Janner to Rita Eker 16 June 1989; Rita Eker to Greville Janner 21 June 1989; and Greville to Rita Eker 20 July 1989.

those MPs willing to adopt a refusenik would be offered names and briefing material and would be asked to liaise with their organization on news and so on. A quarterly meeting would be arranged with MPs on the All-Parliamentary Committee to review progress.[976] Because of the duplication of work between the 35's and the National Council, there were sometimes slip-ups, as MPs were not always informed when refuseniks for whom they were campaigning had been permitted to emigrate. June Jacobs also rebuked Greville Janner for announcing to the Jewish press that he had invited the Levichs to Britain. 'Not only is it a rather meaningless announcement but it makes a bit of mockery of all talk about working together and consulting etc'.[977]

After Andrew Balcombe succeeded June Jacobs as chairman of the National Council, he received a warm letter of congratulation from Peter Archer QC, MP, who headed the All-Parliamentary Committee: 'As you will know, we have enjoyed a close working relationship with the National Council in past years and we shall look forward to continuing our valuable contacts'. He invited Balcombe to attend the next meeting of the Parliamentary group to meet his colleagues, an invitation taken up by the new chairman.[978] Together with Ivan Lawrence MP, Archer sent a letter on behalf of the Parliamentary Committee to Brezhnev in 1981 drawing attention to the plight of eight Jewish activists who had been refused exit visas, the restrictions placed on scientific seminars and Jewish cultural events taking place in Moscow and Leningrad, and the reduction in the number of Jews allowed to emigrate. All of this was in breach of the Soviet Union's compliance

---

[976] LMA, ACC.3087/249 June Jacobs to Tim Sainsbury 29 December 1977; notes of a meeting between the two of them 15 February 1978; and Sainsbury to Jacobs 24 February 1978.

[977] LMA, ACC.3087/249 June Jacobs to Tim Sainsbury 28 February 1978; Jean Karsberg to Tim Sainsbury 8 March and 7 June 1978. June Jacobs to Greville Janner 8 January 1979.

[978] LMA, ACC.3087/249 Peter Archer to Andrew Balcombe 4 March 1980; and same to the same 4 March 1980.

with the Helsinki Agreement on Human Rights and the United Nations Charter.[979] Paul Secher was employed as the full-time clerk to the Parliamentary Committee assisting MPs with the help of Jerry Lewis, a parliamentary agent, in drafting questions for Foreign Office Question Time in the Commons and alerting them to the ongoing situation of Shcharansky and Iosif Begun.[980]

In turn, Andrew Balcombe was succeeded as chairman of the National Council by Arieh Handler, Neil Bradman and John Fenner during which time the relationship with the All-Parliamentary Committee strengthened. Joy Paul, executive secretary of the National Council wrote to Secher, telling him that six refuseniks in Moscow had received final refusals of their applications for exit visas and so had individuals in Leningrad; and that Rita Eker of the 35's 'asked that these cases be brought up in the House', indicating the degree of cooperation between the two Soviet Jewry groups and the fact that sometimes the Women's campaign was beholden to the greater resources of the National Council.[981]

Handler wrote to Peter Archer in 1986, stating that he had arranged for him to 'receive minutes of our Council and Executive Meetings. If you would care to do the same, we might in this way keep each other up to date'. To which Archer replied, 'it was unanimously agreed [by my Committee] that more extensive contacts be made with other groups working on behalf of Soviet Jewry'.[982] Peter Archer wrote to Lawrence O'Keeffe, leader of the UK delegation to the CSCE Review Meeting in Vienna at the behest of Handler, 'to urge you to ensure that the subject of Human Rights and Soviet Jewry be kept at the forefront of

---

[979] LMA, ACC.3087/249 Peter Archer and Ivan Lawrence to President Brezhnev 13 July 1981.

[980] LMA, ACC.3087/249 memorandum of Jerry Lewis 17 January 1983; and Joy Paul to Paul Secher 21 January 1983.

[981] LMA, ACC.3087/249 Joy Paul note to Arieh Handler 20 December 1982.

[982] LMA, ACC.3087/249 Arieh Handler to Peter Archer 8 July 1986; and same to the same 17 November 1986.

the discussions in the coming months'; and that in a number of instances the names of specific individuals should be raised with the Soviet delegation.[983]

At this critical juncture in 1991, however, the Anglo-Jewish campaign for Soviet Jewry was being run down even further and disbanded. Not only had the Jewish Agency and the JIA stopped their financial support of the National Council, but Nan Griefer, who was also subsidised, was dismissed from her post and 'Jews in the USSR' which she edited ceased publication and the Contemporary Jewish Library was closed.[984] The National Council had a budget in excess of £40,000 per annum which it was finding increasingly difficult to raise because of the changed situation in the former Soviet Union with mass emigration and the lifting of the restrictions on Jewish communal life; and in March 1992 its executive director, Lawrence Littlestone, stepped down, despite protests from officials in Exodus and the Lishka.[985] In July, it decided to change its name to the National Council for Jews in the Former Soviet Lands; it was now less a communal body than a corpse lingering on in a drastically shrunken form.

So too, the Women's Campaign gradually phased out its activities after 1992 and transformed itself into the Jewish Aid Committee, whose main aim was to attend to the needs of the Soviet Jews who had settled in Israel. 'The old, the sick (particularly from the Chernobyl area) and the single parent families take longer to settle successfully into their new homes and need extra help while they do so'.[986] Jews from the Former Soviet Union were still arriving in

---

[983] LMA, ACC.3087/249 Arieh Hander to Paul Secher 27 October 1986; meeting of All-Parliamentary Committee with Scientists' Committee 4 November 1986; and Peter Archer to Laurence O'Keeffe 17 November 1986.
[984] LMA, ACC.3087/010 minutes of the executive of the National Council 18 February 1991.
[985] Jewish Chronicle 20 March 1992. LMA, ACC Sara Frankel of the Liaison Bureau to John Fenner 25 March 1992 and Exodus representative to the National Council 6 April 1992.
[986] Southampton, MS254 A980 1/1/29 Rita Eker to Thatcher 1 November 1991 and 18 March 1992.

Israel at the rate of a thousand a month in the summer of 1994. The Jewish Aid Committee, with an office run by the indefatigable Rita Eker, sponsored the One-to-One organization which raised funds through an annual trek in Israel. 'The Mount Sinai to the Promised Land' trek in 1994 netted £250,000; and additional funds were collected through a charity shop which opened in London in 1992. With many reliable contacts in the towns of the Former Soviet Union, the One-to-One organization distributed medicine, clothes, kosher food and money to needy recipients. The requests of the new immigrants in Israel were handled by Keren Klita, a Jerusalem-based charity run by Delysia Jason, a former prominent member of the 35's, and members of ESRA (English Speaking Residents Association).[987] According to Alice Jonah, a former colleague, Delysia was a superb fundraiser, who assisted with the problems of the new olim, many of whom were elderly and housed in the Diplomat Hotel in Jerusalem.[988] Delysia had such a phenomenal memory that it seemed incredible that she could store in it 'all the details concerning personal and family problems of so many people whom she often didn't even know'. Another volunteer for Keren Klita remembered meeting Delysia at a clothing and furniture warehouse run by the Jerusalem municipality. Each new immigrant was welcomed in their home by a smiling volunteer, who greeted them with a laden basket and who tried to befriend them and sort out their problems; and they were also assisted in furnishing their new home. Feeling somewhat overworked as a volunteer, Eleonora Shifrin tried to quit and approached Delysia to inform her of her decision. She replied, 'Do you know what the KGB is? So, she continued innocently, "Keren Klita is like the KGB – you can get in but you cannot quit. As long as you live"'.[989]

---

987 Daphne Gerlis, pp.189-93.
988 Interview with Alice Jonah 7 June 2018.
989 In Tribute to Delysia Jason. A Celebration of her Life (Jerusalem,2010).

Conclusion

When the Bolsheviks seized power in 1917, they nationalised the property of the Russian Orthodox Church by a decree in 1918 and closed many places of worship. Lenin denounced antisemitism without banning it in law and as the revolutionary regime consolidated its power, antisemitism flourished at the local level in the Soviet Union and because of this synagogues were closed in even greater numbers than churches in Belarus and the Ukraine, where the bulk of the Jewish population of the USSR lived. In the inter-war years, Jewish schools and youth clubs were shut down and the teaching of Hebrew and Yiddish virtually ceased, while there were no other communal venues or cafes or hotels for young Jews to meet. As city dwellers, Jews benefited greatly from new educational opportunities thrown open to them after the Bolshevik revolution and were swiftly absorbed into the elite strata of the regime. By 1918 only civil marriages were recognized as valid, but there could also be additional religious ceremonies, though these were frowned upon by the authorities. Jews mixed freely with other nationalities while studying at college and in the workplace, thus becoming more closely integrated with other sections of the population. Before the advent of the Nazis, 44 per cent of the German Jewish population intermarried, in Leningrad by 1936 42.3 of the men and 36.8 per cent of the women married non-Jewish spouses and soon the rates of intermarriage in the Soviet Union surpassed the German-Jewish level and the Jewish community appeared to be on the way to almost total assimilation.[990]

Stalin set off a series of purges of first, second and third-generation Communists in the second half of the 1930s, culminating in great show trials which were based on falsified evidence. Among the many Jews who were tried and perished, were a number of important Old Bolsheviks, including Grigori Zinoviev, Lev Kamenev and

---

[990] Sarah Wobeck-Segev, Homes Away from Home. Jewish Belonging in Twentieth Century Paris, Berlin and St. Petersburg pp.69-71.

Karl Radek; and millions of ordinary Soviet citizens, including Jews, died in the Gulag and prisons as well. Once he was allied with Hitler between 1939 and 1941, Stalin saw that Jews were expendable. During the War years, he was allied with the West and encouraged the formation of the Jewish Anti-Fascist Committee in 1942 in the Soviet Union for fundraising and propaganda purposes overseas, though Stalin did nothing to warn the Jewish population under his control that they were a special target of German atrocities. There was much continuity between the policies followed by Stalin and his post-War successors, but also significant differences in emphasis in their attitude towards the Jews and other faith groups. Having reached a concordat with the Russian Orthodox Church in 1943, Stalin showed little interest after the Second World War in reviving an anti-religious campaign.[991] In the 1920s, convicted Zionists were offered a choice of prison or signing a statement admitting that their activities were counter-revolutionary, for which they were allowed to leave for Palestine. So too, under Brezhnev and Andropov, the Soviet authorities allowed some refuseniks to depart for Israel after serving a prison term.

During the Second World War, the Germans targeted the Jewish population of the Soviet Union, who felt isolated because their neighbours often participated in the genocide, assisting the invaders in the mass killing. Nor were the deaths of these Jews commemorated in any way after the War by the state and all these factors raised Jewish self-awareness. In addition, in the course of the War, the Soviet Union incorporated Latvia, Lithuania and Moldova with a large Jewish population, areas in which religious affiliation and Zionism still enjoyed mass support. In May 1948, the state of Israel was established and in the autumn great crowds of Jews greeted Golda Meyerson (Meir), when she visited the Moscow synagogue. Stalin was concerned that the older generation of Jews were everywhere spreading their Zionist viewpoint to the younger generation and

---

[991] Mordechai Altshuler, Religion and Jewish Identity in the Soviet Union 1941-1964 pp.59-60.

thought that Jews because of their ties to relatives in the West could not be relied on in the event of a war with the United States.

During the early years of the regime, Jews held senior posts in government, the bureaucracy, the Communist party, the army, and the diplomatic service, but in the 1930s they were gradually squeezed out of these positions. In 1949 Stalin ordered an anti-cosmopolitan campaign which attacked rootless wanderers for their lack of appreciation of Soviet culture which was implicitly aimed at Jews. Meanwhile, he ordered the closure of the Jewish Anti-Fascist Committee and the arrest of its members. One of the accused died in prison, while thirteen other defendants were tried in secret and executed. Behind Stalin's motive for the trial was his objective of whipping-up public indignation against the unpatriotic behaviour of Jews. From this trial, sprang the concocted Doctors' Plot, in which a group of high-ranking medical specialists, who were mostly Jewish, were falsely accused of planning to murder senior Soviet politicians. Rumours abounded that Jews had agreed to move out of the sight of the general population and that camps were being prepared to receive them, but before the trial opened Stalin died suddenly and the doctors were released from prison.

When Khrushchev became leader of the Soviet Union, he delivered a secret speech in February 1956 denouncing Stalin's crimes; and there was a period of political relaxation known as the 'Thaw'. As he consolidated his power, Khrushchev implemented an anti-religious drive, closing churches and monasteries as well as synagogues in even greater numbers. Starting in 1961, in an atmosphere where antisemitism and anti-religious sentiment flourished, there were a series of trials of individuals for economic crimes and forty per cent of those executed were Jewish, a suspiciously high number; and Khrushchev continued Stalin's policy of keeping most Jews out of the higher ranks of the Communist party and government.

A few years after the death of Stalin, the Prime Minister of Israel in 1952 set up a secret organization, *Lishkat Kesher,* to assist the migration of Soviet Jews into the newly established state. During the 1930s, heads of the Jewish Agency in Palestine believed that the teeming Jewish masses in Eastern Europe would emigrate to Palestine in their millions and provide the population reserves essential for the foundation and survival of a Jewish state. Now it was necessary to contact the survivors. Shaul Avigur was appointed to head the organization; and members were secretly ensconced in the Israeli embassy in Moscow. On the plus side for the Lishka, Jewish sentiment all over the Soviet Union was ignited because of the mass killing of Jews during the War; and a feeling of isolation and rejection by their neighbours, who sometimes participated in these horrendous crimes, while religious feeling and Zionist sentiments still remained strong in the outlying areas of the USSR which had been recently been brought within its borders. Jewish nationalist sentiment was given a further boost by the foundation of Israel in 1948 in that Jews now had a haven and home to go to. Moreover, the lies and distortions in the Soviet media in the reporting of the 1973 Yom Kippur War and in the news of Israel's impending defeat gave way to the sudden euphoria in the Jewish community, when the Soviet authorities had to admit that their earlier announcements were untrue.

In 1954, the Israeli organization's sphere of operations was extended to Western Countries, where it was known as *Nativ,* but the existence and name of this latter organization were not disclosed for many years. Envoys were then selected in New York, London and Paris to approach interested individuals, who were encouraged to establish campaigning groups and coverage in the press to promote the emigration of Jews from the Soviet Union. It was a two-pronged approach of reawakening Jewish sentiment in the USSR and of prompting and educating Jews in the diaspora to take a much greater interest in the fate of these co-religionists. In these endeavours, the Israeli envoys were assisted by the larger number of Jewish tourists visiting the

Soviet Union by the mid-1950s to seek out relatives or attending services in synagogues, where they made contact with local Jews when on a sight-seeing trip.

In Britain, the poet and novelist Emanuel Litvinoff was asked by one of Avigur's aides, Binyamin Eliav, to publish an article in the *Listener* in 1958 about a trip that he had undertaken to the Soviet Union. Eliav also secured funding for Litvinoff to publish a journal, *Jews in Eastern Europe,* surveying the Soviet Jewish scene. The Israelis then sponsored a series of international conferences of Western intellectuals, starting in 1960 with the limited aim of assisting family reunification and demanding the implementation of the religious and cultural rights of Soviet Jews. Only in February 1971, did the First Brussels Conference on Soviet Jewry pass a resolution demanding that the Soviet government recognize the right of Jews to return to their historic homeland. In turn, Litvinoff encouraged Bertrand Russell, the United Kingdom's most prominent public intellectual, not only to campaign for the enforcement of Soviet Jewry's religious and cultural rights but from this vantage point to take a sustained interest in the plight of individual Soviet Jews.

Fortuitously, international student protests engulfed the 1960s, followed by the Women's liberation movement in the 1970s, which agents of the Lishka utilised for their own purposes by encouraging the formation of student and women's groups for the release of Soviet Jewry. Shortly after the setting up of a national American body for Soviet Jewry on 23 October 1963, Jacob Birnbaum in New York decided to found the Student Struggle for Soviet Jewry in April 1964. In emulation of this organization, Mike Hunter helped to establish the Universities' Committee for Soviet Jewry in Britain in January 1966. Gordon Hausmann played an increasingly important role in the British student pressure group, organizing marches on the Soviet embassy, writing to the Prime Minister Harold Wilson, and securing an interview with embassy officials, when the Board of Deputies had been repeatedly rebuffed. He also organized a non-partisan motion on Soviet Jewry in the House of

Commons, the credit for which was claimed by the Board of Deputies.

These American and British Soviet Jewry organizations were part of the wider international movement of student protest which erupted in the 1960s; and in Britain, the majority of Jewish students shared the same left-wing causes as their gentile colleagues, such as opposition to the Vietnam war, the bomb, and the apartheid regime in South Africa; and adopted many of the same campaigning tactics. Now sizeable in numbers, and cultivated and aided by agents of the Lishka, these young British Jewish students turned their anger against the communal leadership and the government for not doing enough to save Soviet Jews from persecution. They were ashamed of the passivity of their parents at the time of the Holocaust and they were determined that this time they would not fail their co-religionists. However, a smaller number of the youth in the Anglo-Jewish community, enrolled in Young Herut, usually embraced more right-wing views, and espoused more violent tactics. British Jewish students were fortunate that their gentile colleagues among the general student body regarded this as an attractive cause which they were also willing to support, by sometimes joining peaceful demonstrations and signing petitions.

Jewish communities all over the world were enraged when death sentences were decreed against Edward Kutznetsov and Mark Dymshits after the first Leningrad trial for the alleged hijacking of an aircraft to flee from the Soviet Union; and the death sentences were announced on Christmas eve 1970 in the mistaken belief that they would escape notice in the West. But the students demonstrated in London and aroused the whole community in the struggle. Shortly afterwards, British Jewish women formed an organization to participate in the protests; and more generally the international campaign with the slogan of 'Let My People Go' gained momentum across the Jewish world. The death sentences on Kutznetsov and Dymshits were commuted for lengthy terms of imprisonment; the Soviet Jewry movement had gained a significant victory.

However, the students appeared to be somewhat unreliable allies after an incident involving Soviet officials and Ijo Rager, a counsellor at the Israeli embassy in London, turned his attention increasingly to recruiting Anglo-Jewish women. He encouraged them to set up the Women's Campaign for Soviet Jewry better known as the 35's. Its founder Barbara Oberman, who started a protest on behalf of an imprisoned individual, Raiza Palatnik, was associated with the debacle on Soviet premises in London and was encouraged to step down from the leadership of the 35's to avoid a diplomatic incident involving Israel. Under the new leadership of Doreen Gainsford, until her departure for Israel in 1978, the Women's Campaign gained media attention by a series of gimmicks and stunts. Both the Women's Campaign and Barbara Oberman's rival Committee for the Release of Soviet Jewry had their successes in securing the release and emigration of a number of Soviet Jewish individuals, for whom they campaigned. But in some ways, the most successful pressure group for Soviet Jewry in the 1970s in Britain was the independent Committee for the Release of Valery and Galina Panov, manned by ballet enthusiasts and left-wing Jewish activists, who gained the support of Equity and secured the backing of international acting and ballet stars. So powerful were the ripples it caused that the tour of the Bolshoi Ballet Company was almost called off and a diplomatic debacle involving the Soviet Union and the United Kingdom was narrowly avoided.

While the 35's formation was sparked by the international women's liberation movement in the United States and Britain, having interviewed a number of their members, I would conclude that on the whole they were not closely steeped in the ideology of the second-wave feminists but had acquired a similar outlook regarding an enhanced political role for women as part of the general social climate in Britain of the 1970s; and in this more narrow sense the Women's Campaign and Barbara

Oberman's group were part of the British Women's liberation movement. Apart from exceptions such as Margaret Rigal, who was a descendant of an old Anglo-Jewish family, most of the women in the 35's came from comfortable bourgeois families rather than upper-middle class ones and were often the children and grandchildren of immigrants from Eastern Europe. They were more socially comfortable in Britain than their parents' generation and were less inhibited about protesting than the somewhat lethargic male-dominated communal leadership. Like the students, many of the women felt they had a redemptive role to play, by securing exit visas for Soviet Jewry, to atone for what they sensed was their parents' passivity in rescuing Jews from the Continent during the Second World War.

Tired of the stunts and activism of the Women's Campaign both in Britain and in Continental Europe, the Board of Deputies attempted to wrest back control, by setting up the National Council for Soviet Jewry in December 1975, in which all the campaigning groups were represented. Although it was an umbrella organization through which the Board ultimately exercised control, the students and the Women's Campaign remained restive at times and tended to act independently on occasions. But like the Women's Campaign the rank-and-file and leadership of the Board of Deputies were drawn from families descended from migrants from Eastern Europe. Families belonging to the Cousinhood played little part in the Soviet Jewry movement.

In October 1972, Senator Henry M. Jackson 'first proposed linking trade benefits for the Soviet Union with freedom of emigration; the Jackson-Vanik Amendment became law in 1975'. American Jews savoured their political muscle in the 1970s and 1980s compared to their impotence in the 1940s.[992] It was true that before the First World War, American Jews under the leadership of the

---

[992] Elliott Abrams, 'Lessons of the Soviet Jewish Exodus', Jewish Review of Books Spring 2019.

extremely wealthy and influential banker Jacob Schiff helped to secure the abrogation of the Russo-American Commercial Treaty at the end of 1911 because of the persecution inflicted by the Tsarist regime, but since then their political influence had waned. Henceforth the flexing of their political muscle was left to American Jews by the Israelis to put pressure on Presidents and through them on the Kremlin, while the Lishka told British Jews to concentrate on helping individual refuseniks and other facets of the campaign.

With the signing of the Helsinki Final Act on 1 August 1975, which among other matters guaranteed cultural and religious freedom and the right to family reunification, the whole movement for Soviet Jewry gained an added impetus; and the campaign switched from voicing a request to let my people go to the more assured demand for the full implementation of human rights for all citizens, to which the Soviet Union had signed up. The Israelis with the assistance of the international women's movement for the release of Soviet Jewry lobbied diplomatic representatives at the Helsinki talks and strengthened the human rights clauses in the Final Agreement. However, throughout the 1970s, there was a steady flow of Jewish migrants from the USSR which somewhat blunted the effectiveness of the campaigners in the outside world.

Harold Wilson was a very dexterous political operator but also someone sympathetic to the cause of Soviet Jewry, who achieved some success in individual cases before the new human rights regime was properly in place. He emphasised to his Foreign Secretary that he had a free hand in all areas to devise his own policy, apart from Israel and South Africa. The latter because he detested apartheid. 'He was prepared to endanger even his precious relationship with the Russian leaders so as to secure a better deal for Soviet Jewry. He told Martin Gilbert that since 1964 he had been active in trying to get the Jews out of Russia'.[993] His successor as Labour Prime Minister, James Callaghan,

---

[993] Philip Ziegler, Wilson p.388.

was much more concerned about not upsetting the leadership in the Kremlin, by paying too much attention to Soviet dissidents and Jews, and thereby jeopardising the East/West talks on security issues and trade. His replacement as Foreign Secretary, David Owen, was very concerned about human rights issues, writing a book on the subject, but as far as the Jewish campaign was concerned, he had somewhat of a tin ear. He was hypercritical of the Jewish position, not fully appreciating the very substantial role of Soviet Jews in the Helsinki Watch Groups monitoring process and the role of Jews generally in the campaign against unlawful psychiatric detention, nor understanding the ethnic rivalries and the complexities of what happened during the Shoah in the Soviet Union and beyond its borders in Eastern Europe. In both places, members of other ethnic groups had participated on a vast scale in the Nazi extermination of European Jewry. He would not concede that the Soviet government was conducting a broad antisemitic campaign across the whole USSR against Jewish political activists, nor did he seem to realize that this hostility also extended to any expression of Jewish cultural and religious revival. He refused persistently to confront the Soviet Union over individual cases, so that he was far happier discussing broad categories of cases and expected standards of behaviour. He shunned meeting family members pleading for help for their trapped close relatives or members of campaigning groups seeking an interview on their behalf. Meetings with campaigners and freed Soviet citizens were also avoided by ministers and left to civil servants in the Foreign and Commonwealth Office, who started intervening on behalf of individual refuseniks in the CSCE follow-up meetings.

Under June Jacobs, the National Council for Soviet Jewry was not yet able to run a fully coordinated campaign and there was still much rivalry between the National Council, the Women's Campaign and the Inter-Parliamentary lobby group; but she made significant progress, by more closely coordinating the National Council's campaign with that of the MP's on the All-

Parliamentary Committee for the Release of Soviet Jewry. What stands out during these years was the enormous impact of a number of women, who migrated to Israel around 1978, Doreen Gainsford and Barbara Oberman as political campaigners, and Zelda Harris especially in her contributing to the revival of Jewish culture in the Soviet Union; their success in securing exit visas for a few well-known refuseniks; and their protests mounted overseas to secure the implementation of useful human rights provisions in the Helsinki Accords.

Amnesty International was founded in 1961 in London by Peter Benenson, who emphasised the human aspect of his campaign over the word rights, and his organization was joined in Britain in the 1970s by a whole cluster of additional human rights bodies for wrongfully detained psychiatric patients and individuals subjected to religious persecution. Benenson was a Jewish convert to Catholicism, who had a critical but sympathetic attitude towards Zionism, not fully shared by his successors; and following his early death there was increasing tension between Jewish organizations and Amnesty.[994] Benenson strongly believed that human rights were inalienable and could not be restricted by the fiat of governments, a viewpoint which accorded with Jewish and Catholic teaching.[995] This was important because, after Helsinki, the Women's Campaign started to utilise human rights slogans on their placards when they demonstrated; and in this sense of being an auxiliary human rights organization, the 35's were a product of the social climate of the 1970s, quite apart from their connections to the second wave feminist movement. From these heterogeneous campaigning groups, the issue of human rights was taken up by politicians. Above all, President Jimmy Carter after his inauguration in January 1977 began to emphasise the

---

[994]James Loeffler, Rooted Cosmopolitans pp.205,217-19.

[995] J.H. Hertz ed., The Pentateuch and Haftorahs, Genesis (Oxford,1929), p.80 n.6. Samuel Moyn, The Last Utopia pp.50-1,65,67.

478

subject of human rights in his speeches and foreign policy in marked contrast to Nixon and Henry Kissinger; and this approach in foreign relations was adopted in Britain by David Owen and more whole-heartedly by Margaret Thatcher as Prime Minister.

Anatoly Shcharansky suggested the formation of the Moscow-based Helsinki Watch Group which was established on 12 May 1976 to monitor the Helsinki Accords; and there was a proliferation of similar organizations in other parts of the Soviet Union.[996] According to Philip Boobbyer, the dissident movement was primarily one of intellectuals, in which scientists and writers were heavily represented, both groups also contained a high proportion of Jews.[997] Partly because the international women's movement sharpened the text of the human rights clauses in the Helsinki Accords, partly because Shcharansky converted the dissident movement in the Soviet Union to human rights, we would dispute Samuel Moyn's contention that 'the Soviet Jewry movement proved more the beneficiary than the cause of that general transformation'.[998] But Foreign Office officials, although conceding that the Helsinki Final Act made human rights an integral part of detente, were of the opinion that the United Kingdom still had no formal standing to intervene on behalf of individual Soviet citizens with the authorities in the Kremlin.

In 1976, the Politburo under the influence of the hard-line KGB chief Yuri Andropov seems to have decided to put fresh pressure on dissidents and refuseniks to disrupt their communication with the West. At the same time, the discrimination placed on Jews applying for higher education since 1967, broadened the ranks of the dissidents, who wished to emigrate as preference was given to Russians and other Soviet nationalities. Some Jews involved with organizing classes for unemployed scientists

[996] Robert J. Brym, The Jews of Moscow, Kiev, and Minsk pp.14-15.
[997] Philip Boobbyer, Conscience, Dissent and Reform in Soviet Russia p.225.
[998] Samuel Moyn, The Last Utopia p.153.

and the growing movement for the revival of Jewish culture in the Soviet Union were charged with parasitism or received threats that they would be indicted, as some were. Early in March 1977, an article appeared in *Izvestia* denouncing some refuseniks, including Anatoly Shcharansky, for their alleged ties to the American Central Intelligence Agency. Hence Shcharansky was arrested on 15 March 1977 because of his English skills and contacts with Western journalists as a spokesman for the Moscow Helsinki Watch Group and his links to the refuseniks. The Kremlin singled out Shcharansky as a Jew for dire punishment, the threat of execution, in an effort to make an example of him, and to damage both movements. At the same time, other leaders of the Moscow Helsinki Group, such as Dr Yuri Orlov and Ludmilla Alexeyeva, were imprisoned or persuaded to go into exile; and a Jewish physician, Dr Mikhail Shtern, framed on false charges and given an eight-year sentence, was suddenly released from prison to distract Western attention from Shcharansky's detention. Dina Beilin was ordered to go abroad in case she appeared as a defence witness in Shcharansky's trial, which would have upset the prosecution's concocted case against him. Other leading figures in the cultural and scientific wings of the refusenik movement were also arrested and tried, including Vladimir Slepak, Ida Nudel, Dr Victor Brailovsky and Iosif Begun, all of whom were given sentences of internal exile. Although the Jewish defendants in the trials arranged by Andropov were convicted, not all of them buckled under pressure and some made impassioned speeches in favour of Israel and Zionism which were relayed to the refusenik community and bolstered their cause. In addition, the Prisoners of Zion became heroes among the Soviet Jewry campaigning organizations across the globe, who started protests on their behalf which attracted the attention of the media and politicians.

On their release from prison and eventual arrival in Israel or the West, some of the high-profile refuseniks or individuals from the rank and file assisted in the Soviet

Jewry campaign, by speaking at public meetings about their experiences. But other individuals, for whom the Women's Campaign 'had worked incredibly hard over a period of many years', proved to be uncooperative; and unwilling to assist in the protests or even thank the persons, who had worked so assiduously on their behalf.[999]

By the early 1980s, Margaret Rigal and Rita Eker, who were joint leaders of the Women's Campaign, realized that non-stop public protests were becoming counter-productive and switched their attention to building up a strong relationship with the new Conservative Prime Minister, Margaret Thatcher, on a woman to woman basis. During these years, they concentrated on trying to secure the release of two individuals, Shcharansky and Alexander Paritsky, a leader of the movement for Jewish cultural revival in the USSR. A careful study of Avital Shcharansky's approaches to Margaret Thatcher which were arranged by the 35's and Nicholas Bethell shows that the Prime Minister's help for Anatoly was intermittent and only important on one occasion, when Avital was photographed with the Prime Minister on the steps of Downing Street on 29 April 1981. This saved his life by Margaret Thatcher throwing a protective mantle over him, but on another occasion on 15 July 1983 she offered Avital little beyond vague assurances of help and two years later tried to disabuse her of any hope of her husband's early release. Everything was left by Britain to the Americans, but when he was freed in February 1986 the Prime Minister used the opportunity to issue a press statement, painting her own role in glowing terms. She usually followed cautious Foreign Office guidelines, the only difference was that after the installation of Gorbachev as leader she made herself more available to listen to the supplications of wives and mothers for their loved ones; and she was the first head of state to meet refuseniks in Moscow. At a meeting of President Reagan and Soviet dissidents, Avital forced her attention on him, by gripping his hand tightly and refusing

---

[999] Daphne Gerlis, p.178,

to let go until he shook her hand. At the Madrid review meeting, there were exchanges between Max Kampelman, the head of the United States delegation, who tried to secure a deal for Shcharansky's release and Kondrachev, a Soviet delegate with KGB links, though despite promises an agreement did not materialize at this time.

Mikhail Gorbachev became the Soviet leader on 11 March 1985. Young and more appealing than a succession of elderly, ailing predecessors, he was the protege of Andropov. He was a cautious moderniser, without being a closet liberal, and was cut in much the same mould as his mentor. He wanted to preserve the monopoly of power of the Communist party and was prepared to sanction the necessary measures to preserve it intact, even if it meant covering up the Chernobyl nuclear disaster, by placing all the blame on underlings and prosecuting them; and later sanctioning the shooting of unarmed protestors in the Soviet republics. Throughout 1986 and much of 1987, he was not prepared to budge on the issue of the mass emigration of Soviet Jews. He regarded Jews as the state's most educated people, who were crucial to the success of his modernising project and whom he, therefore, wanted to remain in the Soviet Union's borders. Once the nuclear reactor had exploded in Chernobyl on 26 April 1986, he was more willing to make some concessions and negotiated the Intermediate Range Nuclear Weapons Treaty to save money; but not until the full economic impact of the disaster could be comprehended by him, which was some years later, was he prepared to bend on the issue of Soviet Jews. In a spy swap on 11 February 1986 arranged with the United States, he rid himself of the problem of Shcharansky and some of the opprobrium of the international community. In October 1987, he let some other big names go among the refuseniks, including Victor Brailovsky, Ida Nudel and Vladimir Slepak. Perhaps Shevardnadze, the Foreign Minister, understood the message that the Americans were trying to convey to him since his April 1987 session with Shultz on the necessity for the mass emigration of Soviet Jews better than his master; but it is doubtful whether Gorbachev understood the scale of the demand on this issue, even after the mass Jewish rally in Washington organized by Sharansky in December 1987. His reaction was slower. What may have produced this radical turn-around in Soviet thinking was less the strength of the international Soviet Jewry campaign and more the cumulative economic pressure of the Chernobyl disaster and the need for Western financial help; and an additional factor was the dismantling of the central planning apparatus and a new consensus among experts that there would be a labour surplus and widespread unemployment and it would be beneficial if many Jews left.[1000]

In the successful achievement of securing the freedom of the leaders of the refuseniks in the Soviet Union and then mass migration, the British movement played a secondary but important role in comparison to the Americans. But the strategy of the American movement was always based on the belief that 'the road to Moscow was through Washington; that the Soviet Jewry issue could only be resolved by government to government intervention'.[1001] The Women's Campaign had an excellent network of contacts with Jews across the Soviet Union and through these contacts they were able to channel drugs and medical assistance and support in the shape of clothes and goods to needy families and to those with members, who were sick. The National Council in cooperation with the 35's and other organizations helped to sponsor the cultural and religious revival among Jews in the Soviet Union, thus ensuring that large numbers of Soviet Jews were willing to see Israel as their destination of choice; and even if the British movement failed to obtain the release of the big Soviet Jewish names, their essential supportive role was essential in securing their ultimate freedom and their daily campaigning for the freedom of lesser-known figures was eventually successful in many cases. Both Anglo-Jewish bodies struggled to keep abreast of steeply rising

---

[1000] Robert J. Brym, The Jews of Moscow, Kiev and Minsk pp.72-3.
[1001] Sam Lipski and Suzanne D. Rutland, Let My People Go p.137.

expenditure. At the same time, their constant protests on behalf of the refusenik leaders in labour camps and in internal exile helped to sustain their morale; and their dissemination of their defiant utterances at their trials helped to sap the confidence and the self-belief of the men in the Kremlin and the KGB. Both British organizations contributed to the overall success of the campaign by generating their members unflagging interest and enthusiasm in the stagnant years of the 1970s and early 1980s and were not blown off course by diplomatic squalls, a remarkable achievement in itself.

The National Council and the Board of Deputies usually had more direct access to the Prime Minister Margaret Thatcher in the 1980s than the Women's Campaign and Neil Bradman was a formidable chairman of the National Council, who established an excellent rapport with the Prime Minister, when the whole campaign was at its peak. But it was through the letter writing of Margaret Rigal and Rita Eker with their emphasis on human rights and the relationship that they built up with the Prime Minister which kept her in touch with the twists and turns of the campaign and probably at one early point saved Sharansky's life. From speaking of human rights in general terms, they moved on to talking about the specific commitments under international law the Soviet Union had signed up to, including the right of Soviet citizens to emigrate. It was an epistolary love affair. Under Thatcher's leadership Shcharansky's name was mentioned by the British CSCE delegation in Madrid and by Foreign and Commonwealth Office Ministers in discussions with their Soviet counterparts, a break with past practice which followed the American lead. During a visit to Moscow in 1987, Margaret Thatcher had breakfast with a group of refuseniks in the British embassy, establishing another precedent. Meanwhile, because Margaret Thatcher was particularly responsive to the families of trapped refuseniks, her status grew as a mythical mother figure, who could free them from captivity and ease their passage to freedom overseas. Her intervention in the case of the Samoilovich family was especially noteworthy.

The Women's Campaign expressed a regard for human rights which they uttered in general terms or understood as the right to worship freely and not be cast into prison for wishing to leave the Soviet Union. Only later in 1977, after President Carter's outspoken intervention, did they invoke the Declaration of Human Rights and the International Convention on Civil and Political Rights, when trying to safeguard the right to emigrate which they regarded as inalienable. From the position of defending the right to family reunification, the Women's Campaign resolved that under international law all Soviet Jews had the general right to live where they wanted and to emigrate. Gorbachev failed to align Soviet law with international immigration law, although the Soviet Union had signed these documents, and avoided denouncing antisemitism in speeches in the USSR. By sending out muddled signals of sufficient flexibility, Gorbachev, who did at least believe in some form of the rule of law, confused Western leaders and they agreed to hold a human rights conference in Moscow.

Nonetheless, Gorbachev and his bureaucracy and the KGB fought a sustained rear-guard action to delay concessions, despite the economic crisis brought on by the nuclear disaster and the Soviet leader's dithering to switch to a market economy. They wanted to keep the highly trained cadres of Jewish scientists and engineers in the Soviet Union, but as the planned economy collapsed these dissidents eventually became expendable. Even when Jewish emigration from the Soviet Union climbed from 8,155 in 1987 to 18,919 in 1988, and 71,196 in 1989 and then shot up to 181,802 in 1990, there were still 3,000 to 5,000 families caught in the Soviet Union at the end of 1991; but high rates of emigration continued throughout 1991, 1992 and 1993 and the numbers leaving in those years were respectively 178,566, 108,292, and 102,134.[1002] However, the procedural process for the drafting of a new emigration law was constantly delayed, while it was envisaged that the new law was not going to come into force until 1993 in a forlorn attempt to halt the flood of emigrants. Meanwhile, in December 1991, despite President Bush's support for Gorbachev and fear of the dispersal of nuclear weapons if the union was dissolved, the Soviet Union disintegrated and was replaced by a number of independent successor states. Gorbachev's slogans of perestroika and glasnost unleashed the centripetal forces of nationalism which tore the Soviet Union apart. This was not altogether a peaceful transition, as the Soviet Union under Gorbachev had tried in vain to obstruct the independence movements in a hail of bullets in Georgia, Azerbaijan and Lithuania.[1003]

Ultimately, the Women's Campaign was successful in reinforcing Margaret Thatcher's stance of demanding concrete instances of an improvement of the Soviet Union's human rights record before she would agree to a human rights conference being held in Moscow in 1991; and she in turn stiffened President Reagan's resolve in this respect and through their partnership that of their European allies. Shultz, the American Secretary of State, was insisting in 1988 on an enhanced rate of emigration for Jewish families and steps being taken to end the detention of political prisoners and falsely detained psychiatric patients in the Soviet Union. As his term in office was drawing to a close, President Reagan was determined to conclude a deal with the Soviet Union at the Vienna CSCE meeting by January 1989, and after securing what Shultz believed were sufficient concessions, a deal was struck; and Margaret

---

[1002]Pauline Peretz, Let My People Go. The Transnational Politics of Soviet Jewish Emigration during the Cold War (New Brunswick, 2015), p.344.

[1003] Amy Knight review of Vladimir Bukovsky, Judgment in Moscow: Soviet Crimes and Western Complicity 16 January 2020 New York Review of Books .

Thatcher had to follow the President's lead. In these detailed negotiations Richard Schifter (1923-2020) an Under-Secretary in the State Department, a refugee and Jew, played a crucial role with his Soviet counterpart Anatoly Adamishin in bringing these negotiations to a successful conclusion.

What induced Gorbachev to agree to mass emigration from the Soviet Union in 1989 and more markedly from 1990 onwards were the economic repercussions of the Chernobyl disaster, followed by unrelenting Western diplomatic pressure, emanating from the insistence on the implementation of the CSCE human rights provisions; and behind the diplomatic fortitude of Shultz and the British Prime Minister, Margaret Thatcher, were the arrayed ranks of the Soviet Jewry campaigners in the United States and Britain and their relentless pressure which also hardened the resolve of the refuseniks. But in 1990, while much-increased emigration was expected, no one in the Soviet Union, including Gorbachev, could have foreseen its immense scale. While the effects of the British Jewish campaign were generally secondary to those of their American colleagues on the political and diplomatic establishment, in certain respects it was superior. Through Margaret Thatcher's intervention with President Reagan, she reinforced the strength of the allied demand for an improvement in Gorbachev's human rights record and the freeing of those wrongly imprisoned. At the same time, the Union of Councils was exerting pressure on the American government through its contacts with Schifter on the list of detainees he agreed should be freed, after talks with his Soviet counterpart, Adamishin; and their requests were echoed by the Women's Campaign and Martin Gilbert in Britain.

British Jewry's efforts were sustained by affiliated and committed Jews, mainly adherents of Orthodox Jewry in general, the United Synagogue and the Federation of Synagogues, or from the Reform movement with more occasional interest from Liberal Jews. Members of these religious bodies filled the ranks of the National Council, the

487

35's and Exodus. Much of the enthusiasm behind the protests was generated by guilt over what was felt to be non-action by a past generation over saving the Jews of Europe from the Holocaust; but as we have seen, it also merged with the student activism of the 1960s and the feminist rebellion of the 1970s, both of which had wider international ramifications; and the world-wide movement for the implementation of human rights after the signing of the Helsinki Accords which was later highlighted by President Carter. At the same time, the campaign for Soviet Jewry was an attractive one which drew in marginal Jews, such as the persuasive columnist, Bernard Levin, the world-famous violinist Yehudi Menuhin and secular activists such as Pamela Manson. The subject was less contentious than support for Israel and attracted support from non-Jewish movie stars such as Ingrid Bergman and internationally-acclaimed ballet dancers, actors and actresses, such as Laurence Olivier and Vanessa Redgrave, a vocal critic of the Jewish state. Even journalists such as John Pilger, who were condemnatory of Israeli actions, added their support.

The chief British organizations, the National Council and the Women's Campaign reached every section of society through professional bodies, trade unions and Churches, and Amnesty International. Especially noteworthy was the intervention of a large number of gentile elite scientists on behalf of Soviet Jewish colleagues, who happened to be dissidents. Good coverage of the whole campaign appeared in most of the British national dailies and Sunday newspapers, and on the radio and television through the efforts of the campaigners. Among British campaigners, the outstanding personalities were Rita Eker and Margaret Rigal, partly because of the relationship they formed with the Prime Minister, Margaret Thatcher, partly because of all the innovative features they successfully introduced into the British movement. Michael Sherbourne was another formidable figure in the world Soviet Jewry campaign through his dissemination of the latest information from the refusenik leaders to organizations in Britain and the United States and through them to Western governments. Another such figure was Martin Gilbert through his books and articles which were published in newspapers across the globe, but he also invested much time and effort in campaigning for countless individuals. Non-Jewish MPs joined the Inter-Parliamentary Committee for Soviet Jewry in greater numbers than had their predecessors, who worked for the admission of refugees in the 1930s. An Interfaith Committee of Christians, Muslims and Jews under Bishop Richard Harries was reconvened by the National Council in 1987. Although Christian clergy and a number of parishioners had also participated in the earlier interfaith work on behalf of Soviet Jews, the support of the Churches for the Soviet Jewry movement as well as the trade unions can only be summed up as sporadic. Amnesty International more or less shunned the Soviet Jewry campaign after Benenson's demise, apart from a few minor interventions on behalf of individuals.

In line with the new policy of the American National Conference for Soviet Jewry, the National Council shifted its emphasis in 1990 to promoting cultural and religious awareness among Soviet Jews, and as the Soviet Union broke up, there was an increasing need to bolster the supply of food and medicine to needy Jewish families. Already by May 1989, the Jewish Agency had cut its subsidy to the National Council which in turn had to dispense with most of its office staff, and as the funding diminished still further with the success of the emigration campaign, the executive director, Lawrence Littlestone, was dismissed in March 1992; and it renamed itself the National Council for Jews in the Former Soviet Lands but it was no longer a significant body. At the same time, the Women's Campaign was reducing its political activities, since in 1989 it had set up a charitable arm, the Jewish Aid Committee, which sponsored a fundraising organization known as One-to-One. It collected money to promote the integration of Russian and other immigrants into Israel and through its offshoot in Jerusalem, Keren Klita, arranged financial, educational and medical assistance for them and helped to furnish their new homes.

In the fifteen years preceding the First World War, 1.7 million Jews emigrated from Eastern Europe chiefly to the United States, Britain and Argentina.[1004] This was followed by the Holocaust; 'the liquidation of the Jews from the Arab lands'; and the founding of the state of Israel in 1948. The international campaign for Soviet Jewry orchestrated by Israel led to the emigration of almost two million Jews from the former Soviet Union and was on the same scale as the previous mass movement of East European Jews.[1005] By 2020, the Jewish population which had been 409,000 in Russia in 1994 had shrunk to an estimated 155,000 persons.[1006] Moreover, the advent of so many scientists and academics from the Soviet Union enabled Israel to become the start-up nation and a technological and military power; and this may be compared with the contribution made by the emigration of scientists and academics from Germany and Central Europe in the 1930s to Britain and the United States which similarly enhanced their capabilities. These three Jewish population movements were among the defining events of twentieth-century Jewish history along with the Shoah and the founding of the state of Israel in 1948. According to Natan Sharansky, the human rights campaign which led to the exodus of more than a million Jews to Israel and another huge number to the Western world was the most successful human rights campaign in history and was one of the factors which led to the humbling of the Soviet Union, a superpower, and the demise of the Soviet Empire. Equally notable it was a rare example of the reversal of a cultural genocide -- the

---

[1004] Tom Segev, A State at Any Cost, the Life of David Ben- Gurion (London,2019), p.32.

[1005] Antony Polonsky, The Jews in Poland and Russia 1948-2008 vol.3 (London,2019), p.592. Elliott Abrams, 'Lessons of the Soviet Jewish Exodus'. Lucy S. Dawidowicz, What is the Use of Jewish History? p.127.

[1006] Jewish News 22 October 2020.

prolonged Soviet attempt to assimilate their Jews and eradicate all traces of their religion and culture dismally failed, as persecution renewed the search of many for their faith and culture to sustain them.

At first, the Jews from the Soviet Union seemed to be part of a minority culture in Israel, speaking Russian among themselves and reading a multitude of their own newspapers, they ate Russian food in numerous cheap restaurants that sprung up to cater for their tastes and visited specialist bookshops. Numerous Russian musicians entertained the public in the streets and solicited a few coins in payment. The Palestinian terror attacks some thirty years ago, especially on public transport, forced these families to adapt quickly and identify with other Israelis. But they have now assimilated and Russian is heard less often in the street. 'Their children speak Hebrew, fulfil army service, vote and work. Most important of all, they marry other Israelis, creating families, in which Hebraic culture overwhelms Russian', while because of successful integration the Russian newspapers have ceased publication and specialist restaurants have shut their doors.[1007]

Ironically, in Russia today there is a professional mohel (circumciser), Dr Yeshaya Shafit, who flies all over the country circumcising about ten adult men every week.[1008] Above all, the strengthening of Israel's population and economic growth made it into a formidable military power which had to be respected by its neighbours and it could no longer be regarded as an ephemeral Crusader Kingdom. Since the eruption of Russia's war on the Ukraine in 2022, it is estimated that a fresh exodus of 30,000 Ukrainians has entered Israel, a third of whom are estimated to be Jews and more thousands are expected. It is a bonus of trained manpower for Israel, but perhaps sadly

---

[1007] Brian Horowitz, 'Crotchety old academic reflects on the Russian Wave', National Library of Israel Newsletter 5 January 2021.
[1008] Cnaan Liphshiz, 'Russia has a full-time surgeon whose only job is circumcising Jewish men', JTA, 6 August 2020.

marks the passing of a historic Jewish community.[1009] As Lucy Dawidowicz summed it up, Yizhak 'Baer was right: Jewish history follows its own laws. And also Dubnow was right: Jewish history, however dark and catastrophic, has in it the potential for Jewish survival'.[1010]

[1009] JC, 1 July 2022, pp.4-5.
[1010] Lucy Dawidowicz, What is the Use of Jewish History? p.19.

Bibliography

Archives
Central Archives of the Jewish People Jerusalem
Zelda Harris Papers
Rita Eker Papers London
London Metropolitan Archives: Papers of the Board of
Deputies and the National Council for Soviet Jewry
National Archives London
Special Collections University of Southampton
Women's Campaign for Soviet Jewry
Enid Wurtman Papers Jerusalem

Newspapers and Periodicals
Chronicle of Current Events
Daily Express
Daily Mail
Daily Telegraph
Evening Standard
Financial Times
Forward
Guardian
Hamoar
Independent
Insight; Soviet Jews
Jerusalem Post
Jewish Chronicle
Jewish Observer and Middle East Review
Jewish Review
Jewish Telegraphic Agency (JTA)
Jews in Eastern Europe
Listener
Los Angeles Times
Morning Star
New York Review of Books
New York Times
News Portsmouth
New Statesman
Stage and Television Today
Sunday Times
The Times

494

Works Cited

Alexeyeva, Ludmilla, and Goldberg, Paul, *The Thaw Generation. Coming of Age in the Post-Stalin Era* (Boston, 1990).

Altshular, Mordechai, *Religion and Jewish Identity in the Soviet Union 1941-1964* (Waltham, Mass., 2012).

Andrew, Christopher, and Mitrokhin, Vasili, *The Mitrokhin Archive: The KGB in Europe and the West* (London, 1999).

Applebaum, Anne, *Red Famine. Stalin's War on Ukraine* (London, 2018).

Azbel. Mark Y., *Refusenik Trapped in the Soviet Union* (Boston, 1981).

Bartov, Omer, *Anatomy of a Genocide. The Life and Death of a Town Called Buczacz* (Boston,2011).

Baron, Salo W., *The Russian Jews under Tsars and Soviets* (New York, 1987).

Beckerman, Gal, *When They Come for Us, We'll All Be Gone. The Epic Struggle to Save Soviet Jews* (Boston, 2011).

Beizer, Michael, *The Jews of St. Petersburg. Excursions Through a Noble Past* (Philadelphia, 1989).

Ben-David, Joseph, *Centers of Learning. Britain, France, Germany* (New York, 1971).

Berger, Joseph, *Shipwreck of a Generation. Memoirs* (London,1971).

Bergman, Ronen, 'The KGB's Middle East Files: The Fight Against Zionism and World Jewry', https://www.ynetnews.com/articles/07340,L4886594,00.html

Bethell, Nicholas, *Spies and Other Secrets* (London, 1994).

Binard, Florence, 'The British Women's Liberation Movement in the 1970s: Refining the Personal and Political' *French Journal of British Studies* (2017).

Boobbyer, Philip, *Conscience, Dissent and Reform* (London,2005).

Brent, Joshua, and Vladimir P. Naumov, *Stalin's Last Crime. The Plot Against the Jewish Doctors 1948-53* (New York,2003).

Brown, Archie, *The Rise and Fall of Communism* (London, 2010).

Brym, Robert J., *The Jews of Moscow, Kiev and Minsk: Identity, Antisemitism, Emigration* (New York, 1994).

Cantor, Norman F., *The Age of Protest Dissent and Rebellion in the Twentieth Century* (London, 1970).

Caute, David, *Isaac and Isaiah* (New Haven, 2013).

Cesarani, David, *Final Solution. The Fate of the Jews 1933-1949* (New York, 2016).

Conquest, Robert, *The Great Terror* (Harmondsworth, 1971).

Cooper, John, *Raphael Lemkin and the Struggle for the Genocide Convention,* (Houndmills, Basingstoke, 2015).

Courtois, Stephane et alia eds., *The Black Book of Communism. Crimes, Terror, Repression* (Cambridge, Mass., 1999).

Eisen, Wendy, *Count Us In. The Struggle to Free Soviet Jews, A Canadian Perspective* (Toronto, 1995).

Endelman, Todd M., *The Jews of Britain 1656-2000* (Berkeley, 2002).

Galili, Zvi, and Morozov, Boris, *Exiled to Palestine. The Emigration of Soviet Zionist Convicts from the Soviet Union 1924-1934* (London, 2006).

Gavron, Hannah, *The Captive Wife* (London, 1966).

Gerlis, Daphne, *Those Wonderful Women in Black. The Story of the Women's Campaign for Soviet Jewry* (London, 1978).

Feingold, Henry L., *Silent No More, Saving the Jews of Russia, The American Jewish Effort, 1967-1989* (Syracuse, 2007).

Friedman, Murray, and Chernin, Albert D., eds., *A Second Exodus. The American Movement to Free Soviet Jewry* (Hanover, NH, 1999).

Frumkin, Jacob ed., *Russian Jewry 1917-1967* (New York, 1969).

Gilbert, Martin, *The Jews of Hope. The Plight of Soviet Jewry Today* (New York, 1985).

Gilbert, Martin, *Scharansky. Hero of Our Time* (Harmondsworth, 1987).

Griffin, Nicholas ed., *The Selected Letters of Bertrand Russell. The Public years, 1914-1970.*

Hausmann, Gordon, *The Mermelstein Letters 1939-1947*(London, 2014).

Horowitz, Daniel, *Betty Friedan and the Making of the Feminist Mystique* (Amherst, Mass., 2000).

Hosking, Geoffrey, *A History of the Soviet Union 1917-1991* (London,1992).

Howe, Geoffrey, *Conflict of Loyalty* (London,1995).

Hurst, Mark, *British Human Rights Organizations and Soviet Dissent 1965-1985* (London, 2017).

Kalman, Matthew, *The Kids Are Alright. Chapters in the History of the World Union of Jewish Students* (Jerusalem, 1968).

Kavanagh, Julie, *Rudolf Nureyev* (London, 2007).

Kochan, Lionel ed., *The Jews in the Soviet Union* (London, 1970).

Landau, Aviva, 'To Russia With Love and Moseras Nefesh,' *Hamoar* (September 1987).

Laqueur, Walter, *The Long Road to Freedom. Russia and Glasnost* (London, 1989).

Laqueur, Walter, *Stalin. The Glasnost Revelations* (London, 1990).

Levin, Nora, *The Jews in the Soviet Union Since 1917* vol.1 (London, 1988) and vol.2 (New York, 1990).

Levy, Robert, *Ana Pauker* (Berkeley, 2001).

Lipstadt, Deborah, *Denial. Holocaust History on Trial* (New York, 2016).

Litvinoff, Barnet, *A Very British Subject. Telling Tales* (London, 1996).

Litvinoff, Emanuel, *Journey Through a Small Planet* (Harmondsworth, 1976).

Lipski, Sam, and Rutland, Suzanne D., *Let My People Go. The Untold Story of Australia and the Soviet Jews* (Jerusalem, 2015).

Loeffler, James, *Rooted Cosmopolitans. Jews and Human Rights in the Twentieth Century* (New Haven, 2018).

Marshall, Cherry, *The Cat-Walk* (London, 1978).

Morgan, Kenneth, O., *James Callaghan, A Life* (Oxford, 1997).

Moore, Charles, *Margaret Thatcher. Not for Turning* vol. 1 (London, 1978) and *Margaret Thatcher. Everything She Wants* vol. 2 (London, 2015).

Moyn, Samuel, *The Last Utopia* (London, Cambridge, Mass., 2010).

Owen, David, *Time to Declare* (London, 1992).

Panov, Valery, and Feifer, George, *To Dance* (London, 1978).

Peretz, Pauline, *Let My People Go. The Transnational Politics of Soviet Jewish Emigration During the Cold War* (New York, 2015).

Perkins, Ray, *Yours Faithfully, Bertrand Russell. A Lifelong Fight for Peace, Justice and Truth in Letters to the Editor* (Chicago, 2002).

Pincus, Benjamin Jnr, *The Soviet Government and the Jews 1948-67*(Cambridge, 1984).

Pisar, Samuel, *Of Blood and Hope* (London, 1980).

Plokhy, Serhii, *Chernobyl. History of a Tragedy* (London, 2019).

Polonsky, Antony, *The Jews in Poland and Russia 1914-2008 (London, 2019).*

Rich, Dave, 'The Activist Challenge: Women, Students and the Board of Deputies in the British Campaign for Soviet Jewry, vol.29 *Jewish History* (2015):163-85.

Roi, Yaacov, *The Struggle for Soviet Jewish Emigration* (Cambridge, 1991).

Roi, Yaacov ed., *Jews and Jewish Life in Russia and the Soviet Union*(London, 1995).

Roi, Yaacov ed., *The Jewish Movement in the Soviet Union* (Baltimore, 2012).

Rosman, Moshe, *How Jewish is Jewish History* (Oxford, 2007).

Rubenstein, Joshua, and Naumov, Vladimir P. eds., *Stalin's Secret Pogrom. The Post-war Inquisition of the Jewish Anti-Fascist Committee* (New Haven, 2005).

Sachar, Howard M., *A History of Jews in the Modern World* (New York, 2005).

Sacks, Jonathan, *One People? Tradition, Modernity and Jewish Unity* (London, 2001).

Segev, Tom, *A State at Any Cost. The Life of David Ben-Gurion*(London, 2019.

Sharansky, Natan, *Fear No Evil* (London, 1998).

Shindler, Colin, *Exit Visa. Detente, Human Rights and the Jewish Emigration Movement in the USSR* (London, 1978).

Shultz, George, *Turmoil and Triumph. My Years as Secretary of State* (New York, 1993).

Stern, August ed., *The USSR versus Dr Mikhail Stern* *(New York, 1977)*.

Taubman, William, *Khrushchev. The Man and His Era* (London, 2005).

Taubman, William, *Gorbachev, His Life and Times* (London, 2017).

Thatcher, Margaret, *The Path to Power* (London, 1995) and *The Downing Street Years* (London, 2005).

Vilenchuk, Michael, '"My Brother's Keeper". American Jewish Youth and the Making of the Soviet Jewry Movement', Brandeis MA Thesis, 2017.

Vinen, Richard, *The Long '68. Radical Protest and Its Enemies* (London, 2018).

Weisman, Debbie, *Memoirs of a Hopeful Pessimist. A Life of Activism Through Dialogue* (Jerusalem, 2017).

Ziegler, Philip, *Harold Wilson. The Authorised Life of Lord Wilson of Rievaulx* (London, 1993).

Ziegler, Philip, *Olivier* (London, 2013).

Zipperstein, Steven J., *Pogrom. Kishinev and the Tilt of History* (New York, 2018).

About John Cooper

Dr John Cooper is a social historian, specialising in Jewish history and the author of several books. He has written books on Jewish food, Jewish childhood, Jewish professionals and also biographies of Raphael Lemkin and the first Lord Rothschild, as well as a book on the origins of the Welfare State. He has contributed a chapter to David Solly Sandler 'The Pinsker Orphans' (2013) and entries on Jewish sexual attitudes, Chief Rabbi Joseph Hertz and Rabbi Dr Louis Jacobs to the De Gruyter Encyclopedia of Religion. He practised as a solicitor, after studying history at Balliol College Oxford. He received a PhD from Buckingham University in 2021. He is a Fellow of the Royal Historical Society.